WEST VALLEY COLLEGE LIBRARY
3 1216 00202 8442

D1706915

BORDER VISIONS

Identity and Diaspora in Film

Edited by

Jakub Kazecki
Karen A. Ritzenhoff
Cynthia J. Miller

THE SCARECROW PRESS, INC.
Lanham • Toronto • Plymouth, UK
2013

Published by Scarecrow Press, Inc.
A wholly owned subsidiary of The Rowman & Littlefield Publishing Group, Inc.
4501 Forbes Boulevard, Suite 200, Lanham, Maryland 20706
www.rowman.com

10 Thornbury Road, Plymouth PL6 7PP, United Kingdom

British Library Cataloguing in Publication Information Available

Library of Congress Cataloging-in-Publication Data

Border visions : identity and diaspora in film / edited by Jakub Kazecki, Karen A. Ritzenhoff, Cynthia J. Miller.
pages cm
Includes bibliographical references and index.
ISBN 978-0-8108-9050-3 (cloth : alk. paper) — ISBN 978-0-8108-9051-0 (ebook) 1. Boundaries in motion pictures. 2. Identity (Psychology) in motion pictures. I. Kazecki, Jakub. II. Ritzenhoff, Karen A. III. Miller, Cynthia J., 1958-
PN1995.9.B67B67 2013
791.43—dc23 2013007500

∞™ The paper used in this publication meets the minimum requirements of American National Standard for Information Sciences—Permanence of Paper for Printed Library Materials, ANSI/NISO Z39.48-1992. Printed in the United States of America.

The editors would like to dedicate this book to all border crossers searching for a way to share their experience with us.

To my wife, Raluca, my best travel companion—and to my daughter, Iana, who just joined us on our journey.

—Jakub Kazecki

To my mother, Birgit Franz, who taught me the joy of languages and travel.

—Karen A. Ritzenhoff

To my aunt Helen, whose journeys across the world's borders inspired me as a child, and whose sense of adventure, at ninety-eight, inspires me still.

—Cynthia J. Miller

Contents

Foreword

On Love—On Borders

Laila Pakalniņa
Translated by Maruta Z. Vitols

I BELONG TO THOSE DIRECTORS who, when asked, "What is your new film about?" reply, "About love." This is because, when I'm making a film, I'm more interested in the question How? and not About what? Of course, I usually don't even really know what to say, but to respond "About love" seems the most appropriate, since all of my work is always somehow, to some degree, about love.

Yet, now, after becoming acquainted with the contents of the anthology *Border Visions: Identity and Diaspora in Film*, I have gained a new, more appropriate and deeper answer to the question, "What is your new film about?" About borders, of course. And I like this answer much better, because it encompasses both subject and form. Film, as a work of art, comes into existence destroying or overcoming the border between subject and form.

Furthermore, specifically, film always is entirely born from and experienced as the border between darkness and light. One needs both darkness and light to capture and develop cinematic images. Without this recognition of the border between light and darkness, the digital process isn't possible, either—the point of cinema is to create the frame precisely from these borders. From an even more sacred perspective: how does the spectator experience film? In a dark room with a lit screen. From a more personal point of view: what do filmmakers call "the magic hour," the most precious and beautiful time of the day to film? The border between night and day, and day and night. The time when the sun is close to or just below the horizon. Because of this, the light isn't direct, flat, or sharp like it is midday. Instead, it is soft, filtering its beams from the sky. Moreover, the farther away you are from the equator, the longer you can enjoy this "magic." I'm lucky—I live and work in Latvia. And it is far enough away from the equator to permit me to utilize this border time between day and night (light and dark).

In addition, I live in a land not only where it is possible to film during the "magic hours," but also where one experiences all four seasons; that is, enough seasons to pick which one I like the best. Therefore, whenever the production schedule allows, I prefer to film when the seasons are changing, on those borders. For example, I like the time of the year when the leaves on trees are just forming buds, or when they no longer are on the branches. It is then that the tree trunks add a graphic quality to the landscape and become powerful elements of the frame's composition.

Furthermore, without denying that all of my films are about these kinds of borders, I must admit that I have repeatedly been preoccupied with concrete, physical borders as the settings for my films and with how these tangible boundaries create conflicts that serve as subjects for my works. And who knows? Perhaps it is exactly this unconscious obsession with borders that led me to become a film director (or, at least, the kind of director that I am today—I make both nonfiction and fiction films). One of my first documentary films (which would later bring me to the Cannes Film Festival), *The Ferry* (*Prāmis*, 1994), is filmed on the border between Latvia and Belarus. This is where the Daugava River serves as the boundary. We filmed for one year (from summer to summer), showing how the ferry transported people, horses, and cars from one side of the river to the other. In doing so, we actually filmed Latvia's regaining of independence in its everyday, social expression. While Latvia and Belarus are part of the Soviet Union, there really is no border between these two republics—the river is just a river, and people cross it from one shore to the other. They call on relatives, go to the store, visit cemeteries, and so on. It all is so simple and banal, just as how the fly buzzes, how the cow moos, and how the children laugh. And then, suddenly—the river is a border, the ferry no longer runs its course. A border guard sits at the side of the river. Latvia has become an independent state. But, the fly continues to buzz.

Next, when I was working on my first fiction film (as a person who was convinced she would never make fiction films), I was drawn to a particular topic because I suddenly remembered my mother's story about an occurrence during the Soviet era in her (and my) home town of Liepāja. During the Soviet period, this seaside town was an imperial border city, because, on the other side of the Baltic Sea, lived capitalists—the Swedes. This border between socialism and capitalism was very carefully guarded—the inhabitants of the town were allowed to go to the beach only during the day, since the authorities plowed and patrolled the strip to ensure that no enemy of the Soviet Union could secretly creep into the country. However, my mother told me that, during her youth in the 1950s, some girl had fooled the border patrol. During the night, she walked backward across the plowed beach into the water and then stepped in her own footprints to get away. The next morning, an alarm was sounded in the town—the border guards were searching for a spy who had emerged from the sea and had infiltrated Soviet territory. I suddenly remembered this story and understood—this is a movie. I only added a shoe (which, unlike Cinderella's footwear, was very big) that the girl loses on the border, and I called the film *The Shoe* (*Kurpe*, 1998).

And then, of course, there is *The Bus* (*Autobuss*, 2004). Before Latvia became a member of the European Union, the Estonian cameraman Arko Okk and I understood that we had to film the bus route between Tallinn and Kaliningrad, since, during the span of one night, it crosses three borders. This meant that the passengers experienced six real border crossings (and, for example, they required four different currencies in order to use the local rest stops). During the production of this film, I was forced to consider the boundaries of the viewers' patience. One of the scenes that I absolutely had to include in the film was five minutes long, which, perhaps, still isn't so terrible. However, during this scene, nothing happens—people stand in line and don't move. This is the passport control at Russia's Kaliningrad border, where all of the bus passengers have to disembark from the vehicle. They stand in line and wait in absolute silence until the Russian border guard decides to stamp one passport. After five minutes of doing nothing, the guard stamps the passport, and the line moves forward by one person. I had to preserve this humiliation of the passengers in my film, because, without the need for any words, it displayed how the military official enjoyed his power (and, therefore, revealed his small-mindedness). Of course, I couldn't afford to include a five-minute-long scene in the film, not only because the spectators probably wouldn't be able to stand it, but also because this kind of scene would destroy the film's rhythm. Moreover, I still needed space in that work for many other scenes.

And yet, this scene at the Russian border had to be long enough to communicate that which is only felt during the duration of time. Therefore, it couldn't be too long, nor could it be too short. Then, my editor, Kaspar Kallas, and I found our definition of the limits of duration. The scene has to be a duration that allows the viewer's mind to wander off and then to return and realize that the scene is still continuing. It is not necessary to have the scene continue any longer—the person is paying attention to the film again, and we can proceed forward. However, if we cut that scene too short, we would lose the spectator—he would be lost in his own thoughts, while the film would have moved on to something else.

It is very possible, that my interest in the extraordinary and even abnormal qualities of borders is tied to the fact that I grew up in the Soviet Union, when my country, Latvia, was occupied. In school, we all were required to learn a poem, from which I still remember at least one line (probably all Soviet-era children remember this). The line is as follows: "I go across borders with my head held high." Yet, we didn't go anywhere—we didn't walk, drive, or fly. Borders were our prison. It is not hard to imagine what would have happened to a person with his "head held high" who attempted to cross even the border into socialist Poland—the Soviet Union's border.

Perhaps it is precisely because of this, that today, when skiing in the Alps, I particularly enjoy crossing the symbolic boundary between Italy and Switzerland. How simple and normal! And perhaps it is precisely because of this that, the day after Latvia joined the Schengen zone on December 21, 2007 (which meant that European Union citizens could cross into any member country without showing their passports), my family and I drove to the Latvia-Estonia border to enjoy what it felt like to drive across a border without stopping. I remember how people were taking photographs on the border that day. If you think about it, what was there to photograph? Yet, apparently there was something to photograph, something completely fresh and new—an almost tangible freedom and normalcy.

I thought about this and about much more within the context of the collection *Border Visions: Identity and Diaspora in Film*. I see this volume as urging people to recognize borders—the conscious boundaries, but also the borders that we (including myself) haven't even considered yet. Moreover, it encourages us to see these borders by watching films.

And those films that are about love are also about borders.

Acknowledgments

As with any project of this sort, there are many people to thank for their role in helping it come into being. We would like to thank Central Connecticut State University, the Literature/Film Association, and all those who made the Border Visions conference possible. We also appreciate the financial support from the Faculty Development Fund at Bates College that helped us in preparing the volume for print. Thanks, too, go to Laila Pakalniņa, for her thoughtful foreword to the volume, and to Maruta Z. Vitols, for helping to share Laila's thoughts in translation. Their collegiality and generosity of spirit is most appreciated. We would like to thank Stephen Ryan of Scarecrow Press, for his support and patience as the project moved along. We would also like to thank our respective friends, families, and partners for their inspiration, encouragement, and willingness to tolerate the distracted minds, diminished free time, and seemingly endless discussions that were by-products of this volume's creation. Without their understanding, you would not be reading these words now.

Finally, we would like to once again thank each of our contributors for interrogating the notion of borders, both real and imagined, with us, and to express our appreciation for the many forms of collaboration through which this volume has taken shape. This project has been a source of challenge and stimulation as it progressed through its various stages, and without the respective strengths of each member of our editorial trio, it would not be the volume that it has become. We all greatly value the collegiality, support, inspiration, and hard work that has been graciously and generously brought to this project.

Introduction

Jakub Kazecki,
Karen A. Ritzenhoff, and
Cynthia J. Miller

Understanding Borders in Film

OUR COLLECTION, *Border Visions: Identity and Diaspora in Film*, engages with border crossings from diverse cultural, economic, historical, and sociopolitical perspectives. What distinguishes the narratives of travel discussed in this collection from many literary accounts of journeys of discovery and transgression is the fact that the medium of film has the ability to visually capture these processes of (self-)discovery and, through the universality of its language, can have an impact on a wide range of audiences across borders. In an increasingly mobile world, in which communication shifts more and more toward visual language, moving images carry the potential to inform, evoke, cause disdain or relief, and, ultimately, force viewers to react, evoking an impulse that very often defies the audience's expectations, jars their understandings of the world, and fosters social activism. The unique ability of film as a visual medium to depict fictional, as well as nonfictional, journeys of discovery in various cultural contexts is particularly relevant in respect to identity formations: how do people negotiate their differences at home and abroad, while traveling outside their familiar comfort zones?

Filmmakers have addressed the topic of border crossings since the advent of cinema, because the moment of leaving one's home and settling somewhere else is one of the most basic (and sometimes most traumatizing) experiences of human existence. The topics of border crossing and living in diaspora are at once timely and universally relevant. The world in 2013 is far from peaceful, and the echoes of conflicts and tensions from the twentieth century, or even earlier, from the colonial past, are resounding around the globe and forcing many people to relocate and migrate across borders. The delicate balance between the two opposing superpowers, the Soviet Union and the United States, that marked the second half of the last century dissolved in the globalizing world of financial interdependencies, in which the division lines are drawn not always between countries but often between economies. As some national borders are vanishing, other borders are indeed created by the global economy. The global scale of superpower and subordinate power, colonizer and colonized, has changed dramatically in the first decade of the twenty-first century. Hong Kong, Taiwan, some emirates in the Middle East, and Brazil in South America are developing economic muscle that will affect the distribution of wealth and natural resources in decades to come. As China is experiencing a blossoming middle class and Russians are beginning to travel for leisure outside the country, the fissures between the haves and have-nots are becoming increasingly prominent. Some states, such as India and Pakistan, aspire to the ranks of main players on the political scene, while a shrinking American role as a global superpower results in the nation securing its interests by the means of military interventions. Whereas an international economic elite can travel easily across time zones and communicate with ever-increasing ease via modern technologies, the disenfranchised are pushed deeper into poverty, disadvantage, and despair.

Dissolving state borders between East and West Europe after *Perestroika* and the fall of the Berlin Wall almost twenty-five years ago, and the following expansion of the European Union to the east, also brought about new social and economic issues in Europe. As the world financial crisis deepens, we witness increasing tensions within the European Union, related to the tighter economic and political integration within the organization and shifting power relationships between its member states. The European Union is struggling to keep both currency and unity afloat, while facing record unemployment among the young and mounting tensions in Greece, Italy, Spain, and France.

As we conclude our work on this volume, there are several concurrent political conflicts simmering in the world—most visibly, the increasing tensions between Israel and Palestine in the Middle East and the continuing heated debate over the Mexican-American border—which polarize communities and shape agendas. Other political hotspots are the North and South axis in Vietnam, extremist rebels seizing the capital of Congo in Africa, and the violent uprisings in Syria, long-lasting effects of the so-called Arab Spring. The U.S. Army is withdrawing ground troops from Iraq and schedules are in place to pull out of Afghanistan, but the drone attacks that replace them remind us that borders can easily be violated with increasingly dehumanized technology. What is certainly also more visible than even ten years ago is the effect of the information highway, and the role of social media in igniting debate and generating the unprecedented possibility for social movements across state and national boundaries. Filmmakers capture these movements, seeking an opportunity to express their complex nature through images, creating and exploring metaphors of home, travel, and border crossing.

From Screen to Page

Similarly, each author in our volume addresses border crossings as a form of exploration, stretching beyond personal boundaries, as well as the physical transitions that travels entail. Many of these journeys are linked to physical and structural violence as a reason for, or consequence of, the departure from the place called home; many entail personal sacrifices; and many are marked by confusion and doubt. Different ethnic groups, varied economic interests, a sense of inequality in standards of living, diverse religion communities, and postcolonial power plays are only a few factors challenging existing borders around the world.

The chapters in our volume offer a broad spectrum of perspectives on those borders, seen not only as administrative or political boundaries, dividing states and areas of state influence, but also as limits imposed by nature—rivers, oceans, deserts, lakes, and mountains; impenetrable landscapes; and areas of extreme temperatures and vegetation. These liminal spaces created by forces of nature are often seen as "natural" borders of countries, dividing continents and preventing, or slowing down, the natural flows of migration. They test the human ability to survive, but successfully overcoming the challenges they pose fills the traveler with the joy of being alive—it opens up the possibility for telling a story and creates a space for metaphors of crossing borders between life and death, good and evil, or reality and dream.

But looking at borders as features of topography and geopolitics is only one of the perspectives represented in the volume, and it is very often just a starting point for explorations of the wide range of border metaphors in film. Such treatments of borders include labor laws in a dystopic future (in the chapter by Thomas Prasch), variations on existing borders in alternative versions of history (Tanya Shilina-Conte and Dennis Browne), the experiences of guest workers in the post–World War II Europe (María Lourdes Casas and Ayça Tunç Cox), and ethnic wars and their effect on borders in the twentieth century, including their role in creating personal and collective memories (Jane Costlow, Tanya Shilina-Conte, and Katie Davies). Several chapters address borders and contact zones between national, ethnic, and religious groups in Eastern Europe in the turbulent twentieth century (Jane Costlow, Maruta Z. Vitols, Lesley C. Pleasant,

Raluca Cernahoschi, and Dennis Browne). Another group of chapters in the volume, focusing on non-European borderlands, not only hint at a departure from the westernization of border narratives in cinema, but also point out the increasing role of independent films and emerging film industries outside of Hollywood and Europe (Thomas Prasch, Tanya Shilina-Conte, and Sean Allan).

Many chapters included here read the acts of border crossings as filmic metaphors and focus on capturing the common elements of film language that are being used to depict the liminal experience, such as Jane Costlow's exploration of the contrast between colors of the winter landscape in Larisa Shepitko's *The Ascent*, or reflections on dividing horizontal or vertical lines in the film mise-en-scènes, for example, in Tanya Shilina-Conte or Claudia Plasse's chapters on the role of border walls. For other authors in our volume, equally as important is following the narrative process of expressing the transborder experience and its consequences through the means of film: adapting aesthetic devices from other areas of human expression and creativity, other media, and various film genres. Here, music and dance, along with written and spoken texts, come together with film images to create stories that are as multilayered, complex, and transgressive of genre and convention lines as the transcultural journeys they depict. While the volume focuses particularly on film, it also looks at some of the fleeting images provided by television coverage (discussed by videographer and film historian Katie Davies), and the differences offered by that medium.

In our focus on the images of border crossing as universal experience, neither the question of contemporality of borders depicted in films nor the issue of their historicity is of primary importance. The areas of acute crisis in 2012—such as European migrants, Israeli-Palestinian borders, Chinese cultural changes, North-South borders—are embraced in the volume's chapters, but so are the remnants of past conflicts and borders that no longer exist but are still visible in the narratives and collective memory captured through film (see Raluca Cernahoschi, Claudia Plasse, Jane Costlow, and María Lourdes Casas). The sacrifice and disillusionment that often accompany the crossing or transgressing of borders is also a focal point here, as emotional ties are formed and spirits are broken (see Charlotte Christina Fink, María Lourdes Casas, Karen A. Ritzenhoff, and Jakub Kazecki). The inescapable question of whether a borderless society is imaginable is also addressed here, by contributors Thomas Prasch and Charlotte Christina Fink, as their chapters explore futures near and distant in which borders may be rendered irrelevant.

About the Volume

At the heart of all fifteen chapters in the volume is the desire to depict alternative visions of borders as they are represented historically and currently in film. The volume is divided into five sections reflecting different perspectives on envisioning border crossings in film. The opening section, "Utopia and Dystopia: Border Visions and Alternative (His/Her)stories," offers readers the first insights into seemingly limitless ways to express visual and narrative imagination of the filmmakers who create compelling images of alterative realities in order to make optimistic or pessimistic commentary on the existing borders. The section "From the Center to the Margins: Ideological Dominance and Liminal Spaces" reflects the filmmakers' interest in the invisible and ever-changing borders between the center and peripheries of colonial influences—discourses of "small homelands" and multiethnic and multicultural empires—posing questions about possibilities of identity construction in situations of conflicting ideological interests. The third section, "Vanished Borders: Memory, Nostalgia, and Homesickness," focuses on representations of longing for a long-lost home, images of diaspora, and different ways of reconnecting with or creating communities. The chapters in this section examine films depicting the borders and moments of border crossings as past phenomena and nostalgically recreating the boundaries in the narratives. The chapters brought together in "Growing Up on the Road: Crossing Borders and Identity Formation" are linked by their interest in films that comment on personal identity formation as related to border-crossing experiences, choosing children and young adults as their protagonists. The last section, "Narrative Transgressions: Crossing Genres and Border Crossings," aims at showing the representations of borders in cinema also as a form of experimental storytelling, where media and generic conventions are subject to transgression, revealing new formal and aesthetic possibilities.

Regardless of a variety of different perspectives on the borders in this volume, one of the key elements that binds the chapters together is the focus on stories of individuals in transition and how they attempt assimilation in a new environment and different country to develop a sense of home. Although the relocation of peoples was a prominent aspect of war-ridden countries in the aftermath of the First and Second World Wars in Europe, the trajectory of change can hardly be grasped through literary accounts or images of mass movements across borders (as the archival footage television coverage after the fall of the Berlin Wall reminds us). Instead, the contributors to our book seek ways to describe the impact of the border crossings on protagonists, old and young, in these films.

The rationale of the volume goes back to a conference at Central Connecticut State University (CCSU), organized by the three co-editors in October 2011. Cynthia J. Miller, then president of the Literature/Film Association, embraced the topic of "Border Visions" and attracted members of her film studies organization to CCSU, where Jakub Kazecki, now at Bates College, and Karen A. Ritzenhoff taught. The goal of the conference was to draw from scholars bridging different disciplines. This interdisciplinary and multicultural perspective is also reflected by the three co-editors: Cynthia J. Miller is an anthropologist and film historian whose PhD research was carried out in Tamil Nadu, India, and with Tamil immigrants in Boston, Massachusetts. She has been teaching in Emerson College's interdisciplinary program for fifteen years; Jakub Kazecki was born in Poland and completed his PhD in Canada. He teaches German in a Department of German and Russian Studies at Bates College and spent four years on the faculty of Modern Languages at CCSU. Karen A. Ritzenhoff, born in Germany, completed her graduate education in the United States and has been teaching in the Department of Communication at CCSU for almost twenty years. She also works closely with the women, gender, and sexuality studies program as well as cinema studies.

Our multidisciplinary interests and the geographical diversity of our research subjects are reflected in our choices of contributions to this volume. Our exploration opens with Tanya Shilina-Conte's chapter, "*Imaginal* Border Crossings and Silence as Negative Mimesis in Elia Suleiman's *Divine Intervention* (2002)." This chapter takes Israel and the Palestinian border as its geographical focus, as it examines Suleiman's prize-winning film, subtitled as *A Chronicle of Love and Pain.* Three locales are depicted in the film—Jerusalem, Nazareth, and Ramallah—in order to visually render the differences between Christian, Jewish, and Muslim faiths and cultures. Shilina-Conte provides close visual analysis to demonstrate how Suleiman employs strategies of distanciation to illustrate that "the Middle East has proven itself to be one of the world's most conflicted and most dangerous border regions, where the fault lines of religious, ethnic, and historical identity run deep." Suleiman evokes early silent film aesthetics and combines those with art cinema reflexive techniques to create a unique style of "accented" representation.

Next, Dennis Browne's chapter, "Underground Bridges: Tunnels in the Films of Emir Kusturica—*Underground* (1995) and *Life Is a Miracle* (2004)," provides a reading of two films set during the conflicts of the 1990s in former Yugoslavia: *Underground* and *Life Is a Miracle.* Browne focuses on the filmic tropes of bridges and tunnels, and analyzes their narrative functions in validating or contesting the Yugoslav idea of a state of multiple ethnicities and cultures. He interprets Kusturica's employment of tunnels as a successful strategy for questioning the validity of bounded and bordered communities in former Yugoslavia, and the social and political superstructure of late twentieth-century Europe in general. Browne, in his analysis of Kusturica's cast of characters in the two films and other projects by Kusturica, also emphasizes processes of creation, transition, and transformation of the director's self-proclaimed Yugoslav identity.

Disillusionment and abuse is at the heart of a dystopic tale about the Mexican-American borderland in Thomas Prasch's article, "Aquaterrorists and Cybraceros: The Dystopian Borderlands of Alex Rivera's *Sleep Dealer* (2008)." The American Dream has been destroyed by transnational cyber-technology for protagonist Memo (Luis Fernando Peña), who lives in Mexico with his family.

Director Alex Rivera depicts and critiques the failed real-life attempt to allow workers from South America to migrate to the United States as farm laborers by creating a futuristic scenario of mechanized labor. Prasch explains that Rivera combines "the images of technologically displaced workers and of the bracero guest-worker program" and fuses them into "the vision of the *cybracero*." Ultimately, the film deals with lost identity and the fact that a futuristic war between the two countries would cause irreconcilable conflicts of interest.

Raluca Cernahoschi, in her chapter "An Empire of Borders: Central European Boundaries in István Szabó's *Colonel Redl* (1985)," describes two visions of the Austro-Hungarian Empire that dominate the discourse surrounding the Habsburg monarchy in literature and cinema. The first interprets the Dual Monarchy as a centralized open meeting space of peaceful religious, national, and ethnic coexistence, painting a nostalgic image of the lost world of cultural diversity and tolerance; the second offers an image of the empire as defined by the relationship between its core and periphery. Cernahoschi points out that Szabó's film, which traces the career of the empire officer Redl, draws a picture of the empire, in which "the gradual closing-in reduces . . . possibilities of self-actualization to the point of implosion" ending with the outbreak of the First World War.

Jane Costlow's chapter, "Icons, Landscape, and the Boundaries of Good and Evil: Larisa Shepitko's *The Ascent* (1977)," offers a compelling take on borderlands not only as geographical areas subjected to military operations and territorial claims, but also as a terrain of extreme natural conditions and, most importantly, as a metaphor of struggle between good and evil. For Shepitko, Costlow argues, the plot of *The Ascent*, the fate of a partisan unit in Nazi-occupied Belarus during the Second World War, is a starting point in the creation of highly ambivalent images of heroism and sacrifice for community. Costlow's chapter pays particular attention to the aesthetic features of Shepitko's vision, pointing out the parallels between the director's images of human torment and redemption, and the archetypes of Russian identity, and creating a complex dialogue between the inner and outer worlds of individuals and communities.

Maruta Z. Vitols's contribution to the volume, "Negotiating a New Europe: Laila Pakalniņa's *The Bus* (2004) and Transnational Landscapes," explores Pakalniņa's images of borders and border crossings in the zone of the "New Europe" of the Baltic states. Chronicling the journey of a bus from Tallinn, Estonia, to Kaliningrad, Russia, Pakalniņa's documentary investigates postsocialist nations in the era of globalization. Vitols's interest in the processes of new global and European identity constructions results in a reading of the director's work as a testimony to the challenges of such identity reconstructions. In her analysis of *The Bus*, Vitols observes that the redefining of internal and external borders in the liminal, transnational spaces of the postcommunist world in the twenty-first century is hindered by the decades of political and cultural dominance of the their powerful neighbor, the Soviet Union.

Lesley C. Pleasant's chapter, "Zurich Roses: Andrea Staka's *Das Fräulein* (2006)," examines the shifting nature of community and belonging among women struggling to reconstruct or reconfigure their place-based identities. Staka's film focuses on the geographic and emotional boundary crossings of three expatriate women from the former Yugoslavia, who push each other to confront their respective ideas of "home." As the women's lives intersect, they learn that each has her own story to tell about her journey, as well as her own secrets to keep. Pleasant argues that the three deal differently with their senses of *Heimweh* (missing home), as they attempt to balance it with the longing for far away, *Fernweh*. Each of the women chooses different strategies for assimilating or distancing herself from Swiss culture, thereby testing the boundaries of their own abilities to adjust to a new environment, so typical for migrants in the New Europe.

In "A Scar That Vanished: Recollections of the Inner-German Border in German Nonfiction Film," Claudia Plasse adds another perspective to our book by focusing on three documentary filmmakers: One, Holger Jancke, is a former guard along the inner German border who has solicited oral histories from three fellow guards. The second, director Christian Gierke, attempts to evoke nostalgia for the vanished border, through the creation of a politically charged film that challenges mainstream understandings of documentary filmmaking as providing "true" images of reality. The third, Bartek Konopka, stretches the documentary concept even further, incorporating the images of "border bunnies" into a faux documentary of the inner-German border, in the Polish-German coproduction, *Rabbit à la Berlin*. All three films carefully craft images of the now-fallen border and use different approaches to reconstruct both its reality and memory through film.

Ayça Tunç Cox adds to our book an innovative perspective on diasporic and transnational cinema, in her chapter "The Use of Music in Turkish-German Diasporic Cinema." Arguing that the term *diaspora* must be understood differently in the twenty-first century because it has become "diverse and heterogenous," Cox focuses on the use of ethnic music as a cultural signifier in diasporic films. While music is often considered to be a universal language, it is also intimately linked to social and cultural identity. When utilized in films, music serves to signal identities, evoke memories, and frame associations. Its use in Turkish-German film, then, serves to underscore social, cultural, and political identity. Cox's chapter provides a detailed overview of a wide variety of Turkish-German films, their use of diagetic and extra-diagetic music, and the ways in which these films and their content affect and are affected by contemporary identity formations in Europe.

Charlotte Christina Fink's chapter on the romantic comedy *In July*, "Heating Up: Border Crossing and Identity Formation in Fatih Akin's *In July* (2000)," discusses the struggles inherent in crossing, internal as well as external, borders in order to discover one's true self. The film's narrative, while framed as a romantic "road movie," uses the characters' journeys across borders to illustrate the complexities of identity formation in the "new" Europe. Daniel, the protagonist of the film, is an inhibited German high school teacher who heads south to find true love. Through his journey across geographic borders, he acquires both the cultural and self-awareness necessary to embrace difference and achieve true happiness. Fink notes that although the story is a metaphor for the unification of Europe, it also serves as an affirmation of the necessity of the Orient as a reference point for European identity.

Jakub Kazecki's chapter, "Lost Children: Images of Childhood on the German-Polish Border in Christoph Hochhäusler's *This Very Moment* (2003) and Robert Gliński's *Piggies* (2009)," looks at the border between East and West, the German-Polish borderland. He examines the ways in which German directors characterize Poland as lush, unpredictable, and nourishing, while casting Germany as the opposite: cold, sterile, and hostile. Kazecki illustrates this contrast through a discussion of director Christoph Hochhäusler's film *This Very Moment*, which focuses on children whose stepmother drives them from Germany to Poland and then abandons them there—the border functioning as a divide between the rational world and the realm of the unexpected. A second, far less romantic film, *Piggies* by Robert Gliński, offers a grim contrast, framing the Polish-German border as a zone of child prostitution, where teenaged Polish boys sell their bodies to German pedophiles.

Karen A. Ritzenhoff's chapter, "Orphans, Violence, and Identity: Transnational Travel in Cary Fukunaga's *Sin Nombre* (2009), Denis Villeneuve's *Incendies* (2010), and François Dupeyron's *Monsieur Ibrahim* (2003)," examines the legacy of orphaned young adults from Honduras/Mexico, Canada/Middle East, and France who move from North to South, as well as West to East, to discover a sense of belonging, crossing geographical, cultural, and religious boundaries. In each of the three films, the characters seek out the legacy of their parents while choosing new family ties, in order to survive in a potentially hostile environment. The youths struggle with knowledge of both self and "Other," as they create a place for themselves in the world. Violence plays a large part in all three films, as the protagonists experience dangerous journeys in order to connect with their newly found identity.

This is a conflict similar to what the young migrant from Senegal, Alou, experiences in María Lourdes Casas's chapter, "What the Images Cannot Show: The Letters in Montxo Armendáriz's *Letters from Alou* (1990)." Here, the protagonist lives in Spain and experiences the perilous process of entering a country as an undocumented migrant seeking work. Alou explains in his letters his difficult transition from Africa to Spain, both as an act of geographical border crossing as well as a confusing cultural process that affects his sense of identity and belonging. The film—the first Spanish language film to address immigration in Spain—is highly critical of Spain's discrimination against African migrants. Casas argues that the film makes visible, and then erases, the line that separates Alou's ethnic, racial, and geographic identities through the process of migration.

Sean Allan studies the third generation of Chinese film directors in his chapter, "Reflections on China and Border Crossings in Jia Zhang-ke's *Unknown Pleasures* (2002) and *Still Life* (2006)." Allan discusses Jia's films as a means of tracing the transformations in post-Mao China that have resulted from globalization. Known throughout the world for his resistance to governmental control of his films, Jia uses the two films discussed here to explore the intersection of global and local identity, examining the ways in which Jia's films portray the dissolution of cultural borders as negatively affecting the lives of rural Chinese, through changes in economics, morality, sexuality, and aspirations for the future. Allan discusses the director's use of film as cultural critique and social commentary, as well as Jia's commitment to revealing the struggles of rural Chinese in an increasingly global, yet constrained economic environment.

Katie Davies's chapter, "Border Imaging: Revealing the Gaps between the Reality, the Representation, and the Experience of the Border," concludes our volume, ending our collection with the reminder that borders are constantly in flux. Davies's chapter focuses on the small English market town of Royal Wootton Bassett—a town drawn into national significance through its repatriation ceremonies. Davies's short video, *The Separation Line*, which chronicles the enactment and impact of these ceremonies on the local community, explores the performance of commemoration on the town's inhabitants. The modes of representation of borders are challenged in Davies's artwork and installations, as she asks us to think about the institutionalized order that is imposed on the British population in the context of celebrations surrounding the dead soldiers whose bodies are returned from battlefields in the Middle East.

I

UTOPIAS AND DYSTOPIAS

BORDER VISIONS AND ALTERNATIVE (HIS/HER)STORIES

1

Imaginal Border Crossings and Silence as Negative Mimesis in Elia Suleiman's *Divine Intervention* (2002)

Tanya Shilina-Conte

Thus the body stands before the world and the world upright before it. . . . And between these two vertical beings, there is not a frontier, but a contact surface.

—Maurice Merleau-Ponty, *The Visible and the Invisible*

THIS CHAPTER FOCUSES on the depiction of two prominent instances of border transgression, by the Woman and the Red Balloon, in the Palestinian director Elia Suleiman's film *Divine Intervention* (*Yadon Ilaheyya*, 2002). As the title of the film suggests, *Divine Intervention* invokes a spiritual imagination that transcends the nation-state politics in force at the border. I argue that Suleiman supplements a literal portrayal of the divide between the Israeli and Palestinian territories with what I describe as *imaginal* border crossings, drawing on the theory of the *imaginal world* (*mundus imaginalis*) by philosopher and scholar of Islamic mysticism Henry Corbin.[1] I further demonstrate that Suleiman purposefully calls upon the attributes and aesthetics of the silent film era. As opposed to conventional narrative, Suleiman structures his film as a nonlinear series of isolated tableaux, shot with a static tripod-mounted camera. Signaling dispersed and fragmented representation, these cinematic tableaux provide an oblique commentary on disjointed Palestinian realities, while the immobile camera signifies the inability of Suleiman's characters to negotiate their space freely and effectively. Finally, relying on Theodor Adorno's ideas in *Aesthetic Theory*,[2] I contend that the expressive silence of Suleiman's onscreen persona could be interpreted as a form of *negative mimesis* that implies an ideological resistance to dominant culture combined with an aesthetic strategy of meaningful absence.

Elia Suleiman was born in Nazareth in 1960 and raised in a Christian Arab household. An unruly teenager in a Palestinian ghetto under Israeli occupation in the 1970s, he dropped out of school at the age of fifteen. "I became a street kid," he recounted in an interview with Sheila Johnston, "and that was quite an occupation for a while. Then I had to leave the country suddenly because a gang was being busted and I was held in the police records as its leader."[3] Suleiman landed first in London, and then arrived at the age of twenty-one as an illegal immigrant in New York, working menial jobs. His official biography states that he "lived in New York City for a decade (1982–93) before moving back to Palestine to teach Film and Media at Birzeit University near Ramallah, in the West Bank."[4] It is during his sojourn in New York that he became an autodidact in the films of Robert Bresson, Jacques Tati, Michelangelo Antonioni, and Yasujirō Ozu and the writings of Walter Benjamin and Primo Levi.[5] Even though he made a number of worthwhile documentary and short films, Suleiman's main contribution to global cinema is his triptych of chronicles dealing with various aspects of Palestinian existence during and after the 1948 Arab-Israeli war. His first feature film, *Chronicle of a Disappearance* (*Segell Ikhtifa*, 1996), which received the Best First Film Prize at the 1996 Venice Film Festival, marked the return of a Palestinian filmmaker from exile and followed the lives of his family members (including his father, Fuad Suleiman, and his mother, Nazira Suleiman) in the newly formed territories.[6] *Divine Intervention*, subtitled *A Chronicle of Love and Pain* and dedicated to the memory of Suleiman's father (Nazira Suleiman still plays herself in the film), premiered at the 2002 Cannes Film Festival and was awarded the Jury Prize. Similarly, it focuses on the lives of Palestinians under Israeli rule, but also contains a number of border-crossing scenes, accentuating the division between the two territories. Suleiman's latest feature film, *The Time That Remains* (2009) or *Chronicle of a Present Absentee*, likewise received a number of prestigious awards. This film is dedicated to the memory of Suleiman's mother and father and is based on the latter's diaries, providing a more detailed historical account of the changes in Palestine that followed after the formation of the state of Israel in 1948. Suleiman acts in all three films; in the first, he lists his character as Elia Suleiman, while in the other two, he uses the acronym ES for his onscreen persona. Postcolonial film theorist Hamid Naficy observes that Suleiman appears on screen "as a diegetic filmmaker who returns to his homeland" and fashions his films as "personal and autobiographical ruminations about exile and cinema."[7] Naficy coined the term *accented cinema* to designate certain films that are a product of displaced filmmakers. The genre arises due to the coexistence of two cultural discourses of origin and destination and the frictions between them, revealing the *interstitial* nature of accented cinema. As opposed to mainstream cinema, accented cinema does not claim to be universal.[8] According to Naficy, one of the inherent characteristics of accented cinema is the expression of *border consciousness*. He states, "Border consciousness emerges from being situated at the border, where multiple determinants of race, class, gender, and membership in divergent, even antagonistic, historical and national identities intersect. As a result, border consciousness, like exilic liminality, is theoretically against binarism and duality and for a third optique, which is multiperspectival and tolerant of ambiguity, ambivalence, and chaos."[9]

The Middle East has proven itself to be one of the world's most conflicted and most dangerous border regions, where the fault lines of religious, ethnic, and historical identity run deep. "As liminal subjects and interstitial artists," says Naficy, "many accented filmmakers are themselves shifters, with multiple perspectives and conflicted or performed identities. They may own no passport or hold multiple passports, and they may be stranded between legality and illegality. Many are scarred by the harrowing experiences of their own border crossings. Some may be energized, while others may be paralyzed by their fear of partiality. Their films often draw upon these biographical crossing experiences."[10]

The essential topos of such accented films is the journey. In *Chronicle of a Disappearance*, ES indicates that he moved to Jerusalem to be in proximity to the international airport. *The Time That Remains* begins with his character en route from the airport to Nazareth when his taxi driver becomes disoriented in a violent thunderstorm and keeps asking, "What is this place?" and "Where am I?" The principal scenes of *Divine Intervention* are comprised of shorter but more perilous journeys by car through the border checkpoint or through the cities of Jerusalem and Nazareth. And yet, as Naficy observes, films of border consciousness are not simple accounts of international travel but invariably involve "inward, homecoming journeys."[11] It is these latter journeys that Henry Corbin might identify as spiritual quests that can be experienced only through the "imaginative consciousness"[12] that stands between the intellect and the senses. In what follows, I argue that in *Divine Intervention*, the accented filmmaker Elia Suleiman's border consciousness is most clearly expressed not by the literal crossings of people at the checkpoint, who are subject to military harassment and ethnic humiliation, but as imaginal crossings elevated to a spiritual plane.

Imaginal Border Crossings

The international appeal of *Divine Intervention* may be attributed to the transgressive manner in which it presents the tortuous human conflict of

Palestinians and Israelis forced to cohabit in an ancient land that sits at the intersection of Christian, Jewish, and Muslim faiths. In his film, director Suleiman crosscuts between the three diegetic topoi of Jerusalem, Nazareth, and Ramallah. The Jerusalem-based ES (Elia Suleiman) negotiates the borders between this city and the two other locales in order to see his ailing father (Nayef Fahoum Daher) and his romantic partner (Manal Khader). Depicting the clandestine meetings of ES and his Palestinian girlfriend, the Woman, Suleiman sets the key scenes of his film at the al-Ram checkpoint, the border crossing between Israeli-controlled East Jerusalem and the West Bank town of Ramallah that served as the de facto seat of the Palestinian Authority under Yasser Arafat.[13]

In *Divine Intervention* there are two significant instances of imaginal border crossings: the Woman and the Red Balloon. These two figures acquire paranormal, God-like powers through the faculty of ES's imagination that allow them to transcend the guards, who remain in the earth-bound world of border politics. In the first of these instances ES is waiting at the checkpoint's car park to meet the Woman. Although the Arab-Israeli ES can navigate this transnational divide, his Palestinian lover cannot. During their trysts in the barren parking lot strewn with concrete barriers—a liminal *nonplace* that is neither Ramallah nor Jerusalem, neither a Palestinian homeland nor Israel—the couple usually does no more than caress one another's hands and exchange expressive silent glances. As seen in figure 1.1, on one occasion, when the Israeli border guards refuse entry into Jerusalem to all traf-

Figure 1.1. The Woman, played by Manal Khader, walking across the border as the guard tower collapses behind her. *Divine Intervention* (Koch Lorber Films).

fic and turn away cars at gunpoint, the strikingly (even divinely) beautiful, nameless Woman leaves her car and strides directly past the stunned guards. In her fashionable tight-fitting western dress, high heels, and wind-blown uncovered hair, she reminds us of objectified images of female characters in classical Hollywood cinema that, as Laura Mulvey argued, are created for the enjoyment of the male gaze.[14] Indeed, as the Woman walks toward the checkpoint, she wears dark sunglasses that prevent her from returning the gaze, thus rendering her dangerous beauty safe for the male onlookers. And yet, as a double subaltern,[15] a woman and a Palestinian, she makes two negatives a positive by openly confronting the gaze of the dominant power represented by the Israeli men. Approaching the checkpoint, she briskly lifts her sunglasses and with a withering, castrating glance paralyzes the armed guards and topples the phallic watchtower.[16] This scene is based on an actual incident in which the journalist Manal Khader, who plays the Woman in *Divine Intervention*, dared a border guard to shoot her when she was refused entry into Jerusalem.[17] The first piece of nondiegetic music in the film, by British-Bangladeshi dub/dance group Joi, accompanies the Woman as she exits her car and strides through the checkpoint, enhancing the sexual power of what Refqa Abu-Remaileh suggests could be a fashion model's runway walk.[18] The electronic remixed sound emphasizes the multicultural appeal of global fusion music, in contrast to the binarism of Palestinian-Israeli identity that permits some to pass and not others. Yet the dangerous physical beauty of the Woman and her resistant *female Palestinian gaze* only help to explain why the soldiers and their automatic weapons are rendered impotent. Although it is a viable reading of the scene, it is not the Woman's westernized, sexual appeal alone that makes the watchtower collapse. What is more important is that Suleiman invokes the spiritual, imaginal power of the border crossing as the Woman transgresses the divide between two warring patriarchal cultures.

Philosopher and scholar of Islamic mysticism Henry Corbin develops his theory of *mundus imaginalis* based on the visionary spiritual tales by such Sufi mystics as Shihabuddin Yahya Suhrawardi (1155–1191) and Muhyeddin Ibn 'Arabī (1165–1240).[19] Corbin's study of Sufism describes its belief in three worlds, each with its own "organ of perception: the senses, imagination, and the intellect, corresponding with the triad: body, soul and mind."[20] *Mundus imaginalis*, a separate order of reality, was designated by Suhrawardi as "Nâ-Kojâ-Abâd, 'the country of non-where,'" which can only be reached through "imaginative consciousness" or "cognitive Imagination."[21] Describing these spiritual journeys, Corbin stresses that the "*mundus imaginalis* has nothing whatsoever of fantasies projected on some cinematic screen."[22] Borrowing from the Latin expression, Corbin coins the word *imaginal*, distinguishing it from the word *imaginary*, which is often associated with such misleading terms as "unreal," "Utopian,"[23] "fantasy" or "imaginings,"[24] and "illusory fiction or hallucination."[25] Here, my reading of the film differs radically from interpretations in which some scenes in *Divine Intervention*, including the border crossings, have been branded as ES's fantasies or daydreams.[26] I argue that these scenes should be interpreted not as futile fantasies but as "vision-events symbolizing . . . inner states" that are set free by the power of ES's "active imagination."[27] ES's search for the lost country is a spiritual mystical journey, outside of the realm of *where*. As Corbin argues, once the frontier to this intermediate order of reality has been breached, the question of *where* no longer applies to the traveler, as he is not crossing the physical visible boundary but experiencing an inward invisible journey in search of his home.[28] In *Divine Intervention*, again, subtitled *A Chronicle of Love and Pain*, the Woman does not cross the purely arbitrary, political border of the checkpoint (intellect), nor is she merely an erotic fantasy of ES (senses); rather, she is a manifestation of a spiritual love (imagination) that is needed to transcend the earthly plane. The Woman is a representation of what Corbin calls "the Creative Feminine."[29] In *Creative Imagination in the Ṣūfism of Ibn ʿArabī*, Corbin discusses the dialectic of love that leads every human being on the path to an experience of divine love. He says, "By setting in motion the active, creative Imagination, the dialectic of love has, in the world of the creative Imagination, that is, on the theophanic plane, brought about a reconciliation of the spiritual and the physical, a unification of spiritual love and physical love in the one experience of mystic love."[30] The Woman, whose gaze topples the guard tower, exists on the plane of the soul: "a mystic obtains the highest theophanic vision in contemplating the Image of feminine being, because it is in the Image of the Creative Feminine that contemplation can apprehend the highest manifestation of God, namely, creative divinity."[31] As a filmmaker, Suleiman invokes not merely the artistic imagination, but also the spiritual imagination of the *Creative Feminine*, and as such, the Woman crosses an *imaginal* (but not *imaginary*) border.

The second avatar of the Woman with divine powers does not appear in western garb but in the keffiyeh, the checked Arab headdress that is traditionally worn by men,[32] which in itself could be interpreted as a form of defiance on the part of the Woman as a subaltern. This scene, perhaps the most controversial in the film, is set up by another driving sequence in which ES passes a highway billboard advertising a shooting range, "Come Shoot If You're Ready,"[33] with a prominent picture of a knife-wielding Palestinian fedayee[34] in keffiyeh, presumably as the practice target. At a traffic light, a Jewish man flying the Israeli flag from the window of his car pulls alongside the car driven by ES. In this instance, Suleiman employs diegetic music as ES inserts a cassette tape of a Middle Eastern remix of the American pop standard by Screaming

Jay Hawkins, "I Put a Spell on You." This version, signaling his preference for world fusion music of Arabic instrumentation and American blues and rock, is covered by female vocalist Natacha Atlas. If one pays close attention to the billboard image, one can see that the keffiyeh—a traditional emblem of Arab masculinity—reveals the piercing eyes of the Woman. As ES never speaks for himself, the intradiegetic song's lyric performs that task. While some might interpret the song as expressing only an eerie physical love or sexual obsession, the cover version by Atlas—a female artist of the Palestinian diaspora living in Europe—promises a divine intervention: "I put a spell on you, because you're mine. You'd better stop the things that you do. Lord knows I ain't lyin'."[35] If, like the collapsing guard tower, the subsequent scene at the shooting range could be superficially interpreted as a mere fantasy envisioned by ES while driving his car, it is nevertheless an act of what Corbin calls "the creative Imagination."[36] The shooting range targets are standing female figures wearing the keffiyeh, which evokes not only the Arab-Israeli conflict but also a gender conflict between masculine violence and feminine resistance. All but one of the targets fall, and then from a gust of swirling wind and dust emerges the figure of the Woman. After a moment's hesitation—this is now a *live* target—the shooters are instructed to discharge their weapons. However, the Woman stops the bullets fired at her and, as she rises up above the range, they form a halo, or possibly a crown of thorns, around her head. Reflecting the blend of male and female attributes, the Woman's divine power is also ironically signified by a mixing of cultural symbols as she wears both the Arab keffiyeh and the Christian crown of thorns.[37] Just as in the scene in which she lifts her sunglasses, the Woman temporarily sheds her keffiyeh, exposing her feminine essence. With her hair blown by the wind, the divine, Eternal Woman triumphs over death, and rises above the plane of the physical world into the imaginal realm. Just as the wind and the dust recognize no borders, the Woman floats free above the frontier zone, out of human reach, on a spiritual plane that, above sectarianism, may be the director's only hope for peace.

In a second imaginal transgression, ES and the Woman release a red balloon imprinted with an image of Yasser Arafat that drifts across the checkpoint, past the befuddled Israeli guards (see figure 1.2). Spotting through binoculars the disembodied floating image of the Palestinian resistance leader, the guards hurriedly query over their radios whether they should open fire on the balloon. Their response, which obviously comments on the absurdity of the division between the two territories, is militarized and earthbound; they are at a loss to explain and react to the supernatural power of the imaginal realm. In their view, this balloon could be some strange new Palestinian guerilla tactic. Like the Eternal Woman in the guise of a fedayee, the Red Balloon with its image of the keffiyeh-wearing Arafat rises above and across the

Figure 1.2. ES (Elia Suleiman) and the Woman (Manal Khader) releasing a red balloon that floats over the border. *Divine Intervention* (Koch Lorber Films).

political demarcation that is the border and out of the reach of mere physical intervention. The diversion is sufficient to allow ES and the Woman to pass together into Jerusalem. So does the Red Balloon—in one of the few tracking shots in the film—which then grows in size and floats over the Old City before settling on the Dome of the Rock mosque on the Temple Mount, one of the holiest sites for both Islam and Judaism.

Contrary to the claim by one film critic that this scene contributes to a "blissfully surreal" atmosphere in the film,[38] the Red Balloon fails to satisfy the Comte de Lautréamont's famous definition of the surreal as "the chance meeting on a dissecting table of a sewing machine and an umbrella;"[39] that is, as an autonomous and unconscious association of the artistic mind. No matter how absurd the border conflicts between Israelis and Palestinians become, the figure of the Red Balloon is a transport of the spiritual imagination, floating on the unseen breeze of divine love, and not explainable by either the physical senses or the intellect. This imaginal crossing is reminiscent of the short film *The Red Balloon* (*Le Ballon Rouge*, 1956) by Albert Lamorisse, in which a schoolboy is accompanied between home and school, through the threatening adult world, by a red balloon that appears to willfully traverse constructed human boundaries and antipathies. In this scene Suleiman invokes the primitive perception and instinctual psychology of the naive child, before his mind is clouded by experience and the mature world of rational intellect and political discord.

Following this allusion, we can examine both the scene in *Divine Intervention* and *The Red Balloon* according to the work of Jean Piaget in developmental psychology. In *The Child's Conception of the World*, Piaget describes three stages in the attribution of consciousness to things. Initially the child believes "All Things are Conscious"[40] and that movement of the bodies is "self-governed."[41] In the second stage, the child thinks "Things that can move are Conscious."[42] And finally, the child understands "Things that can move of their own accord are Conscious."[43] In the naive representation of the world by the child, inanimate physical objects such as balls, balloons, and clouds move because they are full of intentions, not because they are acted upon by external forces of cause and effect. Thus, a child's perception of phenomena and physical motion is imbued with primitive animism. As Piaget observes in *The Child's Conception of Physical Causality*, when children are asked why balloons rise, they reply, in the first stage, "because they want to fly away." "They go up because 'they like the air. So when you let go they go up in the sky.'"[44] This imputation of animistic consciousness is playfully explored by Lamorisse in *The Red Balloon*, as the balloon not only seems to *follow* the boy—suggesting that the balloon does not belong to the boy, but perhaps the reverse—and appears to avoid capture by adults and a malevolent gang of other children who envy the boy's balloon. The mind of an adult, Piaget tells us, sadly "becomes accustomed to the principle of inertia, [and] we are led to dismiss many forces as imaginary."[45] Children's inquiry of phenomena rarely shows evidence of a search for mechanical causality or logical justification; that is *how* things happen. Rather, in "a world filled and animated with intentions, such as the child conceives it to be, the true cause of a phenomenon is the moral reason for its happening. Every end calls forth the very force which is to realize it, and in looking for the 'why' of things, the child is also exploring the manner of their production."[46] Returning to *Divine Intervention*, we can see that Suleiman's Red Balloon, apparently animated with a consciousness of its own, leads its children to the only moral resolution of the conflict possible. The black screen title card for the scene is "I Am Crazy Because I Love You;" this is also written on one of the yellow sticky notes that ES uses to plot his film and which he affixes to his car's passenger window. While physical love may be the motivation for the trysts and border crossings of ES and the Woman, it is divine love that shows the way to resolution of conflict on the Temple Mount. An inquiry as to *how* such conflict might be resolved occurs only on the plane of the intellect (politics, causality) and has, thus far, been defeated. The Red Balloon, however, asks *why* such things happen and represents the force of moral reason. In his creation of an imaginal world in which balloons float at will and towers collapse untouched, Suleiman's *Divine Intervention* engages in *omnipotent infantilism* as the only way to overcome the politically stagnant dilemma of the Arab-Israeli conflict. Intriguingly, it unites the mode of perception common not only to early childhood developmental psychology but also to the aesthetics of early cinema.

Aesthetics of Silent Film and Negative Mimesis

The cinematic style of *Divine Intervention* is a provocative mélange of silent film aesthetics and art cinema reflexive techniques. It recalls both the one-scene shorts by the forerunners of cinema such as the Lumière brothers, and the deadpan expression and silent physical comedy of Buster Keaton in such films as *Sherlock, Jr.* (1924), as well as the disjointed narrative and other-worldly aura in Michelangelo Antonioni's *Blow-Up* (1966).

Suleiman's evocation of early silent-film aesthetics is prominent in his presentation of images. He resorts to a series of static one-scene shots, proscenium arch framing, and title cards to identify and separate scenes, which is necessitated by the absence of narration and minimal dialogue in the soundtrack. In a reflexive moment in the film, ES, as the diegetic director, stands in front of a wall in his apartment, on which there are a number of yellow sticky notes arranged in a rectangular pattern. He selects one of the notes, seemingly at random, and there follows a black screen title card that announces, "Father Dies." The scene not only introduces critical subject matter but also demonstrates the filmmaker's strategy of arranging his film in a nonlinear series of various tableaux. Suleiman tells postcolonial theorist Hamid Dabashi, "I never really come to a film through the structure. I simply jot down notes and build a story through them. Then I compose tableaux. When I get a tableau that stands by itself, it becomes an image."[47] Film historian Thomas Elsaesser notes that long static shots or tableaux, in which the spectator is imagined as viewing the scene from a centered seat in the theater, were frequently employed in the so-called primitive period of early cinema (1894 to 1908).[48] However, it would be mistaken to regard the primitive vision of early cinema as merely unsophisticated or elementary. Kristin Thompson prefers to "think of primitive films more in the sense that one speaks of primitive art, either produced by native cultures (e.g., Eskimo ivory carving) or untrained individuals (e.g., Henri Rousseau). That is, such primitive art is a system apart, whose simplicity can be of a value equal to more formal aesthetic traditions."[49] While it is true that Suleiman, like Rousseau in painting, was an autodidact in film and had no formal film-school training, his adoption of the tableaux of early cinema is in deliberate pursuit of qualities of vision that we associate with this kind of perception. Thompson suggests that a static long shot reflects the indebtedness of primitive film to vaudeville, and in *Divine Intervention* we can clearly see a vaudevillian assortment of physical comedy, satire, pathetic drama, short skits, music, and repeated actions that would be typical of the variety entertainment in a vaudeville house program, each introduced with title cards.

In addition to his adaptation of the primitive wonderment of early film aesthetics,[50] Suleiman employs a technique that started evolving during the transitional period in early cinema (1909–1917) before the introduction of analytical editing, namely, "editing within the frame"[51] and "staging in depth."[52] Moving away from the shallow tableaux of the primitive period, the films of this era were notable for the "combination of multiple planes of action with multiple views from different distances"[53] as a means of drawing the viewer into the action. A nearly textbook example of this technique occurs relatively early in *Divine Intervention*. The spectator has not been informed directly that Fuad Suleiman lost his business, but because he is a victim of political persecution and arrests by Israeli military police as a purported member of the Palestinian resistance, we can infer that his financial prospects are blighted. In one of the scenes, shot with a static camera and centered on the oblong living room of Fuad's home, we observe three men taking inventory of his property, presumably for repossession in settlement of his debts. One man is seated in the left foreground at the dining table tallying figures on a pad; a second man moves through the right middle ground to examine a china cabinet and takes notes; and a third man, also with a notebook, in the deep middle left of the shot, examines a painting. The foreground and background of the shot are separated by a rectangular archway that evokes a proscenium arch. Through the archway, in the center background, we see Fuad standing motionless with his back to the spectator, watching a football match on the television. His upper body is framed by a window that resembles the woodwork of the archway in the middle distance—a frame within a frame. The spectator, observing this scene from the stasis of the centered camera, must track the movement of the men through four separate planes in the shot. While the Israeli assessors move in and out of the frame, Fuad remains motionless, until he is finally presented with an accounting to sign and the men leave. No one in the room utters a word. The effect of this framing is to draw the viewer—from the static, centered position of the camera—into a sympathetic identification with the similarly static and multiply framed figure of Fuad in the background, rather than with the moving figures of the assessors in the middle and foreground of the shot. Everyone here is involved in the process of observing, but Fuad, watching the football match and not assessing the value of the television that he will soon lose, appears resigned to his fate. The staging in depth, reinforced by planar editing of frames within frames in this scene, strengthens the sense of confinement and melancholic resignation.

As Thompson asserts, the introduction of analytical editing in Hollywood cinema after 1917 marked the transition to classical film, establishing the rules of temporal continuity and creation of three-dimensional space in cinematic narrative. In contrast, Suleiman's deliberate use of static shots signals dispersed and fragmented representation, emphasizing nearly paralyzed moments in Arab lives suspended after the *Nakba* in 1948.[54] Instead of a kinetic movement through time, Suleiman's tableaux present a confined and delimited space that instills an aura of imprisonment similar to the experience of Palestinians under Israeli authority. Relying on the immobile tripod-based camera (with the prominent exceptions of tracking shots in imaginal border crossings and the Woman fedayee scenes), Suleiman provides a subtle commentary on the political stagnation of the infamous Middle Eastern conflict. A characteristic instance of this suspension is, suitably, the final tableau in *Divine Intervention*. ES and his mother (Nazira Suleiman) sit, expressionless and centered in the shot, on a sofa in her home. The scene is protracted, a floating island of nonhappening. A reverse shot reveals a pressure cooker, from which steam and an ominous hissing sound emanate. Finally, and without inflection, his mother utters the last lines of the film: "That's enough. Stop it now." The triple entendre of the line suggests, first, a warning that the repression of the Palestinians in their own lands can only lead to irruptions of violence; second, the recognition of the monotonous sameness of daily life under the occupation that makes time stop; and third, a reflexive comment that the filmmaker has made his point, or exhausted himself in trying to do so, and the film is about to end. Suleiman thus appropriates the mode of perception prevalent in early film grammar and turns it to face both the prolonged suffering of present-day Nazareth and the spectator.

Furthermore, Suleiman denies his main characters the right to speak or engage in dialogue. Noël Burch remarks that early silent film actors "have at their disposal a *language of gestures*."[55] When ES and the Woman meet at the checkpoint, they exchange knowing glances and caress one another's hands, which intertwine across the transmission column, a metaphor for the border that separates them. Suleiman states, "If I have a sensual moment of hands touching, or a gag that makes you laugh, that's already a kind of resistance. You can set up a checkpoint and ask for people's ID, but you cannot capture their imagination."[56] While the silence of actors such as Buster Keaton was imposed by the era's film technology, ES and his lover's refusal to speak could be interpreted as a form of negative mimesis. My understanding of negative mimesis stems from Theodor Adorno's observations in *Aesthetic Theory* on the negative representation of reality in modernity.[57] Adorno advances the possibility of negative mimesis by which modern art or literature expresses the truth through its "resistance to capitalist commodification, a resistance characterized by its opposition to a society that it nevertheless brings back into the artwork by means of indirect critique."[58] By refusing to imitate the false surfaces of mass culture, modern art produces "an uncompromising reprint of reality while at the same time avoiding being contaminated by it."[59] Only by negative mimesis can an artist such as Kafka express his resistance to the authoritarian bureaucracy that destroys modern life in the twentieth century. I propose a broader understanding of negative mimesis that emphasizes the resistance of minority discourse to dominant culture. Although the word *negative* could be used in the sense of *rejection* in opposition to *acceptance*, we should also consider the dialectic of *absence* versus *presence*. I approach negative mimesis not only as an ideological resistance or political objection but also as an aesthetic strategy of meaningful absence.

Absence of speech, manifested by ES's expressive silence and the self-denial of dialogue between the lovers in *Divine Intervention* comments obliquely on the stiflingly repressive regime in which they must live. As Hamid Dabashi poignantly remarks, "At the heart of Elia Suleiman's cinema dwells a dark humor, the frivolity of a pointed anger mutated into laughter, a crisis of mimesis."[60] Suleiman's bonding of the aesthetics of silent film and the nonrepresentational techniques of art cinema offers a unique response to oppression in the historical narrative of Palestine. Dabashi argues that Suleiman's cinema presents the magic of an anodyne in "visual defiance of the metaphysical violence at the roots of any mimetic narrative of a colossal injustice."[61] Mimesis in historical narrative, either in fiction or documentary film—even if the purpose of that representation is to repudiate it—will, to a degree, validate the narrative of dominance by invoking a dialectical response. Instead, Suleiman resorts to negative mimesis because he acknowledges that there can be, as Linda Williams puts it, "traumatic historical truths inaccessible to representation."[62] ES and the Woman therefore refuse to engage in dialogue, neither asserting nor renouncing the antagonistic positions of a colonial power. Suleiman's cinematic aesthetics are a solution to "the *cul-de-sac* of representing the unrepresentable."[63] Silence and secret discourse (ES's father mutters unflattering epithets at his Nazarene neighbors from the privacy of his car) point to the conceptual border that separates absence and presence, exile and residence, life and death. ES's silence avoids a political tendentiousness that might repel some spectators not already predisposed to the Palestinian cause. Suleiman remarks that

> in silence there is a vacuum, and that this vacuum, this empty space, is the potentiality of filling the blank, which in turn raises the question of what is to be filled in the blank. In other words, not too much polluted rigor or speech or that which can be preachy to the spectator, and thus the spectator has that meditative capacity or role or space to actually fill in or participate with the image.[64]

Just like the Woman, Suleiman's silent onscreen persona easily adheres to the figure of the subaltern. According to Gayatri Chakravorty Spivak, the subaltern, as a minority, speaks a different language that is not understood and therefore rejected and silenced by the power structures. Her verdict is concise: "The subaltern cannot speak" because "she cannot be heard."[65] However, the powerlessness of this subordinate position in *Divine Intervention* is replaced by the gesture of silence as an act of resistance that destabilizes the power structure. Silence in *Divine Intervention* is used as a form of negative mimesis and provides deliberate cancellation of all noise, as well as a strategic occupation of the position of a tacit observer as opposed to a speechless victim—a process that is paradoxically empowering. Suleiman's muteness in a modern film with considerable ambient sound is a deliberate tactic that heightens the juxtaposition between absence and presence. Silence, along with the static fragmented tableaux and intertitle cards, works to resist both cinematic diegesis and an oppressive historical narrative.

Coda

On June 15, 1969, in her statement to the *Sunday Times*, former Israeli prime minister Golda Meir famously declared, "There is no such thing as a Palestinian people. . . . It is not as if we came and threw them out and took their country. They didn't exist."[66] By Israeli law, Palestinians who had fled their homes after the 1948 Arab-Israeli war, but returned after the conflict, were not permitted to reclaim their properties and towns, which became instead the property of the new state of Israel. These Palestinians were quizzically deemed *present absentees* because they were considered present on the land but supposedly absent from their homes.[67] In a further irony of this displacement, the Academy of Motion Picture Arts and Sciences determined that *Divine Intervention* was ineligible for consideration in the Best Foreign Language Film category for 2002 because the film "emerges from a country not formally recognized by the United Nations."[68] The decision sparked an international controversy, especially since other territories such as Hong Kong, Puerto Rico, and Taiwan had a long history of nominations in the Academy Awards competition. The silent witness that ES bears toward the Palestinian cause was itself subjected to a form of censorship, and its presentation of the nonplaces at the border of Israel and the West Bank was likewise deemed to emanate from a nonexistent country. As an accented filmmaker, Suleiman observes that there are "[n]ot only the checkpoints in Ramallah, but psychological checkpoints all over the world" that must be overcome.[69] Silent film aesthetics and negative mimesis seem ideally suited to depict the plight of Palestinians who were designated present absentees and made to disappear. Meeting on the roadway between Jerusalem and Ramallah, in a nonplace parking area carved out of a barren hillside, ES and the Woman assert that the harsh border comprised by intransigent national politics and military force can only be subsumed by spiritual leavening, or divine intervention.

Notes

1. Henry Corbin, "Mundus Imaginalis or the Imaginary and the Imaginal," trans. Ruth Horine, 1972, in *The Legacy of Henry Corbin*, October 20, 2009, http://henrycorbinproject.blogspot.com/ 2009/10/mundus-imaginalis-or-imaginary-and.html. Henry Corbin, *The Voyage and the Messenger: Iran and Philosophy*, trans. Joseph Rowe (Berkeley, CA: North Atlantic Books, 1998).

2. Theodor Adorno, *Aesthetic Theory*, trans. C. Lenhart (London: Routledge & Kegan Paul, 1984).

3. Sheila Johnston, "Hey, Heard the One about the Firebomb? Is There a Comic Side to Life across the Palestine/Israeli Divide?" *Independent on Sunday* (London), January 12, 2003.

4. European Graduate School, "Elia Suleiman—Biography," accessed October 24, 2012, http://www.egs.edu/faculty/ elia-suleiman/biography/.

5. Richard Porton, "Notes from the Palestinian Diaspora: An Interview with Elia Suleiman," *Cineaste* 28, no. 3 (2003): 24–27.

6. The dedication of *Chronicle of a Disappearance* reads "To My Mother and Father, the Last Homeland."

7. Hamid Naficy, *An Accented Cinema: Exilic and Diasporic Filmmaking* (Princeton: Princeton University Press, 2001), 116.

8. Naficy, *Accented Cinema*, 4–6.

9. Naficy, *Accented Cinema*, 31.

10. Naficy, *Accented Cinema*, 32.

11. Naficy, *Accented Cinema*, 33.

12. Corbin, "Mundus Imaginalis," 2.

13. Yasser Arafat (1929–2004) was the first president of the Palestinian National Authority.

14. Laura Mulvey, "Visual Pleasure and Narrative Cinema," *Screen* 16, no. 3 (1975): 6–18.

15. Gayatri Chakravorty Spivak. "Can the Subaltern Speak?" in *Marxism and the Interpretation of Culture*, ed. Cary Nelson and Lawrence Grossberg (Urbana: University of Illinois Press, 1988), 271–313. Spivak defines the subaltern as a subordinate subject within the dominant discourse.

16. Suleiman noted in his interview that Palestinian audiences applauded at exactly this very moment. "Interview with Elia Suleiman," *Divine Intervention*, directed by Elia Suleiman (2002, New York: Koch Lorber Films, 2005), DVD.

17. Suleiman recounts the incident to Hamid Dabashi: "I wrote this scene about ten years ago inspired by a moment when Manal [Khader] and I had a rendezvous to have a coffee in Jerusalem. She wanted to defy the checkpoint and a soldier pointed a rifle at her, she said go ahead and shoot, I'm crossing. They didn't shoot." Hamid Dabashi, "In Praise of Frivolity: On the Cinema of Elia Suleiman," in *Dreams of a Nation: On Palestinian Cinema*, ed. Hamid Dabashi (New York: Verso, 2006), 146.

18. Refqa Abu-Remaileh argues that her walk "is more of a glamorous catwalk compared to what we might expect defiance and resistance to look like," overlooking

a feminist reading of the scene. Refqua Abu-Remaileh, "Palestinian Anti-Narratives in the Films of Elia Suleiman," *Arab Media & Society* 5 (Spring 2008), http://www.arabmediasociety.com/countries/index.php?c_article=152.

19. See Corbin, "Mundus Imaginalis," and Corbin, *Voyage*.

20. Corbin, "Mundus Imaginalis," 5.

21. Corbin, "Mundus Imaginalis," 2.

22. Corbin, *Voyage*, 125.

23. Corbin, "Mundus Imaginalis," 1.

24. Corbin, "Mundus Imaginalis," 5.

25. Corbin, *Voyage*, 131.

26. See, for example, Abu-Remaileh, "Palestinian Anti-Narratives," or Suleiman's interview with Richard Porton, "Notes from the Palestinian Diaspora."

27. Corbin, "Mundus Imaginalis," 9.

28. Corbin, "Mundus Imaginalis," 4.

29. Henry Corbin, *Creative Imagination in the Ṣūfism of Ibn 'Arabī*, trans. Ralph Manheim (Princeton: Princeton University Press, 1969), 159.

30. Corbin, *Creative Imagination*, 157–158.

31. Corbin, *Creative Imagination*, 159.

32. The keffiyeh was adopted by Yasser Arafat as the more-or-less official uniform of the Palestinian resistance movement.

33. In Sheila Johnston's film review "Hey, Heard the One about the Firebomb?" Suleiman is quoted as saying that this scene was inspired by a billboard with an advertisement for a shooting range that he saw outside of Tel Aviv.

34. The Fedayeen (pl., Arabic, "redeemers") are members of the armed militia among Arab Palestinians.

35. Natacha Atlas, vocal performance of "I Put a Spell on You" by Screaming Jay Hawkins, on *Intervention Divine,* Milan Music, 2002, compact disc.

36. Corbin, *Creative Imagination*, 157.

37. Perhaps a cross-cultural allusion to Suleiman's own Arab-Christian upbringing.

38. Desson Howe, "A 'Divine' Film Tackles Surreal Life," *Washington Post*, January 31, 2003.

39. Comte de Lautréamont (Isidore Ducasse), *Maldoror (Les Chants de Maldoror)*, trans. Guy Wernham (New York: New Directions, 1965), 263.

40. Jean Piaget, *The Child's Conception of the World*, trans. Joan and Andrew Tomlinson (Totowa, NJ: Littlefield, Adams & Company, 1967), 174.

41. Piaget, *Child's Conception of the World*, 181.

42. Piaget, *Child's Conception of the World*, 179.

43. Piaget, *Child's Conception of the World*, 182.

44. Jean Piaget, *The Child's Conception of Physical Causality*, trans. Marjorie Gabain (Totowa, NJ: Littlefield, Adams & Company, 1969), 110.

45. Piaget, *Child's Conception of Physical Causality*, 116.

46. Piaget, *Child's Conception of Physical Causality*, 120.

47. Dabashi, "In Praise of Frivolity," 135.

48. Thomas Elsaesser, "Introduction," in *Early Cinema: Space, Frame, Narrative*, ed. Thomas Elsaesser (London: British Film Institute, 1990), 20.

49. Kristin Thompson, "The Formulation of the Classical Style, 1909–28," in *The Classical Hollywood Cinema: Film Style & Mode of Production to 1960*, ed. David Bordwell, Janet Staiger, and Kristin Thompson (New York: Columbia University Press, 1985), 158.

50. For a discussion of this phenomenon, see Tom Gunning, "An Aesthetic of Astonishment: Early Film and the (In)Credulous Spectator," in *Film Theory and Criticism*, 7th ed., ed. Leo Braudy and Marshall Cohen (New York: Oxford University Press, 2009), 736–50.

51. Elsaesser, "Introduction," 21.

52. Staging in depth is most notably discussed in David Bordwell, "Exceptionally Exact Perceptions: On Staging in Depth," in *On the History of Film Style* (Cambridge, MA: Harvard University Press, 1997), 158–271.

53. Thompson, "Formulation," 216.

54. The *Nakba* (an-Nakbah), "disaster" or "catastrophe" in Arabic, refers to the Palestinian exodus during the 1948 Arab-Israeli war when nearly three-quarters of a million Arab-Palestinians fled or were expelled from their homes.

55. Elsaesser, "Introduction," 224.

56. Johnston, "Hey, Heard the One about the Firebomb?"

57. Adorno, *Aesthetic Theory.*

58. Marjorie Perloff, "The Aura of Modernism," *Modernist Cultures* 1, no. 1 (Spring 2005). http://marjorieperloff.com/articles/aura-modernism/#ixzz204SqbXY1.

59. Adorno, *Aesthetic Theory*, 28.

60. Dabashi, "In Praise of Frivolity," 135.

61. Dabashi, "In Praise of Frivolity," 135.

62. Linda Williams, "Mirrors without Memories: Truth, History, and *The Thin Blue Line*," in *Documenting the Documentary: Close Readings of Documentary Film and Video*, ed. Barry Keith Grant and Jeannette Sloniowski (Detroit: Wayne State University Press, 1998), 382.

63. Dabashi, "In Praise of Frivolity," 148.

64. Dabashi, "In Praise of Frivolity," 154.

65. Spivak, "Can the Subaltern Speak?" 308.

66. Meir's statement was reprinted on June 16, 1969 in the *Washington Post*, "Golda Meir Scorns Soviets: Israeli Premier Explains Stand on Big-4 Talks, Security. Mrs. Meir Bars Any 'Deal' for Israel's Security."

67. Note that the subtitle of Suleiman's *The Time That Remains*, based on his father's experiences of that time, is *Chronicle of a Present Absentee.*

68. Leela Jacinto, "No Room for Palestinian Film at the Oscars," *ABC News*, December 20, 2002, http://abcnews.go.com/International/story?id=79485&page=1.

69. Porton, "Notes from the Palestinian Diaspora," 27.

Works Cited

Abu-Remaileh, Refqa. "Palestinian Anti-Narratives in the Films of Elia Suleiman." *Arab Media & Society* 5 (Spring 2008). http://www.arabmediasociety.com/countries/index.php?c_article=152.

Adorno, Theodor. *Aesthetic Theory*. Translated by C. Lenhart. London: Routledge & Kegan Paul, 1984.

Atlas, Natacha. Vocal performance of "I Put a Spell on You" by screaming Jay Hawkins. On *Intervention Divine*. Milan Music, 2002, compact disc.

Bordwell, David. "Exceptionally Exact Perceptions: On Staging in Depth." In *On the History of Film Style*, 158–271. Cambridge, MA: Harvard University Press, 1997.

Burch, Noël. "A Primitive Mode of Representation?" In *Early Cinema: Space, Frame, Narrative*, edited by Thomas Elsaesser, 220–227. London: British Film Institute, 1990.

Comte de Lautréamont (Isidore Ducasse). *Maldoror (Les Chants de Maldoror)*. Translated by Guy Wernham. New York: New Directions, 1965.

Corbin, Henry. *Creative Imagination in the Ṣūfism of Ibn 'Arabī*. Translated by Ralph Manheim. Princeton: Princeton University Press, 1969.

——. "Mundus Imaginalis or the Imaginary and the Imaginal." Translated by Ruth Horine. 1972. *The Legacy of Henry Corbin*. October 20, 2009. http://henrycorbinproject.blogspot.com/2009/10/ mundus-imaginalis-or-imaginary-and.html.

——. *The Voyage and the Messenger: Iran and Philosophy*. Translated by Joseph Rowe. Berkeley, CA: North Atlantic Books, 1998.

Dabashi, Hamid. "In Praise of Frivolity: On the Cinema of Elia Suleiman." In *Dreams of a Nation: On Palestinian Cinema*, edited by Hamid Dabashi, 131–160. New York: Verso, 2006.

Elsaesser, Thomas. "Introduction." In *Early Cinema: Space, Frame, Narrative*, edited by Thomas Elsaesser, 11–30. London: British Film Institute, 1990.

European Graduate School. "Elia Suleiman—Biography." Accessed October 24, 2012. http://www.egs.edu/faculty/elia-suleiman/biography/.

Gunning, Tom. "An Aesthetic of Astonishment: Early Film and the (In)Credulous Spectator." In *Film Theory and Criticism*, 7th ed., edited by Leo Braudy and Marshall Cohen, 736–750. New York: Oxford University Press, 2009.

Howe, Desson. "A 'Divine' Film Tackles Surreal Life." *Washington Post*, January 31, 2003.

Jacinto, Leela. "No Room for Palestinian Film at the Oscars." *ABC News*, December 20, 2002. http://abcnews.go.com/International/story?id=79485&page=1.

Johnston, Sheila. "Hey, Heard the One about the Firebomb? Is There a Comic Side to Life across the Palestine/Israeli Divide?" *Independent on Sunday* (London), January 12, 2003.

Joi. Performance of "Fingers." On *Intervention Divine*. Milan Music, 2002, compact disc.

Meir, Golda. "Golda Meir Scorns Soviets: Israeli Premier Explains Stand on Big-4 Talks, Security." Interview by Frank Giles. *Washington Post*, June 16, 1969, A15.

Merleau-Ponty, Maurice. *The Visible and the Invisible* (Studies in Phenomenology and Existential Philosophy). Translated by Alphonso Lingis. Evanston, IL: Northwestern University Press, 1969.

Mulvey, Laura. "Visual Pleasure and Narrative Cinema." *Screen* 16, no. 3 (1975): 6–18.

Naficy, Hamid. *An Accented Cinema: Exilic and Diasporic Filmmaking*. Princeton: Princeton University Press, 2001.

Perloff, Marjorie. "The Aura of Modernism." *Modernist Cultures* 1, no. 1 (Spring 2005). http://marjorieperloff.com/articles/aura-modernism/#ixzz204SqbXY1.
Piaget, Jean. *The Child's Conception of Physical Causality.* Translated by Marjorie Gabain. Totowa, NJ: Littlefield, Adams & Company, 1969.
——. *The Child's Conception of the World.* Translated by Joan and Andrew Tomlinson. Totowa, NJ: Littlefield, Adams & Company, 1967.
Porton, Richard. "Notes from the Palestinian Diaspora: An Interview with Elia Suleiman." *Cineaste* 28, no. 3 (2003): 24–27.
Spivak, Gayatri Chakravorty. "Can the Subaltern Speak?" In *Marxism and the Interpretation of Culture,* edited by Cary Nelson and Lawrence Grossberg, 271–313. Urbana: University of Illinois Press, 1988.
Thompson, Kristin. "The Formulation of the Classical Style, 1909–28." In *The Classical Hollywood Cinema: Film Style & Mode of Production to 1960,* edited by David Bordwell, Janet Staiger, and Kristin Thompson, 155–240. New York: Columbia University Press, 1985.
Williams, Linda. "Mirrors without Memories: Truth, History, and *The Thin Blue Line.*" In *Documenting the Documentary: Close Readings of Documentary Film and Video,* edited by Barry Keith Grant and Jeannette Sloniowski, 379–396. Detroit: Wayne State University Press, 1998.

Films

Blow-Up. Directed by Michelangelo Antonioni. Italy, 1966.
Chronicle of a Disappearance. Directed by Elia Suleiman. Israel, Palestine, 1996.
Divine Intervention: A Chronicle of Love and Pain. Directed by Elia Suleiman. France, Palestine, 2002.
The Red Balloon. Directed by Albert Lamorisse. France, 1956.
Sherlock, Jr. 1924. Directed by Buster Keaton. United States, 1924.
The Time That Remains: Chronicle of a Present Absentee. Directed by Elia Suleiman. United Kingdom, 2009.

2

Underground Bridges

Tunnels in the Films of Emir Kusturica— Underground *(1995) and* Life Is a Miracle *(2004)*

Dennis Browne

THE IMAGE OF A BRIDGE spanning natural obstacles or joining divided frontiers is a frequent symbol of a quest for unity; a prime example is its use on euro paper currency from the five to five hundred euro banknotes. Bridges offer creative artists a palette brimming with visual potential, and they are conspicuous, always adding to the landscape in which they are placed. Tunnels, on the other hand, present a more limited set of options both spatially and luminously. They are, for the most part, inconspicuous, in essence annulling the landscape under which they lie. In his two films set during the conflicts of the 1990s in former Yugoslavia, Emir Kusturica chose the more confining architecture of tunnels to challenge the validity of bounded and bordered communities and to question and even defy the social and political superstructure of late twentieth-century Europe. The subterranean viaducts of *Underground* (*Bila jednom jedna zemlja*, 1995) and *Life Is a Miracle* (*Život je čudo*, 2004) are both framework and freeway for his cast of characters confronting the dissolution of their country.

Ivo Andrić's *The Bridge on the Drina*

Kusturica's use of tunnels can also be seen as a trope for the most famous architectural structure used in Yugoslav literature, the Mehmed Paša Sokolović Bridge on the Drina River, in the eastern Bosnian town of Višegrad. The bridge was a gift to the region from one of the Ottoman Empire's greatest statesmen, Grand Vizier Sokollu Mehmed Paša. When the bridge was completed in 1577, the frontiers of the Ottoman Empire lay far to the north, but historical events would bring the empire's borders much closer, at times turning the bridge's central meeting space, the *kapija*,[1] into a demarcation between empires, religious communities, and emerging nation-states. Mining the rich frontier history of eastern Bosnia and the symbolic potential of bridges, Nobel laureate Ivo Andrić created some of the most memorable images in Balkan literature when he paid tribute to the Grand Vizier's gift in his historical novel *The Bridge on the Drina* (*Na Drini ćuprija*, 1945). Today, a half century after Andrić was awarded the Nobel Prize in Literature (1961) and four and a half centuries after the bridge's completion, filmmaker Emir Kusturica is raising an architectural monument of his own in Višegrad. On a four-and-a-half-acre site just a few meters downstream from the Grand Vizier's gift, Kusturica is overseeing the construction of Andrićgrad, a collection of stone buildings intended to attract tourists and scholars and eventually serve as a setting for a cinematic adaptation of Andrić's masterpiece.[2] The creative efforts of both the novelist and the cinematographer are internationally recognized for their images of everyday life in the Balkans.[3] But where Andrić sets much of his saga's action on the symbolically loaded structure of a bridge, Kusturica, in his two films about the Yugoslav wars of the 1990s, moves the action underground into sewers, cellars, railroad tunnels, and fantastic subterranean labyrinths. These subsurface areas in *Underground* and *Life Is a Miracle*, like the space on Andrić's bridge, emphasize transition and transformation. As characters traverse Kusturica's underground bridges, they experience border crossings not only of a physical and political nature but also those that shape and transform both individual and communal identities. In *Life Is a Miracle* they are also incorporated into the technical aspects of the film's photography, while in *Underground* they offer different visions of the Yugoslav idea.

Life Is a Miracle

Life Is a Miracle is Kusturica's second war film, made almost a decade after *Underground* and the end of the conflict in Bosnia.[4] The time frame and setting of the film are simpler than in the more controversial *Underground*, but the cast of characters in *Life* is more varied, if for no other reason than that in addition to corrupt officials, ignorant western journalists, clueless United Nations soldiers, and local villains, the film has a healthy number of appealing, positive heroes. It is, basically, the story of Luka (played by Slavko Štimac), a Serbian engineer who, after moving back to his birthplace, sees his peaceful family life fall apart as war approaches. First, Jadranka (Vesna Trivalić), his neurotic wife, runs away with a Hungarian musician (Nele Karajlć); then his son Miloš (Vuk Kostić), serving in the Yugoslav army, is captured by Bosnian Muslim forces. His situation seems to worsen when he is given custody of Sabaha (Nataša Šolak), a captured Bosnian Muslim nurse, who is to be used in a prisoner exchange for his son. But as conditions in the region deteriorate, Luka realizes that he prefers the life he has with his Muslim hostage to the one he lost with his Serbian wife and son. His immediate family and his extended Yugoslav family are casualties of the conflict, but Sabaha, whose name is derived from the Bosnian *sabah* (dawn) as well as a combination of the first and last letters of the republics of *Srbija*, *Bosna*, and *Hrvatska* (Serbia, Bosnia, Croatia) reinvigorates Luka, and the two decide to leave the disintegrating Yugoslav community and start a new life together in Australia.

Luka is in charge of reopening an abandoned railway, which runs through the hilly countryside that forms the Serbian-Bosnian frontier.[5] Part of that assignment involves overseeing the completion of a tunnel, one of dozens that cut through the local mountains. Luka knows the details of each and every one of those tunnels. He knows their length, the number of railroad ties in each one, all of their twists and turns, and the elevation changes of the entire system. Luka transfers that knowledge to a detailed scale model he is building in the attic of the stationmaster's house that he and his family occupy. The model of the railway, complete with villages, train stations, ski lifts, and tunnels, is Luka's version of a film storyboard, but in the narrative he creates for his tabletop frontier there are no paramilitaries, corrupt politicians, war profiteers, or ignorant western journalists. His is a miniature *mirna Bosna*, "peaceful Bosnia," a phrase he repeats as if uttering an incantation to ward off the violent reality that is just over the horizon.

When Luka unveils his model to a group of local notables, he draws their attention to one particular tunnel, which, when opened, will overcome one of the project's major engineering obstacles. Kusturica cuts to Luka's son and his drinking buddies as they drive their car into that very tunnel, where they park and proceed to shoot bottles off one another's heads. Staying with this railroad and tunnel motif, the director immediately cuts back to Luka and his friend, the postman Veljo (Aleksandar Berček), as they transport the model back to the stationmaster's house on the trunk of a converted automobile mounted on railroad wheels. They are passing through one of the completed tunnels when they find the track blocked by a donkey standing just at the tunnel's exit. We first meet the donkey—her name is Milica—in the establishing shot of the film, when we see her owner, the coffin maker Vujan (Obrad Đurović), looking for her. Eventually he finds her standing astride a railroad track waiting for a train. She turns out to be a lovesick donkey who has decided to end her misery by letting a train run over her.

Figure 2.1. Luka's presentation of the model and renovation project. *Life Is a Miracle* (Artificial Eye).

Milica is not alone in contemplating intentional death under the wheels of a steam locomotive. Luka and Sabaha have similar ideas. Sabaha's thoughts of suicide occur after she fights with Jadranka, who, having returned from her brief fling with the Hungarian musician, expects Luka to forgive her and accept her back in the family. The two women scuffle, and Sabaha runs away. Luka finds her on a railroad bridge where she tells him that if a train came she would simply let it run over her. Luka has suicidal inclinations twice, both times as he is walking or riding the handcar through a tunnel. His first attempt comes after he learns of his son's capture by Bosnian Muslim paramilitaries; the second occurs after he loses Sabaha in the prisoner exchange

Figure 2.2. Luka's first thoughts of suicide. *Life Is a Miracle* (Artificial Eye).

for Miloš at the film's conclusion. In the first instance, he changes his mind just as the train rushes past only a few inches from his face. In the second, he is saved by Milica, who steps between him and the train, either in a conscious effort to save him or in another failed attempt to end her own life. In either case, the train stops just a few feet short of Luka's long-eared protector.

Life's Tunnels as Cinematic Tools

Kusturica uses tunnels as a framing device and in a variety of scene transitions. All of the central characters, with the exception of Captain Aleksić of the Yugoslav army (Stribor Kusturica) and Sabaha, are introduced on or near the railroad, often with a tunnel framing the actors. Luka appears first at the stationmaster's house, but quickly jumps into his converted automobile and drives off to an orchestra rehearsal. Veljo is introduced skipping through fields as he delivers the mail, and then appears on a handcar driving into a tunnel. Within the first minutes of the film, we see Miloš and his Muslim friend Eso (Adnan Omerović) herding chickens along the tracks, a tunnel looming in the background. The town mayor (Branislav Lalević) and Filipović (Nikola Kojo), a corrupt and unscrupulous lawyer who has the mayor assassinated later in the film, are introduced as they drive through the tunnels in the mayor's converted limousine—also fitted with railroad wheels.

Tunnels offer a natural light-dark contrast for use in scenes with emotional transitions. For example, the scene in which Veljo tells Luka that he observed

Figure 2.3. Veljo entering a tunnel during *Life*'s opening credits. *Life Is a Miracle* (Artificial Eye).

Figure 2.4. Miloš and Eso framed by a tunnel. *Life Is a Miracle* (Artificial Eye).

Jadranka leaving town with the Hungarian musician begins with a natural fade-in, created as the two exit a tunnel into daylight. Veljo mistakenly thinks Luka has arranged his wife's departure to keep her safe, but realizes his mistake when he sees that Luka is emotionally shaken by the news. The camera stays on Luka as the handcar enters a tunnel—at first he is framed against the dark background of the tunnel entrance, then swallowed in its darkness as the screen fades to black.

Tunnels also serve as settings for several scenes of life and death. Life begins in one tunnel when Sabaha delivers the child of a young Serbian woman who, with her family and other local Serbs, has taken refuge there from the

Figure 2.5. Entrance of the mayor and Filipović in the mayor's special limousine. *Life Is a Miracle* (Artificial Eye).

fighting. This simple, almost prosaic depiction of life beginning is contrasted to the bizarre depiction of life ending when Filipović, the corrupt lawyer, murderer, and local Serbian war profiteer, is assassinated while masturbating with the aid of a pay-for-sex telephone service in Germany. He is standing just inside a tunnel, completing his international business, when he is vaporized by an antitank missile fired from a rocket launcher. Filipović had been using the railway to smuggle drugs, cigarettes, and weapons across—more precisely, under—the Serbian-Bosnian border.

Borders and Corruption

Smuggling and human trafficking are present in other Kusturica films: *Do You Remember Dolly Bell?* (*Sjećaš li se Doli Bel?*, 1981); *Time of the Gypsies* (*Dom za vešanje*, 1988); *Black Cat, White Cat* (*Crna mačka, beli mačor*, 1998); and *Promise Me This* (*Zavet*, 2007). In these and his two war films, Kusturica makes it clear that human trafficking and war profiteering are the most loathsome forms of illicit border activity. Most of the characters involved in these or similar criminal transactions meet a violent death or an absurd comeuppance: the Gypsy kingpin Ahmed (Bora Todorović) is killed at his wedding celebration by an entranced fork volant to his throat in *Time of the Gypsies*, Marko Dren (Miki Manojlović) is beaten by his brother and then burned to death in *Underground*, the lawyer/war profiteer Filipović is shot with a rocket launcher in *Life Is a Miracle*, a corrupt Bulgarian border guard (Stojan Sotirov) is hung on a railroad crossing barricade in *Black Cat, White Cat* (also in this film, the gangster Dadan Karambolo [Srđan Todorović] is dropped into excrement), and the crime boss Bajo (Miki Manojlović) is castrated in *Promise Me This*.

Exploitation of borders by the authorities of a state is equally opprobrious. In *The Bridge on the Drina*, Andrić describes a temporary blockhouse the Ottomans build on the *kapija* to control border crossings by Serbian rebels during the early nineteenth-century Karadjordje Uprising.[6] The structure spoils not only the appearance of the *kapija*, but its communal function as well.[7] Similarly, as Luka takes the town mayor on a tour of the railway, Jadranka points out to the mayor and his wife that the entrance of the tunnel is in Bosnia and its exit in Serbia, which means the border is somewhere above them. The mayor makes it clear that he would consider the installation of customs and border controls in the tunnel to be a tragedy. A historical tunnel, like a historical bridge, should not be disfigured with symbols of ephemeral state power.

Bridge and Tunnel in *Life*'s Conclusion

Life Is a Miracle ends with both a bridge and a tunnel as the final two settings of the film. In the penultimate scene on a small footbridge near the banks of the Drina, Luka is reunited with Miloš but he loses Sabaha, who is returned, against her wishes, to the Bosnian Muslim side. The final scene depicts Luka's second attempt to let a train run over him in a tunnel; Kusturica uses a crossfade to join the last two frames of the film. In the frame preceding the fade-out, we see Luka hugging his rescuer, Milica, and looking over his shoulder toward the train. The two are bathed in sunlight coming from low on the horizon. Sunset or sunrise? The fade in of the final frame reveals Luka and Sabaha riding Milica through a tunnel; thus, the light source before the crossfade could represent Sabaha's presence at the moment when Luka is saved. The film freezes on the threesome just as they emerge from the tunnel into natural light, and the final credits begin to roll. The camera is inside the tunnel; thus, the arc of the tunnel walls and ceiling creates a frame around the happy couple.

This crossfade of the final scene invites several interpretations. One possible reading of the conclusion is that Luka does in fact commit suicide; that is, the train runs over him and what we see is a happy afterlife in which he is reunited with Sabaha. A second reading would have the story end when the screen goes to black and everything depicted after the fade in is part of Luka's memory; thus, he is recalling happier moments with Sabaha. That she is dressed as she was when the two tried to escape across the Drina to Serbia

Figure 2.6. Luka, Sabaha, and Milica exit a tunnel in the film's concluding scene. *Life Is a Miracle* (Artificial Eye).

and from there to Australia supports such an interpretation. Finally, there is the possibility that Milica does indeed prevent the train from killing Luka, that Sabaha is on the train, and the Bosnian Muslim Juliet and Serbian Romeo are happily reunited.

Underground and History

In addition to their use as sites for narrative development, the tunnels in *Life Is a Miracle* and the *kapija* and the bridge in *The Bridge on the Drina* have another shared feature—the historical authenticity of the structures: Andrić features an Ottoman bridge; Kusturica, the Austro-Hungarian railway. *Life Is a Miracle*, however, lacks the centuries-long frame of reference of Andrić's historical saga. That feature is better captured in Kusturica's first war film, *Underground* (1995), which rests on a complex network of chronotopes much more intricate and nuanced than the film's tripartite structure suggests. Even the historical references in the film's numerous dialog boxes provide only partial explication of the film's rich historical, social, and political boundaries.[8]

The film's first dialog box sets the place and time of the story as Belgrade on April 6, 1941, the first day of Hitler's retaliatory bombardment of the defiant city. But even before the Roma brass band finishes playing Goran Bregović's "Kalašnikov" and the opening credits fade from the screen, Kusturica draws our attention to an earlier date, which is prominently displayed on the exterior of the building in which one of the film's main protagonists, Petar Popara

Figure 2.7. Vera reacting to the noisy arrival of Crni and Marko. *Underground* (Artificial Eye).

Crni (Lazar Ristovski), lives. In a reaction shot, Crni's wife, Vera (Mirjana Karanović), appears in a second-floor window and looks to her left toward the source of music and commotion being created by her husband and his best friend, Marko Dren. Her gaze highlights the upper right third of the frame in which the date 1928 is displayed.

The last year of the Versailles-denominated Kingdom of Serbs, Croats, and Slovenes was 1928; beginning in January of 1929, King Alexander nullified the country's constitution, prorogued the representative parliament, declared a dictatorship, and renamed the country the Kingdom of Yugoslavia. Several months later, he redrew the internal boundaries of Yugoslavia, instituting nine administrative units called *banovinas*, which were intentionally created so as not to conform to pre–World War I imperial borders or to reflect ethnic boundaries.[9] And in one more step in the direction of *yugoslavism*, the King attempted, by edict, to abolish use of the Cyrillic alphabet.[10]

In one of *Underground*'s final scenes, some fifty years after Vera looks out her window in the film's introduction, we see her husband, Crni, leading a group of war refugees back to Belgrade in a composition reminiscent of an iconic nineteenth-century painting by Serbian Realist painter Paja Jovanović. The painting, *Seoba Srba*, depicts the migration of Serbs in the late seventeenth century from Kosovo. In traditional Serbian historiography, thousands of families left Kosovo with Serbian Orthodox Patriarch Arsenija

Figure 2.8. Paja Jovanović's *Seoba Srba*. Wikimedia Commons/Public Domain.

Figure 2.9. Crni leading war refugees through the tunnels. *Underground* (Artificial Eye).

Čarnojević (both the family name Čarnojević and the sobriquet Crni are based on the Slavic root for "black"). Thus, in addition to the beginning of the Nazi occupation of Yugoslavia (1941), the completion of the Berlin Wall and the establishment of the Non-Aligned Movement (1961), the death of Tito (1980), and the first full year of armed conflict in Yugoslavia (1992), the film comprehends a broad and complex panorama of responses to not only south Slav political and social questions, but to those of Europe, as well.[11]

Underground's Underground

Most readings of the film's subterranean spaces focus attention on the cellar in which Marko first hides, then shelters, and finally interns several dozen of his fellow citizens both during and after the Nazi occupation of Belgrade. The elaborate artifice Marko creates to manipulate and mislead the underground community and the cellar in which they reside are frequently seen as a trope for Tito's Yugoslavia; or Milošević's Serbia,[12] the "only adequate setting for the Balkans"[13]; or Plato's Cave.[14] Here, I suggest a reading that sees a much more consequential and differentiated role for all of the underground spaces: the cellar, the Belgrade sewers, and the fantastic labyrinth of tunnels extending throughout Europe.

The central features of Marko's cellar, if seen as overstated versions of both Tito's and King Alexander's dictatorships, most closely resemble what John Milbank terms *enlightenment* simple space. In suggesting a course for the late twentieth-century Catholic Church to take as it marked a century of Catholic social teaching celebrating the publication of Pope Leo XIII's *Rerum Novarum*, Milbank described two dominant chronotopes of European history, both with implications for states and alliances of the twentieth century. The chronotope he identifies as enlightenment simple space is an artificial construct "suspended between the mass of atomic individuals on the one hand, and an absolutely sovereign center on the other."[15] Opposed to this abstract simple space, Milbank posits a more natural chronotope, which he terms *gothic complex space*. An emphasis on centered verticality and imagined communities is dominant in simple space; whereas, decentered horizontal relationships among intermediate constituents are more characteristic in complex space.[16]

Marko Dren's basement arsenal, as a replica of Tito's Yugoslavia, is then an exaggerated rendering of enlightenment simple space, an organically coherent fictive state, in which the vertical axis between subjects and sovereign dominates. Dina Iordanova speaks of Kusturica's "dichotomies of locale," specifically, his use of an "above and below dichotomy" to reveal superficially constructed edifices of lies, deceit, and duplicity.[17] Peggy Saule analyzes the cellar in Deleuzean terms as a site where crystal images of space-time and real images are parallel and realized as pivotal moments in modifying the course of events.[18] But such interpretations either do not discriminate among the various subterranean spaces, or they focus exclusively on the cellar.[19] Here, I propose a reading that sees the cellar as the vertically centered enlightenment simple space of *yugoslavism*, and the labyrinth as its horizontally decentered gothic complex space. Bridging the simple and complex spaces are the Belgrade sewers, the only conventional subterrestrial spaces in the film.

The incredible expanse of Kusturica's labyrinth is intended to astonish both viewers and the film's main characters. But it is, in essence, a mundane space, noisy, grimy, and teeming with multinational, multilingual travelers from unknown points of origin, all moving across what appears to be a borderless network of roads disdainful of the boundaries of cities, states, commercial, and political alliances dominating the landscape above them.[20] The people traversing the labyrinth appear to be a classless, leaderless collection of individuals who negotiate the network as equals. The cellar is a prosaic space, but one equipped and populated by an astonishing array of technical and human oddities, and controlled by the opportunistic Dren, a bromidic poet and perfidious politician. The denizens of the cellar form a closed, hierarchical community. They are helpless without the authoritarian structure Marko Dren provides, and when given the opportunity to escape, the cellar's inhabitants, with the exception of Crni, choose willingly to remain. The sewers connecting the two hybrid spaces have neither permanent inhabitants nor a constant flow of itinerants. They are used by Marko and Crni in their criminal activities in Nazi-occupied Belgrade, but they are presented without any of the whimsical absurdities of the cellar or labyrinth.

Underground's Pairs and Triads

Moving through Kusturica's *Underground* spaces are six central characters whose relationships are arranged in pairs and triangles, some of which overlap.[21] Individually, each is marked in some way as being essentially different from the other five. Thus, Soni, the monkey rescued by Ivan from the Belgrade zoo, is the only nonhuman in the group, the only one to survive, and the agent for the breach in the cellar walls;[22] Natalja (Mirjana Joković) is the only woman; Jovan (Srđan Todorović) is the only member of the group born in the underground cellar; Ivan (Slavko Štimac) is marked by his stammering speech and limp; Crni cannot be killed; and Marko is the agent of the film's narrative trajectory and a close personal associate of another narrator, Josip Broz Tito. The six form three familial pairings: the husband-wife pair of Marko and Natalja; the father-son pair of Crni and Jovan; and the adoptive father–adopted son pair of Ivan and Soni. There are onomastic pairs, as well: Ivan and Jovan are united by their names, Jovan being the Serbian variant of Ivan; Soni and Crni have names that are phonetically similar.

Finally, there are two important triangles: the "love" triangle of Crni, Marko, and Natalja; and the "brothers" triangle of Crni, Marko, and Ivan (Crni and Marko being best friends, *kumovi*; Marko and Ivan being brothers). Marko establishes the nature of this relationship with Crni and Ivan in the opening scene of the film. As he and Crni ride through Belgrade, they refer to one another as *kum*. As the carriage passes the zoo and Ivan's house, Marko calls out to Ivan using the colloquial *burazer*; Ivan clarifies their relationship when, speaking to a parrot, he describes Marko as his *brat* (brother), and Marko and Crni as *kumovi* (the plural form of *kum*). There is some latitude in using any of the three terms within certain types of male social relationships, but *kum* is "godfather" or "best friend" and *brat* is "brother." *Burazer* is the least marked and can be used in the widest range of situations.[23] The importance in the opening scene is that all three words are used; however, in part three, when Ivan returns to war-torn Yugoslavia and beats Marko with his cane, Marko speaks to Ivan using *brat*. Similarly, when Crni realizes that the war profiteers he has ordered to be executed are Natalja and Marko, he, too, refers to Marko as his *brat*. Thus, the emphasis shifts from the casual and colloquial use of the term to the more specific, thereby reinforcing Marko's dying words that there is no war until brother kills brother. The death of the *burazer-kum-brat* relationship also reflects the way in which brother Slavs—

be they the Muslim, Catholic, or Orthodox Slavs of Bosnia and Herzegovina, or the Slavs of the original south Slav federation of the Kingdom of Serbs, Croats, and Slovenes—chose the most violent means to end their political union.

How these six traverse the various underground spaces is important. Crni and Jovan live in the cellar and move through the sewers, but together as a pair, never enter the labyrinth. Natalja and Marko live on the surface and visit the cellar; Natalja for special occasions such as Jovan's wedding, Marko as part of his gun-running activities. Like Crni and Jovan, their final exit from the cellar is through the sewers. Marko tells Natalja that they have no future in Tito's Yugoslavia, and then he destroys the cellar. When the two reappear years later in a Mercedes with German license plates, it is clear that they have settled somewhere in the country of the former enemy. Natalja and Marko are never shown in the labyrinth, a sign that Marko's control over life in the broader underground world is limited, and, by extension, a comment on Tito's control over Yugoslavia and Milošević's over Serbia. Only Ivan and Soni reside in the cellar, depart through the sewers, and find their way to the labyrinth where they are at first separated and then, after many years pass, reunited.

Ivan maps the subterranean highways, albeit inaccurately with respect to surface geography. The map he creates for one of the Berlin psychiatrists shows the tunnels of the underground labyrinth connecting Warsaw, Moscow, Cracow, and Vienna, but the cities are not in their proper positions relative to one another. Ivan's understanding of late twentieth-century European politics and history does not inform his travels through the labyrinth. Not only is he unclear as to what lies above him as he crosses the Cold War frontiers underground, but he is also ignorant of the types of territories he is leaving and/or entering. For example, as the result of Marko's deception, when Ivan leaves Belgrade in 1961, he believes that he is leaving a Nazi-occupied city, and, as far as he knows, Berlin is still the capital of Hitler's Third Reich. When Ivan finally leaves Berlin on New Year's 1992, it is a unified, unoccupied city; Germany is a free country; and he is returning to a disintegrating Yugoslavia. Ivan's journey through the gothic complex space of the labyrinth is not sufficient to save him, but his is the most eventful and transformative experience, for it is Ivan who crosses borders and experiences the multilingual, international feel of the labyrinth.

Marko's control over his brother, Ivan, and best friend, Crni, lasts only as long as the two victims are interned in the enlightened simple space of the cellar. In addition to being deceived by Marko, Ivan and Crni share certain experiences and feelings. They both want Marko dead: Ivan after he learns of his brother's duplicity and various crimes as an arms smuggler; Crni when he

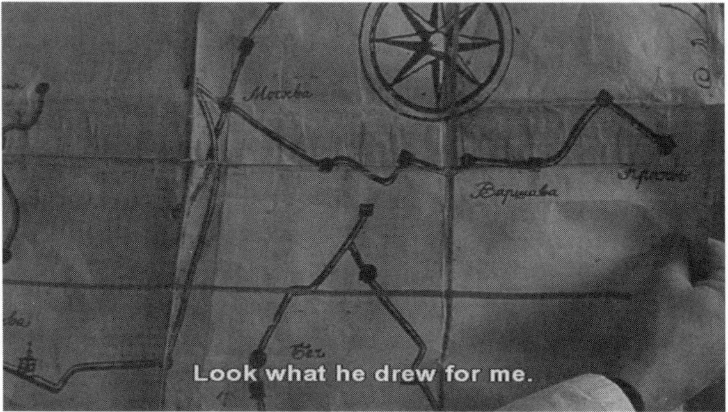

Figure 2.10. Ivan's map of the labyrinth. *Underground* (Artificial Eye).

finally understands the infidelity of his best friend. There is a difference in so far as Ivan's desire for retribution comes after his travels through Europe's underground; Crni's occurs prior to his setting foot in the labyrinth. Both men eventually have a hand in Marko's death: Ivan when he beats Marko almost to death with a walking cane, and Crni when he orders one of his soldiers to kill a pair of gun runners, who turn out to be Natalja and Marko. Ivan and Crni also take their own lives: Ivan by hanging himself in a deserted, bombed-out church on a Slavonian battlefield; Crni when he throws himself into the well in the bombed-out and deserted cellar in Belgrade. Ivan returns to see his country in ruins, Crni returns to see the cellar in ruins. Marko's grand narrative, like Tito's Yugoslav experiment, has failed. When, in the film's final scene, the dead of *Underground* emerge from the Danube and reunite on its banks, it is Ivan, the most widely traveled of the underground community, who assumes a new role.

Ivan is seated at a table full of revelers, the resurrected inhabitants of the Belgrade cellar, who are dressed as if at a wedding party. The camera tracks clockwise around Ivan, who now speaks to the viewer in the confident, smooth voice of a storyteller. He is the only character to experience all of *Underground*'s spaces, its gothic complex labyrinth, its enlightened simple cellar, and its transitional system of sewers. Ivan's passage through these zones is marked by both vertical and horizontal movement, and his border crossings include the physical, social, political, and, with his death and resurrection, the metaphysical one, as well. It is fitting, therefore, that the last words of the film are his and are spoken in a new voice, clear and sure of himself. He speaks as if telling us a fairy tale and ends with the words

Figure 2.11. Ivan, the poised fabulist. *Underground* (Artificial Eye).

that are the film's original title, "Once upon a time there was a country" (*Bila jednom jedna zemlja*).

Conclusion

Kusturica is quick to speak of Ivo Andrić as the writer one must read to understand the Balkans.[24] He himself is arguably the most celebrated and widely recognized contemporary filmmaker from the Balkans, but to elevate him to the status he assigns Andrić would be contentious and controversial, even in his adopted Serbia.[25] The cinéaste does, however, share a number of biographical details with the Nobel laureate. Both were born in Bosnia, both lived and worked abroad, and both finally settled in Serbia—Andrić in Belgrade, Kusturica in rural Serbia—and they are probably best known for works they produced about and during times of war. Andrić, however, became and remained a Yugoslav, writing his most famous work, *The Bridge on the Drina*, in Nazi-occupied Belgrade, the city that served as the primary setting for Kusturica's most famous work, *Underground*. The fates of Ivan in *Underground* and Luka in *Life Is a Miracle*, both played by actor Slavko Štimac, best epitomize the trajectory of the filmmaker's Yugoslav identity. From the nostalgic fabulist Ivan, who drifts down the Danube on an island of ghosts, to the disillusioned Luka, who chooses love and self-exile, there seems to be little left of Yugoslavia-as-bridge. Their journeys through the chaotic subterranean world created by Emir Kusturica echo the director's own odyssey, and suggest that another metaphor for the border-laden Balkans is possible—one that takes the well-worn thoroughfares underground into tunnels and subterranean labyrinths.

Notes

1. The term *kapija*, from the Turkish *kapi*, generally means "gate." In Andrić's historical novel, *kapija* refers to the central section of the bridge where the roadway widens and a raised U-shaped divan is located. The *kapija* and its divan are a focal point of many scenes in the novel. In peaceful times, it is a space where town notables gather, students discuss distant and local events, lovers meet, and coffee is brewed and sold. In times of war, the primary meaning of a gate is more important, as the *kapija* becomes a checkpoint for authorities to control traffic into and out of Višegrad and crossing the new borders between Bosnia and Sebia.

2. In a 2011 interview with *Vesti online*, Kusturica was asked whether he considered himself a modern-day Mehmed Paša (the Grand Vizier was from a Serbian Orthodox family in the Višegrad region, and was taken as a child to be raised and educated in Istanbul as part of the Ottoman practice of *devşirme*, by which Ottoman bureaucrats took young boys from Christian families, converted them to Islam, and prepared them for service in the Sultan's military and governmental corps). Kusturica, who was born a Bosnian Muslim but converted to Orthodoxy in 2005, replied, "Yes, but in reverse." See B. A., "Kusturica: Ja sam novi Mehmed-Paša," *Vijesti.ba*, September 12, 2011, http://www.vijesti.ba/intervjui/51319-Kusturica-sam-novi-Mehmed-pasa.html.

3. Andrić was awarded the Nobel Prize in Literature in 1961. Kusturica has received several international festival awards, but is best known for having won the Palme d'Or at Cannes in 1985 for *When Father Was Away on Business* and 1995 for *Underground.*

4. The dissolution of Yugoslavia began de jure in 1991 with the secessions of Slovenia and Croatia, and continued with declarations of independence by Macedonia (also 1991) and Bosnia-Herzegovina (1992). The most violent departures from the Yugoslav federation took place in Croatia (1991–1995) and Bosnia and Herzegovina (1992–1995), where ethnic Serbs refused to recognize the authority of the fledgling countries in which they found themselves, and in some regions even voted to secede from the newly formed post-Yugoslav states. Armed belligerents included the Yugoslav National Army, official defense forces of the new states, regional guards units, and numerous paramilitary organizations. In Bosnia-Herzegovina the situation became even more complicated after a Bosnian Muslim-Croat alliance broke down and Croat forces fought with the Army of the Republic of Bosnia and Herzegovina in and around the city of Mostar. The Dayton-Paris Agreements of November–December, 1995 ended the military hostilities but left the former Yugoslav republic divided into political entities: the Republika Srpska and the Federation of Bosnia and Herzegovina.

5. The story of *Life Is a Miracle* supposedly takes place on the western (Bosnian) side of the Bosnian-Serbian border, but the film was actually shot in western Serbia in the Mokra Gora Park region. See Matthieu Dhennin, *Le Lexique Subjectif*

d'Emir Kusturica (Lausanne: Editions L'Age d'Homme, 2006), 63. The film used a picturesque section of the old narrow-gauge railway line, the Šargan Eight, which was intended to connect central Serbia to the Adriatic coast near Dubrovnik. See Илија Мисаиловић и Радован Гибетић, *Шарганска Осмица:Железничка Пруга Ужице-Вардиште* (Београд: Географски институт "Јован Цвијић" САНУ, 2010), 491.

6. Djordje Petrović, known as Karadjordje (Black George), was one of the leaders of the first Serbian uprising against the Ottoman Empire. The rebellion resulted in a short-lived independent Serbian state (1804–1813). Andrić refers to this uprising in chapter six of *The Bridge on the Drina*, when he cites songs sung by the rebels and mentions the distant rumbling of Karadjordje's cannon.

7. Ivo Andrić, *The Bridge on the Drina*, trans. Lovett F. Edwards (New York: Signet/New American Library, 1967), 85.

8. All references, unless otherwise noted, are from the standard Yugoslav-era history: Ivan Božić, Sima Cerović, Milorad Ekmečić, and Vladimir Dedijer, *Istorija Jugoslavije*, 3rd ed. (Beograd: Prosveta, 1973).

9. Božić et al., *Istorija Jugoslavije*, 433–438.

10. "To Use Latin Alphabet: King Alexander Issues Order for Its Adoption in Yugoslavia," *New York Times*, March 23, 1929.

11. The controversy surrounding the film and Kusturica's stance vis-à-vis the breakup of Yugoslavia is well documented. For summaries, see Goran Gocić, *The Cinema of Emir Kusturica: Notes from the Underground* (London: Directors' Cuts/Wallflower Press, 2001); Dina Iordanova, *Cinema of Flames: Balkan Film, Culture and the Media* (London: British Film Institute, 2001); and Dan Halpern, "The (Mis) Directions of Emir Kusturica," *NY Times.com*, May 8, 2005, http://www.nytimes.com/2005/05/08/magazine/08EMIR.html. For the original text of one of the first post-Cannes attacks on Kusturica, see Alain Finkielkraut, *Dispatches from the Balkan War and Other Writings* (Lincoln: University of Nebraska Press, 1999). More recent studies by Tomislav Longinović, "Playing the Western Eye: Balkan Masculinity in Post-Yugoslav War Cinema," in *East European Cinemas*, ed. Aniko Imre (New York: AFI Film Readers/Routledge, 2005), 35–47; Marcos Farias Ferreira, "Nation as Narration: the (*De*)construction of "Yugostalgia" through Kusturica's Cinematic Eye," *Comunicação & Cultura* 1 (2006): 135–55; and Sean Homer, "Retrieving Emir Kusturica's Underground as a Critique of Ethnic Nationalism," *Jump Cut: A Review of Contemporary Media* 51 (2009), http://www.ejumpcut.org/archive/jc51.2009/Kusterica/text.html have gone beyond the Kusturica-as-Serb-nationalist debate and have looked at the film as meta-narrative.

12. Gocić, *Cinema of Emir Kusturica*, 32.

13. Iordanova, *Cinema of Flames*, 118.

14. Emir Kusturica and Serge Grunberg, *Il était une fois . . . Underground* (Paris: Cahiers du Cinéma CIBY 2000, 1995), 108.

15. John Milbank, "Against the Resignation of the Age," in *Things Old and New: Catholic Social Teaching Revisited*, ed. Francis P. McHugh and Samuel M. Natale (New York: University Press of America, 1993), 10.

16. Milbank, "Against the Resignation," 10.

17. Iordanova, *Cinema of Flames*, 114–115.

18. Peggy Saule, *Le Baroquisme d'Emir Kusturica, un cinema de la metamorphose* (Paris: Editions universitaires européennes, 2010), 158–159.

19. Iordanova does draw attention to the tunnels of the labyrinth but focuses the reading on the hypocrisy, as Kusturica supposedly sees it, of Cold War public relations—above ground the great powers are enemies, but below the surface they allow commerce and borderless migrations: see Iordanova, *Cinema of Flames*, 161. Her work also predates *Life Is a Miracle*; thus, her comments about tunnels are restricted to *Underground*.

20. The analyses in this paper are based on the theatrical releases of *Underground* and *Life Is a Miracle*. Both films were serialized for Serbian television in longer versions (*Underground*: five hours, forty minutes, *Life Is a Miracle*: five hours). In the TV version of *Underground*, there are signs of borders in the labyrinth; for example, there is a hand-operated barricade at the entry into Berlin, and Ivan encounters a character who looks like Franz (Ernst Stötzner), the chief Nazi villain of occupied Belgrade. This tunnel version of Franz appears as a type of customs agent. The scene includes a payoff to Franz, but it is more about the ubiquitous German officer himself, or at least his likeness, than it is about customs and borders. He was Crni's rival for Natalya in occupied Belgrade, he survived a gunshot at point-blank range when Crni steals Natalya from the theater, he is strangled to death by Marko in an asylum where partisans are tortured, and he materializes in postwar Belgrade as a character in a movie about Crni's life! For more information on the TV scenes of *Underground*, see Matthieu Dhennin's site kustu.com, "*Underground*—Long Version," www.kustu.com/w2/en:underground_long_version.

21. Most critics ignore Soni's role. Judith Keene, for example, identifies five central characters: Marko, Crni, Natalja, Ivan, and Jovan. See Judith Keene, "The Filmmaker as Historian, Above and Below Ground: Emir Kusturica and the Narratives of Yugoslav History," *Rethinking History* 5, no. 2 (2001): 235–236.

22. Soni, who fires two rounds from the underground tank blasting a hole in the cellar walls, is never mentioned by critics, who typically describe the scene in ambiguous language leaving their readers to assume that the cellar self-destructs or collapses from the frenzied wedding party. See Iordanova, *Cinema of Flames*, 113; Pavle Levi, *Disintegrating in Frames: Aesthetics and Ideology in the Yugoslav and Post-Yugoslav Cinema* (Stanford: Stanford University Press, 2007), 94–95; David A. Norris, *In the Wake of the Balkan Myth: Questions of Identity and Modernity* (New York: St Martin's Press, 1999), 161.

23. As a foreign student living in Belgrade, I was often called *burazer* by my male friends; I could be called *brat*, but only in informal situations when the word was used in the vocative case and had no familial connotations; but I was never referred to as *kum*.

24. Емир Кустурица, *Смрт је непровјерена гласина* (Београд: Новости, 2010), 335.

25. Tamara Skrozza, "Gazda od Drvengrada," *Vreme* 856, May 31, 2007, http://www.vreme.com/cms/view.php?id=500496.

Works Cited

Andrić, Ivo. *The Bridge on the Drina*. Translated by Lovett F. Edwards. New York: Signet/New American Library, 1967. First published 1945 by University of Chicago Press.

B. A. "Kusturica: Ja sam novi Mehmed-Paša." *Vijesti.ba*, September 12, 2011. http://www.vijesti.ba/intervjui/51319-Kusturica-sam-novi-Mehmed-pasa.html.

Božić, Ivan, Sima Cerović, Milorad Ekmečić, and Vladimir Dedijer. *Istorija Jugoslavije*. 3rd ed. Beograd: Prosveta, 1973.

Dhennin, Matthieu. *Le Lexique Subjectif d'Emir Kusturica*. Lausanne: Editions L'Age d'Homme, 2006.

——. "*Underground*—Long Version." *Куступедија* August 12, 2012. www.kustu.com/w2/en:underground_long_version.

Ferreira, Marcos Farias. "Nation as Narration: the (*De*)construction of "Yugostalgia" through Kusturica's Cinematic Eye." *Comunicação & Cultura* 1 (2006): 135–155.

Finkielkraut, Alain. *Dispatches from the Balkan War and Other Writings*. Lincoln: University of Nebraska Press, 1999.

Gocić, Goran. *The Cinema of Emir Kusturica: Notes from the Underground*. London: Directors' Cuts/Wallflower Press, 2001.

Halpern, Dan. "The (Mis)Directions of Emir Kusturica." *NY Times.com*, May 8, 2005. http://www.nytimes.com/2005/05/08/magazine/08EMIR.html.

Homer, Sean. "Retrieving Emir Kusturica's Underground as a Critique of Ethnic Nationalism." *Jump Cut: A Review of Contemporary Media* 51 (2009). http://www.ejumpcut.org/archive/jc51.2009/Kusterica/text.html.

Iordanova, Dina. *Cinema of Flames: Balkan Film, Culture and the Media*. London: British Film Institute, 2001.

Keene, Judith. "The Filmmaker as Historian, Above and Below Ground: Emir Kusturica and the Narratives of Yugoslav History." *Rethinking History* 5, no. 2 (2001): 233–253.

Kusturica, Emir, and Serge Grunberg. *Il était une fois . . . Underground*. Paris: Cahiers du Cinéma CIBY 2000, 1995.

Кустурица, Емир. *Смрт је непровјерена гласина*. Београд: Новости, 2010.

Levi, Pavle. *Disintegrating in Frames: Aesthetics and Ideology in the Yugoslav and Post-Yugoslav Cinema*. Stanford: Stanford University Press, 2007.

Longinović, Tomislav. "Playing the Western Eye: Balkan Masculinity in Post-Yugoslav War Cinema." In *East European Cinemas*, edited by Aniko Imre, 35–47. New York: AFI Film Readers/Routledge, 2005.

Milbank, John. "Against the Resignation of the Age." In *Things Old and New: Catholic Social Teaching Revisited*, edited by Francis P. McHugh and Samuel M. Natale, 1–39. New York: University Press of America, 1993.

Мисаиловић, Илија и Радован Гибетић. *Шарганска Осмица:Железничка Пруга Ужице-Вардиште*. Београд: Географски институт "Јован Цвијић" САНУ, 2010.

Norris, David A. *In the Wake of the Balkan Myth: Questions of Identity and Modernity*. New York: St Martin's Press, 1999.

Saule, Peggy. *Le Baroquisme d'Emir Kusturica, un cinema de la metamorphose.* Paris: Editions universitaires européennes, 2010.

Skrozza, Tamara. "Gazda od Drvengrada." *Vreme* 856, May 31, 2007. http://www.vreme.com/cms/view.php?id=500496&print=yes.

"To Use Latin Alphabet: King Alexander Issues Order for Its Adoption in Yugoslavia." *New York Times,* March 23, 1929.

Films

Black Cat, White Cat. Directed by Emir Kusturica. CiBY 2000/Pandora/Komuna/France2 Cinema. France, Germany, Yugoslavia, 1998.

Do You Remember Dolly Bell? Directed by Emir Kusturica. Sutejska Film Sarajevo/TV Sarajevo. Yugoslavia, 1981.

Life Is a Miracle. Directed by Emir Kusturica. Les Films Alain Sarde/Rasta. France, Italy, Serbia, 2004.

Promise Me This. Directed by Emir Kusturica. Fidélité. Serbia/France, 2007.

Time of the Gypsies. Directed by Emir Kusturica. Forum Sarajevo/TV Sarajevo/Smart Egg. Yugoslavia, 1988.

Underground. Directed by Emir Kusturica. CiBY 2000/Pandora/Novofilm. France, Germany, Hungary, 1995.

When Father Was Away on Business. Directed by Emir Kusturica. Forum Film. Yugoslavia, 1985.

3

Aquaterrorists and Cybraceros

The Dystopian Borderlands of Alex Rivera's Sleep Dealer *(2008)*

Thomas Prasch

When main character Memo Cruz (played by Luis Fernando Peña) first directly encounters a "sleep dealer" shop—one of the sites where node-attached Mexicans labor in eerie technosuspension, moving their own limbs to pilot distant robots—the foreman of the operation (Jake Koenig) gives potential recruits the tour: "This is the American dream. We give the United States what they've always wanted, all the work—without the workers. Jose is in a slaughterhouse in Iowa. Maria is a nanny for a little girl in Washington. You three will be on a big job in San Diego. Plug in, your future starts today." Memo does plug in: he attaches the wires to the nodes implanted in his own flesh, dons the oxygen mask ("to keep you alert," the instructional sign informs him), and pops in the opaque eye covers that allow him to see his distant virtual task. "I got a job," he tells his brother later, "I think it's in California." That Memo is not even certain where he (or his robot avatar) is working underlines the new forms of alienation that come with the technologized labor of *Sleep Dealer*'s projected future. In the futuristic sci-fi dystopia of *Sleep Dealer* (2008), multiple forms of technologically mediated bodies—people with implanted nodes connecting to computer networks in order to labor from afar as workers, drone pilots, and technojournalists—are employed to comment on a range of contemporary border issues, including immigrant labor, economic inequalities, control of water resources, and modern drone warfare.

In the commentary track on the DVD version of *Sleep Dealer*, Alex Rivera, the film's director (and writer, with David Riker), recalls the origins of the project in his more or less simultaneous encounter with two prodding influences.

The first was an article on how technology was leading to the possibility that all work would be done from home. For Rivera, this had significant implications, reversing the traditional terrain of robotic sci-fi films; as he told an audience at the 2008 Sundance Film Festival, "If you look at *Blade Runner* or *I, Robot*, the drama comes from the idea that the robots will wake up and want to kill the people. In my film people use machines to exploit each other. The robot doesn't want to kill you. The robot wants to take your job."[1] Interestingly and ironically, the film's dark vision of "telepresence" strongly appealed to the group of technology-focused authors of *Starting an iPhone Application Business for Dummies*, who saw in *Sleep Dealer* a "fascinating look at the potential future of telepresence" and an "amazing vision for how a person's entire set of senses could be digitized and transmitted through the Internet to distant locations," while assuring readers that this future need not be as "grim" as Rivera's dystopian vision implied.[2] The context for the original article that inspired Rivera was Japanese and oriented toward high-tech office work, but his response, as the son of parents who were labor immigrants to the United States, pushed his thoughts in a different direction.

The second prod for the project was when Rivera saw a documentary on the bracero program, that brief-lived (1942–1964) American experiment in creating a controlled, temporary guest worker program, mainly for work in the agrarian sector.[3] That program had followed a Depression-era campaign of full-scale deportation of immigrants, which had in turn, and predictably, been followed by a labor crisis, especially pronounced in the agrarian sector and exacerbated by the enhanced labor needs that came with the commencement of World War II. The job crunch forced government action (in this case, a cooperative intergovernmental program between U.S. and Mexican governments) to bring official temporary workers across the border, alleviating the labor crisis in the north and ensuring the regularized flow of migrant-labor earnings back to Mexico. As Rivera himself summarizes the program and its impact,

> Bracero, in Spanish, means a man who works with his arms and hands. Under the Bracero Program Mexican workers . . . would be invited to participate in the American economy as farm hands. Government buses and trains transported Braceros from the Mexican border to American farm lands. Unfortunately, while solving America's farm labor problems, the Bracero Program contributed to several other problems. . . . The presence of Braceros contributed to a climate of racial and economic suspicion. Evidence of major tension was not hard to find.[4]

The bracero program, of course, existed alongside continued extralegal immigration from Mexico throughout the period and American efforts to control that flow of undocumented migrants, most notably with Operation Wetback, a U.S. program aimed at identifying and deporting illegal immigrants.[5]

To these two originating impulses can be added other concerns Rivera expressed as he was developing the project and since it has been released. As he was working on *Sleep Dealer*, Rivera talked about the role of transnational corporations in redefining and remobilizing labor across traditional geopolitical boundaries.[6] As Rivera has also noted,

> Other present-day realities inspired my futuristic fantasy: violent reality shows like *COPS*, private military contractors like Blackwater, remote control drones like the Predator Drone, the trend of outsourcing jobs over the web, the impending global water crisis, and the ubiquity of video sharing sites like YouTube, to name a few. This is a science-fiction film with many anchors in today's reality.[7]

More broadly, Rivera's project seeks to rework the character of a familiar genre, the science-fiction movie; in essence, he wants to make science fiction take its political labels seriously. As he told audiences at Sundance, "What I'm really interested in is speculative fiction. I wanted to use this film to ask the question, 'Where are we going?' . . . Films like *Star Wars* use terms like *empire* and *rebellion*, but they are bandied about in bland ways—powerful words used to describe nothing."[8] In *Sleep Dealer*, Rivera works to give those words real meaning.

To destabilize the generic conventions of speculative-fiction film, Rivera shifts the focus of attention in two distinct ways. First, he relocates the film's center, taking us from traditional metropoles to the Third-World fringes of transnational labor mobilization. As he put it at Sundance, "Science fiction always tells outsider stories, with people coming into conflict with the system. But I wanted to create a science-fiction point of view that we've never seen before. . . . Just yanking the point of view out of London, or New York, or Los Angeles and dropping it somewhere else is a powerful gesture."[9] He explained to another reviewer, while discussing his film as "third world cyberpunk," "We've never seen the future of the rest of the world, which happens to be where the majority of humanity lives."[10] Second, he blocks viewer expectations by refocusing on an atypical sort of hero. As Rivera recalled,

> I started to conceive of [the film] as a provocation, as an attack, as a kind of joke, really, saying, "What would it be like if this genre that is the terrain of Harrison Ford and Tom Cruise was flipped completely upside down, and instead of making Tom Cruise the hero, we made that guy in the background of *Blade Runner*—the guy riding a bicycle and speaking, you know, Spanglish—what if we made that person the protagonist?"[11]

So it is through the eyes and memories of a Mexican menial laborer that we enter Rivera's film. The undermining of science-fiction norms is cemented by Rivera's commitment to small-budget independency, against the genre's trend toward megamillion-dollar blockbusterism.[12]

Combining in Rivera's imagination, the images of technologically displaced workers and of the bracero guest-worker program fused to become the vision of the *cybracero*. In its earliest incarnation, in 1997, he explored the theme in a semi-animated short, "Why Cybraceros?" (the title parodying that of the promotional film "Why Braceros?" from 1959 about the bracero program), a work essentially devoted to giving visual embodiment to the idea of disembodied labor (his robotized laborers working in orange orchards, in that early version).[13] Finally, he elaborated the idea into the full-length film *Sleep Dealer*, which had its debut at the Sundance Film Festival in 2008, and was released (albeit never widely) the following year.[14]

The film's title itself constitutes another sort of dislocation, as it comes from art historian John Berger's examination of migrant labor in Europe. As Rebecca Carroll explains, "Rivera came upon the title of the film, *Sleep Dealer*, in a book by art historian and theorist John Berger—the term refers to early 20th-century migrant workers who walked from southern Europe to northern Europe for jobs, forced to rent beds along the way from 'sleep dealers.'"[15] Within the film, the term shape-shifts to become the Mexican slang for the factories that house node laborers. As Memo, the central character, explains, in his expository voiceover narration, "We call the factories 'sleep dealers,' because if you work long enough, you'd collapse." As realized in its full-length version, *Sleep Dealer* constitutes both a provocative meditation on the political front of the U.S.-Mexican border and the issues raised by immigrant labor and border security, and a fanciful futurism in which technology enhances the effect of labor alienation first discussed by Marx in his analysis of industrial capitalism.[16]

The film has received decidedly mixed press. Summarizing some of the more negative reviews, Jamie Oliver and Tony Goodwin write, "*Time Out Chicago* called it 'impressive but unsatisfying,' the *San Francisco Chronicle* said it was 'flawed but still vibrant and inventive,' while the *New York Post* reported the film as 'a well-meaning failure.' Film reviewing website nerve.com summed it up thus: 'The film culminates in an unconvincing finale whose hopefulness seems not only fanciful but . . . short-sighted.'"[17] *Village Voice* reviewer Aaron Hillis dismissed the film: "Science fiction easily lends itself to allegory, but while the dystopian near-future of co-writer/director Alex Rivera's feature debut focuses, admirably, on how globalization affects the third world, his ideas are as subtle as a light saber to the face. . . . From imperialist villains and their humanitarian abuses to the laborers dying on their feet, what's so clever about tricking out this worn-out tale of woe into a genre flick?"[18] On the other hand, A. O. Scott, in the *New York Times*, called the film "an unusually thoughtful science fiction film, using the speculative energy of the genre to explore some troubling and complex contemporary issues." While conceding that "[t]he plot of *Sleep Dealer* is a bit thin, and the performances . . . are earnest and dutiful," Scott insists, "there is sufficient ingenuity in the film's main ideas to hold your attention, and the political implications of the allegorical story are at once obvious and subtle. Mr. Rivera's vision of Tijuana, in particular, is pointed and intriguing, an unsettlingly plausible extrapolation of what that city already represents."[19] And, in the Manchester *Guardian*, B. Ruby Rich declared *Sleep Dealer* "my favorite kind of sci-fi, just enough into the future for things we recognize to have become grotesque, untenable, and dangerous," concluding with even higher praise: "Rivera revives the promise of an American independent cinema that can intervene in our world, imagine the worst, hope for the best—and entertain like mad along the way."[20] For a film that presents such challenging political ideas while at the same time undermining genre conventions, such a divided reception is perhaps no surprise.

Technoalienation takes multiple forms in the dystopic future envisioned in *Sleep Dealer*, all in ways that play upon and amplify existing political/cultural concerns. Most are centrally fixed along the border between the United States and Mexico, but more broadly echo wider issues that separate (but still connect) first and third worlds. First, and most critically, that vision of the exploitation of Mexican labor without having to deal with the actual Mexicans who contribute it provides a hyperbolic nightmare vision of the existing conditions for undocumented Mexican workers in the north today: that combination of exploitation and insecurity, the dream of jobs and the realities of low-level menial employment, and that subjection to the mechanics of the security state (with all the peril of illegal border crossings on one side and arrest and deportation on the other that this entails) that constitute the conditions of today's undocumented work force. As Ronald Mize and Alicia Swords argue—using another film, Sergio Arau's mockumentary *A Day without a Mexican* (2004) to make their point—exploitation of Mexican labor is closely connected to consumer demand on this side of the border: "The 2004 mockumentary A Day without a Mexican [*sic*; title not italicized in original] satirized omnipresent anti-immigrant sentiments by challenging us to seriously think about how our economy would operate without Mexican immigrants in our midst. . . . [The movie] dramatizes the economic standstill that would result if nobody was present to pick crops, clean houses, operate leafblowers, tend lawns, build roads and structures, and provide childcare."[21] Labor demand in the United States, the authors insist, is at the root of Mexican immigration across the border.

By separating worker from work in his futuristic fantasy, Rivera accomplishes Arau's satiric aim with a decisive difference: in *Sleep Dealer*, labor demands can be fulfilled even as laborers themselves are kept away. Melissa Lopez, noting that "national space still, in many ways, correlates quite strongly to national race," argues that "Alex Rivera makes the same point in his film *Sleep Dealer* . . . , a futuristic dystopia depicting a world connected by technology but yet divided by geopolitical borders."[22] Labor, rather than race, however, seems to be at the center of Rivera's vision. The futuristic conditions of labor underline and amplify the existing problem for the undocumented worker, exploited as laborer but unable to participate fully (politically, socially, or economically) in the American Dream because of the constant threat of deportation.

Second, and in close connection with the envisioned new form of labor, the film projects the comprehensive (and presumably successful) completion of the sealing off of the Mexican border, the hugely controversial fencing project endorsed by the U.S. Congress in 2006 and still a favored topic on campaign trails today. Rachel St. John tracks a history of fence-building going back to 1909, with a fresh explosion of fence-building in the 1940s, a new wave responding to new concerns about immigration in the 1990s, and the most current phase dictated by a combination of immigration and terrorism concerns.[23] In his critical account of the border-fence project, its "simple solution" logic, and its comprehensive failure to solve the underlying problems of the border, Robert Maril notes, "In whatever form, the border fence between Mexico and the United States, its notorious history, its rationalizations and justifications . . . [its] construction, operation, and maintenance are all an embodiment of competing individuals, institutions, and forces. As such, this border fence is a clear reflection of American polity."[24] The consequences, either in terms of the failure to stop immigration or the amplification of border violence, lead Maril to suggest utterly alternative strategies. Tony Zavaleta even more forcefully argues, "In my forty years of studying the U.S.-Mexico border I have never seen anything suggested by either government that is so wrong headed and destructive to our communities and our people as this border wall."[25] In *Sleep Dealer*, however, the fence is finished and is taken as genuinely impermeable, a real case of science-fiction fantasy. Within the parameters of the film, at any rate, the border is genuinely, securely sealed.

Third, the film hypothesizes the metropolitan exploitation of Mexico's water resources. U.S.-controlled corporations, backed by the U.S. military, have imposed control over the water resources of Mexico through a combination of dams and reservoirs, fenced off and guarded from locals. Recurrent shots of pipelines heading north underline the principal aim of the water projects: supplying the waters of Mexico to the metropolitan centers of the north. Indigenous people, meanwhile, are forced to buy water to fulfill their own needs from the transnational corporations, at increasingly usurious prices. Early in the film, Memo and his father are shown buying water, paying credits to gain access through the fence, and filling their few water containers under the watchful eyes of both guards and electronic surveillance cameras. Local subsistence agriculture has suffered from the repurposing of local water supplies to fulfill metropolitan needs. Again, Rivera's arguments in the film reflect larger concerns, especially focused on privatized exploitation of Third-World water resources by global capitalism. As Maude Barlow argues in relation to the rise of corporatized models of water development,

> The shift from a public to a private model of water services can be traced to the rise of neo-liberal, market-based ideology first manifested in Margaret Thatcher's Britain, then adopted by Ronald Reagan in the United States. . . . By the late 1970s, the stage was set for an emerging global regime based on the belief that liberal market economics constitutes the one and only choice for the whole world, including the developing world.[26]

Barlow and Tony Clarke have also insisted that "disputes over the control and use of groundwater beneath the U.S.-Mexican border threaten to create major tensions between the two countries."[27] Into such tensions, Rivera's projections fit perfectly. The damming project in *Sleep Dealer* primarily serves the interests of a water-hungry metropole, as we repeatedly see images of the pipeline trailing north from the dam project in Santa Ana del Rio, the small Oaxaca town whose name becomes ironic when they lose control of their river. Secondarily, the dams further exploit the now-water-deprived indigenous populations, who have to buy back their own water at ever more outrageous prices.

The control of water resources, contested by Mexicans—the film alludes to armed conflict as the dams were installed and continuing "aquaterrorist" attacks on the water infrastructure—necessitates an ongoing military policing of the reservoirs and pipelines. The militarization of the border projected into the future in *Sleep Dealer* is an already-accomplished fact. As Douglas Massey has noted, "The boundary between Mexico and the United States has become perhaps the most militarized frontier between two nations at peace anywhere in the world."[28] This involvement of armed force in the policing of the border links to the fourth theme of the film: the use of drone attack craft as the principal method of military intervention.

The drone-dominated military apparatus alludes to the present tendencies of American armed conflict abroad; drone attacks have by now become routine in the so-called War on Terror, but they have figured in American operations in Afghanistan and against identified Al Qaeda targets elsewhere since 2001 and regularly in Pakistan border areas since 2004, well within the timelines of the inception of the film.[29] At the same time, drone warfare parallels the alienated technologized labor regime of the film. Drone pilots work through essentially virtual-reality environments to carry out attacks, making war increasingly look like a video game. Strikingly, even official congressional hearings on the subject of drone warfare cannot seem to evade a sci-fi/video-game language, as in the hearing before the congressional Subcommittee on National Security and Foreign Affairs that titled its report, à la *Star Wars*, *Rise of the Drones*.[30] In *Sleep Dealer*, the game-ology of new war is enhanced by the fact that a TV show, *Drones*, covers the attacks live for entertainment, like a high-tech version of *COPS* (1989–present).

But drone warfare also presents a new range of ethical issues. For example, Steven Lee explores the ethics of drone warfare, where (much as is envisioned in *Sleep Dealer*) "the drone's weapons are fired by members of the CIA in the United States, sitting before computer screens using joysticks, as if playing computer games." He concludes that such practices "create a moral quandary for just war theory, undermining its very logic."[31] Rivera's film explores one variation of the ethical dilemma technologically mediated warfare presents.

Fifth and finally, *Sleep Dealer* conjectures the marketing of human memories, culled from the brain of the supplier by computer technologies and made into marketable commodities. The theme echoes the commodification of memories in Kathryn Bigelow's *Strange Days* (1995), as well as the node-based connectivity of David Cronenberg's *eXistenZ* (1999). Within *Sleep Dealer*, the mechanics of futuristic nodalized journalism also provides a secondary perspective on the same character and an opportunity for journalistic exposition.

All that would seem to be a lot of themes to juggle in one low-budget sci-fi movie, but a single strand of sci-fi plotting binds together most of the major thematic elements and a single simple character arc unites all three central figures in the film. The key themes dovetail around the conceit of the technologized body: the central notion that nodes implanted in humans allow them direct interface with machines for a range of possible purposes. Thus Memo (his name suggests memory, and the film is, essentially, his remembrances) plugs in to the "sleep dealers" to sell his labor abroad without leaving Tijuana to do it; Luz (Leonor Varela), again with a referential name (signifying light), uses the same nodes to upload her memories and narration into instant digitalized stories that she posts to TruNode, a web-based platform just a shade more futuristic than YouTube, in a form of technologized journalism (although she insistently still refers to herself as "a writer"); Rudy Ramirez (Jacob Vargas) pilots his drone through precisely the same node technology. Since the fencing off of North America necessitates the technologized solution to the labor problem, and since the drone attack craft above all else defend the water expropriation through the damming of rivers, all the thematic elements finally constellate around the technologized body, a conjunction consolidated by the fact that the story is told retrospectively through two of those bodies: Memo's, in what, at the outset, seems like a state of tech-induced suspension (re-dreaming from his plugged-in state back to "when it all began"), and Luz's, posting her stories about Memo's journey to the TruNode web.

The central thematic device is reinforced by a constant pattern of displacement, where current concerns and language are translated (often with a dark playfulness) into new terms to fit the technologized new borderlands. Thus new arrivals in Tijuana are met in back alleys by "coyoteks" (instead of coyotes) offering to supply them with black-market node implants in lieu of actual border crossing ("Know how to drive? I'll get you a cab in London. Or how about picking oranges in Florida," one backstreet seller importunes). At the node bar, buzzing neon promises "Live Node Girls," and the barkeep supplies exhausted node workers with "teki" instead of tequila, plugging directly into their systems. The sign on the sleep-dealer factory labels the work "Cybraceros," wedding new technology and old labor solution. What passes for traditional music at a village festival is tech-edged hip-hop.

Meanwhile, in terms of plot structure, all three characters share essentially the same basic arc in their interactions with the new technology, while the story simultaneously itself intertwines their lives. They begin their engagement with the nodes innocently, with what seem reasonable, limited goals. Imbedded in the node realm, they lose their course, themselves, control of their own destinies. Each has a share of guilt to bear. In the end, brought together by the events that connect their lives, they combine to strike a Luddite blow against the system.

Memo, seeking work, still heads to Tijuana; it remains, Luz's narrative of his story tells us, "the biggest border town in the world. It pulls people in like magnets. Even today, long after the border has been closed, wondering millions keep coming, carrying nothing but their dreams." Memo, she adds, "looked like they all do, a little lost, holding on to whatever was left behind." In Memo's case, although he has from the outset craved an escape from his small, desolate town into the wider world, tragedy and his own responsibility for that tragedy drives him finally into it. As we learn through an extended flashback in Memo's narrative, his amateur computer hacking had allowed him to plug in to the satellites that control communication among the attack drone forces, but that in turn drew an attack on his own home, as his interception of signals was designated aquaterrorist activity. His home, after all, is the site of one of the dams; the information screen on the attack aircraft responding to his hacking filled in the background on the site: "Water concession reservoir. Local population: Mexican. Threat level: high. History: armed insurgency upon initial construction of the dam." While Memo was away from home visiting an uncle at a nearby village, he watched the destruction of his home and the death of his father (José Concepción Macías) live on *Drones*. On the program, the narrator (Greg Lucas) excitedly relates, "Dams all around the world are a security risk . . . and often come under attack by legions of aquaterrorists, like the Mayan Army of Water Liberation." Tonight would be one drone pilot's first mission, to "eliminate a terrorist intercept and blow the hell out of the bad guys." But in this case, the blown-away "bad guy" was Memo's innocent father. After his father's funeral, Memo made a redemptive promise to his mother (Metzli Adaminia): "I told her I'd go to the city, find work, help them any way I could." And his work does indeed allow him to send significant amounts of money home, albeit with high levels of fee deductions from the techno-banking system. But, nodes implanted, working as a robot on a construction site in San Diego, he begins to lose his way; after a Skype-ish call home, he narrates, "How could I tell her the truth. I was just finding it out myself. My energy was being drained, sent far away. What was happening to the river, was happening to me." Only his love for Luz keeps him connected to the world.

Luz, meanwhile, begins her cyberjournalism with good motives, reflected in her choice of stories (her first four posted stories treat a battle over a well, a visit with a witch doctor, and interviews with rebels, as well as her own node implantation), but nobody buys them, and her student loans are coming due. Her vision of a technojournalistic future recalls bygone vistas of the open Internet, as she tells Memo, trying to explain her work: "[T]here's so much distance between people. The only thing nodes are good for is to destroy that distance, to connect us, to let us see." And nodes are also an interesting sex toy, as Luz then shows him. But, when her story about Memo, who she has met on that Tijuana-bound bus, gets not just a buyer but someone willing to commission follow-ups, she becomes, essentially, a spy, sharing Memo's story to an unknown Internet consumer without telling Memo what she is doing. A first attempt to bring him in on the secret—by sharing one of her other stories—elicits so negative a reaction ("She invited you into her house and you sold her memories?" an appalled Memo asks) that she cannot bring herself to tell him that he has become her new subject. He discovers it on his own, with all the sense of betrayal that could be expected.

Drone pilot Rudy, meanwhile, is the secret consumer of Luz's uploaded version of Memo's tale, searching for answers to salve his own conscience after that first drone strike. Rudy has, quite simply, followed family tradition in joining the military, but with new technology, the rules have changed. As he recalls for the interviewer on *Drones*, "When I was young, all I wanted was to be a soldier, like the rest of my family. So I signed up, and a second later, I'm a pilot." But that initial strike has been different in one key way: after the first explosion, Memo's wounded father had crawled out of the house, and a second strike was needed to finish him off, but in the meantime, the distant pilot had seen what distant pilots usually do not: a human face. The program's narrator underlines the point: "This is unusual. Rarely does a drone pilot get to see the enemy face-to-face." That accidental humanization of what has become increasingly dehumanized mechanics of war haunts Rudy, forcing him to look for answers, hoping first to find that he had indeed killed a dangerous aqua-terrorist, forcing him finally to recognize that he had murdered an innocent man.

If accidents draw them together—the coincidence of the drone strike, the happenstance meeting on a Tijuana-bound bus—the film's denouement coincides with all three characters' rediscovery of purpose. Rudy travels to Tijuana to find Memo—Luz's stories and visual images provide him with the clues he will need to locate him amid the town's millions—to confess and offer his assistance in making good on his now-perceived crimes. Memo concocts a plan that requires good tech assistance, bringing him back to Luz's door for the first time since he had discovered her violation of his personal life in the uploaded memories. The three of them conspire to break into the cybracero sleep factory, hook Rudy into the system, hack into the military machines, and arrange a rogue attack that destroys the Santa Ana del Rio dam, restoring (at least for a time) water to Memo's home community.

The hopeful tenor of the film's end—the successful dam attack; the reconciliation among all three characters; Memo himself finding a new way forward in re-creating his father's way of life, planting along the border—is ameliorated, of course, by what we know of past Luddite adventures. The machines never stay away. Rudy cannot return home; neither can Memo. But the film's closing voiceover reconnects to the deeper strands of Mexican identity that the new technological age has sought to wipe away. Near the film's outset, in the flashback sequence, Memo's father had wondered aloud, "Is our future a thing of the past?" and then lamented that when they build the dam, "they cut off our future." In the film's closing moments, as he plants seeds along the border fence, Memo meditates, "But maybe there's a future for me here. On the edge of everything. A future with a past." In such slim hopes, the prospects for real reconciliation, real justice, real border crossings, real connection perilously hang.

Notes

1. Quoted in Dennis Lim, "At the Border between Politics and Thrills," *New York Times*, March 12, 2009, AR12.

2. Aaron Nicholson, Joel Elad, and Damien Stolarz, *Starting an iPhone Application Business for Dummies* (Indianapolis: Wiley Publishing, 2010), 43.

3. For more on the bracero program, there are two extensive internet archives: the Farmworkers website, which includes historical background, documents, and some oral testimonies (http://www.farmworkers.org/benglish.html) and the Bracero History Archive, a collection of oral histories (http://braceroarchive.org/). See also the chapter "The Bracero Program, 1942–1964" in Ronald L. Mize and Alicia C. S. Swords, *Consuming Mexican Labor: From the Bracero Program to NAFTA* (Toronto: University of Toronto Press, 2011), 3–24; Richard B. Craig, *The Bracero Program: Interest Groups and Foreign Policy* (Austin: University of Texas Press, 1971).

4. Alex Rivera, "Why Cybraceros?" AlexRivera.com, accessed October 12, 2012, http://alexrivera.com/project/why-cybraceros/.

5. See the chapter "Operation Wetback, 1954" in Mize and Swords, *Consuming Mexican Labor*, 25–42. See also Juan Ramón García, *Operation Wetback: The Mass Deportation of Mexican Undocumented Workers in 1954* (New York: Praeger Press, 1980).

6. Carlos Ulises Decena and Margaret Gray, "Putting Transnationalism to Work: An Interview with Filmmaker Alex Rivera," *Social Text* 24, no. 3 (2006): 131–138.

7. Director's statement on the page "Synopsis," *Sleep Dealer*, accessed October 12, 2012, http://www.sleepdealer.com/synopsis.html.

8. Quoted in Jason Silverman, "*Sleep Dealer* Injects Sci-Fi into Immigration Debate," Wired.com, January 24, 2008, http://www.wired.com/entertainment/hollywood/news/2008/01/sleep_dealer.

9. Silverman, "*Sleep Dealer* Injects Sci-Fi."

10. Quoted in Rebecca Carroll, "Independents Day," Papermag.com, March 18, 2009, http://www.papermag.com/arts_and_style/2009/03/independents-day-5.php.

11. Quoted in Lim, "At the Border," AR12.

12. The strategies Rivera and his production designer, Miguel Ángel Álvarez, employed to develop a convincingly futuristic look on a shoestring budget are discussed in Mick Hurbis-Cherrier, *Voice and Vision: A Creative Approach to Narrative Film and DV Production*, 2nd ed. (Burlington, MA: Focal Press, 2011), 127–128.

13. Rivera discusses this genealogy of the film and includes excerpts from the earlier short "Why Cybraceros?" in "Before the Making of *Sleep Dealer*," a short feature included on the *Sleep Dealer* DVD. The short feature also includes excerpts of "Why Braceros?" the 1959 promotional documentary that served as one of his inspirations. That film can also be viewed online, both at YouTube and at the Open Video Project (here: http://www.open-video.org/details.php?videoid=4503).

14. The Internet Movie Database lists it as playing 18 screens on its opening weekend, and grossing rather less than its $2.5 million estimated budget (http://www.imdb.com/title/tt0804529/business).

15. Carroll, "Independents Day."

16. For Marx's view on alienation of labor, see the chapter "Estranged Labor" in Karl Marx, *The Economic and Philosophic Manuscripts of 1844*, trans. Martin Milligan (New York: Prometheus Books, 1988), 69–84. See also Herbert Marcuse's discussion of the concept and its relationship to commodity fetishism in Herbert Marcuse, "Marx: Alienated Labor," in *Reason and Revolution: Hegel and the Rise of Social Theory* (Amherst and New York: Humanity Books, 1999), 273–322.

17. Jamie Oliver and Tony Goodwin, *How They Blew It: The CEOs and Entrepreneurs behind Some of the World's Most Catastrophic Business Failures* (London: Kogan Page, 2010), 86. The reviewing sample is slanted toward the negative in this account, however, because Oliver and Goodwin's main interest is in trashing the film's executive producers, Guy Naggar and Peter Klimt, who were about to become involved in the collapse of the Dawney, Day financial empire. So, for example, they leave out *San Francisco Chronicle* reviewer Peter Hartlaub's final note: after quoting his judgment that the film was "flawed, but still vibrant and inventive," they omit his conclusion that "Rivera is definitely a filmmaker to follow" (Peter Hartlaub, "Sci-Fi Border Saga," *San Francisco Chronicle*, June 19, 2009, http://www.sfgate.com/movies/article/Review-Sci-fi-border-saga-3294715.php).

18. Aaron Hillis, "Sleep Dealer as Subtle as a Light Saber to the Face," *Village Voice*, April 15, 2009, http://www.villagevoice.com/2009-04-15/film/sleep-dealer-as-subtle-as-a-light-saber-to-the-face/full/.

19. A. O. Scott, "Tale of an Anxious Wanderer," *New York Times*, April 16, 2009: C10, http://movies.nytimes.com/2009/04/17/movies/17slee.html.

20. B Ruby Rich, "Back into the Light," *Guardian*, January 28, 2008, http://www.guardian.co.uk/film/2008/jan/29/sundancefilmfestival.festivals.

21. Mize and Swords, *Consuming Mexican Labor*, xiii.

22. Melissa K. Lopez, *Chicano Nations: The Hemispheric Origins of Mexican American Literature* (New York: New York University Press, 2011), 202.

23. Rachel St. John, *Line in the Sand: A History of the Western U.S.-Mexico Border* (Princeton: Princeton University Press, 2011), 203–205.

24. Robert Lee Maril, *The Fence: National Security, Public Safety, and Illegal Immigration along the U.S.-Mexico Border* (Lubbock: Texas Tech University Press, 2011), 22.

25. Quoted in Robert Edwin Koulish, *Immigration and American Democracy: Subverting the Rule of Law* (New York: Routledge, 2010), 104.

26. Maude Barlow, *Blue Covenant: The Global Water Crisis and the Coming Battle for the Right to Water* (New York: The New Press, 2007), 37.

27. Maude Barlow and Tony Clarke, *Blue Gold: The Battle against Corporate Theft of the World's Water*, rev. ed. (London: McClelland and Stewart, 2010), 70.

28. Douglas S. Massey, "The Wall That Keeps Illegal Workers In," *New York Times*, April 4, 2006, http://www.nytimes.com/2006/04/04/opinion/04massey.html. Quoted in Justin Akers Chacón and Mike Davis, *No One Is Illegal: Fighting Racism and State Violence on the U.S.-Mexico Border* (Chicago: Haymarket Press, 2006), 210.

29. For a handy summary, see Rachel Martin, "An Open Secret: Drone Warfare in Pakistan" National Public Radio, September 6, 2011, http://www.npr.org/2011/09/06/140216985/an-open-secret-drone-warfare-in-pakistan.

30. U.S. House of Representatives Subcommittee on National Security and Foreign Affairs of the Committee on Oversight and Government Reform, *Rise of the Drones: Unmanned Systems and the Future of War: Hearing before the Subcommittee on National Security and Foreign Affairs of the Committee on Oversight and Government Reform, House of Representatives, One Hundred Eleventh Congress, Second Session, March 23, 2010* (Washington: U.S. Government Printing Office, 2011), I.

31. Steven P. Lee, *Ethics and War: An Introduction* (Cambridge: Cambridge University Press, 2011), 224.

Works Cited

Barlow, Maude. *Blue Covenant: The Global Water Crisis and the Coming Battle for the Right to Water.* New York: The New Press, 2007.

Barlow, Maude, and Tony Clarke. *Blue Gold: The Battle against Corporate Theft of the World's Water.* Rev. ed. London: McClelland and Stewart, 2004.

"Box office/business for *Sleep Dealer*." IMDb. Accessed October 12, 2012. http://www.imdb.com/title/tt0804529/business.

"Bracero History Archive." Center for History and New Media. Accessed October 12, 2012. http://braceroarchive.org.

Carroll, Rebecca. "Independents Day." Papermag.com. March 18, 2009. http://www.papermag.com/arts_and_style/2009/03/independents-day-5.php.

Chacón, Justin Akers, and Mike Davis. *No One Is Illegal: Fighting Racism and State Violence on the U.S.-Mexico Border.* Chicago: Haymarket Press, 2006.

Craig, Richard B. *The Bracero Program: Interest Groups and Foreign Policy.* Austin: University of Texas Press, 1971.

Decena, Carlos Ulises, and Margaret Gray. "Putting Transnationalism to Work: An Interview with Filmmaker Alex Rivera." *Social Text* 24, no. 3 (2006), 131–138.

García, Juan Ramón. *Operation Wetback: The Mass Deportation of Mexican Undocumented Workers in 1954.* New York: Praeger Press, 1980.

Hartlaub, Peter. "Sci-Fi Border Saga." *San Francisco Chronicle*, June 19, 2009. http://www.sfgate.com/movies/article/Review-Sci-fi-border-saga-3294715.php.

Hillis, Aaron. "*Sleep Dealer* as Subtle as a Light Saber to the Face." *Village Voice*, April 15, 2009. http://www.villagevoice.com/2009-04-15/film/sleep-dealer-as-subtle-as-a-light-saber-to-the-face/.

Hurbis-Cherrier, Mick. *Voice and Vision: A Creative Approach to Narrative Film and DV Production.* 2nd ed. Burlington, MA: Focal Press, 2011.

Koulish, Robert Edwin. *Immigration and American Democracy: Subverting the Rule of Law.* New York: Routledge, 2010.

Lee, Steven P. *Ethics and War: An Introduction.* Cambridge: Cambridge University Press, 2011.

Lim, Dennis. "At the Border between Politics and Thrills." *New York Times*, March 12, 2009, AR12. http://www.nytimes.com/2009/03/15/movies/15denn.html.

Lopez, Melissa K. *Chicano Nations: The Hemispheric Origins of Mexican American Literature.* New York: New York University Press, 2011.

"Los Braceros, 1942–1964." Farmworkers website. Accessed October 12, 2012. http://www.farmworkers.org/benglish.html.

Marcuse, Herbert. "Marx: Alienated Labor." In *Reason and Revolution: Hegel and the Rise of Social Theory*, 273–322. Amherst and New York: Humanity Books, 1999. First published 1941.

Maril, Robert Lee. *The Fence: National Security, Public Safety, and Illegal Immigration along the U.S.-Mexico Border.* Lubbock: Texas Tech University Press, 2011.

Martin, Rachel. "An Open Secret: Drone Warfare in Pakistan." National Public Radio, September 6, 2011. http://www.npr.org/2011/09/06/140216985/an-open-secret-drone-warfare-in-pakistan.

Marx, Karl. *The Economic and Philosophic Manuscripts of 1844*. Translated by Martin Milligan. New York: Prometheus Books, 1988.

Massey, Douglas S. "The Wall That Keeps Illegal Workers In." *New York Times*, April 4, 2006. http://www.nytimes.com/2006/04/04/opinion/04massey.html.

Mize, Ronald L., and Alicia C. S. Swords. *Consuming Mexican Labor: From the Bracero Program to NAFTA*. Toronto: University of Toronto Press, 2011.

Nicholson, Aaron, Joel Elad, and Damien Stolarz. *Starting an iPhone Application Business for Dummies*. Indianapolis: Wiley Publishing, 2010,

Oliver, Jamie, and Tony Goodwin. *How They Blew It: The CEOs and Entrepreneurs behind Some of the World's Most Catastrophic Business Failures*. London: Kogan Page, 2010.

Rich, B. Ruby. "Back into the Light." *Guardian*, January 28, 2008. http://www.guardian.co.uk/film/2008/jan/29/sundancefilmfestival.festivals.

Rivera, Alex. "Synopsis." Sleep Dealer. Accessed October 12, 2012. http://www.sleepdealer.com/synopsis.html.

———. "Why Cybraceros?" AlexRivera.com. Accessed October 12, 2012. http://alexrivera.com/project/why-cybraceros/.

Scott, A. O. "Tale of an Anxious Wanderer." *New York Times*, April 16, 2009, C10. http://movies.nytimes.com/2009/04/17/movies/17slee.html.

Silverman, Jason. "*Sleep Dealer* Injects Sci-Fi into Immigration Debate." Wired.com. January 24, 2008. http://www.wired.com/entertainment/hollywood/news/2008/01/sleep_dealer.

St. John, Rachel. *Line in the Sand: A History of the Western U.S.-Mexico Border*. Princeton: Princeton University Press, 2011.

U.S. House of Representatives Subcommittee on National Security and Foreign Affairs of the Committee on Oversight and Government Reform. *Rise of the Drones: Unmanned Systems and the Future of War: Hearing before the Subcommittee on National Security and Foreign Affairs of the Committee on Oversight and Government Reform, House of Representatives, One Hundred Eleventh Congress, Second Session, March 23, 2010*. Washington: U.S. Government Printing Office, 2011.

Films

"Before the Making of *Sleep Dealer*" (short). Directed by Alex Rivera. United States, Mexico, 2008.

Blade Runner. Directed by Ridley Scott. United States, 1982.

COPS (TV show). Created by Malcolm Barbour and John Langley. United States, 1989–present.

A Day without a Mexican. Directed by Sergio Arau. United States, Mexico, Spain, 2004.

eXistenZ. Directed by David Cronenberg. Canada/United Kingdom, 1999.

I, Robot. Directed by Alex Proyas. United States, 2004.

Sleep Dealer. Directed by Alex Rivera. United States, Mexico, 2008.
Star Wars. Directed by George Lucas. United States, 1977.
Strange Days. Directed by Kathryn Bigelow. United States, 1995.
"Why Braceros?" (short). Produced by Council of California Growers; no director listed. United States, 1959.
"Why Cybraceros?" (short). Directed by Alex Rivera. United States, 1997.

II

FROM THE CENTER TO THE MARGINS

IDEOLOGICAL DOMINANCE AND LIMINAL SPACES

4

An Empire of Borders

Central European Boundaries in István Szabó's Colonel Redl *(1985)*

Raluca Cernahoschi

In his preface to *The Cinema of Central Europe*, Hungarian director István Szabó evokes an ideal image of Central Europe as a "world of diversity and tolerance, a world of living together where dissimilarity was honoured." Its symbolic space is a "small Hungarian town," whose

> main square is surrounded by six churches. The Town Hall is flanked by a Catholic, a Greek Orthodox and a Calvinist church, and a Presbyterian School and chapel. Opposite, on the other side of the square, there is a synagogue, and to the right, on the corner of a small street there is yet another Catholic church and convent. The town's people did not build their churches away from each other, locked into small communities but all together, grouped on the main square. In the middle of the square there is a park, with one building only, a café: the only café for all the different churchgoers, where they could gather, read the papers, have coffee, play cards and billiards.[1]

This elaborate vision of Central Europe as an open meeting place where denominational, ethnic, linguistic, and political differences are suspended through mutual sociability is overshadowed by only one drawback: it was not meant to last. This best version of Central Europe, Szabó underlines, only existed before World War I ushered in the catastrophes of the twentieth century. It is centered—geographically, temporally, and socially—in the Austro-Hungarian Empire, which is also the setting of *Colonel Redl* (*Oberst Redl/Redl ezredes*, 1985), Szabó's film chosen by volume editor Peter Hames as one of "24 seminal films that, taken together, best represent the artistic, industrial and technological development of that territory's cinema."[2]

While the coincidence of Central Europe with the social and geographical space of the Austro-Hungarian Empire may not surprise, Szabó's two versions of the region—one essayistic, the other cinematic—are very different. Written two decades after the production of the film, the essay paints a much more optimistic vision of the Dual Monarchy, even carrying a whiff of the Habsburg nostalgia first described by Claudio Magris.[3] Peter G. Christensen has argued that the film's attempt at historical reconstruction cannot avoid evoking this nostalgia,[4] yet the invocation is necessary for the critique of the empire ultimately embedded in the film. The most salient difference between the two depictions of the empire (and, by extension, Central Europe), however, is one of geography. The essay imagines Central Europe literally as a center: a town square in which all citizens meet. In the center, the citizens divide neatly into categories (Catholic, Greek Orthodox, Calvinist, etc.) but they are on equal footing, despite their differences, which can be resolved through friendly frissons, such as a game of cards. The film, by contrast, emphasizes the periphery, as it is there that the identity of the protagonist is constructed and his and the monarchy's fate are set in motion. The periphery engenders a citizen who feels marginal and yearns for the protection and stability of the center, but who never truly arrives in the center nor feels at home in the periphery.

Colonel Redl: Mapping the Rise and Fall of an Imperial Servant

The second film collaboration between the director and Austrian actor Klaus Maria Brandauer, *Colonel Redl*, traces the rise of the titular officer (played by Brandauer) from an obscure background, to the highest ranks of the Royal and Imperial Army, to his eventual fall from grace and suicide. The narrative arc is based loosely on the biography of real-life Chief of the General Staff Alfred Redl, who was discovered to have sold sensitive military information to the Russian Empire and committed suicide in May 1913. The film takes large liberties with the historical record, however.[5] As is typical for Szabó's films, the protagonist of *Colonel Redl* is both an individual (due in no small part to Brandauer's visceral performance) and a type. His demise parallels that of the monarchy that he serves and ultimately embodies: Redl's suicide is followed closely by the murder of the crown prince (Armin Mueller-Stahl) in Sarajevo, suggesting that the two acts taken together are the beginning point of the empire's disintegration.[6] Szabó's Redl can further be read as a representative of a certain class,[7] of a particular ethnicity and sexual orientation,[8] or as an illustration of Central European historical experience[9] within the framework of the Habsburg Dual Monarchy. But the film also maps the empire in a more direct way in its choice and treatment of settings. A key to understanding how Redl functions as its representative is to look at the relationship between the geo-social spaces he inhabits—the cores and peripheries of the empire—and the social boundaries that define him.

The film maps Redl's career across the expanse of the empire, from his humble Galician home, to a royal and imperial cadet school, to an early post on the Adriatic, to a promotion on the Russian border, and, intermittently, to the capital. Most of these spaces are peripheries, far from the glittering center of the empire to which Redl aspires. His peripheral existence throws the character's social limitations and aspirations into relief. Like several other characters in Szabó's films—including Hendrik Höfgen in *Mephisto* (1980) and Erik Jan Hanussen in *Hanussen* (1988), both also played by Brandauer,[10] and the Sonnenscheins of *Sunshine* (1999), played by Ralph Fiennes—Redl is an outsider, who sets out from the geographic and social periphery and journeys to the core of power, wealth, and privilege in search of fortune and fame. If Höfgen, Hanussen, and the older Sonnenschein move rather quickly from the periphery to the center, where their fates play out, however, Redl stands out for his circuitous route to the seat of power, spending more than half of the film on the margins of the empire.

Also set partially in the Dual Monarchy, *Sunshine* provides an illuminating contrast to the director's handling of geographic space in *Colonel Redl*. Despite their shared historical interest, *Colonel Redl* and *Sunshine* depict the geography of the empire very differently. The story of the Sonnenschein/Sors family through three generations, *Sunshine* begins in a nameless village in the Austro-Hungarian Empire, defined generically through its hillside landscape, traditional architecture, and Jewish culture. Although the village could be Galician, as Sandra Theiß suggests,[11] the narrative seems to purposely eschew such specificity. Where the Sonnenscheins come from is far less important to the development of the story than where they are going: Budapest, one of the empire's two political, cultural, and social centers. Here, three generations of Sonnenschein heirs embody the triumphs and trials of a Jewish family through the three regimes—monarchy, fascism, communism—that defined Central Europe from the middle of the nineteenth to the middle of the twentieth century. With Budapest dominating the geographic setting of the film, *Sunshine* depicts a specific Hungarian as much as a more general Central European experience.[12] By contrast, *Colonel Redl* is a decentered film, avoiding the Transleithanian capital entirely and offering only glimpses of the Cisleithanian one.

Geographically speaking, this is the most mobile of Szabó's films, moving freely between locations as widely disparate as Ukrainian Galicia, Vienna, and the Adriatic coast. The movement is facilitated both by the setting of the film in the multinational Habsburg Empire (an entity at least theoretically devoid of internal borders) and by the filmmaker's real-life access to shooting locations in Hungary, Austria, and the former Yugoslavia. However, the sense of freedom in this free-floating spatial construction is at odds with the limited social horizons of the characters. The border scenes generate an important source of the tension between the two, as the opportunities inscribed in the marginal spaces of the empire remain unrealized in the life of the protagonist.

Galicia and the Crisis of Identity

The film's most important settings are the two extreme borders of the empire, the northernmost and southernmost crown lands: Galicia, on the border with the Russian Empire, and the Austrian Littoral, on the Adriatic Sea. The two borders appear at first in direct opposition. Galicia can be read in multiple ways: as a political divide, a remote area, or a contact zone in which subjectivities are variously constructed, deconstructed, and reconstructed through a number of social forces. By contrast, the Austrian Littoral appears as almost no boundary at all: like the sea to which it is exposed, the Littoral seems to promise freedom from any constraints on identity.

As a region of "shifting alliances and identities," Galicia takes a privileged position in Szabó's film.[13] It is Redl's birthplace, but also as the place where the identity of the young officer—and his subsequent fate—begins to crystalize. Today divided between Poland and Ukraine, Galicia was created by decree as a buffer zone between Austria-Hungary and the Russian Empire during the First Partition of Poland in 1772. The last province to be added to the Habsburg Empire and the only one with no historical identity of its own, it occupied, from the very beginning, a special role in the imperial imagination.[14] Home to Poles, Ukrainians, and Austrian Germans, Galicia also had the biggest Jewish population, and its material poverty but cultural richness became, over the next one hundred years, the two pillars of a steadfast mythologization.[15] Remote from the imperial centers of Vienna and Budapest, the region affectionately dubbed "half-Asian" by Karl Emil Franzos,[16] came to be seen as an alternative model to, and a source of criticism of, the core. From the second half of the nineteenth century on, Galicia stood

> not for picturesque poverty and foreign-seeming Chassidic traditions or misty-eyed recollections of the tolerant coexistence of different cultures in a far-away place beyond civilization and reality but for the questioning of hegemonic concepts of progress. . . . Not deprivation but an abundance of possibilities spring forth from this border region on the periphery. The fascinating thing about the literature [about Galicia] is the problematization of normative propositions,

> especially at the intersection of nationality and modernity. The distance to the geographic and political center allows for a distancing from the historical and cultural norm.[17]

In *Colonel Redl*, Galicia appears very differently from this space of potential resistance. Seen through the eyes of the protagonist, the province is at first a childhood haven. Like the historical Alfred Redl, Szabó's protagonist is born in or near Lemberg (today Lviv), eastern Galicia's largest and most significant city.[18] Yet other than the location of the fictional Redl's birth and the occupation of his father, a civil servant employed by the Imperial Royal Railways, the sequence that establishes the protagonist's roots and that opens the film bears no resemblance to the historical record. Instead of a sizeable urban center, Redl's place of birth appears as an isolated hamlet; instead of the prosperous family of a railway inspector, Redl's family appears impoverished, his father's position diminished to that of a stationmaster. Still, the vision is a happy one. Set to the gently swaying tune of the "Emperor Waltz," the sequence shows a series of vignettes, centering on Redl's home and family life: his father (not credited) saluting from his post, his mother (Éva Szabó) getting water or putting the children to bed, his siblings playing, the family eating dinner. The camera's gaze, looking onto this familial world from a slightly low angle, is that of young Redl, who does not himself appear in this sequence. Family members respond to the child's gaze by looking into the camera and smiling, as if answering the boy's own smile.

Constant reminders that the private world the viewer witnesses in this sequence is embedded in the social and political world of the empire subvert the seeming idyll of Redl's childhood world, however; the safe haven of Redl's home is already inculcated with the norms of the empire. These childhood vignettes are framed by close-up shots of the adult Redl in uniform, as he appears later in the film in the last moments before his suicide. This framing suggests that the happy images of childhood are fragmentary (reconstructed?) memories of the isolated and desperate officer. As the adult Redl stares into the camera, mirroring the gaze of the child, the sequence gathers the force of a search for answers: how did he arrive at his impasse? Underlying the complex answer offered by the subsequent narrative is a thread borrowed from the variegated tapestry of Habsburg myth: the special connection between the peripheral individual to the central authority figure of the emperor. From the dialog of the opening sequence, we learn of the family legend, according to which the emperor befriended the boy's grandfather, a simple peasant. The child's gratitude for this act of imperial condescension is expressed in a poem that brings him to the attention of his teacher, who later recommends him for the royal and imperial cadet school. On the eve of his departure for the school, his mother further enjoins him to always be grateful to the emperor, who has done so much for their family. Having thus internalized gratitude toward the emperor from an early age, Redl continues to defend and strengthen his relationship to the core of the empire throughout his life.

This story of imperial benefaction and eternal gratitude bears more than a passing resemblance to one of the lynchpins of Habsburg myth, Joseph Roth's 1932 novel *Radetzky March* (*Radetzkymarsch*).[19] Like the Trotta family of *Radetzky March*,[20] the Redls are burdened with a special distinction. The premise of the narrative that sets young Redl on his path is the establishment of a direct link between the emperor and one of his subjects, however lowly, which subsequently ennobles the subject to a standard-bearer of the empire. This connection between core and periphery is of the purest order: the only contact occurs between the emperor and the subject. Like the isolated train station that can only be reached by imperial trains and the family whose only demonstrated contact is to imperial institutions, Redl's early view of the margin is that of a discrete entity tethered to the imperial enterprise by the umbilical cord of Franz Joseph's benevolence.

A different view of Galicia is revealed later in the film, when Redl, now a promising young officer, is sent from his first post on the Adriatic to serve on the Austrian-Russian border. The sequence of his Galician sojourn, during which he is promoted to district commander, ends at the midpoint of the film, dividing it neatly into a before and after, and is thus of special significance in the understanding of the character's construction. Redl's return to Galicia appears, at first, to offer no break from his previous life as an officer. The shot of his and his friend Kubinyi's (Jan Niklas) entry into Lemberg/Lviv pans over a cobbled square flanked by a Gothic church and other representative buildings, comforting in the conventionality of their Central European architecture. The very next scene, however, sets out to complicate the image of the Galician border. As Redl, Kubinyi, and the district commander, Colonel Ruzitska (László Mensáros), toast the young men's arrival, the latter expounds on the problems of this border: prostitutes, Gypsies, thieves, and Jews, the last of which are especially troublesome, since they stand in contact with their "brothers" on the Russian side, with whom they engage in illicit and subversive trade. Ruzitska's Galicia is a space inhabited primarily by marginal groups, both a geographical and social periphery prefigured by the map in the colonel's office. Located on the wall behind the officers in the interview scene, the map takes up the center of the image. Its most prominent feature—a thick line slashing across its upper right—appears, at first, to be the political border between the two inimical empires but is revealed, upon closer inspection, to be a boundary of a different kind. The heavy line follows the contours of the Carpathian Mountains, which mark Galicia's southern edge and thus its division not from the Russian but from the rest of the Austro-

Figure 4.1. The Carpathians separate Galicia from the rest of the empire on the commander's map. *Colonel Redl* (Starz/Anchor Bay).

Hungarian Empire, a visual reminder of the province's remoteness from the imperial center.[21]

While borders are political divides between states, they are also "markers of the actual power that states wield . . . over their own societies."[22] This power is negotiated between the state (the center) and the population of the borderland (the periphery) and is as such inherently "restricted and unstable."[23] The power of the center must be continually reinforced, a task to which Redl feels particularly called. He takes it upon himself to discipline the officers of the garrison for neglecting their duties or performing them badly, as well as for transgressions against civilian and military authority. Redl's actions speak of the distance that he perceives between the imperial center and this remote area, with its poor connection to the empire's center.[24] In Galicia, Austrian culture is not so much nonexistent as poorly replicated. The viewer observes, from Redl's point of view, the breakdown in decorum at a local ball held in a shabby mansion and attended by drunken officers and disgruntled agitators. The breakdown threatens to engulf even Redl. When he witnesses Kubinyi also agitating against the emperor, Redl forgets both his status as an officer and their friendship, and tackles Kubinyi to the ground. It takes Kubinyi's ambiguous remark—"Trying to play switchman, are you?"[25]—to remind Redl of his position and cause him to desist. After a brief moment of reflection, Redl then flees the premises. Edward Plater has interpreted Kubinyi's poisoned comment as an allusion to Redl's humble provenance—his father's "lowly position with the railroad"[26]—and this is certainly the case. But the remark can also be read as an allusion to Redl's efforts to switch the course of the monarchy and, in the process, ingratiate himself with the emperor. Finally, Kubinyi's remark points to Redl's own switching of sides, which will also manifest itself in the end of the two officers' friendship.

Redl's paradoxical position with respect to the border makes him indeed a "switchman." He starts out as indigenous to the periphery—a poor but robust "peasant boy," who, through his "native" gifts, attracts the benevolence of the emperor—but returns to it as a functionary of the center. He chooses the privilege of the latter, but cannot escape the former. The son of a poor minor functionary and a man of ambiguous ethnicity and sexual orientation, Redl understands social divisions only too well. The childhood story with which the film endows him illustrates his efforts to overcome them by hiding his provenance and assiduously studying and copying the behaviors and accomplishments that buy him admittance into the rarefied circle of Austrian and Hungarian nobility. By the time he returns to the border, he seems to have accomplished his goal. Hidden behind the great equalizer of the uniform, Redl hopes to "pass" as an Austrian officer and throws himself zealously into the work of upholding the social divisions that make his passage possible.

Images foregrounding barriers or partitions visually emphasize the segregation Redl attempts to enforce between the officers and the townspeople, especially Jews. When the newly arrived Redl first interviews the Jewish innkeeper, for instance, the camera positions him behind a partition that draws a physical barrier between Austrian officer and Jewish civilian. Other partitions, too, such as doors, curtains, tables, or chairs, soon separate Redl from all human contact, including with the townspeople, fellow officers, his friend Kubinyi, and even his family.

Redl's fear of contamination reaches a crisis point in a scene at the local restaurant where the officers take their meals. The mimicry of Viennese *joie de vivre* in the restaurant's setting exposes the remoteness of the border and highlights the inescapable inequality between core and periphery: while the restaurant may have a sultry chanteuse performing the Strauss waltz "Viennese Blood" ("Wiener Blut"), the audience, composed of Hasidic Jews and lonely exiled officers drawn from every corner of the empire, is pointedly lacking in the precious commodity. Against this setting, a Jewish trader's request of the officer's company at Shabbat dinner is perceived by Redl as a public compromise. When a fortune-telling Gypsy simultaneously approaches him, he seeks to defend himself by shaking off both Jew and Gypsy in a violent outburst. Redl's attempts at safeguarding himself from contamination have, of course, the exact opposite effect: the more the officer seeks to distance himself from those he construes as Others, the more Other he becomes. Rumors about his Jewish roots—never previously suggested in the film—start to abound and to ultimately construct him as Jewish.

Figure 4.2. The table protects the officer from contact with his sister (Flóra Kádár). *Colonel Redl* (Starz/Anchor Bay).

To his alarm, Redl ultimately finds that Galicia is a contact zone, in which "subjects are constituted in and by their relations to each other."[27] Redl's panicked defense against his identification with the Jewish inhabitants of the Galician border stands in stark contrast to his friendship with the Jewish doctor, Sonnenschein (András Bálint),[28] with whom he served on the Adriatic. In an earlier scene, Redl and Sonnenschein are shown strolling arm in arm along a boardwalk and discussing the doctor's planned subversion of imperial military norm through an open and public declaration that he is a "Hungarian Jew." After admitting that his father used to "play cards with the Rabbi of Lemberg," Redl joins his friend in this flight of fancy by declaring himself ready to embrace the "beautiful holidays" of Yom Kippur and Passover.

The Adriatic: The Empire's Gateway

Set against the openness of the Adriatic Sea, the self-fashioning of identity to which the two young officers aspire seems possible. Indeed, throughout the film, the scenes on the southern border of the empire hint at the possibility of unlimited social freedom. Although the Adriatic coast has a mythology of its own as a meeting place of nations and a laboratory for the study of cultural interaction,[29] the film does not allude to it. The mutability and penetrability of the sea—long associated with fluidity and the feminine—seem to make the Adriatic an open border, along which the two men test out interchangeable identities.

The scenes on the Adriatic are often medium close-ups of intimate conversations between two people against the backdrop of sea and sky, simultaneously suggesting the intimacy and the openness of the social transfer. The framing of the shots also reminds us, however, that such a transfer between equals is only possible in isolation, away from the influence of social institutions. Indeed, the sun-drenched Adriatic scenes seem to offer the southern border of the empire as a means of escape not only from the hierarchical order of the center but also from border natives. This is where Redl goes when he seeks a respite and where he meets his only two disinterested friends: Dr. Sonnenschein and Redl's confidante and sometimes mistress, Katalin Kubinyi (Gudrun Landgrebe). The progressively more distancing camera work in the second half of the film, which replaces the intimate-but-open close-ups from the beginning with framed long and medium shots, suggests Redl's increasing inability to open up to the possibilities offered by this border. He refuses Katalin's offered route of escape to America over the open sea, locking himself into an arranged marriage instead. In the sequence following his wedding, Redl is seen closing the triple window on the sea with grim determination, as if shuttering himself up against an outside world that once held such great promise.

As tempting as it is to conclude that the polarity between the two borders proposed by the film is an absolute one, there is also evidence that suggests otherwise. In a discussion on the future of the monarchy, the skeptical Katalin points to the Roman ruins among which the pair is strolling as an example of the fate of past imperial ambitions. Her gesture and the long camera shot of the towering ruined structures superimposing themselves between the human actors and the sea reveal not just the vain ambition of peoples past but also the true nature of the border as a contact zone, in which the cultural transfer—both constructive and destructive—is inscribed into the very landscape.

As Katalin points out, the borders of the empire are highly penetrable, and Redl—the *Grenze* soldier—is continually engaged in sequestering them. Indeed, closing things in and out is one of the dominant visual and narrative motifs of the film. Whatever Redl's motives may be—whether one regards Redl as a ruthless careerist, or a hapless victim of the system, or both—he is continually engaged in maintaining separation, both as a soldier and as a human being. This is his defense strategy, both for the empire and for himself, except the gradual closing-in reduces his possibilities of self-actualization to the point of implosion. Not coincidentally, the film portrays the explosion of World War I as following the implosion of the protagonist and of the empire itself.

Figure 4.3. Redl and Katalin walk in the contact zone of past empires. *Colonel Redl* (Starz/Anchor Bay).

Notes

1. István Szabó, "Preface," in *The Cinema of Central Europe*, edited by Peter Hames (London: Wallflower Press, 2004), xiii.
2. Quote taken from the dust jacket of Peter Hames, ed., *The Cinema of Central Europe* (London: Wallflower Press, 2004).
3. Claudio Magris, *Der habsburgische Mythos in der österreichischen Literatur* (Salzburg: Otto Müller Verlag, 1966).
4. Peter G. Christensen, "Szabó's *Colonel Redl* and the Habsburg Myth," *CLCWeb: Comparative Literature and Culture* 8, no. 1 (2006), http://clcwebjournal.lib.purdue.edu/clcweb06-1/contents06-1.html.
5. For a thorough discussion of the film's departures from the historical record, see Peter C. Christensen, "Szabó's *Colonel Redl.*" Christensen shows how the director manipulates both the sense of time and the depiction of historical characters to enhance a mythical representation of the Austro-Hungarian Empire.
6. For a developed analysis of this parallel, see Edward M. V. Plater, "István Szabó's Film of Inner Conflict and Political Prophecy: The 'Poseur' in István Szabó's *Colonel Redl*," *Hungarian Studies Review* 19, nos. 1–2 (1992): 43–57.
7. Hildegard Nabbe has analyzed the film's creation of a "rootless individual in a rigid class system." Hildegard Nabbe, "Verrat und Verfall in der kaiserlich-königlichen Monarchie: István Szabós Film *Oberst Redl*," *Modern Austrian Literature* 32, no. 4 (1999): 64.

8. Dagmar C. G. Lorenz, "Ethnicity, Sexuality, and Politics in István Szabó's *Colonel Redl* and *Mephisto*," in *Insiders and Outsiders: Jewish and Gentile Culture in Germany and Austria*, ed. Dagmar C. G. Lorenz and Gabriele Weinberger (Detroit: Wayne State University Press, 1994), 263–279.

9. Katherine Arens, "Central Europe's Catastrophes on Film: The Case of István Szabó," in *History of the Literary Cultures of East-Central Europe: Junctures and Disjunctures in the 19th and 20th Centuries*, ed. Marcel Cornis-Pope and John Neubauer (Amsterdam: John Benjamins, 2004), 548–558.

10. As a part of an informal trilogy featuring Brandauer, *Colonel Redl* is often compared to *Mephisto* and *Hanussen*. The stories of an actor and a clairvoyant, respectively, who seek to establish careers in 1930s Berlin by arranging themselves with the Nazis, the two latter films share a protagonist who becomes entangled in the machinations of a regime he believes to control—or at the very least evade—with *Colonel Redl*.

11. Sandra Theiß, *Taking Sides: Der Filmregisseur István Szabó* (Mainz: Bender Verlag, 2003), 219.

12. Theiß, *Taking Sides*, 219. Sandra Theiß offers a compelling reading of the film as part of the director's examination of Hungarian history and an explicit return to "Hungarian" topics.

13. David Robinson and Peter Hames, "*Redl Ezredes / Colonel Redl*," in Hames, *Cinema of Central Europe*, 209.

14. Larry Wolff, *The Idea of Galicia: History and Fantasy in Habsburg Political Culture* (Stanford: Stanford University Press, 2010), 1–6.

15. For the development of the Galician myth, see the study by Larry Wolff, *Idea of Galicia*; also the article by Dietlind Hüchtker, "Der 'Mythos Galizien': Versuch einer Historisierung," *Kakanien Revisited*, August 5, 2003, http://www.kakanien.ac.at/beitr/fallstudie/DHüchtker2.pdf.

16. Karl Emil Franzos, *Aus Halb-Asien: Kulturbilder aus Galizien, der Bukowina, Südrußland und Rumänien* (Stuttgart: J. G. Cotta, 1901).

17. Hüchtker, "Der 'Mythos Galizien,'" 13 [my translation].

18. Lemberg/Lviv was the capital of Galicia until the addition of Cracow and adjacent regions to the province in the Third Partition of 1795. By the beginning of the twentieth century, Lemberg/Lviv was a sizeable metropolis of some two hundred thousand (the fourth largest urban area in the empire) and an important political and cultural center. The city's evolution under the Dual Monarchy is detailed in Markian Prokopovych, *Habsburg Lemberg: Architecture, Public Space, and Politics in the Galician Capital, 1772–1914* (West Lafayette, IN: Purdue University Press, 2009).

19. Joseph Roth, *Radetzkymarsch* (München: Deutscher Taschenbuch Verlag, 2002). The novel is discussed in the context of Habsburg myth by both Magris and Wolff.

20. The novel centers on young Carl Joseph Trotta von Sipolje, a young lieutenant, whose grandfather—a Slovenian peasant—saves the emperor's life and is ennobled as the "Hero of Solferino." Under pressure from his father, Baron Trotta, to show gratitude to the emperor for his special connection to the family, Carl Joseph embarks on a military career and dies meaninglessly at the beginning of the war.

21. Mountains are one of the features identified by anthropologist Edwin Ardener that "conventionally add to the 'remoteness' experience." Edwin Ardener, "'Remote Areas': Some Theoretical Considerations," in *Anthropology at Home*, ed. Anthony Jackson (London: Tavistock Publications, 1987), 41.

22. Michiel Baud and Willem van Schendel, "Toward a Comparative History of Borderlands," *Journal of World History* 8, no. 2 (1997): 215.

23. Baud and van Schendel, "Toward a Comparative History of Borderlands," 215.

24. "The lesson of 'remote' areas is that this is a condition not related to periphery, but to the fact that certain peripheries are by definition not properly linked to the dominant zone" (Ardener, "'Remote Areas,'" 50).

25. This translation follows the subtitles. The German original—"Was bist denn, du Weichensteller?"—translates more directly as "Who are you, you switchman?" calling even more strongly into question Redl's identity.

26. Plater, "István Szabó's Film," 47.

27. Mary Louise Pratt, *Imperial Eyes: Travel Writing and Transculturation* (London: Routledge, 1994), 7.

28. Like Brandauer, Bálint is a recurring actor in Szabó's films, having starred in three of the director's early films. The character's name, later picked up in *Sunshine*, also points to a persistent interest in the fate of Central European Jews in Szabó's work.

29. See Dominique Kirchner Reill, *Nationalists Who Feared the Nation: Adriatic Multi-Nationalism in Habsburg Dalmatia, Trieste, and Venice* (Stanford: Stanford University Press, 2012), 81–114.

Works Cited

Ardener, Edwin. "'Remote Areas': Some Theoretical Considerations." In *Anthropology at Home*, edited by Anthony Jackson, 38–54. London: Tavistock Publications, 1987.

Arens, Katherine. "Central Europe's Catastrophes on Film: The Case of István Szabó." In *History of the Literary Cultures of East-Central Europe: Junctures and Disjunctures in the 19th and 20th Centuries*, edited by Marcel Cornis-Pope and John Neubauer, 548–558. Amsterdam: John Benjamins, 2004.

Baud, Michiel, and Willem van Schendel. "Toward a Comparative History of Borderlands." *Journal of World History* 8, no. 2 (1997): 211–242.

Christensen, Peter G. "Szabó's *Colonel Redl* and the Habsburg Myth." *CLCWeb: Comparative Literature and Culture* 8, no. 1 (2006). http://clcwebjournal.lib.purdue.edu/clcweb06-1/contents06-1.html.

Franzos, Karl Emil. *Aus Halb-Asien: Kulturbilder aus Galizien, der Bukowina, Südrußland und Rumänien*. Stuttgart: J. G. Cotta, 1901.

Hames, Peter, ed. *The Cinema of Central Europe*. London: Wallflower Press, 2004.

Hüchtker, Dietlind. "Der 'Mythos Galizien': Versuch einer Historisierung." *Kakanien Revisited*, August 5, 2003. http://www.kakanien.ac.at/beitr/fallstudie/DHüchtker2.pdf.

Lorenz, Dagmar C. G. "Ethnicity, Sexuality, and Politics in István Szabó's *Colonel Redl* and *Mephisto*." In *Insiders and Outsiders: Jewish and Gentile Culture in Germany and Austria*, edited by Dagmar C. G. Lorenz and Gabriele Weinberger, 263–279. Detroit: Wayne State University Press, 1994.

Magris, Claudio. *Der habsburgische Mythos in der österreichischen Literatur*. Salzburg: Otto Müller Verlag, 1966.

Nabbe, Hildegard. "Verrat und Verfall in der kaiserlich-königlichen Monarchie: István Szabós Film *Oberst Redl*." *Modern Austrian Literature* 32, no. 4 (1999): 60–73.

Plater, Edward M. V. "István Szabó's Film of Inner Conflict and Political Prophecy: The 'Poseur' in István Szabó's *Colonel Redl*." *Hungarian Studies Review* 19, nos. 1–2 (1992): 43–57.

Pratt, Mary Louise. *Imperial Eyes: Travel Writing and Transculturation*. London: Routledge, 1994.

Prokopovych, Markian. *Habsburg Lemberg: Architecture, Public Space, and Politics in the Galician Capital, 1772–1914*. West Lafayette, IN: Purdue University Press, 2009.

Reill, Dominique Kirchner. *Nationalists Who Feared the Nation: Adriatic Multi-Nationalism in Habsburg Dalmatia, Trieste, and Venice*. Stanford: Stanford University Press, 2012.

Robinson, David, and Peter Hames. "*Redl Ezredes / Colonel Redl*." In *The Cinema of Central Europe*, edited by Peter Hames, 203–212. London: Wallflower Press, 2004.

Roth, Joseph. *Radetzkymarsch*. München: Deutscher Taschenbuch Verlag, 2002.

Szabó, István. "Preface." In *The Cinema of Central Europe*, edited by Peter Hames, xiii–xv. London: Wallflower Press, 2004.

Theiß, Sandra. *Taking Sides: Der Filmregisseur István Szabó*. Mainz: Bender Verlag, 2003.

Wolff, Larry. *The Idea of Galicia: History and Fantasy in Habsburg Political Culture*. Stanford: Stanford University Press, 2010.

Films

Hanussen. Directed by István Szabó. Hungary, West Germany, Austria, 1988.

Mephisto. Directed by István Szabó. Hungary, West Germany, Austria, 1981.

Colonel Redl. Directed by István Szabó. Hungary, West Germany, Austria, Yugoslavia, 1985.

Sunshine. Directed by István Szabó. Germany, Austria, Canada, Hungary, 1999.

5

Icons, Landscape, and the Boundaries of Good and Evil

Larisa Shepitko's The Ascent *(1977)*

Jane Costlow

Some of the finest Russian films of the Soviet era focused on World War II. In the four and a half decades during which they were made, these films ranged from glorifications of Soviet heroism, to psychological studies of traumatized veterans, to explorations of the moral and emotional dilemmas of what Americans might call the "home front." The boundary between war zone and home front was never as clear in the Soviet Union, where Nazi forces occupied vast stretches of land, effectively pushing Soviet borders to a line that ran just west of Moscow.[1] Larisa Shepitko's *The Ascent* (*Восхождение*), released in 1977, takes place in this vulnerable and dangerous terrain, somewhere in Nazi-occupied Belarus. A violently contested borderland, this is a landscape of life-and-death choices, in which characters must make extraordinarily difficult decisions under torture and threat of death. Shepitko's camera emphasizes the brutality of winter and the danger of the landscape itself, but also focuses with penetrating compassion on her characters' faces, caught in moments of communion, epiphany, and torment. Landscape and faces are the visual medium of the film's ethical and psychological drama; understanding how Shepitko crafted this profoundly unsettling narrative about the boundary between good and evil, choice and necessity will form the focus of this chapter. Shepitko's film draws richly on key archetypes of Russian identity: a landscape understood as the "homeland" or "motherland"; human faces shot in ways that evoke Russian icons. References to these archetypes, however, confound more than confirm any conclusions about heroism and identity. Shepitko's unflinching vision captures a terrain of choice not unlike the physical landscape of her film: the few landmarks that suggest direction are quickly covered over or obscured by driving snow; characters must chart their paths through an unremittingly hostile landscape, guided less by absolutes than by compassion and an ethic of care. The clarity and gentle grace of Shepitko's own filmic eye becomes a kind of compass in this difficult terrain.

Larisa Shepitko and *The Ascent*

Larisa Shepitko was born in 1938 and died in 1979, in an automobile accident while returning from a film shoot.[2] She entered the All-Union Film Institute in Moscow at age sixteen, insistent on studying to be a director despite pressure to follow the more conventional female route into acting. She studied for a year and a half with Alexander Dovzhenko, one of the giants of early Soviet filmmaking.[3] For Shepitko, Dovzhenko represented integrity and allegiance to film as a vehicle of conscience; despite enormous ideological pressure in the 1930s and '40s, he had continued making films of artistic value, many of which incorporated elements of visual lyricism and Ukrainian culture.[4] Shepitko made five films in her tragically brief life. Her 1963 diploma film *Heat* (*Зной*) is based on a novella by the Kirgiz writer Chingiz Aitmatov; the 1969 *Motherland of Electricity* (*Родина электричества*), based on a short story by Andrei Platonov, was filmed in Astrakhan using nonprofessional actors. Intended as one part of a film triptych celebrating the fiftieth anniversary of the Revolution, Shepitko's film, like Platonov's extraordinary story, was too unheroic for the authorities, who had the film shelved.[5] Her 1966 film *Wings* (*Крылья*) focuses on a female fighter pilot struggling with the tedium and conformity of provincial Soviet life. At the time of her death, Shepitko was making a film based on Valentin Rasputin's *Farewell to Matyora*. This 1979 novel draws an idyllic portrait of Siberian village life, implicitly challenging the cultural and environmental consequences of Soviet industrial development. Each of these films suggests Shepitko's desire to make probing films about complex subjects, revisiting key aspects of late Soviet identity: war veterans and the experience of war; meanings of *motherland*; the social contract of postwar Soviet life, with material comforts supposedly won by war but with palpable costs to the human psyche and the natural world. All of Shepitko's films have the capacity to seduce viewers with their visual beauty, and then to discomfort them with unresolved and probing questions.

The Ascent recounts a foraging expedition that ends with death rather than sustenance. The film opens in a punishingly cold landscape of field and forest, shot by Shepitko as a minimalist study in white on white, with skeletal traceries of black and gray. Rybak (Vladimir Gostyukhin) and Sotnikov (Boris Plotnikov), two partisans sent in search of food, shoot a farmer's sheep, only to abandon it after Sotnikov is wounded in an encounter with Nazi police. Rybak gets his comrade to a village house where their presence endangers a woman and her three children. Sotnikov, ill clad and racked by fever, gives away their hiding place when he coughs. He, Rybak, and the woman who had sheltered them are taken prisoner; Sotnikov is questioned and tortured by a Russian named Portnov (Anatoly Solonitsyn) who has turned collaborator and is doing the Nazis' dirty work. Rybak accepts Portnov's offer to work for the *Polizei*, the Nazi police forces, rather than suffer the fate that awaits Sotnikov: execution by hanging. Branded with a Soviet star, Sotnikov survives his final night in an underground cellar with three others who will hang with him. Shepitko's camera transforms the suffering Sotnikov into a Christ-like figure with enormous, suffering eyes. He begins his journey to the hanging (filmed to evoke associations with Golgotha and Christ's Passion) by declaring his desire to die for the others. The Germans spurn his offer, and all of the prisoners, save Rybak, are hung. The hanging scene is presented as a montage of close-ups shot with expressionist intensity, backed up with tonally and emotionally discordant music by Alfred Schnittke. The camera moves slowly among the faces of those in attendance: women in shawls and headscarves, a weeping young boy in a Soviet cap, a cluster of German officers talking among themselves, an anguished Rybak. When there is nothing left but swinging feet, we head back down the hill to *Polizei* headquarters with the Nazis and their collaborators; in a moment of grotesque pathos, Rybak tries and fails to hang himself in an outhouse. In a film that has focused repeatedly on tragic, suffering faces, the camera conveys one more—the distorted grimace of Rybak as he tries to slip the belt over his head. The final frames of the film return us to the film's beginning, as we, like Rybak, get one last glimpse of the world his choice has apparently separated him from forever: a broad, flat landscape with an Orthodox church in the distance, slowly obscured by blowing snow and streaks of white.

Empathy, Heroism, and Betrayal: Rybak or Sotnikov?

Much of the critical discussion of the film focuses on Rybak's choice—and the apparently stark and clear contrast between Sotnikov, the film's Christ figure, and Rybak, the film's traitor. Andrei Goncharov declares that the film "is about sacred things: the Motherland, loftier values, conscience, duty, spiritual heroism," while Valerii Golovskoi sees the film as being about "practical and impractical heroism," claiming that Shepitko is "entirely on the side of Sotnikov."[6] After the hanging, as Rybak begins his descent down the hill and back to Nazi headquarters, an old woman snarls a whispered "Judas" at him. Her condemnation is quick, direct, and in some sense justifiable—and certainly ties in with the Golgotha imagery of this sequence. But this, I would suggest, is a condemnation that we as viewers aren't invited to share, at least not without a strong measure of uncomfortable recognition that we ourselves might be closer to Rybak than to Sotnikov. Olga Denisova hints at a more complex perspective, one that sees betrayal in more diffuse terms: "Larisa Shepitko's film is about traitors. About how different they were, how many different factors could lead a man to betrayal. . . . Each of the film's heroes, except Sotnikov, is either a traitor or ready to become one."[7] The woman's denunciation, the sanctification of Sotnikov, the final anguished separation from the beloved landscape: all of these might turn our hearts against Rybak. But much of the film has worked to forge identification with this Judas. Such identification makes it hard wholly to condemn him; the film asks for compassion and empathy rather than judgment. Such empathy is also key to the viewer's feeling the full force of Shepitko's desire to implicate *us* in this drama.

Shepitko's film is based on the story "Sotnikov" by Vasil Bykov, published in 1970 in the progressive journal *Novyi mir*.[8] Shepitko first read the story while hospitalized with a concussion during pregnancy; as she read it Shepitko "grasped that this was a story about the questions most troubling her: the mortality and spiritual immortality of man, the choice between life and conscience, moral maximalism akin to heroism, amoral conformity that slips into betrayal."[9] Bykov, a Belarusian writer and World War II veteran, published a number of stories and novellas in the early 1970s, philosophical and psychological studies that presented the war "in a completely new light," posing ethical dilemmas whose resolutions were far from clear.[10] In translating Bykov's story for the screen, Shepitko retained much of his plot, but her narrative sequence and the visual and aural repertoire of film make the film very much her own. Bykov's title suggests that Sotnikov is the story's hero, but it is told in alternating first persons—a chapter in Sotnikov's voice followed by one in Rybak's. Readers' sense of identification and empathy, in other words, is evenly distributed, if not slanted toward Rybak, especially in the first half of the story, in which Rybak is a capable and patient pathfinder, saddled with a dangerously sick and poorly equipped companion. Working in film, Shepitko handles the matter of identification and empathy differently. While Bykov's tale begins with the men already en route, *The Ascent* opens with landscape and the partisan band, giving us a vivid sense of who and what Rybak and Sotnikov are defending (something Bykov does with flashbacks). Shepitko launches her film with scenes that emphasize the extraordinary difficulties of life and movement for the partisans and the civilians who are with them: we see their faces in close-up, asking us to consider how the drama of Rybak and Sotnikov emerges from that place and those people.[11]

In this opening sequence Shepitko uses visual strategies that mark the film as a whole: landscape, faces, and the periodic breaking of the boundary between character and audience. Jagged streams of white ripple against a gray background, a saw-toothed band of white marks the right limit of the screen. Whistles of wind are interrupted by machine-gun fire. We see an Orthodox church in the distance and more blowing snow. There's a slow montage of images: great crevasses of snow; a line of trees in the distance; telephone poles at awkward angles; and finally, a classic landscape of winter Russia—a row of birch and one lone oak with leaves still hanging on its branches. More whistling wind, machine guns, German voices. For a minute or more there are no human forms in this landscape—and then someone rises from the white, looks slowly about, and gestures for others to run for the woods' protective cover. The sound of German voices is replaced by Schnittke's score, a chorus of swelling voices that builds, wave-like, and into which is finally cut the sound that will become a hallmark of the film: humans laboring through heavy snow.

This is a landscape that is inherently hostile: it's a killing field. The body's dark contours are themselves a form of visual betrayal; standing up means giving yourself away. Movement is extraordinarily difficult, and direction is often obscured. Even someone who knows the landscape (like Rybak) can get lost; at several different moments he wonders aloud, "Where the hell is that village?" Once the opening skirmish has ended, Shepitko brings us into a forest grove where the partisan commander orders a halt for rest; once everyone has collapsed into the snow, backs against the sheltering trees, the film makes one of the transitions that will be its hallmark: from acute physical danger and alarm to a moment of stillness and almost mystical communion. The commander tells the keeper of provisions to "get out what's left"; a scruffily bearded man in a worker's cap draws a tiny bag from under his coat, spills its contents into a pot, and begins to share what there is.

This shared "meal" is shot as a succession of faces, faces that—like Sotnikov's later in the film—we might call iconic. Knit together into a communal scene of suffering and care, the frames evoke a shared communion. Each man, woman, and child is given a ration of seeds from a spoon (used in Russian Orthodox liturgy to distribute wine at Eucharist). The spoonfuls fall into open hands whose stillness suggests almost preternatural endurance. Again and again the camera rests in close-up on faces. We watch men and women lost in meditation, slowly masticating their meager handfuls of seeds. Sometimes they lean together, sometimes they are separate; in a particularly powerful image, one man separates a single seed to place on the lips of a man recumbent, injured, perhaps dying. In two arresting final frames the people we are watching are no longer lost in thought or attending to each other; they are looking at *us*, across the fourth wall of the screen.

Figure 5.1. The forest meal in Larisa Shepitko's *The Ascent*. Courtesy of Mosfilm.

The faces that Shepitko frames in this opening are echoed throughout the film in moments when the camera rests on the human face—in moments of meditation, epiphany, and anguish. After being shot, the wounded Sotnikov lies on the snow, looking up into a distant sky, where a veined moon floats; later he rests against a tree and looks toward us, his focus resting first on the distance (at a mist-shrouded sun that we, too, are shown), and then in close, at ice-covered branches. And throughout the night that Sotnikov and others spend in a cellar, awaiting their death, we are shown his increasingly gaunt and ethereal face. These faces are reminiscent of icons, religious images fundamental to Orthodoxy, whose cultural significance in Russia cannot be understated. While Sotnikov's is perhaps the most obviously iconic image, *all* of the faces in the film are seen in reference to holy images, including the face of the tormentor Portnov and that of the anguished Rybak at the film's end.

Sotnikov is, however, the film's most obvious icon. By the end of the film, in the night spent in the cellar with Rybak and the others, Sotnikov's already gaunt face has turned into an icon not merely of suffering but of illumination. As Denise Youngblood puts it, "[b]y this point in the picture, Sotnikov is openly portrayed as Christlike, through the staging, editing, and especially the lighting of the extreme close-up shots of his suffering face, lit with a holy glow."[12] In the final moments before the guard thrusts open the doors of the cellar, we become increasingly aware of the extent to which the light in Shepitko's canvas emerges from human faces, hanging like beacons in the darkness—and most insistently from Sotnikov's face, until

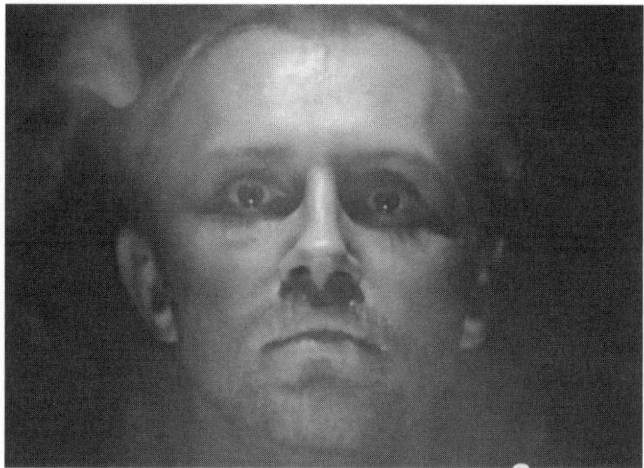

Figure 5.2. The suffering Sotnikov. Courtesy of Mosfilm.

the luminescence of his regard, directed straight at us, occupies all but the tiniest corner, where we see the nose and chin of the village elder, gazing down at Sotnikov.[13] Alfred Schnittke's score accompanies this sequence in a mounting braid of voices, seemingly chanting, and the bell-like sounds of a celeste.[14] The luminous severity of Sotnikov's face at the end does indeed suggest that he is Christ-like—but the visual reference can be made even more specific: these frames give us Sotnikov in a fashion that mimics a particular icon, the Christ Not Made by Human Hands (*Spas nerukotvornyi*) with its huge eyes, direct *en face* composition, and severe gaze.[15]

The iconic quality of Sotnikov's face also derives from how Shepitko handles light sources throughout the scene. Most dramatically in the final frames, light comes *from the faces themselves.* Icons, for the Orthodox, are not paintings but images of the divine, sometimes called "windows to Heaven." They are not intended to be realistic representations. Their aim is to show forth not material form but the divine light as it is manifest in the human.[16] As such, the light they make visible to us comes not from somewhere in the natural world but from the divine itself. Icons represent the possibility of transfiguration, a form radically changed through the light of the divine.

Shepitko's film often seems to study the human face as though it alone might hold the answer to the riddle of human identity. "Human scum," says Portnov, "that's what man is." Is Portnov right? Are human beings "scum"? The film's response to this is not spoken but seen: Sotnikov's transfigured face but also the faces of partisans, women, and children, or even Rybak's own tormented visage at the film's end. *All* of these faces challenge Portnov's claim

Figure 5.3. Christos Acheiropoietos (Christ Not Made by Human Hands; *Spas nerukotvornyi*): A twelfth-century Novgorod icon from the Assumption Cathedral in the Moscow Kremlin. Tretiakov Gallery, Moscow/Wikimedia Commons/Public Domain.

that humans are but scum.[17] The image the film ends with is not, however, a transfigured face; it ends not with ascent but with descent. During the scene of hanging, Sotnikov is virtually sanctified, but after the hanging, Rybak follows the Nazis and their Soviet collaborators back down the hill, into the compound where he had spent the night imprisoned with those who have just died. The film ends with the character who has been denounced as a Judas, in a world that is deeply compromised; viewers are left, with Rybak, in the "fallen" world. Three visual images in particular shape these final moments of the film: Rybak's anguished face; a long, stark shot of the dark cellar from which Sotnikov and the others had emerged; and the final frames of landscape. Each of these echoes the film's central concerns—but they also return us to the man who is, in a sense, at the moral center of the film, not Sotnikov but Rybak.

Throughout *The Ascent* Rybak is the film's caregiver and sustainer. He is the peasant to Sotnikov's intellectual, a man who lives deeply in the present, defined by his physicality and endurance. Stockier and sturdier, Rybak moves more confidently through the landscape than the frail, intellectual Sotnikov. Sotnikov seems ill prepared for their venture, both because he's sick and because he's ill clad. Rybak bemoans his companion's clothing and sickness, but despite this remains patient with Sotnikov to the point of endangerment. When Sotnikov is shot, Rybak turns back to save him, even though saving him involves dropping the sheep they're taking back to camp. Turning back to take care, however, seems to be deeply a part of Rybak's constitution.

The weight of guilt for ultimate betrayal falls on Rybak, a weight we see him bearing at the end of the film. Rybak's face turns to an anguished grimace when he looks (in two extended shots) at the empty cellar from which he had so recently emerged. That vision of the cellar's empty blackness seems to prompt his next act, an attempted suicide. With an increasingly agitated track of German voices singing, fragments of Russian ("I want to eat"), and Schnittke's intense and powerful music, Rybak tries to hang himself with his belt. Twice

Figure 5.4. The despairing Rybak. Courtesy of Mosfilm.

we see him make a loop over the outhouse roof beam, then slip it over his head. The first time the belt simply slips off the beam; the second time he can't force the belt over his head—and we see an extended shot of his distorted, pained face. When he emerges from the outhouse, he is left staring dumb-faced out through the compound gate, through which a horse has just pulled a cart. We alternate between shots of his profoundly expressive face, with its mixture of pain, regret, and horror that is truly beyond words, and the landscape toward which he is looking. Shepitko finally takes us out toward where Rybak may not go: into the bleak wintry landscape that had opened her film.

What we are presented with in these final minutes of the film is the absolute anguish of a man who realizes the full weight of what he has done. That "weight" can't yet be put into words—perhaps never can be—so we see icons, images that help us grasp the horror of his situation. This is a soul, truly, in torment, and we must be witness not just *to*, but *with*, him. Each of these moments might be given a name; the empty cellar recalls what is no longer there: the companions, Sotnikov and the others, who are now dead, who had been icons of human beauty only a few hours earlier. And if we consider the symbolic thread of Christian imagery in the film, this is also an empty tomb, one that registers for Rybak not as a symbol of hope but as a seal of absolute loss. The face we see as he attempts and fails to commit suicide, or weeps in anguish, is an icon of absolute suffering, Shepitko's portrait of despair. The world from which he is separated is the landscape of the film, what he had known better than anyone else, that he had been able to navigate and find shelter in. It is also, symbolically, the motherland, a Russia he is now cut off from. Shepitko brings the viewer down from the exalted death of martyrs, leaving us with Rybak to await the solitary "dog's death" Sotnikov feared when he was wounded. With Rybak, she brings us back into the compromised world, a world in which survival means a betrayal of conscience.

The Landscape: Motherland as Borderland between Life and Death

The landscape of this film is extraordinarily rendered. Part of what is so arresting about *The Ascent* is, in fact, its rendering of the natural world; there is a visceral quality to Shepitko's filming of this motherland. The film was shot just outside of Murom, an ancient city 185 miles east of Moscow, which for Shepitko and the whole film group became "Belarus in the winter of 1942." Shot in January, conditions were brutal: it was often as much as forty below during the shooting. This punishingly cold landscape is what is being fought for: just before he is led to his death, Sotnikov answers the question of who he is by responding that he has "a mother, a father, and a motherland [*rodina*]." Put that way, the land becomes a political abstraction, something it never is in this film: in Shepitko's vision the land is a medium of both experience and identity, beloved terrain (as when Rybak stands silently in a burnt-out farmstead, pondering a small mirror that is all that's left of a woman he had loved), space of ever-present danger, and paradoxical site of near-mystical revelation. The film opens and closes with that scene of an obscured landscape, with the church in the distance a reference point and cultural icon, what in someone else's hands would be a visual banality. At the center of the film, on the other hand, is an enigmatic moment of immersion in the landscape, a scene both intimate and exhausting.

When Sotnikov is shot by German soldiers, we see him both giving fire and preparing to die: he will shoot himself rather than be taken prisoner. Rybak has made it into the woods, but he hears the gunfire, realizes Sotnikov is in danger, and returns for him. The sequence begins with a startling and eerie vision of the moon; it continues through an almost impossibly arduous scene when Rybak drags his wounded companion through heavy snow. The physicality of this sequence is almost unbearable; the viewer is tormented by the slowness of Rybak's efforts until both men can finally catch their breath in a clump of ice-covered bushes. The floating, beautiful moon is then replaced by another visionary, almost mystical sequence. Sotnikov stares vacantly into space, his back against the tree. We initially see him through a net of branches encased in ice; our eyes track his as their focus shifts from the distance to the near foreground. With Schnittke's unearthly music increasingly agitated in the background, Sotnikov suddenly lashes out at the branches between him and us: thrashing with a piece of wood, he bursts into violent action and then as suddenly sinks back into inertia. Rybak returns from scouting out where they are, only to discover that Sotnikov has been frozen to the tree: in an extraordinarily intimate sequence, Rybak gently cups Sotnikov's head in his hand, blowing gently on the back of his neck.

Rybak's isolation at the end of the film contrasts not only with the communion of the opening but also with the physicality and intimacy of this remarkable scene. The two men's closeness is resolutely nonerotic but deeply tactile. The sequence veers back and forth between submission and struggle: Sotnikov seems mentally to retreat into some space of interiority that intensifies the otherworldly calm of his face.[18] Shepitko frames Sotnikov first against the snow and then the tree, as though he is dissolving into the more-than-human world. While the camera lets us see what Sotnikov is watching (the moon, the sun), we also see his gaze refocus, from looking *beyond* the icy branches to the branches themselves. His striking of the ice-laden branches is a gesture as powerful and visually arresting as it is inscrutable, quickly followed by Rybak

Figure 5.5. Intimacy in a punishing landscape. Courtesy of Mosfilm.

blowing gently against Sotnikov's neck. Denise Youngblood has suggested that this moment marks a transition for Sotnikov, an epiphanic moment in which he "has accepted the certainty of his death."[19] If so, then this pivotal moment in Sotnikov's journey involves not anything otherworldly, but a profoundly tactile immersion in the natural world—in the very *rodina* (motherland) for which he is fighting. The physical, almost maternal intimacy of Rybak only intensifies our sense of that immersion.

The Horrors of War

The American critic Susan Sontag, in her discussion of the role of photographic images in understandings of war, points to *The Ascent* as evidence of what narrative can bring to that understanding: "A narrative seems likely to be more effective than an image. Partly it is a question of the length of time one is obliged to look, to feel." In the original version of this essay, published in the *New Yorker*, Sontag concluded this way: "*The Ascent* [is] . . . the most affecting film about the horror of war I know."[20] When she revised the essay for inclusion in her book *Regarding the Pain of Others*, she changed the word *horror* to *sadness*: "*The Ascent* [is] . . . the most affecting film about the sadness of war I know."[21] The shift, which I take to refer to a kind of ambivalence on Sontag's part, seems deeply right: Rybak's death, and the final frames of the film, leave us caught between horror and sadness, both connected to the fate of this decent, caring, life-giving man. We experience the horror and sadness with such intensity and immediacy in part because of the "length of time" we have been made to look and feel—not just *at*, but *with* these characters. The woman who calls Rybak "Judas" has not come to love him as we have, and that makes all the difference.

As I noted at the beginning of this chapter, by the time the film was made, Soviet war films as a genre included a wide array of approaches. Particularly in the period of "the Thaw"—from the mid-1950s to Krushchev's fall from power in 1964—a new generation of Soviet directors had expanded the genre significantly beyond straightforward renderings of heroic sacrifice.[22] Shepitko was cognizant of the fact that she was making a war film for a generation that had by and large not experienced the war firsthand. Soviets watching the film in 1977 were citizens of an ideological state in which survival was regularly at odds with individual conscience. In this sense, Rybak's story might be their own, the enclosure at the end a paradigm of their own lives. How many comfortable citizens of Brezhnev's stagnant Soviet Union could be made uncomfortable by the counterpoint of a Russian voice saying "I want to eat," while all the while, in the distance, the motherland is obscured? Shepitko herself commented that the film went "beyond a war picture" and would achieve its aim to the extent that it was directed *at our own days*.[23] When Shepitko's characters look out across the screen, not at some mystical vision or into a vague beyond, but straight *at the viewer*—are they calling their descendants to a moral accounting?

Eight years after *The Ascent* was released, Shepitko's husband, Elem Klimov, released his harrowing film of the Nazi occupation of Soviet Belarus, *Come and See* (*Иди и смотри*, 1985). Klimov's film is about monsters, all of whom are German. Shepitko's film is not about monsters but about desperate situations that lead good men and women to spiritual disaster. When we see Rybak's distorted face at the film's end, we see one last icon of pain, human suffering, and desolating isolation. Sotnikov is given the chance to die a martyr's death rather than dying "like a dog, in a field" because Rybak saved him. No one has saved Rybak from the choice he had to make—and which he makes, in some sense, in complete consonance with his character. He has chosen life and care throughout the film. The film ends with pity rather than judgment, and with that final glimpse of the motherland. The horror of the film isn't war as such but situations we like to call "inhuman." Surely it was intentional on Shepitko's part that the end of the film takes us back down the hill. It ends, that is, with descent rather than ascent, into the world where all her viewers live: a place of compromise and enclosure, where even Rybak's intimate caring might seem an icon of a laudable world.

Notes

1. World War II is commonly referred to in Russia as the Great War of the Fatherland. Vast stretches of the western Soviet Union were occupied by Nazi forces, including the whole of Belarus, where the film is set. For a discussion of Soviet war films, see Denise J. Youngblood, *Russian War Films: On the Cinema Front, 1914–2005* (Lawrence: University Press of Kansas, 2007).

2. Sources used in this brief account of Shepitko's biography include Elem Klimov, ed., *Larisa: Vospominaniia, vystupleniia, interv'iu, kinostsenarii, stat'i: Kniga o Larise Shepitko* (Moscow: Iskusstvo, 1987); Andrei Goncharov, "Shepit'ko, Larisa Efimovna," Chtoby-pomnili.com, accessed January 4, 2013, http://chtoby-pomnili.com/page.php?id=162; Josephine Woll, *Real Images: Soviet Cinema and the Thaw* (London: I.B. Tauris Publishers, 2000).

3. Along with Sergei Eisenstein, Vseovolod Pudovkin, and Dziga Vertov, Dovzhenko was one of the great Soviet filmmakers of the 1920s. Dovzhenko is best known in the West for *Earth* (Земля, 1930), a beautifully rendered evocation of the passing of traditional peasant life with the arrival of collectivization and mechanical agriculture; *Earth* justifies David Thomson's designation of Dovzhenko as "the first intensely personal artist in Russian cinema." See David Thomson, *The New Biographical Dictionary of Film* (New York: A.A. Knopf, 2004), 257.

4. George Liber emphasizes Dovzhenko's ability to navigate the treacherous waters of Stalin-era censorship, but also suggests that in the process Dovzhenko engaged in considerable self-censorship. See George O. Liber, *Alexander Dovzhenko: A Life in Soviet Film* (London: British Film Institute, 2002), 25.

5. Denise Youngblood suggests that Shepitko's *Motherland of Electricity* was "banned for its alienated style and desacralization of the sacred subject of electrification." See Youngblood, *Russian War Films*, 155.

6. Goncharov, "Shepit'ko, Larisa Efimovna"; Valerii Golovskoi, *Kinematograf 70-kh: Mezhdu ottepel'iu i glasnost'iu* (Moscow: Materik, 2004), 264.

7. Olga Denisova, "*Voskhozhdenie* Larisy Shepit'ko protiv *Proverki na dorogakh* Alekseia Germana," Olga Denisova: Knigi, April 30, 2009, http://vyritsa-lend.livejournal.com/17580.html.

8. *Novyi mir* played a major role in the period of liberalization known as "the Thaw," and continued to be a vehicle of relatively progressive thought even after Krushchev's downfall.

9. Goncharov, "Shepit'ko, Larisa Efimovna."

10. N. N. Shneidman also notes the extent to which Bykov's treatment of the war differed from mainstream Soviet war literature. See N. N. Shneidman, "Soviet Prose in the 1970s: Evolution or Stagnation?" *Canadian Slavonic Papers/ Revue Canadienne des Slavistes* 20, no. 1 (1978): 67–68.

11. There are other ways in which Shepitko's film differs strikingly from the story: *The Ascent* significantly extends the scene of interrogation and torture (the film's

"naturalistic" treatment of violence occasioned some criticism), and her deployment of Christian symbolism, while it is rooted in Bykov's story, is much more elaborate.

12. Youngblood, *Russian War Films*, 182.

13. This sequence also calls to mind the work of Georges de la Tour, a seventeenth-century painter whose work is referred to in the films of Andrei Tarkovsky, a contemporary of Shepitko's.

14. Bells have a particular significance within Russian Orthodoxy, where they are the only instruments used in churches—the liturgy itself is sung without accompaniment.

15. Shepitko's framing may also allude to the "Savior of the Fiery Eye." In the Fiery Eye icon Christ's gaze is directed at the viewer, while the eyes of the nerukotvornyi spas look to the viewer's right. *See* Leonid Ouspensky and Vladimir Lossky, *The Meaning of Icons* (Crestwood: St. Vladimir's Seminary Press, 1982), 69–72.

16. "[A]n icon is an external expression of the transfigured state of man, of his sanctification by uncreated Divine light" (Ouspensky and Lossky, *The Meaning of Icons*, 38).

17. Jason Merrill gives an insightful account of the interrogation scene, relating the onesided "dialogue" of Portnov and Sotnikov to Dostoevsky's treatment of human nature, freedom, and evil in "The Grand Inquisitor." See James Merrill, "Religion, Politics, and Literature in Larisa Shepit'ko's *The Ascent*," *Slovo* 18, no. 2 (2006): 156–160.

18. Several moments in this sequence are reminiscent of Tolstoy's *War and Peace*, where Prince Andrei lies wounded at the battle of Austerlitz, staring up into a vast sky. The scene from Tolstoy's great epic is echoed in other Soviet films of World War II, including *The Cranes Are Flying* (in which the hero looks upward into a whirling grove of birch trees as he falls) and a scene in *Fate of a Man* by Sergei Bondarchuk (1959) in which a soldier escaping from a Nazi prisoner of war camp briefly hides in a hay field; there's a long, stunning shot of him lying in the field, as the camera lifts skyward, followed by a shot from his point of view, looking up toward the sky itself.

19. Youngblood, *Russian War Films*, 180.

20. Susan Sontag, "Looking at War," *New Yorker*, December 9, 2002, http://www.newyorker.com/archive/2002/12/09/021209crat_atlarge?currentPage=all.

21. Susan Sontag, *Regarding the Pain of Others* (New York: Picador, 2003), 122. Originally published as "Looking at War" in the *New Yorker* on December 9, 2002, the essay was republished in 2003 as *Regarding the Pain of Others.*

22. By 1964, as Denise Youngblood puts it, "wonderful and innovative war films, rich in genuine humanity and pathos, had graced the screens for a number of years." (Youngblood, *Russian War Films*, 140). Her discussion includes, among others, *The Cranes are Flying, The Fate of a Man, The Ballad of a Soldier, Clear Skies*, and *Ivan's Childhood.*

23. "Moe proizvedenie—nash fil'm." (Klimov, *Larisa*, 130).

Works Cited

Bykov, Vasil'. *Sotnikov: Povest'. Novyi mir* 5 (1970).

Denisova, Olga. "*Voskhozhdenie* Larisy Shepit'ko protiv *Proverki na dorogakh* Alekseia Germana." Olga Denisova: Knigi, April 30, 2009. http://vyritsa-lend.livejournal.com/17580.html.

Golovskoi, Valerii. *Kinematograf 70-kh: Mezhdu ottepel'iu i glasnost'iu*. Moscow: Materik, 2004.

Goncharov, Andrei. "Shepit'ko, Larisa Efimovna." Chtoby-pomnili.com. Accessed January 4, 2013. http://chtoby-pomnili.com/page.php?id=162.

Klimov, Elem, ed. *Larisa: Vospominaniia, vystupleniia, interv'iu, kinostsenarii, stat'i: Kniga o Larise Shepitko*. Moscow: Iskusstvo, 1987.

Liber, George O. *Alexander Dovzhenko: A Life in Soviet Film*. London: British Film Institute, 2002.

Merrill, James. "Religion, Politics, and Literature in Larisa Shepit'ko's *The Ascent*." *Slovo* 18, no. 2 (2006): 147–162.

Ouspensky, Leonid, and Vladimir Lossky. *The Meaning of Icons*. Crestwood: St. Vladimir's Seminary Press, 1982.

Shneidman, N. N. "Soviet Prose in the 1970s: Evolution or Stagnation?" *Canadian Slavonic Papers/ Revue Canadienne des Slavistes* 20, no. 1 (1978): 63–77.

Sontag, Susan. "Looking at War." *New Yorker*. December 9, 2002. http://www.newyorker.com/archive/2002/12/09/021209crat_atlarge?currentPage=all.

——. *Regarding the Pain of Others*. New York: Picador, 2003.

Thomson, David. *The New Biographical Dictionary of Film*. New York: A. A. Knopf, 2004.

Woll, Josephine. *Real Images: Soviet Cinema and the Thaw*. London: I. B. Tauris Publishers, 2000.

Youngblood, Denise J. *Russian War Films: On the Cinema Front, 1914–2005*. Lawrence: University Press of Kansas, 2007.

Films

The Ascent (*Восхождение*). Directed by Larisa Shepitko. Soviet Union, 1976.

Ballad of a Soldier (*Баллада о солдате*). Directed by Grigorii Chukhrai. Soviet Union, 1959.

Clear Skies (*Чистое небо*). Directed by Grigorii Chukhrai. Soviet Union, 1961.

Come and See (*Иди и смотри*). Directed by Elem Klimov. Soviet Union, 1985.

The Cranes Are Flying (*Летят журавли*). Directed by Mikhail Kalotozov. Soviet Union, 1957.

Earth (*Земля*). Directed by Alexander Dovzhenko. Soviet Union, 1930.

The Fate of a Man (*Судьба человека*). Directed by Sergei Bondarchuk. Soviet Union, 1959.

Heat (*Зной*). Directed by Larisa Shepitko. Soviet Union, 1963.

Ivan's Childhood (*Иваново детство*). Directed by Andrei Tarkovsky. Soviet Union, 1962.

Motherland of Electricity (*Родина электричества*). Directed by Larisa Shepitko. Part of triptych *Beginning of an Unknown Century* (*Начало неведомого века*) Soviet Union, 1967.

Wings (*Крылья*). Directed by Larisa Shepitko. Soviet Union, 1966.

6

Negotiating a New Europe

Laila Pakalniņa's The Bus *(2004) and Transnational Landscapes*

Maruta Z. Vitols

THE YEAR 2004 WAS MONUMENTAL for the Baltic states, with Estonia, Latvia, and Lithuania joining the European Union (EU) and The North Atlantic Treaty Organization (NATO). In many respects, this moment in history was as significant to these countries as the collapse of communism thirteen years before. These events immediately affected the economies, politics, and cultures of these three postsocialist countries, and the ensuing changes in conceptualizing place, space, and identity appeared in Latvian documentary cinema that same year. One film in particular, Latvian filmmaker Laila Pakalniņa's 2004 work *The Bus* (*Buss*), explores borders and border crossings in the zone of the "New Europe."

Chronicling the journey of a bus from Tallinn, Estonia, to Kaliningrad, Russia, Pakalniņa's documentary investigates postsocialist nations in the era of globalization. As the bus makes stops in various villages and cities in Estonia, Latvia, Lithuania, and Russia, the director demonstrates how some real and imaginary borders, such as those between Western (capitalist) and Eastern (formerly communist) Europe, are rapidly eroding, while others, such as the demarcation between Russia and the former Soviet Union, intensify. These transformations also reveal the consequential dialogues between the past and the present, as well as the shifting relationships of the center and the periphery.

Through a close reading of *The Bus*, this study examines the ways Pakalniņa's film comments on the construction of identity and the redefining of internal and external borders in the liminal, transnational spaces of the Baltic states. It also contextualizes the documentary's arguments within the contemporary political, economic, and cultural climates in order to reveal the ways the inhabitants of the New Europe negotiate their lives in the twenty-first century.[1] In other words, the study participates in the current debates on globalization, transnationalism, and identity formation, particularly in regards to cinema and the representation of space. Film scholar Meta Mazaj explains:

> [T]he significance of small national cinemas and the need to remap the relationship between European and Eastern European cinema . . . sheds new light on the relationship between the national and the levels that operate beyond and above the national (international, transnational, post-national, global). . . . This contentious relationship exists in a particularly intense form in Europe, both in political and cultural spheres. If the formation of the European Union can be seen as the geopolitical manifestation of the homogenizing process of globalization, it was on the other hand accompanied by the fragmentation and emergence of many new nation states in Central and Eastern Europe. . . . [T]he spatial trope assumes a significant role in the cinematic imagination of new European identity.[2]

Finally, this chapter endeavors to inspire more critical attention to Pakalniņa's work. Part of what makes Pakalniņa's oeuvre so compelling is the ambiguity and openness of her filmic texts, allowing for multiple, often contradictory readings. This chapter provides only one possible interpretation of her film and invites further academic investigation and debate.

Laila Pakalniņa and Her Filmmaking Style

Latvia's most internationally recognized and critically successful contemporary filmmaker, Laila Pakalniņa (born 1962) is synonymous with the reconstruction of Latvian cinema in the postcommunist era. Working in both fiction and nonfiction modes, Pakalniņa and her cinema have become a ubiquitous presence at such festivals as the Cannes Film Festival, the Venice International Film Festival, the Venice Biennale, and at the Berlin Film Festival.[3] Pakalniņa graduated with a degree in television journalism from the Moscow University and a degree in film directing from the Moscow Film Institute (VGIK), beginning her career as a documentary filmmaker. At the end of the 1990s, she completed her first feature-length fiction motion picture, *The Shoe* (*Kurpe*, 1998), and has since simultaneously produced feature-length and short films, as well as documentaries and fiction works. To date, her filmography includes over twenty-two motion pictures made since 1988, each featuring Pakalniņa's unique style as arguably Latvia's most prolific contemporary cinematic auteur.

Figure 6.1. Director Laila Pakalniņa. Courtesy of Laila Pakalniņa.

At the heart of Pakalniņa's oeuvre one finds the celebration of the everyday. All of her works encourage spectators to appreciate the mundane, emphasizing the beauty that lies in the quotidian. While aesthetically akin to Chantal Akerman's *Jeanne Dielman, 23 Business Offices, 1080 Brussels* (*Jeanne Dielman, 23 quai du Commerce, 1080 Bruxelles*, 1975), Michael Snow's *Wavelength* (1967), Andrei Tarkovsky's *Stalker* (*Стáлкер*, 1979), and Michelangelo Antonioni's entire catalogue (among others), Pakalniņa's cinema extols the banal, highlighting the exquisite and charming qualities of the simple objects, peripheral spaces, and the socially peripheral people one encounters in daily life. Truly, "[f]or Pakalniņa, inspiration lies in the commonplace, her camera seeking to show the extraordinary qualities of the ordinary."[4]

Nowhere is this more obvious than in her documentary work. Former managing director of the Rīga Film Museum Elīna Reitere describes Pakalniņa's nonfiction films: "[I]n her documentary projects the camera functions as the revealer of the world for the viewer and the sound accents this vision."[5] Film critic and festival programmer Mārtiņš Slišāns agrees, claiming, "If poetry was written in pictures, [Pakalniņa's] works would be the first to be quoted. The material they are made of is pure ambience; things that you cannot define but feel very clearly, things that you live and breathe. Simple everyday trivia turned into a masterful audio-visual narrative."[6] It is precisely this emphasis on atmosphere, visual associations, and rhythmic and tonal qualities that characterizes *The Bus*, and situates it within Pakalniņa's oeuvre. Critic Leslie Felperin, reviewing the film for *Variety*, notes, "Affection for ordinary people shines through, particularly in posed portraits where various subjects stand and stare back at the lens for 30-seconds or so, little filmic snapshots that often end with laughter and smiles breaking through."[7]

Aesthetically, *The Bus* features Pakalniņa's typical long takes, carefully composed frames, and a marked lack of any real action or dialogue. As the film advertises in its trailer, the work contains "No Action, No Heroes."[8] Indeed, *The Bus*, like most of Pakalniņa's work, is more concerned with creating an atmosphere than it is with developing a narrative. Pakalniņa's camera dwells on individuals on and off the bus, creating cinematic portraits that break the fourth wall when the subject acknowledges the presence of the filmmakers by smiling or addressing the crew. Spectators are forced to devote attention to the things and people that they would otherwise ignore, such as border guards, with Pakalniņa encouraging viewers to see the beauty in them.

The Bus and Political Meaning

Though Pakalniņa's work superficially seems primarily preoccupied with aesthetics, there is a clear, albeit subtle, political statement in the film. *The Bus* may be seen as expressing the optimism, hopes, and aspirations of the three Baltic states after becoming members of the EU. The Baltic states have always considered themselves as having more in common culturally, artistically, and politically with the European West. Thus, their acceptance into the EU and NATO was perceived as a form of a "homecoming" for the Baltic people. For example, in a post-1991 world, the Latvian state urgently feels the need to minimize its political, economic, and cultural associations with Russia, and to be seen (again) as a member of Europe. Consequently, Latvians have gone out of their way to emphasize their "westernness." Physically, this appears in the reconstruction and rehabilitation of many sections of Rīga that bear a German influence, such as the medieval section of the city (and the various *Jugendstil* buildings that adorn the city center). Sociologist Daina Stukuls Eglitis explains the crucial and complex relationship between space and the construction of national identity in post-1991 Latvia:

> [S]pace and place offer links between the present and the past through the representation of that past. The normalization of place and space apparently falls in the domain of a temporal conception of normality: space can be used to establish and capture a temporal continuity between present and past. The elevation and veneration of this continuity, in the case between prewar and post-Communist [*sic*] Latvia, are core imperatives contained in the vision of temporal normality.

> . . . [R]ather than simply being a backdrop against which change was played out, space and place were (and are) fundamental parts of transformation, embodying aspirations and symbolizing and structuring processes of change.[9]

Economically, the need to identify with the West is displayed in the uncontrolled adoption of neoliberal capitalism. Culturally, western television programs and films dominate local communities, and Latvian theater companies usually favor productions of plays written by westerners.

Meanwhile, a public discourse on its Soviet past has remained largely absent in Latvia since 1991.[10] Media scholar Kriss Ravetto-Biagioli explains this situation:

> The collapse of state socialism generated an enormous amount of historical revisionism; images of democracy and nationalism lying dormant through the Cold War have resulted in the collective forgetting of history, which not only erases the accommodation and collaboration with the former Soviet regime but also, as in the Soviet regime's practices of the past, revises current national identity by removing monuments, names, and events from public space and official history. As Barbara Einhorn argues, nationalist self-identification offers a convenient legitimization for this collective erasure and forgetting because "it defines the former Soviet Union as the quintessential Other, and state socialism as a foreign system imposed from outside."[11]

These collective attitudes clearly emerge in Latvian cinema. Film scholar Irina Novikova describes the postcommunist film culture in the Baltic states: "Popular cinemas as parts of national cultural productions, in my view, turned the imploding post-socialist ambivalences and controversies within nations into the essentialised [*sic*] idea of nation as an 'organic' and exclusive historical and cultural continuity, and of its 'return to Europe' (delimited by the politically charged meanings of the trauma-recovery discourse)."[12] Ravetto-Biagioli and Novikova's arguments regarding national and popular cinemas, respectively, are relevant in Pakalniņa's case, though her work is far from mainstream in Latvia. One may read Pakalniņa's *The Bus* as illustrating the contemporary Latvian euphoria about "officially" returning to Europe, while trying to distance itself from its communist history. The filmmaker highlights the westernness of the Baltic countries by underlining how they differ from Russia, the definitive "Other" in this cultural dichotomy. This aspiration of merging into a unified, utopian European identity while simultaneously striving to downplay any connections to Russia already appears on the poster for the film, which has now become its DVD cover.

Underneath the film's title and above the cartoon of a bus, the text "Borders/No Borders" is visible. The inclusion of these particular words is very revealing. Pakalniņa signals to her potential audience the subject of her film—the liminal

Figure 6.2. Poster for *The Bus*. Courtesy of Laila Pakalniņa.

and transnational space that the Baltic states occupy in 2004. On the one hand, there are still borders, both literal demarcations between individual countries and metaphoric boundaries. The Soviet past, embodied by Russia's industrial landscapes and the seemingly abandoned Sovetsk bus station, borders the European present, represented by the colorful capitalist signs and the modern, clean stations in Estonia, Latvia, and Lithuania. On the other hand, there are no more philosophical borders between Western Europe and these three former socialist countries, cinematically represented by the easy passing across the Estonian/Latvian and the Latvian/Lithuanian border controls. In a way, Pakalniņa presciently envisions a Schengen world three years before the agreement would go into effect in the Baltic states.[13] The political border of the Iron Curtain is gone, and the Baltic states may rejoin their intellectual and artistic brethren, or so was the optimistic belief of many in Estonia, Latvia, and Lithuania.

Pakalniņa illustrates all of these hopes and aspirations in the opening sequence of *The Bus*. The film begins in the interior of a maintenance facility, where the bus that will be the central feature of the film is being washed. Instead of presenting spectators with a typical long shot of workers hosing down the bus, Pakalniņa offers a shot from the interior of the bus, with viewers watching water stream down the windshield of the vehicle as the bus moves forward into the daylight. Not only does this choice identify the bus itself as the true protagonist of the film, but one may also interpret this as Pakalniņa's poetic representation of a rebirth of the Baltic countries, a cleansing of their turbulent past.

Furthermore, the landscapes featured in *The Bus* echo the differences between the Soviet past and the European present, as seen by many ethnic Lithuanians, Latvians, and Estonians. Each of the Baltic bus stations appears vibrant, bustling with people and activity, and well kept.[14] On the other hand, the Sovetsk station looks filthy, in disrepair, and almost deserted. Even a feral dog chases pigeons in the shabby and empty bus terminal. Moreover, the bucolic countryside through which the bus passes in Estonia appears peaceful and charming, if not completely pastoral. Robust cows graze as geese noisily run around in Estonia, while Russia's unkept fields, presented as industrial wastelands, are full of oil pumps and machinery.

Meanwhile, the border crossings from Estonia into Latvia and from Latvia into Lithuania all appear uneventful and standard. Passports are collected, scanned, verified in a computer database, and stamped before the bus and its passengers are allowed to cross into the next country. By contrast, the border control between Lithuania and Russia looks like a traveler's nightmare: passengers have to stand in a seemingly endless line to await their turn at the passport control officer's desk. The line remains almost completely static throughout the duration of the shot, and no one speaks. The buzzing of the fluorescent lights is occasionally broken by a curt announcement over the intercom system and the ominous echoing of a forceful stamp. Pakalniņa also films a sign on a wall that declares, "Payment for Border Control Service Prohibited!"

Even the bus itself that the passengers ride on belongs to the EuroLines company, whose advertising slogan is "Your Connection Across Europe."[15] Instead of enduring the voyage through the Baltics in a dilapidated, Soviet-era motor coach, the passengers enjoy their trip sitting in newly upholstered seats in a clean vehicle that could as easily be at home in the Termini Central Station in Rome as it is in Rīga's Central Station. One might even see the physical bus as representing the Baltic states at this particular time in history—a liminal space in transit striving to connect to Europe.

Furthermore, the presence of capitalism in the Baltic countries as Pakalniņa depicts it in *The Bus* paints these postsocialist states as "western." At every stop along the bus route until Russia, Pakalniņa presents bus riders casually purchasing various consumer goods at convenience stores, cafes, and kiosks. Display cases are full and the shelves always appear stocked with an assortment of goods. Passengers effortlessly buy coffee, beer, candy, Camel cigarettes, Coca-Cola—many of the things that either were not readily available during the Soviet era, were only acquired via the black market, or were obtained by standing in line for hours. Indeed, Coca-Cola's presence throughout the Baltic countries (and the film) is ubiquitous, whether appearing in the form of

Figure 6.3. Production still from *The Bus*. Courtesy of Laila Pakalniņa.

branded umbrellas, signs, or the drink itself. Western capitalism also is visible on the bus. One rider is seen sleeping next to her jacket, which prominently features the luxury label Escada. Another passenger that Pakalniņa's camera highlights wears a Ché Guevara shirt, perhaps to emphasize how even communism, once a lived reality for the Baltic states, has now been co-opted by western capitalism and consequently reduced to the level of merchandise.[16]

Latvia and Postcolonialism

It is understandable why Pakalniņa and other Latvians would want to draw attention to the western qualities of the Baltic states, as opposed to aligning themselves with Russia. Though the "official" Soviet occupation of this region ended in 1991, postcolonial Russian imperialist efforts continue to this day. Russian politicians repeatedly attempted to block the expansion of the EU and NATO into the Baltic countries, successfully redrew the geographical borders in these states (so that Russia gained more land), and they still maintain that Russian minorities are discriminated against and denied their human rights in Estonia, Latvia, and Lithuania. Finnish diplomat and political commentator Max Jakobson explains,

> What exactly are Russia and the Baltic countries at odds about? . . . It is no longer about the borders, since that question has been settled. The dispute is about the past. Russia demands that the Baltic countries acknowledge that they willingly and by a large vote joined the Soviet Union, and at the same time accepted the communist system as their own. For the Russians mean, without saying so overtly, that the Baltic countries are still a part of Russia.[17]

Given such a tense and volatile contemporary sociopolitical climate, it is no surprise that Pakalniņa would endeavor to stress Estonia, Latvia, and Lithuania's similarities with and allegiances to Europe, the West, democracy, and to capitalism to demonstrate how the Baltic states are distinctly "un-Russian." Indeed, many residents in the Baltic states considered their countries' membership in the EU and NATO as political and military insurance against any possible future acts of Slavic aggression or threats to the Baltic states' regained independence. Political scientist Boyka Stefanova notes, "The Baltic states . . . continue to regard the security situation in Europe as based on the assumptions that the Baltic sub-region is a bridge between the East and the West, and that they are two mutually opposed entities. In order to eliminate strong power asymmetry in their geopolitical situation, they have sought integration with the West."[18] Yet, Pakalniņa acknowledges in *The Bus* that the seemingly omnipresent western capitalism cannot erase the traces of the Soviet era in these transitional countries. For example, one hears Russian, Estonian, Latvian, and Lithuanian languages spoken onboard. However, the most frequently heard language is Russian, a vestige of the Soviet colonization when Russian was considered the "international language." The communist past appears again at the terminal in Sovetsk, where a man tries to board this European bus for free, insisting that the driver accept his "war veteran certificate." The man argues that his certificate grants him gratis travel, including between cities, while the driver attempts to explain to him that his certificate only applies to the local coach network and that this particular bus is international (and not intercity). Finally, the film ends with the credits rolling across the screen, and the voice of the bus driver complaining about the lack of traffic signs on the street, telling someone, "Back then, in a Soviet-era driver's license class . . ." Audiences never hear the rest of the driver's sentence, with his voice gradually becoming inaudible on the soundtrack. One may only speculate that the man's critique of the traffic sign situation today led to his eulogizing of the superior vehicular conditions under communism.

These vestiges of the Soviet past remind viewers of the Baltic states' current postcolonial position, displaying the countries' contemporary liminality. Cultural theorist Homi K. Bhabha labels this contingent in-between space as "'the unhomely' [,] a paradigmatic colonial and post-colonial condition."[19] Scholar Kathleen Cassity elaborates Bhabha's ideas:

> Bhabha describes the "unhomely moment" as the state of being "un-homed," which is not to say "homeless." In Bhabha's use of the term, the 'unhomed' subject lives somewhere in the purely physical sense, yet figuratively occupies an intermediary space which makes it difficult for her to know where she belongs, socially and culturally. The "unhomed" subject dwells in a border zone, "as though in parenthesis."[20]

Pakalniņa's documentary cannot hide or disavow Estonia, Latvia, or Lithuania's unhomeliness. As much as Pakalniņa and her fellow Baltic brethren may wish to highlight the ways that the three Baltic states resemble their Western European counterparts, the communist past has not been eradicated from collective memory metaphorically, nor has it been erased from the physical landscape. They cannot escape their reality of existing in a cultural and economic border zone, somewhere in between East and West, past and present. In other words, *The Bus* chronicles how the Baltic states live in parenthesis, constantly in flux and perpetually in the process of negotiating their identities within the New Europe.

Conclusions

The Bus offers a snapshot of an optimistic and hopeful time in the Baltic states, when many citizens saw their countries' admittance to the EU and

NATO as the beginning of a new, positive era of economic rejuvenation and cultural revitalization. Many Estonians, Latvians, and Lithuanians viewed these political developments in 2004 as a return to their rightful place as part of a Europe that was the binary opposite of the Putin-ruled Russia.[21] However, the initial euphoria and confidence of regaining independence was quickly replaced by disappointment in democracy and disillusionment with western capitalism. Instead of being embraced and considered as European citizens, completely equal to the original members of the EU, the inhabitants of these postcommunist states encountered a new form of economic and cultural imperialism. Film scholar Dina Iordanova characterizes this situation:

> The reality of contemporary Europe is one where the established links within the former Soviet bloc's "sphere of influence" were severed overnight and replaced by new, often rushed, affiliations that essentially formed another sphere where disparities persist; a contested pecking order has been removed to be replaced by another, equally challenging one. In the new configuration, economic inequalities and cultural incompatibilities not only persisted but also predefined the outcomes of many undertakings; many peripherally located countries were reassigned from their previous dependencies into the position of satellites to emerging sovereigns. The ongoing redistribution of wealth and power was often disguised through a Europe-wide rhetoric of deficiency of supposedly culturally inferior areas that are traditionally located in the South East or East of Europe.[22]

In other words, "earlier colonization by powerful socialist entities [has been] gradually replaced by new subtle forms of colonization by the West."[23]

By all accounts, political, economic, and social integration of the Baltic states into the New Europe has not occurred. While a wave of nostalgia for the "good old days" of communism, with its guaranteed jobs and economic stability, passes over postsocialist countries like Latvia twenty years after the collapse of the Union of Soviet Socialist Republics (USSR), Pakalniņa's film reminds spectators that the ability to change decades-old physical and cultural borders does not come easily. As the situations in the Baltic states have demonstrated, optimistic enthusiasm alone cannot redefine such boundaries. In lieu of minimizing or attempting to escape their Soviet pasts, these countries would instead benefit from embracing a future that strives to openly negotiate the borders between their recent communist identities and their subsequent European selves. Perhaps then Pakalniņa's bus will finally arrive at its desired destination.

Notes

1. The term *New Europe* refers to the postcommunist states in Central and Eastern Europe. Contemporary politicians, historians, and economists have labeled these

countries as "new" because of their relatively recent transformation into capitalist democracies. While the residents of the New Europe have seen this moniker largely as a positive description, in the context of the Iraq War, the idea of the New Europe stands in opposition to the Old Europe (i.e., France, Germany, etc.), according to former U.S. Secretary of Defense Donald Rumsfeld. He criticized the countries of the Old Europe for opposing the Unites States' invasion of Iraq in 2003, praising the New Europe states for their support of the war effort, a categorization that would later become pejorative as the global antiwar protests increased. This chapter considers the New Europe outside of the Iraq war context, and, instead, utilizes this term in a positive way to refer to current postcommunist states. See "Secretary Rumsfeld Briefs at the Foreign Press Center," U.S. Department of Defense, January 22, 2003, http://www.defense.gov/transcripts/transcript.aspx?transcriptid=1330.

2. Meta Mazaj, "Freewheeling on the Margins: The Discourse of Transition in the New Slovenian Cinema," *Studies in Eastern European Cinema* 2, no. 1 (2011): 8–9.

3. In October 2011, Pakalniņa not only had her latest documentary 33 Animals for Santa Claus (2011) included in the competition for Best Mid-Length Documentary at the prestigious International Documentary Film Festival Amsterdam, the filmmaker herself also served on the festival's jury for the Best Feature-Length Documentary.

4. Maruta Z. Vitols, "Alternative Spaces, Alternative Voices: The Art of Laila Pakalniņa," *Acta Academiae Artium Vilnensis* 56 (2010): 34.

5. Elīna Reitere, "Pakalniņa's World of Objects," *Film News from Latvia*, Special Issue Laila Pakalniņa/Infinity FF/Italy, 2005, 6.

6. Mārtiņš Slišāns, "Painting with the Senses," *Film News from Latvia*, Special Issue Laila Pakalniņa/Infinity FF/Italy, 2005, 8.

7. Leslie Felperin, "Review of The Bus (Buss)," *Variety* 395, no. 11 (August 2, 2004): 29.

8. Buss DVD, trailer no. 2, 2004.

9. Daina Stukuls Eglitis, *Imagining the Nation: History, Modernity, and Revolution in Latvia* (University Park: The Pennsylvania State University Press, 2002), 132–133.

10. For more information on how contemporary Latvian documentarians address the Soviet past in their films, see Maruta Z. Vitols, "Investigating the Past, Envisioning the Future: An Exploration of Post-1991 Latvian Documentary," in *The Blackwell Companion to East European Cinema*, ed. Anikó Imre (Malden, MA: Blackwell Publishing, 2012), 325–343.

11. Kriss Ravetto-Biagioli, "Reframing Europe's Double Border," in *East European Cinemas*, ed. Anikó Imre (New York: Routledge, 2005), 182.

12. Irina Novikova, "Baltic Cinemas—Flashbacks in/out of the House," in *Via Transversa: Lost Cinema of the Former Eastern Bloc*, ed. Eva Näripea and Andreas Trossek (Tallinn: Studies in Environmental Aesthetics and Semiotics, 2008), 262.

13. The Schengen Agreement is a treaty signed in 1985 in Luxembourg, by five members (Belgium, France, Germany, Luxembourg, and the Netherlands) of the European Economic Community (the precursor to today's EU). The agreement allowed for no internal border controls within the Schengen zone, ensured common rules on visas, and ensured police and judicial collaboration. As the EU accepted more countries into its membership, the Schengen area expanded, and, since 2007, it has included the Baltic states.

14. The exception is the Šiauliai station, which is quiet and empty since it is the middle of the night when the bus arrives.

15. EuroLines Company Austrian and Czech Republic websites, accessed October 23, 2012, http://www.eurolines.at/en/home/ and https://www.elines.cz/en/.

16. One should note that, while this study interprets Pakalniņa's film as depicting western capitalism in a positive or, perhaps, innocuous light, the filmic text is ambiguous enough to also allow a reading that is highly critical of the unrestrained neoliberal capitalism that swept through (or "colonized") Eastern Europe after the fall of communism.

17. Max Jakobson, quoted in Jukka Rislakki, *The Case for Latvia: Disinformation Campaigns against a Small Nation* (Amsterdam: Rodopi, 2008), 203.

18. Boyka Stefanova, "The Baltic States' Accession to NATO and the European Union: An Extension of the European Security Community?" *Journal of International Relations and Development* 5, no. 2 (June 2002): 158.

19. Homi K. Bhabha, *The Location of Culture* (London and New York: Routledge, 1994), 13.

20. Kathleen J. Cassity, "Emerging from Shadows: The 'Unhomed' Anglo-Indian of 36 Showringhee Lane," accessed October 2, 2012, http://home.alphalink.com.au/~agilbert/chowri~1.html.

21. For more information on the acrimonious relationship between the Baltic States and Russia in the twenty-first century, see Mykolas Cherniauskas, "Accession to the EU through the Eyes of the Baltic States: Addressing the Enlargement, the Convention on the Future of Europe, and the Constitution," Slovo 17, no. 1 (2005): 49–63.

22. Dina Iordanova, "Migration and Cinematic Process in Post–Cold War Europe," in European Cinema in Motion: Migrant and Diasporic Film in Contemporary Europe, ed. Daniela Berghahn and Claudia Sternberg (Basingstoke: Palgrave Macmillan, 2010), 52.

23. Iordanova, "Migration and Cinematic Process," 52.

Works Cited

Bhabha, Homi K. *The Location of Culture*. London: Routledge, 1994.

Cassity, Kathleen J. "Emerging from Shadows: The 'Unhomed' Anglo-Indian of *36 Showringhee Lane*." Accessed October 23, 2012. http://home.alphalink.com.au/~agilbert/chowri~1.html.

Černiauskas, Mykolas. "Accession to the EU through the Eyes of the Baltic States: Addressing Enlargement, the Convention on the Future of Europe, and the Constitution." *Slovo* 17, no. 1 (2005): 49–63.

Eglitis, Daina Stukuls. *Imagining the Nation: History, Modernity, and Revolution in Latvia*. University Park: The Pennsylvania State University Press, 2002.

"EuroLines Company Austrian website." EuroLines. Accessed October 23, 2012. http://www.eurolines.at/en/home/.

"EuroLines Company Czech Republic website." EuroLines. Accessed October 23, 2012. https://www.elines.cz/en/.

Felperin, Leslie. "The Review of *The Bus* (*Buss*)." *Variety* 395, no. 11 (August 2, 2004): 29.

Iordanova, Dina. "Migration and Cinematic Process in Post-Cold War Europe." In *European Cinema in Motion: Migrant and Diasporic Film in Contemporary Europe*, edited by Daniela Berghahn and Claudia Sternberg, 50–75. Basingstoke: Palgrave Macmillan, 2010.

Mazaj, Meta. "Freewheeling on the Margins: The Discourse of Transition in the New Slovenian Cinema." *Studies in Eastern European Cinema* 2, no. 1 (2011): 7–20.

Novikova, Irina. "Baltic Cinemas—Flashbacks in/out of the House." In *Via Transversa: Lost Cinema of the Former Eastern Bloc*, edited by Eva Näripea and Andreas Trossek, 247–266. Tallinn: Studies in Environmental Aesthetics and Semiotics, 2008.

Pakalniņa, Laila. Poster and DVD cover for *Buss* (*The Bus*). Tallinn: Acuba Film Collection, 2004.

Ravetto-Biagioli, Kriss. "Reframing Europe's Double Border." In *East European Cinemas*, edited by Anikó Imre, 179–196. New York: Routledge, 2005.

Reitere, Elīna. "Pakalniņa's World of Objects." Film News from Latvia, Special Issue Laila Pakalniņa/Infinity FF/Italy, 2005, 6–7.

Rislakki, Jukka. *The Case for Latvia: Disinformation Campaigns against a Small Nation*. Amsterdam: Rodopi, 2008.

"Secretary Rumsfeld Briefs at the Foreign Press Center." U.S. Department of Defense, January 22, 2003. http://www.defense.gov/transcripts/transcript.aspx?transcriptid=1330.

Slišāns, Mārtiņš. "Painting with the Senses." *Film News from Latvia*, Special Issue Laila Pakalniņa/Infinity FF/Italy, 2005, 8–9.

Stefanova, Boyka. "The Baltic States' Accession to NATO and the European Union: An Extension of the European Security Community?" *Journal of International Relations and Development* 5, no. 2 (June 2002): 156–181.

Vitols, Maruta Z. "Alternative Spaces, Alternative Voices: The Art of Laila Pakalniņa." *Acta Academiae Artium Vilnensis* 56 (2010): 33–39.

——. "Investigating the Past, Envisioning the Future: An Exploration of Post-1991 Latvian Documentary." In *The Blackwell Companion to East European Cinema*, edited by Anikó Imre, 325–343. Malden, MA: Blackwell Publishing, 2012.

Films

33 Animals for Santa Claus (*33 zvēri Ziemassvētku vecītim*). Directed by Laila Pakalniņa. Latvia, 2011.

The Bus (*Buss*). Directed by Laila Pakalniņa. Estonia, Lithuania, Latvia, Finland, 2004.

Jeanne Dielman, 23 Business offices, 1080 Brussels (*Jeanne Dielman, 23 quai du Commerce, 1080 Bruxelles*). Directed by Chantal Akerman. Belgium, France, 1975.

The Shoe (*Kurpe*). Directed by Laila Pakalniņa. Germany, Latvia, France, 1998.

Wavelength. Directed by Michael Snow. Canada, United States, 1967.

Stalker (*Ста́лкер*). Directed by Andrei Tarkovsky. Soviet Union, 1979.

III

VANISHED BORDERS

MEMORY, NOSTALGIA, AND HOMESICKNESS

7

Zurich Roses

Andrea Staka's Das Fräulein *(2006)*

Lesley C. Pleasant

Hau ab! (Get lost)

—*Das Fräulein*

ANDREA STAKA'S *Das Fräulein* (2006) is not a political film about globalization and its discontents. It does not judge its three main characters, but rather asks its viewers to see them as Orhan Pamuk regards them in his novel: with "compassion for their fear and insecurity,"[1] understanding their processes of coming to terms with displacement. The Swiss director focuses on the geographic and emotional boundary crossings of three expatriate women from the former Yugoslavia, "charting a complex renegotiation of identity."[2] Winner of the Golden Leopard at the Locarno International Film Festival in 2006, *Das Fräulein* deals with the space between "[d]welling/[d]rifting,"[3] as Serbian Ruža[4] (Mirjana Karanović), Croatian Mila (Ljubica Jović), and Bosnian Ana (Marija Škaričić) push each other to confront the uncanny[5] that their respective ideas of home have become. Their temporary community embodies the transitory and unsettling nature of "feeling at home," as well as the resilience of home-seekers' ability to "re-think" home,[6] to find the familiar in the unfamiliar in their "present time and space."[7] Providing a personal look at the "possibility of [home] . . . beyond place,"[8] *Das Fräulein* "remove[s] the spaces from the fence and build[s] of them a residence."[9]

To clarify, the previously quoted line, taken out of context from Christian Morgenstern's poem "The Picket Fence" ("Der Lattenzaun") as translated by Max Knight, refers to making a home out of the spaces between the fence pickets, not a home out of the remaining pickets themselves. As such, it reads

Figure 7.1. English film poster. Ana in the foreground and Ruža peering through her office blinds (her "picket fence"). Courtesy of Film Movement.

almost custom-made for this film, at once realistic and fairy tale–like. Gray Zurich is shown in its bleak concrete coldness, as are banal and routine activities and chores.[10] Staka's "narrative shorthand," which "presents immigrant lives with significantly more empathy than detail,"[11] shows a city and its people both intimately and from a birds-eye view; gives glimpses of "boundaries . . . [that] are the edges at which something begins its 'unfolding.'"[12]

Seeking to find a better life for herself, Serbian Ruža immigrated to Zurich, Switzerland, twenty-five years earlier, from what was then Yugoslavia. At the last minute, her then-fiancé refused to accompany her. Since then, she has achieved financial success as the autocratic manager of a canteen in Zurich, but otherwise leads a lonely, stark, and "rigidly structured existence,"[13] containing her "unspoken pain"[14] behind a distant, cold demeanor. Mila, who has been working at Ruža's restaurant from its beginning, had originally moved to Switzerland with her husband (Zdenko Jelčić) with the intention of returning to their Croatian homeland after making enough money to retire comfortably to a new house. As her husband's retirement approaches, however, a distance grows between the couple, as she realizes that she no longer shares his homesickness for Croatia and that she is unwilling to cut herself off from the place and the people she now considers home.[15] Ana, a young, energetic Bosnian, grew up in Sarajevo during the Bosnian War. Adept at crossing boundaries and at waking up somewhere else every morning, she is running away both from the dead in her past and from her own impending death from leukemia. Home left her as much as she left home, first through the destruction of the war,[16] and then, more recently, through the suicide of her brother after the war. Ana hitchhikes her way to Switzerland and by chance ends up working for Ruža. The trio's boundaries change as they move through time and space, and Ruža, Mila, and Ana must come to terms with their respective forms of "Swiss sickness,"[17] an old term for homesickness, which in the film is simply called longing. All three experience home as *uncanny*, "in an ambiguous way,"[18] and must adapt to "the shifting meanings of home,"[19] and its precarious, yet tenacious, existence.

Staka's "Swiss Miss"

That longing is central to the film is clear from the opening shot: the first frame of the film is of very thin branches reaching upward into the sky as Slavic music plays. Several of these new growth branches are then shown being cut from pollarded[20] trees, as nondiegetic, somewhat melancholic Slavic music is heard. The viewer sees a freshly cut branch being thrown onto a pile of other sawn-off branches, then a close-up of the saw sawing off another branch. At the moment when the branch is separated from its base, the film cuts to a black screen, onto which the title of the film appears. In fact, the entire film takes place in this space of separation that leads in time to home "being . . . unfolded in terms of abyss,"[21] the concept "designat[ing] at once a limit, a negative limit and a chance . . . which is the opening of its identity into the future."[22]

The title of the film that appears in white on the black screen does not just refer to Ana and Ruža (who are both called *Fräulein* during the film), but also to *das Heimweh*, the German word for homesickness, which, in Croatian, is also neuter.[23] *Heimweh* is at the same time *Fernweh* (longing for far away), since both refer to the longing to be somewhere where one is not presently. This longing is represented well by the word *Fräulein*[24] (Miss). If one uses this word to refer to a woman it can suggest that the woman has *Fernweh* and *Heimweh* for a home of her own making. In this context, *Fräulein* is learning to navigate the world on her own, by leaving home "when home isn't home"[25] anymore in order to find it. The title stresses that Ruža and Ana are at a threshold, regardless of their different ages. Similarly, Mila, who has family ties in Zurich, is also at a boundary line: she chooses to venture into new territory for her, finding and using her voice to change the dynamics of her relationships; to determine where, what, and whom she calls home.

The black screen with the title *Das Fräulein*, which followed the images of the pollarded tree being sawn, cuts into the image of Ruža's white inner curtains. Shot from a low angle, the curtains form a wall, whose folded and hemmed ends are emphasized. The viewer sees light from behind these curtains but cannot discern anything behind them but a murky space. Then, the camera frames the sleeping Ruža from above, forcing her closed eyes open, as her head rests between green pillows adorned with a pattern of bunches of fernlike branches. In hindsight, it seems that the first images of the trees being cut were Ruža's dream and that the cut to the black screen and the abrupt end to the music indicated the end of her dream as she awoke and saw the white curtain in her apartment in Zurich.

Unfinished Houses

This white curtain separates Ruža from the rest of the world. It is a protective border behind which she hides her Yugoslavian self and her Yugoslavian memories. Although Ruža wakes up to the same curtains every morning and follows the same morning routine—brushing her hair, putting on her watch, cinching her coat tightly in the mirror by the door as if to hold herself up—she has not really found a home in Zurich and is not "at home" there. Ruža's "space" is "dead"; neither she nor it is "open to the world."[26] Nothing personal hangs on the walls; it is practical and cold like her canteen, although at least the canteen has living plants and one hanging photograph of a young Ruža smiling in front of the restaurant.[27] Her sheets, patterned with the bundles of leaves, are the most personalized things in her apartment, perhaps because in her dreams Ruža can let herself long for new growth, long for home. Ruža's "fortress," her behavior toward the world, and her literal walls prevent her from "produc[ing] a new set of mental images" (of her old home), which in turn could "induce a new way of seeing her everyday environment."[28]

Mila and Ana must also come to terms with their own struggles against "graves"—both figurative and literal—whether Mila's feeling of being boxed in to an ending to her life story that she does not want, or Ana's attempt to outrun her own grave and those of her family. In the still of the scene in figure 7.2, Mila is holding a picture of an unfinished house in Croatia in her hand under her bandaged finger. She always has this picture in the pocket of her apron, proudly showing it to anyone who will look, explaining that this is the house that her husband is building for their retirement. The picture shows the lone concrete frame of a house of empty rooms on a cliff overlooking the ocean. Seeing it, Ana responds with, "It will be nice someday." Although the house is on a cliff similar to one depicted on a poster of Croatia in Mila's apartment,[29]

Figure 7.2. Mila holding the picture of "the dream house"; Ana, cutting a radish rose. Courtesy of Film Movement.

it is not inviting but cold, dead—a skeleton, not a home. Mila seems to sense this when looking at Ana, the woman associated with the bandaged wound on Mila's finger.

Mila had cut her finger quite badly while working. Ana, who happened to be a customer at the restaurant at the time, had run to help her, soothed her by speaking to her in Serbo-Croatian, bandaged it for her, and temporarily took Mila's place in the canteen serving line, which had been stalled as Ruža stood helpless, frozen behind the cash register. Ruža did not ask Mila how she was doing, but instead called out her name as if admonishing her. It was as if both women realized in that moment what the future would be like when Mila has gone. Ruža's well-functioning everyday comes to a standstill when Mila is not in her place, and Mila gets a glimpse of the canteen—so familiar to her—functioning, unfamiliarly, without her.[30] On the one hand, once retired, Mila would not have to endure Ruža's condescension. On the other hand, if she would leave, she sees how easily replaced she would be.

Noticing that Ana is carving a radish rose for Ruža's take-home dinner, Mila dismisses the gesture, telling Ana that Ruža will not appreciate it. Ana replies that it is prettier that way and finishes the radish, which, as she holds it in her hand, looks more like a heart with scars than a rose. Mila is jealous of Ana and of her ability to reach Ruža in ways that Mila has not been able to. The cut on her finger is not only a real wound but also symbolic of Mila's desire for Ruža and her husband to appreciate Mila's contribution to the lives they have made in Switzerland. As Ana cuts into the radish, Mila anticipates feeling similarly "cut off" if she leaves Zurich.

Upon opening the plastic container of food at home, Ruža sees the radish, which on top of the food now actually looks like a rose, garnishing a not-so-attractive-looking meal. Ruža takes a deep breath and quickly recloses the container; she appreciates the radish rose, but also fears it. Ruža means rose.[31] The radish rose is a symbol of the Ruža she had been, the Ruža who left not only her home but also her fiancé, the Ruža with "heart scars," cut off from home like the branches from the pollarded trees. At the same time, it represents her potential to become a Ruža beyond her former self, a Ruža who can "split" and grow out of the carapace she made to protect herself from homesickness. Indeed, by the end of the film, the white showing in the radish rose is not the protective white of Ruža's white curtains and office blinds: Ruža energetically opens both sets of curtains in her apartment, to stand looking at the view she has chosen without the need of the protective "lens" of the inner white curtain. She has made something of the empty space that was Zurich, of the absence of her former friends and family. When Ruža finally takes the box of old pictures off her dresser, she discovers that to "make a residence" of her empty spaces she must include those of her past, as well. She builds a "fence," a narrative that includes the pictures of her youth, whose "absent presence,"[32] together with the empty spaces between them on the wall of her Zurich apartment, create her home. What is no longer present is the radish, the pieces of which—cut out, but remembered—help give shape to the rose.

Carved by Bosnian Ana for Serbian Ruža, this radish rose might also allude to the Sarajevo Roses—scars in concrete caused by shell explosions from the Bosnian War and filled by red resin by those wishing to remember the dead—that can still be seen on some streets of Sarajevo.[33] What connects the scars of real war with the cuts in the radish is that both are memorials to the struggle for independence and to survivors. Both roses remember the dead and symbolize attempts at eradicating the familiar by making it unfamiliar. By carving a rose out of a radish, Ana almost seems to flaunt her ability to deal with the war. If asked about it—which she is, by everyone except Ruža—she responds unemotionally, "It was shit. . . . My grandmother said that I would always stop and stare at the dead." Explaining why she has not followed through on plans to go to New York with her brother, she remains detached: "My brother killed himself after the war." Some see her as a type of Sarajevo rose herself—a young woman scarred from the war, someone exotic who needs to be taken care of.[34] Not yet scarred over and playing the strong, well-adjusted, free spirit, Ana wants empathy, not pity. Like Ruža, however, she clings to the idea that survival means repressing weakness, hurt, and longing. She needs to feel homesick and, especially, feel the loss of her brother, which she does when her leukemia symptoms become acute. Only then can she, in some sense, fill in her wounds, literally, with the blood transfusion Ruža risks everything to give her.

In German, the verb *abhauen* has the connotation of running away, leaving everything familiar behind, fleeing from problems, consequences, or responsibilities; but it also is associated with freedom, with ripping out one's roots and choosing to start anew. The third-person singular form also sounds like "skin off." We find it used in the film with this connotation by an old man feeding seagulls, as he cruelly pushes Ana away. He drops the bag of bread from which he is feeding the birds. Ana, who had been sitting on a bench nearby, hurries to pick it up. He grabs it away from her, asking her gruffly what she wants from him, telling her to leave him in peace, to *hau ab*—get lost. The camera focuses on the rejected Ana, as she struggles to make sense of this unnecessary and biting dismissal, and reveals a person stung by this tearing off of her skin. Alone and homeless, she turns to look at the lake and the seagulls through the pay-per-view binoculars rooted at the shore. She has just focused on a pigeon, which is separated from the flying gulls beyond, when the film cuts to black as the binoculars' time "runs out." Both Ruža and Ana share this literal black screen in the film—an end, a grave, a total destruction of their "worlds."[35] There is no home to which she can fly; like the everyday pigeon she needs to adapt and find her place in the urban landscape of Zurich. Experiencing the end of her belief in the stability of home as happy ending is uncanny, but necessary, in order to find a home in real time and space.

Alps in Snow

Even seemingly "eternal," constant places change. For this reason, Staka brings Ruža and Ana to the Alps, in an ironic nod to the genre of *Heimatfilm*,[36] which often portrayed the Alps as timeless, traditional simplicity and beauty, the epitome of home, and an attainable utopia. In *Das Fräulein*, the mountains certainly are a place of longing, but they are a temporary stop, not the ultimate goal, a means to see the familiar differently.

It is Ana's journey, but, oddly, she invites Ruža to accompany her. The first shot of Ana shows her staring out the window of a car, looking at the mountains at dusk on her way to the city limits of Zurich. Mountains make clear borders; they hem in valleys, but they also provide more expansive views. For Ana, mountains seem to represent her longing to escape the death of the valley, much as the first image of the film focused on branches pointing straight up into the sky. For someone without a home, the mountains may symbolize

Figure 7.3. At the threshold. Courtesy of Film Movement.

a sort of extreme rootedness in place. They also provide Ana and Ruža a setting in which to "step out of the 'everyday' and experience nature as . . . the . . . realm of the poet," which, to Heidegger, is necessary for "dwelling."[37] And indeed, Staka does allow the matter-of-fact, no-nonsense Ruža to experience the Alps as "poetic." The film, however, does not focus on panoramic shots or the fierce beauty of the Alps, but on the shift in the relationship between the two women. Not framed as tiny insignificant beings in the face of giant Nature, Ana and Ruža are shown moving through space, coming closer to rearranging the empty spaces of the fence (the boundary of the unfamiliar) into something they can live in, not write poems about or sentimentalize.

While Ana rushes to the viewing platform that juts out over the abyss, Ruža hesitates to go to the edge, responding to Ana's jarring "Are you afraid that I'll push you, or that I'll jump?" with "I don't like the emptiness down there." Neither, it seems, does Ana. That Ana sees death, sees the war, sees all the dead in her past when looking out is clear when she turns to Ruža and asks her, "Don't you want to know about the war? Everyone else asks me about it." To Ruža's "Only if you want to," Ana realizes, "No, not really." Ana is scared. She tries to engage Ruža more directly and asks her whether she is scared of dying, admitting that it is the one thing of which she (Ana) is scared.

Where Ana sees "the inevitability of . . . annihilation" when looking into the abyss, Ruža recognizes that leaving home, and the "anticipatory nostalgia"

Figure 7.4. "Don't you want to ask me about the war?" Courtesy of Film Movement.

she feels before looking down into the valley "is a necessary component of experience the wonder of life."[38] Ruža is no longer "overcome" by "this primal fear"[39] of the loss of home, a death of that self who felt at home there. Where Ana sees "the nothing of the abyss," Ruža sees the emptiness as "something 'positive.'"[40] The birds-eye view of her home allows her to see it from above instead of from the daily familiar views. Home, according to Young's reading of Heidegger, is "a state of mind: experiencing the 'nearness,' 'wonder,' 'uncanniness' of being."[41] Instead of seeing Zurich as the grave she chose when she cut herself off from home, as a place for which she should no longer feel longing, the view from above allows her to see Zurich in an unfamiliar way, strangely nearby yet being so far.

In this significant role reversal, Ana remains serious and looks down, while Ruža looks up and sees the view. Once she has the courage to look at the view from the railing, she breaks out into a smile, recognizing that the "emptiness down there," the emptiness of the black screen that she had experienced when "cut off" from her "family tree" by choosing to go to Zurich, are things she no longer fears. What she sees before her is the murkiness of potential, not something to keep at bay behind white curtains and blinds. She can look into the gray cloud cover before her, as well as the peaks above it, and realize that instead of being the space of a freshly sawn-off limb, the round gray area has scabbed over and is familiar in a new way; it is no longer an area she fears to see. Ruža realizes she is looking at the valley in which she now feels more at home than she does in Belgrade.

Although Ruža seems to dismiss Ana's fear of death, by laughing and responding with a seemingly inadequate "at your age" in German, Ruža's reaction helps bring Ana back to the present, makes her look up, see a smiling Ruža, then look back at that which made Ruža smile. Ana asks Ruža about how the view will look in the spring, to which the matter-of-fact Ruža replies, "There's no snow." She lets Ana (and herself) focus on what remains, even as places and people change over time. At this, Ana takes a handful of snow, a handful of the present, as it were, and starts a snowball fight with Ruža. Both literally and spontaneously grab and experience the transient present, something that Ruža has not been able to do for a long time. But their spontaneous togetherness in the snowball fight does not last, and the distance grows between them again in the Alpine restaurant. Staka is not promising a happy ending, nor providing a sentimentalized mother-daughter-like relationship blossoming in a beautiful setting. Home comes in fleeting moments, in the form of a snowball. The mountains—for Ana, perhaps, a means to move as far away as possible from the grave below, or an indication of the borders she plans to cross and has crossed—become emblems of the change and continuity. They will remain when the snow is gone, yet they will look different without snow, or from a different outlook point, illustrating that "[t]he identities of place [and the people within them] are always unfixed, contested and multiple."[42]

Money Rolls and Money's Roles

Even after this trip to the mountains, Ruža's most precious item, it seems, is kept in her safe at the office: an oval metallic box with a smiling young woman on the cover, along with Serbian writing. Within this box are the rolls of money she has earned. Every morning, she opens the safe, in a ritual of sorts, and touches the money. This money is what she left home for, what she, in part, longed for. It is her "proof" that she "needs no one," as she claims. The money, in itself, however, is not a satisfactory replacement for the home she left—a fact that becomes clear to her after she reluctantly accompanies Ana to a casino. After watching the impulsive Ana lose all of her chips, she flees to an underground parking lot. Ruža then tries to convince Ana (and herself) that although she had been so homesick at the beginning of her life in Zurich that it took everything in her not to run back home, she had persevered and become the strong example of how money can lead to independence. Ana, however, is not impressed. She tells Ruža that she is not like her; that she does not care about money; that she is scared. Ana, who had kept the disease hidden from everyone else until this point, also confesses to Ruža that she has leukemia. Ruža simply stares, speechless. It is as if she suddenly sees Ana—this embodiment of life, energy, and hope—as its opposite, as the embodiment of death. Faced with the uncanny, in the form of the unexpectedly dying Ana, Ruža is shaken. Her convictions about money, about safety, about independence lose their familiarity and "develop towards an ambivalence, until . . . [they] finally coincide with . . . *unheimlich*."[43] Standing in front of Ana, who cuts off her attempt at dispensing advice with "You don't know me," Ruža recognizes the enormity of the space, not only between herself and Ana, but also between Ruža the young immigrant and the Ruža expounding the virtues of "need[ing] no one." Confronting the quarter of a century she has spent hiding, Ruža is suddenly acutely aware "of how [her] . . . own body intimates [her] mortality."[44]

Ruža does not reach out to Ana, although she does care for her.[45] Ana disappears without another word; she does not come back to work. Mila and Ruža come to work as usual, yet feel Ana's absence. Significantly, the film literally loses focus for a short moment, when showing Ruža in her office after her experience with the uncanny. The film blurs the usually clear and well-defined lines of Ruža's office and blinds. Ruža's borders, which until now have been so rigidly maintained, are changing and becoming more fluid. Despite her attempts at protecting herself in the confines of her office, Ruža learns that "there never was a place that was a container,"[46] except perhaps a coffin. Her recognition of Ana's mortality puts her own into perspective, as well. It is as if she is trying to see through the blinds in her office or through the curtains in her apartment—to push through them and away from her attempt to exist as "a self-enclosed or encapsulated entity"[47]—in order to be more open to the world. All the murkiness and gray she kept at bay outside by her blinds seems to enter the room.[48] She has come to accept and appreciate that "we are, despite being characterized by 'mineness,' thrown into the lived . . . possibilities of how we are with others and who we can become."[49]

One morning Ruža arrives at the canteen to find Ana sitting at one of the tables with all of her belongings. This time, Ruža does not pause. It is clear that the young woman is very sick. Ana can no longer deny her illness and has moved through the "gap between knowledge and nausea,"[50] between rationally knowing she has leukemia and will die and living its reality.[51] Ruža immediately runs to her safe and takes out all of the money from her box. On the way to the hospital, Ana looks out of the taxi window, on which can be seen reflections of leafless branches, reminding the viewer of the leafless branches that were cut at the start of the film. She asks Ruža, "Do you know that feeling when you think you are thirsty but you realize that what it is, is longing?" Ruža does not need to respond; both Ana and the audience know that she does.

Mila also experiences revelations and growth through the uncanny. While hosting a dinner party, Mila is fascinated by a close-up image of a spider weaving its web around a twig on her TV screen. The fact that the TV is on, albeit muted, during the party is interesting in itself. Did she seek a distraction from the talk about Croatia? She stands separated from her seated husband and the Croatian guests who discuss how the Croatia of today has become so expensive while they were away. The undercurrent of this scene is strong. Mila watches the spider, seemingly fascinated. She then "weaves" her way around the guests to sit at the head of the table, where she unwraps her bandage to show herself the scar on her finger. There is a sense of calm in this scene. She is alone in company, but it is not the loneliness of the outsider looking in at the dinner party before her; it is the comfort of introspection. Mila no longer looks outward, to others, to make her decisions, but inward, to herself.

The spider on the TV screen is literally making a residence out of nothing, weaving its web out of the empty spaces of the fence. Mila realizes that she has made a home for herself in Switzerland, a home she is not willing to leave for the emptiness of the unfinished house in Croatia. Croatia is a scar, a part of her, but no longer a wound that is open and bleeding; it has become a bridge between her past and her present. Before her "molting," Mila tells her husband that he will miss his children when he moves to Croatia. However, her mind is made up, regardless of his future plans or his feelings. She will miss her children, and so decides to stay.

This newly confident Mila will no longer accept Ruža's disrespect, either. While Ruža is at the hospital with Ana, Mila manages the restaurant. Upon her return, Ruža walks into her office to find Mila sitting behind her desk, counting the day's revenue. When Ruža reacts suspiciously, Mila does not respond bitterly, but tells Ruža point-blank that she was only doing Ruža's job because she was not there, and that her boss should be "grateful" for Mila's help. Mila does not cower when Ruža walks in on her but smiles and speaks to her in Croatian, rather than in the usual German in which Mila-the-employee addresses, and is addressed by, her boss. Mila speaks to Ruža in Croatian and German, and Ruža responds in both, as well. Their fluid switching between the two languages[52] also indicates that they feel at home in both worlds.

By the end of the film, Ruža comes to realize that she has treated Mila, with whom she has worked since the beginning, as she has treated her own inner immigrant self. In turn, Mila recognizes that she has let Ruža treat her that way. Not randomly, the Mila who demands respect, and who literally stands on the threshold of Ruža's door as Ruža finally thanks her, wears a shirt patterned with blue roses.

Homesick

The strongest metaphor for an identity at odds with itself is Ana's leukemia. Leukemia is a disease in which white blood cells, which are meant to protect the body by attacking "invasions" of the unfamiliar, fail to recognize the body as familiar, and instead, attack it as an enemy. Ana's own marrow, which creates her blood, her core, has turned against her and has become uncanny. Despite her movement, her energy, her dancing, and her drinking to life, she is unable to contain her illness and bleeds from her gums and nose.

Ignoring her leukemia prevents Ana from really dwelling, as well as from really moving. Much like Ruža, she is "stuck" in a past that does not fit her and cannot move into the present. Ana's leukemia symptoms become so acute that she is forced to stop running from them. It is the unfamiliar, the uncanny within her, her own strange blood in the bus station sink; herself as fluid, as death, as Other, which she must confront before she can move into and then through the space that is Zurich.

Ana does not choose Zurich. Once she receives the blood transfusion at the hospital, she is shown in a hospital gown, looking out the window through a crack in the curtains, much as Ruža had earlier from her office blinds. She looks out over Zurich but does not see home. Despite finding Ruža, despite finding friendship, Ana still longs for somewhere else. Feeling at home is temporary; it is not a constant, unchanging stasis. "Home . . . is always in the process of being 'made.'"[53]

After being told that she needs to begin chemotherapy the next day, Ana admits to the visibly shaken Ruža, "You know, all hospital rooms smell the same; the only difference is the view." Ruža, sitting in her open coat, responds, "Yes, the best view is the one you choose yourself." She knows Ana will not stay, that Ana needs to find her own view. She does not ask Ana to stay, but lets her go. The film ends with Ana hitchhiking toward her future, strengthened by the Zurich "resin" that both the city and Ruža added to this Sarajevo "rose." Ultimately, all three women have faced the uncanny and realized that, for them, home is not a safe room designed to protect them from the rest of the world, but the view they choose to make out of the empty spaces.

In *Das Fräulein*, home is "a fluid idea . . . a striving for"[54] the familiar in the unfamiliar, being able to make dwelling places out of the empty spaces between mountains, clear border markers. For Staka and his characters, "dwelling takes place as this openness" to "the space between us,"[55] where the "us" is the shifting identities of a home-seeker within herself and with other home-seekers, as they all move through space and time. Ruža, Mila, and Ana

Figure 7.5. The view you choose. Courtesy of Film Movement.

have become more comfortable with bridging spaces, stepping out into the unknown like the branches reaching up into the sky in the first image of the film. "[T]hey dwell near to one another, on mountains farthest apart."[56]

Notes

1. Orhan Pamuk, "The Two Souls of Turkey," *New Perspectives Quarterly* 26, no. 4 (Fall 2009): 75.

2. David Fleming, "*Das Fräulein*," *Cineaste* 32, no. 3 (2007): 64.

3. See Charlie Hailey, "Building/Dwelling/Drifting," *Antioch Review* 60, no. 4 (2000): 688. This chapter does not pretend to analyze Heidegger's idea of "dwelling," although the film does thematize something aķin to "being-in-the-world," "being-with-others" and "being-towards-death." See Heidegger (1962), Dallmayr (1993), Fynsk (1982), Gray (1952), Hailey (2000), and Young (2011). The three figures learn to "be" more "authentically" during the course of the film, by recognizing that not only they themselves but their ideas of home shift in space and time after being confronted with the uncanny. Compare Sigmund Freud, "The Uncanny," in *On Creativity and the Unconscious: Papers on the Psychology of Art, Literature, Love, Religion*, edited by Benjamin Nelson (New York: Harper & Row, 1958), 122–161.

4. Ruža in Serbian means 'rose.'

5. See Freud, "The Uncanny," 122–161. Freud discusses several definitions of the words *heimlich* and *unheimlich*, showing that while seemingly opposites, the one actually can come close to meaning the other, depending on use and context. Freud discusses E. T. A. Hoffmann's *Der Sandmann* (*The Sandman*) and analyzes the story's uncanniness, especially with regard to the protagonist and his recurrent uncomfortable encounters with Coppola. Freud explains how the story creates its effect. That which is uncanny is something that is very familiar but has been repressed. It is recognized as familiar but in an unfamiliar context.

6. Heike Henderson, "Re-Thinking and Re-Writing Heimat: Turkish Women Writers in Germany," *Women in German Yearbook* 13 (1997): 225.

7. Fleming, "*Das Fräulein*," 64.

8. Doreen Massey, "The Possibilities of a Politics of Place beyond Place? A Conversation with Doreen Massey," ed. Sophie Bond and David Featherstone, *Scottish Geographical Journal* 125, nos. 3–4 (2009): 401.

9. Christian Morgenstern's poem "Der Lattenzaun" (The Picket Fence), quoted in Hailey, "Building/Dwelling/Drifting," 697.

10. Such activities include sawing off branches; cutting vegetables; paying for lunch in a canteen; brushing hair and teeth; waiting for the bus; getting into an elevator and watching the door close; draining the sink after washing dishes; picking up after a tiny dog in a coat; and watching a game show on TV. These images share space with falling snow; branches on an advertisement that look like bloody synapses; a radish rose; a living room ceiling lamp that starts moving spontaneously after a secret has been shared; a box of a dead brother's baby teeth; a pigeon coming into focus in

the foreground of the view through binoculars following seagulls in the background before a cut to black; empty boxes of dreams; a young woman smiling and yelling "I live" at the city from a hilltop at sunset; a close-up of a spider weaving its web around a twig framed in a muted TV set; the joy on a canteen customer's face as he dances to the music of his homeland; the lost look of an old woman standing still in the bustle at a busy bus station; and an unexpected view into the abyss under a sea of clouds instead of the expected panoramic view of the Swiss Alps from a viewing platform.

11. Jeannette Catsoulis, "Three Disparate (and Desperate) Women," September 18, 2008, www.movies.nytimes.com/2008/09/19/movies/19frau.html.

12. Hailey, "Building/Dwelling/Drifting," 699.

13. Jay Weissberg, "Film Review: *Fraulein*," *Variety* 404, no. 2 (2006): 69.

14. Director's statement in "Fraulein (Das Fraulein), Directed by Andrea Staka," Film Movement, accessed November 30, 2012. http://www.filmmovement.com/downloads/press/FRAULEIN_FM_Press_Kit.pdf.

15. It is unclear whether even her husband still really wants to go, despite his disdain for the country in which he has lived and worked for decades. Currently not working, because of a hurt foot, he literally stays in place, relying on others to finish his dream house. He waits for retirement but perhaps mostly out of habit.

16. See Nicol Ljubic, "Wo ist Ratko Mladic?" *Geo* 10, no. 2 (2010): 84–111; Doug Schwartz, "Sarajevo, the Rose of Bosnia, Rises from Ruin," *Christian Science Monitor* 90, no. 12 (1997): 7.

17. Widespread homesickness among mercenary Swiss soldiers between 1400 and 1800 caused the illness to be associated with Switzerland, although it was obviously not confined to the Swiss military. See Anne Herrmann, "*Heimweh*, or Homesickness," *Yale Review* 95, no. 3 (2007): 23–25.

18. Andrew Warsop, "The Ill Body and *das Unheimliche* (The Uncanny)," *Journal of Medicine and Philosophy* 36, no. 5 (2011): 484.

19. Laura Huttunen, "'Home' and Ethnicity in the Context of War: Hesitant Diasporas of Bosnian Refugees," *European Journal of Cultural Studies* 8, no. 2 (2005): 180.

20. Pollarding is a special type of pruning, which ensures that trees take on a certain shape and do not "outgrow" their given space. New growth is cut to limit the width of the tree; the branches that are left point almost vertically upward from trunk. See Debbie Macklin, "Return of the Living Dead," *Geographical* 72, no. 5 (2000): 14–21; "Pollarding," Royal Horticultural Society, November 4, 2011, http://apps.rhs.org.uk/advicesearch/profile.aspx?pid=156..

21. Mikko Joronen, "Dwelling in the Sites of Finitude: Resisting the Violence of the Metaphysical Globe," *Antipode* 43, no. 4 (2011): 1127–1154.

22. Jacques Derrida, *The Other Heading: Reflections on Today's Europe* (Bloomington: Indiana University Press, 1992), 35; quoted in Elizabeth Boa and Rachel Palfreyman, *Heimat, A German Dream: Regional Loyalties and National Identity in German Culture 1890–1990* (Oxford: Oxford University Press, 2000), 28.

23. "Results for: Nostalgija," EUditc: Croatian-German Dictionary, accessed November 29, 2012, http://www.eudict.com/?lang=croger&word=nostalgija.

24. For more on the word see Bastian Sick, "Hallo, Fräulein!" SpiegelOnline, February 8, 2006, http://www.spiegel.de/kultur/zwiebelfisch/zwiebelfisch-hallo-fraeulein-a-395538.html; "Fräulein, das," Duden, accessed October 16, 2012, www.duden.de/rechtschreibung/Fraeulein.

25. Dieu Hack-Polay, "When Home Isn't Home: A Study of Homesickness and Coping Strategies among Migrant Workers and Expatriates," *International Journal of Psychological Studies* 4, no. 3 (2012): 62.

26. Hack-Polay, "When Home Isn't Home," 68.

27. Even the name of the restaurant is no-nonsense, impersonal and practical; it is simply Restaurant.

28. Ayaka Yoshimizu, "Chopsticks, Phone Bells and Farms: Fuyuko Taira's Diasporic Spatial Practice," *Gender, Place, and Culture: A Journal of Feminist Geography* 19, no. 3 (2012): 316.

29. Mila's apartment is personalized. There are pictures hanging on the walls. It is a lived-in space.

30. Ruža offers Ana money for her "work" behind the counter, which Ana rejects, saying she just wanted to help out. Ruža then offers Ana a job, which Ana also does not accept at first. Later, having experienced Zurich's "cold shoulder," Ana returns to a place where she is welcome. Yet as Ana changes the dynamics of the canteen, Mila becomes jealous.

31. "Ruža," Behind the Name: The Etymology and History of First Names, accessed October 16, 2012, http://www.behindthename.com/name/ruz18a.

32. Laura E. Tanner, *Lost Bodies: Inhabiting the Borders of Life and Death* (Ithaca: Cornell University Press, 2006), 89; quoted in Karen Wilson Baptist, "Diaspora: Death without a Landscape," *Mortality* 15, no. 4 (2010): 304. Baptist writes of physical "sense" of the dead, of landscape as a "dwelling place place of diasporic grief," of "death without a landscape" but also of "particular landscapes [which] become imbued with hyper-real signification. These offer temporary dwelling places for the dead." See Baptist, "Diaspora," 299. This relates to the film in that Ana feels the "dead" not only in her own physical illness but also in the landscapes she passes through, specifically the view from the top of the mountain. The dark valley becomes a grave for her dead, as well as a physical reminder of her own "open" grave. Ruža sees the view as one of promise. At the end of the film she can view the pictures of her past as well as the view of Zurich from her window as two views of "emotional investment," two views of home. See Eric Paul Meljac, "The Poetics of Dwelling: A Consideration of Heidegger, Kafka and Michael K.," *Journal of Modern Literature* 32, no. 1 (2008): 70.

33. Spencer Burke, "Sarajevo Rose," *Harvard Advocate*, Spring 2011, http://www.theharvardadvocate.com/content/sarajevo-rose.

34. The Swiss filmmaker in the bar responds to this assumed need by making a quick exit. The man in the disco, however, takes her home and tells her the next day that he would like to take care of her again. To this, Ana responds by making her quick exit.

35. Mila has her children and her home; she is not as unmoored as Ana or Ruža. However, she, too, almost "blacks out" when she cuts her finger.

36. For a general overview of *Heimatfilm* see Michelle Langford, *Directory of World Cinema*, vol. 9, *Germany* (Bristol, UK: Intellect, 2012), 94–121.

37. Julian Young, "Heidegger's *Heimat*," *International Journal of Philosophical Studies* 19, no. 2 (2011): 287.

38. Young, "Heidegger's *Heimat*," 287–288.

39. Young, "Heidegger's *Heimat*," 288.

40. Young, "Heidegger's *Heimat*," 288.

41. Young, "Heidegger's *Heimat*," 280.

42. Doreen Massey, *Space, Place, and Gender* (Minneapolis: University of Minnesota Press, 1994), 4; quoted in Yoshimizu, "Chopsticks, Phone Bells and Farms," 317.

43. See Freud, "The Uncanny," 131.

44. See Warsop, "The Ill Body and *das Unheimliche* (The Uncanny)," 485. Ana, Ruža, and Mila all confront their mortality in this film: Ana through her illness; Mila as she realizes she is about to step into the last phase of her life "retirement"; Ruža when she recognizes how much time has passed in Switzerland.

45. Proof that she cares for Ana is her smiling when Ana comes to get her wages; her reaching out to Ana by speaking to Ana in Serbian rather than in German after Ana had asked her why she insisted on only speaking German with her; her joining Ana on an outing to the mountains and the casino; her giving Ana the key to the canteen when she realizes that Ana has no place to stay, but is too proud to say it.

46. Massey, "Possibilities of a Politics," 416.

47. Martin Heidegger, *Sein und Zeit* (Tübingen: Niemeyer, 1967), 45; translated from German and quoted in Fred Dallmayr, "Heidegger and Freud," *Political Psychology* 14, no. 2 (1993): 237.

48. Mila is also associated with white cloth—with the gauze over her cut finger; with the crocheted white blanket on her sofa, whose fringe she plays with trying to come to terms with the empty space building between herself and her husband. Similarly, Ana tries to escape the dead she saw growing up during the war in Sarajevo, in the spaces/blocks of light the disco-ball reflects every night on a dance-floor. She, too, is learning to "make a residence" out of the spaces between the baby teeth her dead brother left.

49. Warsop, "The Ill Body and *das Unheimliche* (The Uncanny)," 486.

50. Noam Israeli, "Reflections on Freud's *The Uncanny*," *Existential Analysis: Journal of the Society for Existential Analysis* 16, no. 2 (2005): 385.

51. Shortly before she appears in Ruža's restaurant, the viewer has seen her throwing up violently in an alley.

52. The title and one of the languages of the film is German, although the lead actors are not Swiss or German. Indeed, the three leads do not speak German. See "*Fraulein* (2006): Did You Know?" IMDb, accessed October 16, 2012, http://www.imdb.com/title/tt0476999/trivia. Both they and the film as a whole self-reflexively perform crossing borders, which the film does on the content level, as well. These well-known, familiar actors in their respective homelands cross borders to find "home" in a Swiss film. The actresses learned their German lines phonetically, thereby literally taking words that untranslated are meaningless to them and turning the unfamiliar into the familiar in communicating their meaning through their intonation not only within the film "world" itself, but also to a German-speaking audience.

53. Yoshimizu, "Chopsticks, Phone Bells and Farms," 316.

54. Uta Larkey, "New Places, New Identities: The (Ever) Changing Concept of Heimat," *German Politics & Society* 26, no. 2 (2008): 24.

55. Paul Harrison, "The Space between Us: Opening Remarks on the Concept of Dwelling," *Environment and Planning D: Society and Space* 25, no. 4 (2007): 642–643.

56. A paraphrase of a line from Johann Christian Friedrich Hölderin's hymn "Patmos," used by Heidegger to describe the relationship between thinkers and poets.

Quoted in J. Glenn Gray, "Heidegger's 'Being,'" *Journal of Philosophy* 49, no. 12 (1952): 420.

Works Cited

Baptist, Karen Wilson. "Diaspora: Death without a Landscape." *Mortality* 15, no. 4 (2010): 294–306.

Boa, Elizabeth, and Rachel Palfreyman. *Heimat: A German Dream: Regional Loyalties and National Identity in German Culture 1890–1990.* Oxford: Oxford University Press, 2000.

Burke, Spencer. "Sarajevo Rose." *Harvard Advocate,* Spring 2011. http://www.theharvardadvocate.com/content/sarajevo-rose.

Catsoulis, Jeannette. "Three Disparate (and Desperate) Women." *New York Times,* September 18, 2008. www.movies.nytimes.com/2008/09/19/movies/19frau.html.

Dallmayr, Fred. "Heidegger and Freud." *Political Psychology* 14, no. 2 (1993): 235–253.

Derrida, Jacques. *The Other Heading: Reflections on Today's Europe.* Bloomington: Indiana University Press, 1992.

Fleming, David. "*Das Fräulein.*" *Cineaste* 32, no. 3 (2007): 64.

"Fräulein, das." Duden. Accessed October 16, 2012. www.duden.de/rechtschreibung/Fraeulein.

"Fraulein (Das Fraulein), Directed by Andrea Staka." Film Movement. Accessed November 30, 2012. http://www.filmmovement.com/downloads/press/FRAULEIN_FM_Press_Kit.pdf.

Freud, Sigmund. "The Uncanny." In *On Creativity and the Unconscious: Papers on the Psychology of Art, Literature, Love, Religion,* edited by Benjamin Nelson, 122–161. New York: Harper & Row, 1958.

"*Fraulein* (2006): Did You Know?" Internet Movie Database. Accessed October 16, 2012. http://www.imdb.com/title/tt0476999/trivia.

Fynsk, Christopher. "The Self and Its Witness; On Heidegger's *Being and Time.*" *Boundary 2* 10, no. 3 (1982): 185–207.

Gray, J. Glenn. "Heidegger's 'Being.'" *Journal of Philosophy* 49, no. 12 (1952): 415–422.

Hack-Polay, Dieu. "When Home Isn't Home: A Study of Homesickness and Coping Strategies among Migrant Workers and Expatriates." *International Journal of Psychological Studies* 4, no. 3 (2012): 62–72.

Hailey, Charlie. "Building/Dwelling/Drifting." *The Antioch Review* 60 no. 4 (2002): 688–700.

Harrison, Paul. "The Space between Us: Opening Remarks on the Concept of Dwelling." *Environment and Planning D: Society and Space* 25, no. 4 (2007): 625–647.

Heidegger, Martin. *Being and Time.* New York: Harper, 1962.

——. *Sein und Zeit.* Tübingen: Niemeyer, 1967.

Henderson, Heike. "Re-Thinking and Re-Writing Heimat: Turkish Women Writers in Germany." *Women in German Yearbook* 13 (1997): 225–243.

Herrmann, Anne. "*Heimweh,* or Homesickness." *Yale Review* 95, no. 3 (2007): 23–32.

Hoffmann, E.T.A. *Der Sandmann.* Stuttgart: Reclam, 1986.

Huttunen, Laura."'Home' and Ethnicity in the Context of War: Hesitant Diasporas of Bosnian Refugees." *European Journal of Cultural Studies* 8, no. 2 (2005): 177–195.

Israeli, Noam. "Reflections on Freud's *The Uncanny.*" *Existential Analysis: Journal of the Society for Existential Analysis* 16, no. 2 (2005): 378–389.

Joronen, Mikko. "Dwelling in the Sites of Finitude: Resisting the Violence of the Metaphysical Globe." *Antipode* 43, no. 4 (2011): 1127–1154.

Langford, Michelle. *Directory of World Cinema.* Vol. 9. *Germany.* Bristol, UK: Intellect, 2012.

Larkey, Uta. "New Places, New Identities: The (Ever) Changing Concept of Heimat." *German Politics & Society* 26, no. 2 (2008): 24–44.

Ljubic, Nicol. "Wo ist Ratko Mladic?" *Geo* 10, no. 2 (2010): 84–111.

Macklin, Debbie. "Return of the Living Dead." *Geographical* 72, no. 5 (2000): 14–21.

Massey, Doreen. "The Possibilities of a Politics of Place Beyond Place? A Conversation with Doreen Massey." Edited by Sophie Bond and David Featherstone. *Scottish Geographical Journal* 125, nos. 3–4 (2009): 401–420.

——. *Space, Place, and Gender.* Minneapolis: University of Minnesota Press, 1994.

Meljac, Eric Paul. "The Poetics of Dwelling: A Consideration of Heidegger, Kafka and Michael K." *Journal of Modern Literature* 32, no. 1 (2008): 69–76.

Pamuk, Orhan. "The Two Souls of Turkey." *New Perspectives Quarterly* 26, no. 4 (2009): 72–76.

"Pollarding." Royal Horticultural Society, November 4, 2011. http://apps.rhs.org.uk/advicesearch/profile.aspx?pid=156.

"Results for: Nostalgija." EUditc: Croatian-German Dictionary. Accessed November 29, 2012. http://www.eudict.com/?lang=croger&word=nostalgija.

"Ruža." Behind the Name: The Etymology and History of First Names. Accessed October 16, 2012. http://www.behindthename.com/name/ruz18a.

Schwartz, Doug. "Sarajevo, the Rose of Bosnia, Rises from Ruin." *Christian Science Monitor* 90, no. 12 (1997): 7.

Sick, Bastian. "Hallo, Fräulein!" SpiegelOnline, February 8, 2006. http://www.spiegel.de/kultur/zwiebelfisch/zwiebelfisch-hallo-fraeulein-a-395538.html.

Tanner, Laura E. *Lost Bodies: Inhabiting the Borders of Life and Death.* Ithaca, NY: Cornell University Press, 2006.

Warsop, Andrew. "The Ill Body and *das Unheimliche* (The Uncanny)." *Journal of Medicine and Philosophy* 36, no. 5 (2011): 484–495.

Weissberg, Jay. "Film Review: *Fraulein*" *Variety* 404, no. 2 (2006): 69–70.

Yoshimizu, Ayaka. "Chopsticks, Phone Bells and Farms: Fuyuko Taira's Diasporic Spatial Practice." *Gender, Place, and Culture: A Journal of Feminist Geography* 19, no. 3 (2012): 313- 326.

Young, Julian. "Heidegger's *Heimat.*" *International Journal of Philosophical Studies* 19, no. 2 (2011): 285–293.

Film

Das Fräulein. Directed by Andrea Staka. Dschoint Ventschr Filmproduktion AG Switzerland, 2006.

8

A Scar That Vanished

Recollections of the Inner-German Border in German Nonfiction Film

Claudia Plasse

Twenty years after German reunification, physical evidence of the border that divided the two German states has mostly disappeared. Its political and legal repercussions have likewise faded. Yet, as the dust has begun to settle over the notorious German "scar," concerns about its fall into oblivion have risen. During the past decade, documentary filmmaking in Germany has become noticeably involved in the endeavor of recollecting the physical, political, and psychological implications of the former border. My chapter explores three such documentaries, each with a distinctive approach to recalling the border past and legitimizing the perspectives they present. The 2004 film *Grenze—Lebensabschnitt Todesstreifen* (Border—Part of Our Lives, Death Zone)[1] by Holger Jancke represents a rather emotional attempt by a former East German border guard and some of his former colleagues to come to terms with their involuntary deployment at the demarcation line between East and West. More distanced and sober, the 2005 documentary *Freedom's Frontier: Traces of the Inner-German Border* (*Halt! Hier Grenze—Auf den Spuren der innerdeutschen Grenze*) by Christian Gierke tries to find physical and historical traces of the former border. And finally, deviating from more traditional documentary styles, Bartek Konopka has chosen an innovative and decisively ironic approach for his 2009 Polish-German co-production *Rabbit á la Berlin* (*Mauerhase*), which presents the former borderland from the perspective of the rabbits that inhabited it.

My analysis compares the different means through which the three films collect evidence from the past and "convert" it into filmic language. In this context, I explore the selective processes and persuasive strategies that the documentaries utilize to present the "truth." Lastly, I discuss the filmmakers' potential motivations for crafting these particular representations of the history of the inner-German border.

Visualizing the Past

At the outset, the directors of all three films faced the same challenge: their camera crews could not just go out and start to record their desired thematic subject. The 1,393-kilometer (840-mile)-long demarcation line between the two sovereign German states vanished with the collapse of the German Democratic Republic (GDR), and the consecutive accession of the five "new" *Länder* (federal states) to the Federal Republic of Germany (FRG). After the last of the once almost fifty thousand GDR border troops left their posts, more than one thousand kilometers (six hundred miles) of wire fences, over one hundred kilometers (sixty miles) of concrete walls, about six hundred watch towers, and five hundred bunkers were left for demolition.[2] As Rainer Eppelmann, a known former GDR dissident, states in his introduction to Jürgen Ritter and Peter Lapp's *Die Grenze. Ein deutsches Bauwerk*, "The dismantling of the border installations along the former inner-German demarcation line took place so thoroughly that not a single remain would have survived for future generations, if it would not have been for the various private initiatives that were committed to preserve parts of the construction."[3]

Remarkably, two of the documentaries examined here base their strategies for visualizing the past on the preservation efforts of these initiatives and the museum-like spaces they created. Most noticeably, this is accomplished in *Freedom's Frontier*, where the director Gierke composed his film without utilizing any (evident) archival footage. In fact, the documentary's narrative consists of a filmic quest for physical remnants of the former border. Beginning in Bavaria, in Germany's south, and ending at the Baltic Sea in the north, the documentary highlights ten locations along the former demarcation line where civic and private initiatives have kept small stretches of the fortifications "alive." The film is rather slow and ponderous in its visual representation of the past, capturing its evidence through long takes such as lasting pans over barbed-wire fences, slow zooms forward on watchtowers, and enduring distance shots of the picturesque landscapes that surround the fortification remnants. These long takes, uninterrupted by editing, seem particularly able to render "the real."

However, this impression is deceiving. Undoubtedly, the filmmaker renders a subjective view of the past. He presents history as an impersonal occurrence that is disconnected from individual experience. Furthermore, for Gierke, historical developments are driven by fate rather than human interference. Therefore, in his representation of the border history, he deemphasizes social power struggles and subjective experiences. Instead, he stresses the importance of physical locations. He conveys his argument with carefully selected filmic means. Images of looming watchtowers, seemingly endless fences, and picture-perfect landscapes that are deprived of any signs of human existence are a reoccurring theme in the documentary. Historian Charles Maier has termed this focus on physical locations as "geography as destiny,"[4] a paradigm central to conservative German historiography. According to its perceptions, historical processes are determined by "geographic situation" rather than "social structures."[5] The latter concept, in turn, has been pivotal to historians who oppose the conservative point of view and who focus on interplays between societal groups as a driving force of history.[6] By adhering to the paradigm of geographic destiny, Gierke explains the division of Germany being a result of the country's location rather than the product of any rational human act. In addition, the filmmaker only hesitantly points to Germany's Nazi past. It takes until almost the end of the documentary, when the narrator mentions that Hitler's aggressive military strategies started the Second World War.

Symbolism also plays an essential role in Gierke's film. The powerful exposure of the border's bare remnants is designed to signify history's cruelty and far-reaching impact. The narration supplies a dramatic undertone: "Where in former times the middle of Germany had been, now the end of the world was established."[7] The border's eventual erasure and East Germans' consequent freedom are also symbolized by static objects, disconnected from their human origin—a long pan over a wire fence reveals a discarded Coca-Cola can (which is meant to be a symbol for American freedom) that rests at the fence's bottom.

By primarily relying on artifacts' ability to speak truth about the past, Gierke seeks to discredit human accounts of history as untrustworthy. This intention becomes even more apparent when it is supported by statements from interviewees in the film. Berthold Dücker, a representative of the memorial site Point Alpha (a civil initiative that is located at the former frontier line between the German *Bundesländer* Hesse and Thuringia), underlines the significance of museums as authentic locations for remembrance and understanding. At the same time, he dismisses the value of public memory for historical insights by criticizing its tendency to create nostalgic transfigurations of the truth. Nonetheless, he claims his own right to interpret the past. Thus, Dücker's assertion, although intended to bolster the filmmaker's strategy, actually results in the opposite, revealing a central problem of Gierke's approach: the filmmaker wants to devalue human interpretations of history yet he seeks to persuade his audience of his own point of view.

The documentary *Grenze—Lebensabschnitt Todesstreifen* also attempts to recollect the past through depictions of surviving sites of border history. Director Jancke, who served as a GDR border guard, bases his film's narrative on an arranged reunion with some of his former colleagues. Together, they revisit the places where they completed their compulsory army service. The barracks in which the guards first had been trained are among these locations. Now, the former army buildings are used as temporary housing for foreign nationals who seek asylum in Germany. Jancke depicts the location with its new inhabitants, intertwining evidence of present and past actualities. The film displays the sober surroundings of the facility and its run-down condition with a variety of shots, as the former guards walk through hallways and enter rooms. In their quest for the past, the men cross paths with the asylum seekers. This encounter appears accidental, but perhaps is not. As former border guards and current border penetrators meet, it becomes evident that only one frontier has disappeared while others still exist and that all borders create hardship. Nevertheless, the asylum seekers remain as silent witnesses in Jancke's film while it maintains its focus on its protagonists.

Following the former guards' sequence of deployment, the film's next location is the stretch of prior borderland that the five soldiers once had been assigned to protect. Here, watch towers and fences also have been preserved through a civil initiative. Jancke depicts his friends climbing up to the towers, sitting inside their small watch areas, and peeking through the dusty windows at the former death zone. It has turned into a serene countryside scene now, exhibiting stretches of meadows that are lined with trees. But in order to highlight the remarkable contrast between present and past actualities, the filmmaker focuses on the protagonists. The emotional expressions of the former guards (in both their testimonies and body language) reveal the location's problematic history. Only occasionally, Jancke displays remains of the former border fortification. They mainly serve to establish the authenticity of the surroundings—and, more importantly, the authenticity of the memories that they trigger in the former guards. To further support his claim of portraying the truth, the filmmaker also includes in the documentary photos of himself and his youthful brothers-in-arms from his personal archives. Although Jancke uses these old images to create connections between the present and the past, the private and intimate character of the photos highlights the documentary's emphasis on the individual as a force in history. By shining a spotlight on the human element and social structures, Jancke's approach stands in sharp contrast with that of filmmaker Gierke.

Bartek Konopka's *Rabbit á la Berlin* also stresses societal factors in the construction of history, yet differs in significant ways from the other two documentaries. Konopka rarely uses images of fortification remains to reflect on the past. Instead, he draws on archival material to construct a unique story about rabbits that become trapped in the no-man's-land between the two walls of Berlin's border fortification.[8]

Konopka portrays historic events in the divided city exclusively from the perspective of the rabbits. Chased away by humans from parks and backyards in postwar Berlin, the rabbits eventually find refuge in the small stretch of land between East and West. Unharmed by Cold War power plays, in fact protected by them, the critters begin to flourish in their unusual habitat. Konopka portrays their fate in conjunction with major developments at the border. However, he keeps the specific histories of humans and rabbits as two separate narrative lines. This strategy is evident by the type and content of archival material that he employs. On the one hand, the filmmaker uses historical footage from established, traditional archives, including both well-known and little-known images of Berlin's border history from 1945 to 1989.[9] On the other hand, Konopka presents filmic images of rabbits, which display them roaming on meadows and resting in holes in a variety of shots. These images mostly appear arbitrary with regard to their location as they miss any indications that would link them to a specific site. Since Konopka has explained that he only produced "a few shots, like four or five in the whole film"[10] by himself, it must be concluded that most, if not all, of the rabbit footage stems from other private or public sources.[11] The rabbit scenes are cast in black and white, altered from their original colored version to enhance their status as historical documents. However, Konopka's partially fabricated representation of the historical past does not mean that the rabbits in his film lack a historical referent. Seemingly, bunnies have existed on the grasslands between the border fortifications. In fact, Konopka presents one photographic image in his film that shows an encounter between a soldier and a rabbit on border territory. The occurrence of border bunnies is also mentioned in the German documentary *Walled In! What the Cold War Frontier That Divided Germany Was Really Like* (*"Eingemauert!" Die innerdeutsche Grenze*, 2009).[12] Since Konopka's rabbits have a historical referent, the film should be distinguished from so-called mockumentaries. In these false documentaries, the subjects mostly do not refer to actual historical beings.[13] Rather, *Mauerhase* resembles those documentaries that have employed (professional) performers to reenact occurrences in the historical world (to which the films for different reasons had no access) and convey assumed experiences of authentic subjects.[14] However, Konopka's reenactments (of border rabbits' lives) are distinct. They are not created by the filmmaker's own recording but by the use and reorganization of already existing images. Furthermore, *Rabbit á la Berlin* with its main focus on animals differs from the human-centered approach of other, unconventional documentaries.

To indicate the separate "habitats" of humans and rabbits, and the parallelism of the events in both spheres, Konopka mostly utilizes the editing technique of parallel montage throughout the film. He selects single shots and sequences from his pool of archival images and arranges them into a new structure that accords with his film's narrative. However, as Michael Renov has discussed, the process of montage as a procedure of "plucking and recontextualizing profilmic elements"[15] calls into question its ability to represent the truth. In the case of Konopka's documentary, the problem of manipulation through montage is particularly evident, due to the arbitrary relationship of his source material. Rabbits, presumably taken from one or the other kind of nature film, and humans, plucked from archival material that carries "society's memory,"[16] are bound to meet each other for narrative purposes. The filmmaker's emphasis on the montage technique could perhaps be criticized in the same way in which André Bazin has targeted works of Russian formalism: "The final significance of the film was found to reside in the ordering of these elements much more than in their objective content."[17] Yet it also appears likely that Konopka chose his documentary's approach to question society's reliance on its "storage spaces of memory" and its belief in the ability of nonfiction film to represent the historic truth.[18]

Commentaries, Experts, and Witnesses

Certainly, the three documentaries cannot solely rely on the portrayal of physical evidence to recollect the existence of the former inner-German border. Its social, psychological, and emotional repercussions continue even though the physical manifestation of the border has vanished. After all, the frontier not only divided territory but it also divided people who belonged to one nation. For the majority of GDR citizens, the existence of the highly fortified border also meant that they were imprisoned in their state and the socialist system. Over one thousand people were killed while trying to escape or seeking to assist refugees.[19] Due to the horrific events at the border, it received its notorious label *Todesstreifen*—death zone. Many victims died after stepping on land mines or after triggering one of the automatic firing devices that were mounted to the fences. Others were shot or left to die by GDR border guards who, as Corey Ross points out, "were told to fire on would-be escapists since 1958."[20] To recall the border in this broader context, all three documentaries mainly rely on oral sources of information; all utilize voice-over commentary, yet in distinctive ways.

In *Grenze—Lebensabschnitt Todesstreifen*, director Jancke narrates the film from a first-person perspective. Although he does not appear on the screen for the most part, Jancke uses his commentary to express his personal connection to the documentary's topic. In so doing, he clearly signals the film's bias. In stark contrast, filmmaker Gierke strives hard to express seemingly unbiased views on the history of the border and its effects in his *Freedom's Frontier*. He chooses a dark-voiced narrator who slowly and pompously recites historical facts that appear indisputable. The mode of narration clearly reminds viewers of "that 'detached, authoritarian male voice'"[21] that has been the trademark of many televised historical documentaries.[22] Conversely, the soothing voice of the female narrator in *Rabbit á la Berlin* evokes the impression of a fairy tale being told, rather than an account of reality. Filmmaker Konopka clearly has revealed his intention to conquer new ground in documentary production. In an interview with the International Documentary Association, he noted, "[N]obody had done this kind of documentary before. We had to invent this fairy tale-allegory-docu genre, and it had to find its own language."[23] Certainly, Konopka's claim is a little bit misleading. *Rabbit á la Berlin*, as mentioned earlier, is not the first documentary that relies heavily on techniques of fictional genres. Yet, perhaps the director's assertion reflects his belief in the inseparable bond between nonfictional and fictional representations.[24] Part of Konopka's specific language is the importance of voice-over commentary. In its third-person perspective, it functions as an explanatory link between the two storylines of the film and also as an interpreter of the rabbits' experience of border history.

Each of the films also relies on experts and witnesses, as well as other major sources of oral testimony. As Alan Rosenthal notes, "[T]he use of witnesses is one of the key methods for bringing visual histories alive," yet he also reminds us "how manipulative this process can be."[25] All three films prove him to be right, and they apply their strategies with varying degrees of transparency. Predictably, *Freedom's Frontier*, with its rather authoritative approach and unwillingness to rely on everyday accounts of history, presents its oral testimony through experts rather than "ordinary" witnesses. Director Gierke chose four major representatives of border museums to explain the history of their sites and of the border in general. By stressing the interviewees' official function, the filmmaker attempts to establish their "unbiased" expert position. At the same time, Gierke conceals his interviewees' potential for providing accounts of personal experience. For instance, interviewee Berthold Dücker only speaks in his function as representative of the memorial site Point Alpha. However, his personal history as a GDR escapee who crossed the border by cutting through the wire fence, and who lived separated from parts of his family for many years,[26] is not revealed in the film. Also not disclosed is Dücker's close relationship to Germany's conservative Christian Democratic Party,[27] whose actions in support of border remembrance are mentioned in the film, while other interest groups' efforts are not addressed. Similarly, the other interviewees also are exclusively presented in their expert roles, although they, too, possess worthy individual experiences (and, in one case, an undisclosed affiliation with the conservative party).[28] Gierke seeks to highlight the "objectivity" (and consequently the credibility) of his film's content by avoiding accounts of oral history and concealing his interviewees' subjective position. In looking at viewers' responses to Gierke's film, his strategy seems to work. One schoolteacher states, "Finally, once again a real documentation that one also can show in the classroom without any problems! . . . The students . . . learn facts: 'this' is how it was at this border. . . . One does not get distracted by eyewitnesses who always attempt to remember something that one can believe or not."[29]

In contrast, eyewitness accounts stand at the center of Jancke's documentary about the former guards revisiting their pasts. At the beginning of the film, one of the protagonists reads a personal statement that relates his memory of pledging allegiance to the GDR army. The mocking tone of the recital and its unconcealed criticism of the event indicate the film's argumentative direction and its carefully constructed rhetoric: the former guards attempt to refute public accusations of the soldiers' unquestioning, absolute loyalty to their state. Some of the film's personal accounts, however, are less transparent. Just a few scenes further into the film, Jancke outlines the difficulties he encountered reuniting his former colleagues: "When I started after sixteen years to research for this film and to contact the former soldiers, one of them threatens to hire a lawyer; another one wants to avoid the camera because he is a civil servant now. Yet Boja, Lohengrin, Mückfried and LSD-Wölfi [former nicknames of his friends] agree to come."[30] By highlighting these problems, the filmmaker not only points to the delicacy of his documentary's topic but also, implicitly, claims that his main witnesses, that is, the ones who have agreed to come have nothing to hide. Thus, they are presented as trustworthy. Rosenthal argues that documentaries mainly create such a "framework . . . to bring the witnesses within the audience's sympathies so that their stories will be believed."[31] While Gierke, in *Freedom's Frontier*, attempts to convince his audience with an authoritative, experts-based approach, *Grenze—Lebensabschnitt Todesstreifen* tries to win over its viewers through the personal testimonies of "credible," ordinary people who have lived the experience.

In their accounts, the former guards allude to their "victimization" by the GDR's totalitarian system. They also try to highlight the absurdity of the East German state, which was founded on a socialist ideology, that is, to establish the rule of the working class. As Jancke explains in his narration, the regime's propaganda claimed that the soldiers who protected the border were the "guards of the proletariat."[32] Yet, by socialist definition, the soldiers were also members of the working class. Thus, they protected their own alleged rule and, ironically, at the same time fell victim to it (according to Jancke's accounts). The filmmaker asserts that he and his former colleagues were ordered to serve as border guards by the GDR authorities and had little choice other than to obey the order. "We were told [by the hated officers] that we have to protect the Western border of the socialist camp against any attack with all means. We avoided listening, if somehow we were not already falling asleep from exhaustion. Let these idiots talk."[33] As the testimonies convey, the protagonists were well aware of the fact that they mainly had to defend the demarcation line from people who tried to cross it from the inside (i.e., GDR citizens), rather than to protect it from the officially alleged "attacks" from the capitalist West.

Apparently, the young soldiers' "worst fear"[34] came true when they encountered a man who crossed the border while they were on duty. Jancke managed to find this prior escapee and to interview him for the documentary. The man, whose name is not revealed in the film, states that his dissatisfaction with the supply of consumer goods in the GDR led to his decision to flee the state. Yet, he emphasizes that West Germany was also a disappointing experience for him and that he returned to his former home as soon as the border had disappeared.

The documentary's presentation of this witness as "the sole authority for the facts"[35] further highlights the filmmaker's political agenda. It implies that the exhibited escapee is the *typical* escapee, with *typical* motives and *typical* negative experiences of life in the West. Rosenthal argues that "the *choice* [his emphasis] of witness can be crucial where history is in dispute."[36] Several scholars have also pointed out that history is in dispute when it comes to the question of the GDR border guards' accountability for the atrocities committed at the border. *Grenze-Lebensabschnitt Todesstreifen* enters that debate in order to question, if not downplay, the former guards' responsibility by depicting them as innocent victims and exposing attempts at escape as ultimately not having been worth the risk. At the same time, the film's narrative emphasizes the man's attempt to cross the border as the highlight of its dramatic arc. This strategy not only contradicts the documentary's attempt to downplay border-crossing incidents, but it also suggests that in order to appeal to audiences, a film about border guards needs a border violation as an ultimate element of suspense. In this regard, Jancke exploits acts of human tragedy to sensationalize his film.

Similarly, in *Rabbit á la Berlin*, Konopka also utilizes tragic events at the frontier to heighten his film's appeal. However, this documentary largely raises eyebrows by vigorously challenging conventional notions of documentary filmmaking. The film's appeal lies in its interlude between the alienation and the fascination of its viewers. The documentary deliberately creates discomfort with its format and content, yet dismisses concerns about the factuality of its representations at the same time. A set of experts and eyewitnesses addresses the living conditions of the border rabbits and thus confirms their existence. The statements make up for part of the film's questionable visual authenticity. Moreover, by focusing on the unique habitat of rabbits on border territory, the statements are informative. However, for the audience, it is disorienting to witness accounts of border history that only address the fate of animals.

The irony of the film's narrative becomes particularly evident when both a former GDR border guard and a former West Berlin hunter insist that nobody, on either side of the frontier, was eager to fire on the rabbits. According to these testimonies, any unnecessary shot at the border could have caused a major international disturbance. Shortly after these statements are made, the images of lifeless human bodies, carried away by GDR guards, appear on the screen. Yet these horrific scenes, and the fates of the humans displayed in them, are not addressed. Rather, an expert zoologist asserts that the rabbits "were not really caring about the human refugees that occasionally passed them by on the death zone, and that these people did not influence the rabbits' ideological perceptions."[37] Through the use of this profound irony, Konopka, in a Brechtian way, attempts to prevent his film's audience from engaging in an act of uncritical reception. He intends to call his viewers' attention to analogies between the critters and their human counterparts, both submissive to an oppressive political regime. As Konopka underscores, the rabbits symbolize the majority of the people behind the Iron Curtain:

> This was for me like a mission to speak on behalf of the rabbits-people of the world. I mean those people who want to have a simple life and want to have at least some area of fresh grass. What is most important about this film for me is that it is mostly about people from Poland, the Czech Republic, and from East Germany, people who lived in a system which was very oppressive and pushed them in such a role.[38]

However, *Rabbit á la Berlin* is not only an allegory about the illusion of freedom but also an avenue through which to clarify the absurdities of social life. At one point in the film, the narrator claims that the rabbits seem to have accepted their entrapment. The soothing female voice suggests that they, perhaps, have acknowledged their imprisonment as a measure designed to keep them safe from predators. This notion recalls the rhetoric of the GDR government, which tried to justify the enforced imprisonment of its citizens as protection against malicious influences from the West (socialist authorities termed the Berlin Wall an "antifascist protection wall").[39] Also, at the end of the documentary, when the border is opened and the rabbits gain freedom, they struggle to adapt to their new, free, but often hostile surroundings, just as many East Germans had difficulties adapting to Western conditions and prejudices. It is obvious that Konopka's rabbits have famous "predecessors" in literary dystopias like George Orwell's *Animal Farm* (1954) and Richard Adams's *Watership Down* (1974).

All three documentaries display a distinct way of recollecting the history of the inner-German border, and all three filmmakers seek to persuade their audiences of the "truths" of their concepts and messages. Each of the directors has created a distinct filmic rhetoric, with which they attempt, as Spence and Navarro put it, "to mold the reality we see on the screen."[40] Part of that persuasive strategy, of course, is the nonfiction film format itself, with its reputation for authenticity. In *Freedom's Frontier* and *Grenze—Lebensabschnitt Todesstreifen*, the respective directors, Gierke and Jancke, have utilized similar approaches to recall the existence of the border in its physicality, but the two differ greatly in their perception of its history. Gierke intends to convey an authoritative conceptualization of border history, distant from everyday human experience and interference. Hence, he avoids personal accounts of history, regarding them as unreliable and unable to render historic truth. Assumedly, with this strategy, Gierke attempts to counteract the trend of *Ostalgie*[41] in Germany, which tends to emphasize the more positive aspects of everyday life in former East Germany while downplaying the oppressive character of the state. In contrast, Jancke highlights the "human side" of history and the ability of eyewitnesses to evaluate the past in significant ways. He uses a corresponding strategy in his film to refute the widely held perception of GDR border guards as perpetrators and murderers. With *Rabbit á la Berlin*, Konopka forces his audience to critically engage with culturally common strategies for accessing knowledge about the past, encouraging his film's viewers to reexamine their acquired interpretations of history. By attempting to carefully and creatively construct a credible truth about the history of the inner-German border, all three documentaries seek not only to encourage its remembrance but also to influence the way it will be remembered.

Notes

1. My translation since the film offers no English title.
2. For a detailed list and description of all installations and constructions of the GDR border protection system, refer to Jürgen Ritter and Peter Joachim Lapp, *Die Grenze: Ein deutsches Bauwerk* (Berlin: Ch. Links Verlag, 2009), 100–116, 196–197; the minefields were removed by the GDR in 1985, and the automatic firing devices were dismantled by the GDR in 1984.

3. Ritter and Lapp, *Die Grenze*, 10 (my translation). At many former border locations the landscape changed so drastically that for an onlooker today, it is hard to believe a monstrous line of fortification ever has existed here before. Ritter and Lapp offer an array of photos that depict the same geographic locations once when the border was still in place and once after its removal.

4. Charles S. Maier, *The Unmasterable Past: History, Holocaust, and German National Identity* (Cambridge, MA: Harvard University Press, 1988), 115.

5. Maier, *Unmasterable Past*, 115.

6. Particularly in chapter 4 of *The Unmasterable Past* (100–120), Maier explains the two rivaling concepts of German historiography, their respective origins, and their influences on and interactions with contemporary and consecutive scholarly research and engagement.

7. Christian Gierke, *Freedom's Frontier: Traces of the Inner-German Border* (my translation).

8. The Berlin Wall actually consisted of a system of two parallel walls that created a no-man's-land in between. GDR border guards patrolled this no man's land since it was perceived to belong to the GDR's fortified borderline.

9. West Berlin was a West German enclave within the GDR. It was enclosed by a 155-kilometer-long (about 100 miles) ring of border fortifications that mostly consisted of concrete walls.

10. Bartek Konopka, "Interview with Bartek Konopka," Visions du Réel, accessed February 8, 2012, http://www.art-tv.ch/3823-0-Visions-du-Rel-Rabbit-la-Berlin.html.

11. Jeannette Catsoulis claims in her *New York Times* article that some of the film's footage depicting the rabbits was taken from YouTube. See Jeannette Catsoulis, "Out of Paradise and into the Pot: A Post-Communism Parable," *New York Times*, December 8, 2010, C5(L).

12. The film that is produced by the German public broadcaster *Deutsche Welle* is entirely computer animated. Therefore, it also does not show images of actual border rabbits.

13. Examples of classic, obviously constructed mockumentaries include Woody Allen's film *Zelig* (1983) and Christopher Guest's *Best in Show* (2000), while faux documentaries include films such as Peter Delpeut's *Forbidden Quest* (1993), which also utilizes archival footage to support a fictional narrative.

14. An example of this type of documentary is Errol Morris's film *The Thin Blue Line* (1988). By using provocative new approaches (such as employing professional actors and omitting archival footage), some filmmakers have openly questioned conventional styles of documentary. The latter frequently are associated with generic, unimaginative, and impersonal accounts of history. For instance, Bill Nichols claims in this context, "By avoiding reenactments, the use of interviews to recount events together with archival footage . . . avoids the problem of a 'body too many,' where actors double for historical figures. . . . Instead, historical documentaries that rely on archival footage are faced with a 'body too few,' lacking both actors and the historical figure." Bill Nichols, "'Getting to Know You . . .': Knowledge, Power, and the Body," in *Theorizing Documentary*, ed. Micheal Renov (New York and London: Routledge, 1993), 177.

15. Quoted in Stella Bruzzi, *New Documentary: A Critical Introduction* (London: Routledge, 2006), 3.

16. Michael Chanan, *The Politics of Documentary* (London: British Film Institute, 2007), 257.

17. André Bazin, "The Evolution of the Language of Cinema," in *Film Theory and Criticism: Introductory Readings*, ed. Leo Braudy and Marshall Cohen (Oxford: Oxford University Press, 2009), 44.

18. Chanan, *Politics of Documentary*, 257.

19. Ritter and Lapp, *Die Grenze*, 199.

20. Corey Ross, *The East German Dictatorship: Problems and Perspectives in the Interpretation of the GDR* (London: Arnold, 2002), 193. Ironically, but not surprisingly, the most famous border victim has become the last one, Chris Gueffroy, who was shot by GDR border guards in 1989. Gueffroy's case led to the first trial of border fatalities that was initialized after German unification. The trials of former border guards were accompanied by heated debates in Germany because the soldiers were prosecuted without first evaluating their superiors' legal accountability. For the case of Chris Gueffroy and the border guard trials refer to Ross, *East German Dictatorship*, 194–195; Ritter and Lapp, *Die Grenze*, 96–97.

21. Jeffrey Youdelman, "Narration, Invention, and History," in *New Challenges for Documentary*, ed. Alan Rosenthal and John Corner (Manchester: Manchester University Press, 2005), 397.

22. Youdelman, "Narration, Invention, and History," 397. In this context, Youdelman refers to the U.S. newsreel series *The March of Time* that was shown in movie theaters from 1935 to 1951. A further example is the British television series *The World at War* that was shown in 1973–1974. More recently, the U.S. documentary filmmaker Ken Burns has produced several TV documentaries focusing on history (including the 2007 television series *The War*) that feature this specific type of narration.

23. Thomas White, "Meet the Filmmakers: Bartek Konopka—*Rabbit á la Berlin*," Documentary.og, accessed October 25, 2012, http://www.documentary.org/content/meet-filmmakers-bartek-konopka-rabbit-a-la-berlin.

24. With regard to this interconnection, Michael Renov stresses that "in a number of ways fictional and nonfictional forms are enmeshed in one another—particularly regarding semiotics, narrativity, and questions of performance." Michael Renov, "Introduction: The Truth about Non-Fiction," in *Theorizing Documentary*, ed. Micheal Renov (New York: Routledge, 1993), 2.

25. Allen Rosenthal, ed., *New Challenges for Documentary* (Berkeley: University of California Press, 1988), 428.

261. "Curriculum Vitae: Berthold Dücker," Konrad-Adenauer-Stiftung, accessed February 14, 2012, http://www.kas.de/upload/dokumente/2009/06/Duecker.pdf.

27. "Curriculum Vitae: Berthold Dücker."

28. The interview partner Arnd Schaffner not only served as a founder and representative of the *Deutsch-deutsches Museum Mödlareuth* (German-German Museum Mödlareuth; my translation), but also was a (West German) photographer and documentary filmmaker who spent a lot of his lifetime collecting visual evidence of

border history (Schaffner died in 2007). The expert of the *Grenzlandmuseum Eichsfeld* (Borderland Museum Eichsfeld; my translation), Wolfgang Nolte, also has served for consecutive terms as the Christian Democratic Party's mayor of Duderstadt, a major town in the Eichsfeld region. In contrast, Dr. Frank Stucke, the director of the memorial site *Gedenkstätte Deutsche Teilung Marienborn* (Memorial Site German Marienborn; my translation) was born and educated in the GDR.

29. Angelo [pseud.], "Kommentare zur DVD 'Halt hier Grenze,'" *Forum DDR Grenze* (blog), October 13, 2008, accessed May 7, 2011, http://www.forum-ddr-grenze.de/t240f53-Halt-Hier-Grenze-Auf-den-Spuren-der-innerdeutschen-Grenze.html [my translation].

30. Holger Jancke, *Grenze—Lebensabschnitt Todesstreifen* (my translation).

31. Jancke, *Grenze.*

32. Jancke, *Grenze.*

33. Jancke, *Grenze.*

34. Jancke, *Grenze.*

35. Rosenthal, *New Challenges*, 429.

36. Rosenthal, *New Challenges*, 429.

37. Bartek Konopka, *Rabbit á la Berlin* (my translation).

38. Konopka, "Interview."

39. Ritter and Lapp point out that the GDR authorities tried to legitimize the installment of border fortifications "as protection against the class enemy in the West and potential attacks from the outside." However, the authors emphasize that from the beginning, the real reason for erecting the border was the number of people fleeing from East Germany's socialist system (Ritter and Lapp, *Die Grenze*, 30 [my translation]). Ross explains that in the GDR "the uprising of 17 June [1953] was officially denigrated as a 'fascist putsch attempt'" and that "anti-fascism served to legitimize a range of repressive measures" which included fortifying the (Berlin) demarcation line "against Western revanchism" (Ross, *East German Dictatorship*, 179).

40. Louise Spence and Vinicius Navarro, *Crafting Truth. Documentary Form and Meaning* (New Brunswick, NJ: Rutgers University Press, 2011), 143.

41. The term *Ostalgie* (ostalgia) refers to nostalgic memories of the GDR.

Works Cited

Angelo [pseud.]. "Kommentare zur DVD 'Halt hier Grenze.'" *Forum DDR Grenze* (blog), October 13, 2008. Accessed May 7, 2011. http://www.forum-ddr-grenze.de/t240f53-Halt-Hier-Grenze-Auf-den-Spuren-der-innerdeutschen-Grenze.html.

Bazin. André. "The Evolution of the Language of Cinema." In *Film Theory and Criticism: Introductory Readings*, edited by Leo Braudy and Marshall Cohen, 41–53. Oxford: Oxford University Press, 2009.

Bruzzi, Stella. *New Documentary: A Critical Introduction*. London: Routledge, 2006.

Catsoulis, Jeanette. "Out of Paradise and into the Pot: A Post-Communism Parable." *New York Times*, December 8, 2010, C5(L).

Chanan, Michael. *The Politics of Documentary*. London: British Film Institute, 2007.

"Curriculum Vitae: Berthold Dücker." Konrad-Adenauer-Stiftung. Accessed February 14, 2012. http://www.kas.de/upload/dokumente/2009/06/Duecker.pdf.

Konopka, Bartek. "Interview with Bartek Konopka." Visions du Réel. Accessed February 8, 2012. http://www.art-tv.ch/3823-0-Visions-du-Rel-Rabbit-la-Berlin.html.

Maier, Charles S. *The Unmasterable Past: History, Holocaust, and German National Identity*. Cambridge, MA: Harvard University Press, 1988.

Nichols, Bill. "'Getting to Know You . . .': Knowledge, Power, and the Body." In *Theorizing Documentary*, edited by Micheal Renov, 174–191. New York: Routledge, 1993.

Renov, Michael. "Introduction: The Truth about Non-Fiction." In *Theorizing Documentary*, edited by Micheal Renov, 1–11. New York: Routledge, 1993.

Ritter, Jürgen, and Peter Joachim Lapp. *Die Grenze: Ein deutsches Bauwerk*. Berlin: Ch. Links Verlag, 2009.

Rosenthal, Allen, ed. *New Challenges for Documentary*. Berkeley: University of California Press, 1988.

Ross, Corey. *The East German Dictatorship: Problems and Perspectives in the Interpretation of the GDR*. London: Arnold, 2002.

Spence, Louise, and Vinicius Navarro. *Crafting Truth: Documentary Form and Meaning*. New Brunswick, NJ: Rutgers University Press, 2011.

White, Thomas. "Meet the Filmmakers: Bartek Konopka—*Rabbit á la Berlin*." Documentary.org. Accessed October 25, 2012. http://www.documentary.org/content/meet-filmmakers-bartek-konopka-rabbit-a-la-berlin.

Youdelman, Jeffrey. "Narration, Invention, and History." In *New Challenges for Documentary*, edited by Alan Rosenthal and John Corner, 397–408. Manchester: Manchester University Press, 2005.

Films

Freedom's Frontier: Traces of the Inner-German Border (*Halt! Hier Grenze—Auf den Spuren der innerdeutschen Grenze*). Directed by Christian Gierke. Germany, 2005.

Grenze—Lebensabschnitt Todesstreifen. Directed by Holger Jancke. Germany, 2004.

Rabbit á la Berlin (*Mauerhase*). Directed by Bartek Konopka. Germany, Poland, 2009.

Walled In! What the Cold War Frontier That Divided Germany Was Really Like ("*Eingemauert!*" *Die innerdeutsche Grenze*). Produced by Deutsche Welle. Germany, 2009.

9

The Use of Music in Turkish-German Diasporic Cinema

Ayça Tunç Cox

THE CONCEPTS OF DIASPORA and diasporic cinema are highly contested. While terminology varies when it comes to the definition of diasporic cinema—*cinema of transvergence*, *accented cinema*, *interstitial cinema*, *cinema of displacement*, *intercultural cinema*, and so on—there are certain characteristics of this cinema that are discernible regardless of the label used. In brief, diasporic cinema is a cinema of multiple allegiances and affiliations.[1] It is a cinema located across subnational and transnational levels, foregrounding transnational mobility and perpetual interconnectedness. Consequently, it is hybrid in character and aesthetics, drawing on, first and foremost, the cinematic traditions of homeland and hostland, but also on a larger, widely available universal language of cinema. It is a cinema that privileges places of transit and nonspaces as the projections of diasporic experience. It focuses on language as one of the signifiers of identity. It can be market oriented, commercial, or marginal, and so it comprises a wide range of films from the socially conscious to the celebratory that highlight the delights of hybrid existence. Yet, either way, it is a cinema that is politically engaged. It is interstitial in the sense that it operates in between. It is mostly seen as the means of self-representation for long-silenced diasporic subjects and, therefore, is considered autoethnographic and accented.

The term *diaspora* has almost always had negative connotations, grounded in the Jewish diasporic experience as the "ideal type." Correspondingly, diaspora is primarily identified with pain and trauma: displacement, landlessness, alienation, and the loss of homeland, of the sense of security, and of power. Inasmuch as the concept of diaspora is traditionally associated with a sense of loss and an accompanying longing for the homeland, diasporic subjects are often assumed to suffer from homesickness and "nostalgia," which, simply put, is "a longing for a home that no longer exists or has never existed. Nostalgia is a sentiment of loss and displacement."[2] Svetlana Boym argues, "[T]he nostalgic had an amazing capacity for remembering sensations, tastes, sounds, smells, the minutiae and trivia of the lost paradise that those who remained home never noticed. Gastronomic and auditory nostalgia [are] of particular importance."[3] In this respect, one would expect all diasporic films to be fraught with cinematic images of nostalgia, juxtaposing idealized images of homeland culture and customs with the unpleasant everyday routines of the hostland through dreams, flashbacks, and various other narrative techniques—all set to a nostalgic deployment of music or soundtrack.

As much as music is regarded as a universal language, it is also considered to be strongly related to one's social and cultural identity.[4] When music is shared, "the experience becomes public, shared and exterior. Such a reification of feeling and sensation, in turn, endows musical sound with a social existence coded as identity (our music) and shared associations."[5] This is not to assert an essentialist understanding of music in relation to identity, but to underscore that as a means of communication, "music is a peculiar lens into cultural identity. Its focal length, together with other ethnographic and ethnologic elements, provides a context for lived experiences, generational relationships, and moreover, it reflects and catalyzes the dynamics of political and economic environments."[6] Moreover, in the context of diasporas, "music can bond displaced peoples, effectively bridging the geographic distance between them and providing a shared sense of collective identity articulated by a symbolic sense of community."[7] Yet, when used appropriately, it might also go beyond simply reflecting individuals and their cultural associations, and function as a powerful tool to shape or challenge identities and form relationships between disparate cultures, as seen in some diasporic films.

Before moving onto the discussion of the use of music in Turkish-German diasporic films, it is useful to consider why this particular cinema was chosen for analysis.[8] Turks have settled in Germany for five decades now and have partaken in the political, cultural, and social institutions of the host society. Turkish men were invited to Germany as guest workers and were expected to stay only temporarily. By the time they changed their status from guest workers to claimants for citizenship as members of a permanently settled community, second and third generations with different cultural, social, educational demands and expectations from their parents had taken over. These young people were not workers anymore. A Turkish middle class was slowly emerging. They attended German schools and pursued higher education in order to cultivate careers in diverse occupational areas, much as any German citizen might. Thus, the "contemporary Turkish diaspora can no longer be simply considered temporary migrant community who lives with the 'myth of return' or passive victims of global capitalism who are alienated by the system. They have rather become permanent settlers, active social agents and decision-makers."[9] The Turkish-German population now constitutes a significant force in the social and cultural life of Germany, as in the case of filmmakers, who have undoubtedly changed the face of German national cinema. They have been prolific, especially during the past two decades, and their films have garnered critical acclaim and awards, both nationally and internationally. Therefore, Turkish-German cinema has been chosen here as a representative example of contemporary diasporic cinema in Europe, since it has proved to be one of the most prominent and successful ones.

While the pioneering filmmakers of the second generation of Turkish immigrants functioned as cultural mediators between their predecessors and those who came after, the third, and latest, generation of Turkish-descent filmmakers in Germany represent increasing layers of cultural difference. They are primarily German citizens who were born and raised in Germany, and thus, the entirety of their socialization process was in the German education system. Not only does the third generation have the opportunity for total integration, they are also very likely to remember the migration process via "prosthetic memory"—a received, mediated relationship with the past, rather than direct experience or "postmemory" of the second generation—determining their particular perception of the events and shaping their self-consciousness and self-representation.[10]

These diasporic subjects do not form a single entity, but rather, constitute a diverse, heterogeneous, and multilayered demographic that cuts across various dynamics and components such as gender, class, religion, politics, and generation. Accordingly, the role of nostalgia in the formation and definition of diasporic subjectivity can be expected to undergo a transformation across generations, since "affective cultural memories diverge between social constituencies and even between generations in accordance with the different pasts to which they are able to connect the present."[11] How does this, then, affect the use of music in diasporic films? How do the second and third generations of Turkish-German filmmakers register nostalgia and cross borders between generations, cultures, and musical styles?

Changing Music Scene: Toward Reflective Nostalgia

It is possible to argue that second-generation Turkish-German cinema largely serves as a platform to showcase the idiosyncratic music style and preference of this generation, as well. In this context, the transnationality of diasporic cinema is reinforced with the global characteristics of the music these filmmakers use.

The memorable staged shot of Istanbul in Fatih Akin's award-winning film *Head-On* (*Gegen die Wand*, 2004) is one such example. In this scene, a group playing Turkish *fasıl*, or Ottoman, music—with musicians (the renowned clarinet virtuoso Selim Şeşler and his orchestra) dressed in black suits while the female singer (İdil Üner) in front of them wears a red dress—performs a song by the Golden Horn, in between two continents, with a well-defined mosque behind. As Sujana Moorti observes, this type of visual grammar makes the self-expression of diasporic subjects possible, working as a visual interpretation of reflective nostalgia—looking constantly at different worlds and moving in different directions simultaneously—expressing both the duality of diasporic subjects and the character of diasporic films.[12] Here, music is directly implicated in that duality, as the band, poised between continents and traditions, draws simultaneously on East and West, tradition and modernity.

The postcard-like image just described opens the film and is used as a transition scene that recurs several times throughout an otherwise linear narrative, in order to create connections between sequences. It also reveals a sense of nostalgia, since the *fasıl* band players and the singer, along with the mise-en-scène, seem to belong to a rusty, forgotten, but still captivating past—a utopian image of "the homeland that is uncontaminated by contemporary facts"—even though the rest of the scenes set in Istanbul do not create

Figure 9.1. Between two continents: a song by the Golden Horn in *Head-On* by Fatih Akin. *Head-On* (Strand Releasing).

a glorified homeland image at all.[13] As Göktürk observes, Akin endows this nostalgic image with a reflective character by perpetually linking the chronotopes of Turkey and Germany through music: "[T]he fourth interlude, a short clarinet solo by Selim Şeşler, conveys temporal and spatial transition in a highly condensed fashion, namely Sibel's (Sibel Kekilli) journey from Hamburg to Istanbul . . . [while] the fifth interlude . . . parallels the fluid transition in a reversed direction."[14] That is, it is not only the cinematic images that cross continents, cultures, and nations, but the music also functions across these diverse elements, creating an ironic and hybrid mix.

The combination of homeland and hostland music in the films made by second-generation Turkish-German filmmakers conveys more of a sense of humor and pleasure than misery and a melancholic longing for a lost past or homeland. Therefore, these films seem to provide an audiovisual interpretation of reflective nostalgia by highlighting the duality of, rather than overemphasizing differences and disparity between, the two cultures they simultaneously inhabit. The Turkish elements are ingrained in noticeably German lifestyles, daily routines, and appearances.

> If restorative nostalgia ends up reconstructing emblems and rituals of home and homeland in an attempt to conquer and specialize time, reflective nostalgia cherishes shattered fragments of memory and temporalizes space. . . . Reflective nostalgia can be ironic and humorous. . . . Reflective nostalgia does not pretend to rebuild the mythical place called home; it is enamored of distance, not of the referent itself. This type of nostalgic narrative is ironic, inconclusive and fragmentary.[15]

The music used in the films of the second generation of diasporic Turkish filmmakers is not only a vehicle for nostalgia seen as the means for a playful engagement with possibilities. It not only combines the music traditions of home and host country but also underscores the heterogeneity of Turkish music and culture, challenging any homogenizing characterization of the Turkish community.[16]

Dorit Klebe points out the popularity of a wide range of traditional Turkish music among the migrants in Germany: "Within the musical world of the Turkish migrants in Germany traditional *halk müziği* (folk music) plays an important role, and about 50 per cent of the young Turks listen to it. Further genres are pop müzik, sanat müziği and klasik müzik (two specific genres of Turkish traditional art music), dini müzik (religious music), and özgün müzik (political songs)."[17]

Correspondingly, we see a diverse range of music genres—from folk, to Turkish, to foreign pop—used by the filmmaker, sometimes in a single film. Traditional arabesk, as Stokes notes, is "a music of the city and for the city. . . .

It describes a decaying city in which poverty-stricken migrant workers are exploited and abused, and calls on its listeners to pour another glass of raki, light another cigarette, and curse fate and the world."[18] In *Head-On*, Akin effortlessly switches from this traditional mode to popular Turkish music, as well as the songs of internationally recognized stars such as Depeche Mode.

In a similar manner, Buket Alakuş mingles overtly western tunes composed for violin, cello, and percussion with discernibly Turkish popular music in *Offside* (*Eine andere Liga*, 2004). The film tells a universal love story between a Turkish-German girl, Hayat (Karoline Herfurth),[19] whose life revolves around football until she is stricken by breast cancer, and a German amateur football coach, Toni (Ken Duken).[20] Like many of her Turkish-German colleagues, Alakuş refuses to be seen as exclusively Turkish. The filmmaker argues that in *Offside*, "it is not important whether Hayat is German or Turkish. Her plight—surviving a severe illness and dealing with the consequences—could happen to anyone in the world."[21] This outlook is most certainly reflected in the film through a wide range of music, including a song performed by the first female Turkish-German rapper, Aziza A., who is widely associated with the genre Oriental hip-hop—a hybrid form that cuts across several continents and various genres. Unmistakably multilayered and complex, the genre combines "African-American techniques of rapping and making beats with self-consciously Turkish-sounding melodic samples and motifs taken from Turkish folk and popular music."[22]

To put it differently, in correlation with this new generation of diasporic subjects' identities, their music has become "hyphenated." Hybrid music genres, such as rap or hip-hop blended with Turkish folk or arabesk, provide a complex and multireferential musical ground corresponding to the generic characteristics of Turkish-German cinema; an idiosyncratic vernacular music language in tune with their peculiar "third space" positioning.[23] As Bhabha suggests, theirs is a fluid space, from which new meanings and new identities may be negotiated.[24] Reflecting their experiences, Turkish-German musicians underscore their transnational connections and multiple allegiances. In this respect,

> Aziza A. and others like her get away from becoming exotic fragments of migrancy and emerge as part of a comprehensible normalcy. Their names become not signs of counterfeit Americana or an aberrant modernity manifest in Berlin but symptoms of connectedness and of sharing and participating in the discursive spaces of hip-hop. They write on the walls in Berlin, leaving individual, aesthetic inscriptions for us to see. They rap in English, Turkish and German, inviting us to common projects of social justice, solidarity, and cultural resonance.[25]

The multilingual and multicultural character of this particular type of music offers resistance against homogeneity by using diversity as a discursive weapon to challenge fixed meanings. It also has strong links with the politically engaged and conscious Kanak Attak movement in Germany. *Kanak* was a derogatory German term, which has been appropriated by Turkish-German rappers and writers, who use it as a mark of resistance against prejudices in Germany.[26] By deploying this specific genre, as well as other musical traditions, Turkish-German filmmakers depart from the convention commonly seen in earlier films that used music as a primarily nostalgic device and, instead, use it to underscore multiplicity.

Subversive Potentials: Diversified Use of Music

The new generation of diasporic Turkish filmmakers retains their artistic autonomy, delving into difficult questions of identity, belonging, agency, and calling many contentious issues into question, not only in their country of residence, but also in their country of origin. Thus, unlike most of their Turkish counterparts who work in Turkey, they audaciously investigate more controversial issues that have been taboo in Turkey, such as homosexuality and the Kurdish-Turkish conflict. While doing so, they employ music to convey their messages, because "if musical sound has the potential to speak socially as well as individually, then its sounds may turn out to be potent icons of social practice as well as of personal experience. Music becomes as much a political tool as it is a language of feelings."[27]

In her road movie *Tour Abroad* (*Auslandstournee*, 1999), Ayşe Polat boldly chooses unconventional characters for her narrative: Zeki (Hilmi Sözer), a Turkish homosexual performer in his forties, and newly orphaned Şenay (Özlem Blume), a cute eleven-year-old girl who is the daughter of Zeki's ex-colleague. Zeki finds himself responsible for taking Şenay to find her real mother, Çiçek (Özay Fecht), who abandoned her long ago. Even though Zeki is not eager to assume this responsibility, they set off on a long journey in search of Çiçek that turns into a journey of self-discovery and leads to a strong connection between the two. As they travel through various European cities such as Stuttgart, Paris, and Istanbul, "the history of migration is revisited through the lens of travelling performers."[28] One evening, after Şenay has had her first period and Zeki has been beaten up by some homophobic attackers, they listen to Zeki's idol, Bülent Ersoy, a singer of traditional Turkish music, while Zeki smokes marijuana. Ersoy was the first transsexual in Turkey, daring to undergo a sex change to become a woman in 1980. Subsequently, Ersoy was banned from Turkish national television and radio channels and was forced to live in exile in Germany, but she managed to become very popular back home in the 1990s. In this context, it is not the songs that constitute narrative significance, but Bülent Ersoy herself, who, with her controversial public persona, manipulates the entire meaning of the scene.

Against this background, Zeki's name is clearly charged with implications for viewers familiar with Turkish culture and history; he is the namesake of the most celebrated and respected Turkish singer of all time, Zeki Müren, who was also a cross-dressing homosexual. However, unlike Ersoy, he never came out or changed his sex, and it was speculated that the two had a secret relationship. Ersoy symbolizes trans-ness, and Zeki, as the gay character in the film, underlines diverse queer sexualities. Thus, the music here is deftly used to deconstruct fixed gender categories. The diegetic music rises and the pair dance—Zeki in the front, Şenay behind him, both in fancy dresses—signifying and celebrating the trans-ness across sexes, cultures, and identities.

Another example of challenging and subversive use of music in Turkish-German cinema can be seen in the 1998 film *April Children* (*Aprilkinder*) by Yüksel Yavuz. The film tells the story of Cem (Erdal Yıldız), who is the eldest son of a Kurdish family in Germany and is forced to marry his cousin from the family village in Turkey, although he is in love with a German prostitute, Kim (Inga Busch). Toward the end of the film, scenes of family members preparing for Cem's wedding in the arranged marriage with his cousin from Turkey are edited in parallel with scenes of lovemaking between Cem and Kim, as if she is the true bride. The film then cuts to the wedding ceremony, accompanied by traditional instruments, drum, and clarion. Daniela Berghahn observes, "[W]edding ceremonies bring the customs, traditions and the music from the Heimat to life in the context of the adopted culture and thus create a sense of nostalgia and collective identity."[29] However, the wedding in *April Children* is not simply used to convey the cultural traditions of the homeland, but rather to reinforce the drama in the narrative. Soon, the music, and, subsequently, the entire mood of the scene, changes. Cem, walking next to the bride, with whom he is not in love, sees everything in slow motion. Later, while the pair is dancing, the camera starts spinning in ever-faster circles, framed by the guests, and the slow dance music fades into a Kurdish dirge, communicating Cem's state of mind—his ambivalence and grief—to the audience. Irony is inserted by transforming what should have been a happy gathering into a poignant event, via a sly employment of music. The wedding becomes the site of rupture, rather than convergence or collectivity, focusing on Cem's alienation from the crowd.

Similarly, Yavuz's 2003 film *A Little Bit of Freedom* (*Kleine Freiheit*) features a considerable amount of Kurdish music, as well as the songs of Kardeş Türküler, a folk band that blends the music of every ethnic group in Turkey. The film focuses on the friendship between Kurdish Baran (Çağdaş Bozkurt) and African Chernor (Leroy Delmar), who are both in Germany illegally. In one scene, while Baran delivers food by bike for the *döner*—the Turkish fast food place where he works—images of the German city, streets, bars, and construction sites are all superimposed. These images are accompanied by a very rhythmic melody with religious lyrics that recall the name of prophets and salient religious figures in Turkish/Kurdish/Shiite/Sunni culture. This striking audiovisual collage functions as a compact capsule of the very complex culture of the Turkish diaspora in Germany, unmasking its internal diversity, with sounds, "superimposed just like images," evoking, as Göktürk notes, "deep, subconscious connections and resonances in meaning."[30]

Alternatively, in *En Garde* (2004) by Ayşe Polat, a film that narrates the complex relationships among isolated, displaced youth in Germany, the female lead Berivan (Pınar Erincin) sings in Kurdish, totally isolated from the rest of the characters in the frame, with her eyes locked on a distant point, signifying a moment of recollection. A sense of yearning is detectable. Unlike Turks, who generally migrated in pursuit of a prosperous life, Kurds were more often expelled from their villages as a result of ethnic conflict and thus sought asylum status in Germany. This is referred to many times in Yavuz's and Polat's films, illustrating how diverse subject positions, even in one diasporic community, are addressed through the use of music.

The use of music is also, very often, creatively combined with the oral tradition of storytelling, which constitutes an indispensable part of Turkish culture. The figure of the *ozan*, who can be described as a singing poet in the Turkish context, has played a significant role, transferring information and cultural values from one generation to another. Songs and lyrics still constitute an inherent part of Turkish popular culture today, and Fatih Akin deploys this tradition in almost all of his films. In the fairy tale–style road movie *In July* (*Im Juli*, 2000), the narrative focuses on a science teacher, Daniel (Moritz Bleibtreu); a hippie saleswoman, Juli (Christiane Paul); and a mysterious Turkish woman, Melek (İdil Üner).[31] Thinking that Melek is "the one," Daniel decides to set off for the "unfamiliar" Istanbul, leaving the familiar shelter of Hamburg in order to find her. Thus begins a long journey that spans several border crossings, spiritual transformation, and self-discovery. In one scene, when Melek and Daniel go to a restaurant, an explanatory Turkish folk song, which acts as an impelling sign in the narrative, is heard while she talks about *yakamoz*, sea sparkle. Then the pair goes to a beach, where Melek sings another Turkish song that reveals coming events: "your eyes should follow and find me, and your lips should kiss me . . ."[32]

Another example can be seen in Akin's *Short Sharp Shock* (*Kurz und schmerzlos*, 1998); when the intercultural couple Gabriel (Mehmet Kurtuluş) and Alice (Regula Grauwiller) make love, the soundtrack features Sezen Aksu, a prominent Turkish pop music artist, her symbolic lyrics depicting lusty and sensual sex. Akin skillfully combines Turkish symbolism devised to avoid controversial and taboo issues with a literal and manifestly western narrative style that allows direct depiction of the actions, including nudity.

This employment of songs as narrative devices evokes the term *juke-box narrative*, coined by Jeff Smith,[33] in order to explain that "whilst the pop song may be used in a conventional way to reinforce or comment upon a character or their emotions, it always retains an autonomous identity and resists full integration into the narrative. This means that recognition of songs by audiences will influence interpretation of narrative events."[34] Many examples in Turkish-German cinema incorporate jukebox narratives. For instance, *Rage* (*Wut*, 2006) by Züli Aladağ, a controversial film that ignited audiences with portrayals of its Turkish villain, uses this technique. The film explores the multilayered and complicated nature of intercultural and racial relationships in Germany through the story of a German nuclear family, the Laubs, and a violent Turkish teenager, Can (Oktay Özdemir), who is full of hatred and harasses the Laubs' only son, Felix (Robert Höller). The tragedy caused by Can's departure from home after being disowned by his father is intensified by a soundtrack that translates his feelings: "I am walking towards longing and sorrow . . . the happiness of my heart has faded away . . ."[35] Similarly, in *April Children*, when Dilan (Senem Tepe) wants her lover Arif (Kaan Emre) to stay for dinner but cannot articulate her desire, the voice of Tarkan, probably the most popular pop music singer in Turkey,[36] speaks on her behalf. The romantic song "Gitme" discloses Dilan's feelings: "If I say don't go, will you stay with me my darling . . ."[37] Likewise, in an earlier scene, Cem goes to a brothel, where music by Orhan Gencebay, referred to as the king of arabesk, is being played. Kim chooses another song in the jukebox and starts dancing, while the lyrics "turn around turn around, it is never gonna change . . ." foreshadow the fate of their relationship.

The same strategy regarding the use of music can be detected in the films made by third-generation filmmakers of Turkish descent. One salient example is seen in Kemal Görgülü's film *My Sorrowful Village* (*Benim dertli köyüm*, 2005), which focuses on the problems of the filmmaker's village, rather than the genealogy of a diasporic family and their experience in their host country. In the final scenes of the film, Çerkez—the filmmaker's grandfather and the main character of the film—is captured walking in the morning while the soundtrack features a song by Aşık Mahzuni, a highly political Shiite figure, considered to be one of the greatest minstrels of the century. The folk song "Benim dertli köyüm" is also the Turkish title of the film and basically condenses the film's story.

Of all Turkish-German films, Fatih Akin's feature documentary *Crossing the Bridge: The Sound of İstanbul* (2005) unquestionably stands out, owing to its direct engagement with the diverse music genres and the associated cultures shaping the cosmopolitan lifestyle of the titular city. Akin collaborated with musician Alexander Hacke in order to trace disparate music traditions coexisting in the city. The film mobilizes an entirely unexpected image of Turkey—young, active, developed, modern, vibrant, and most definitely heterogeneous—by exploring the country's music. It begins with a voice-over on black screen, encapsulating the theme and the narrative trajectory of the film: "Confucius says that you should listen to a place's music first if you would like to understand what kind of place it is." From the outset, postcard images of the city are juxtaposed with crammed concrete buildings. The dichotomy portrayed in these visuals is reinforced by the comments of various interviewees who describe Istanbul as a city of binary contradictions. The city of seven hills is presented as an eclectic synthesis through a musical mix of neo-psychedelic, modern electronic, hip-hop, rock, arabesk, and more: an idiosyncratic habitat that permits the togetherness of incompatible and disparate elements.

German bass guitar player Alexander Hacke,[38] of the band *Einstürzende Neubauten*, leads the narrative as a modern nomad who sets off to explore the musical treasures of Turkey. While he introduces the musicians, a handheld camera records their rehearsals or live performances staged for the film. First, Baba Zula, a neo-psychedelic music group, performs on a boat between the Anatolian and European sides of the city, rather than on either shore, claiming that the Bosporus is what Istanbul is about. For them, the city is understood through a conceptualization not of "either/or" but of "across," and the band aims to reflect this character by combining western and eastern musical techniques and melodies. Their performance is disrupted by inserted images of Orhan Gencebay, who is called "the Elvis of arabesk—Father Orhan." Hacke's regular interpretative voice provides a context for the images, but no subtitles are used for any of the languages spoken—Turkish, English, German—as though the universal language of music suffices to communicate. Akin leaves the task of creating a "pure language" out of musical harmony to the musicians and their music.

An array of bands and musicians appear on the screen, one by one, conveying the intended message of diversity through a visual and audio pastiche: multinational band Orient Expressions; punk-rock group Duman; rock group Replikas, with a more intellectual concept and attitude; rapper Ceza and his sister Ayben; İstanbul Style Breakers; the father of Turkish rock Erkin Koray; the so-called digital dervish Mercan Dede; the queen of Turkish popular music Sezen Aksu, a source of inspiration for younger generation of musicians; the legendary Turkish classic music artist Müzeyyen Senar; Canadian musician Brenna MacCrimmon, who unearthed some long-forgotten Turkish songs; a group of street musicians, Siyasiyabend, who claim to be marginalized and made "Other" by the authorities, yet keep inhabiting the streets to deliver their message; Kurdish singer Aynur, whose music is informed, in part by her nation's life; and the renowned clarinet virtuoso Selim Şeşler. The sound of one is linked to images of the other, highlighting the connectedness of all, despite apparent differences between them. Istanbul, as their shared habitat, is what gives them their identity. Meanwhile, Hacke blends into the daily life of the city, encountering all types of people from street peddlers to transvestites. A sense of imperfection created by the filmmaker's mobile, handheld camera and the abundance of close-ups and medium shots gives the film an amateur feel. Also, the music is recorded by Hacke and edited on his computer, and we observe the entire process. Occasionally, some archival nonfiction footage and scenes from old Turkish films like those of Orhan Gencebay and Sezen Aksu, who also acted in movies owing to their popularity, are inserted while the musicians are interviewed or perform. The chaotic, disorganized structure of the film suggests and underpins the city's frenzied, muddled, yet vivid character, in which everyone can feel at home. In the end, inasmuch as Istanbul is considered a microcosm of Turkey, the filmmaker deconstructs prejudicial perceptions attributed to Turkey and Turks by playfully deploying the varied musical traditions of his country of origin, calling for the convergence of the two sides of his identity. "The emphasis in the title *Crossing the Bridge* must therefore lie on the 'crossing' rather than on the 'bridge,' on mobility and flux across borders."[39] These new diasporic generations are no longer located at a painful position of in-betweeness but are comfortably and constantly across, and the filmmakers use every necessary means, including music, to clarify their new subject positions, to assign resistance.

In conclusion, diasporas not only occupy substate, subnational, subcultural positions of social space, but also have increasingly become more transnational, disturbing and reshaping the borderlines between local and global. "The diasporic public spheres are no longer small, marginal or exceptional. They are part of the cultural dynamic of urban life in most countries and continents."[40] In this context, diasporic subjects define the new sociocultural space in European capitals and major cities, which is a site of fresh encounters and constant flow. One of the main platforms reflecting this change is diasporic cinema. While the early films made by those whom I have called "observers/outsiders" mostly contribute to the discourse and narrative of victimhood in terms of the construction and representation of diasporic identity, the films of succeeding generations seem to render a more complicated understanding of diasporic identity and experience, providing multilayered and often celebratory representations of diverse diasporic subjectivities.

This is also evident in the varying use of music in the films over time. Music serves to emphasize characters' ethnic and/or cultural constituency, to differentiate between cultures and to indicate a sense of nostalgia in early films. By contrast, the later generations of filmmakers use music in a more playful way, to enrich their cinematic language, subvert stereotypes, challenge fixed meanings and incorporate humor and irony into the narrative. All in all, these younger generations of diasporic Turkish filmmakers seem to make the most of their transnational, cross-cultural allegiances by drawing on a wide range of musical traditions.

Notes

1. Will Higbee, "Beyond the (Trans)national: Towards a Cinema of Transvergence in Postcolonial and Diasporic Francophone Cinema(s)," *Studies in French Cinema* 7, no. 2 (2007): 79–91; Hamid Naficy, "Situating Accented Cinema," in *Transnational Cinema: The Film Reader*, ed. Elizabeth Ezra and Terry Rowden, 111–130 (London: Routledge, 2006); Bishnupriya Ghosh and Sarkar Bhaskar, "The Cinema of Displacement: Towards a Politically Motivated Poetics," *Film Criticism* 20 nos. 1–2 (1996): 102–113; Laura U. Marks, *The Skin of the Film: Intercultural Cinema, Embodiment, and the Senses* (Durham, NC: Duke University Press, 2000).

2. Svetlana Boym, *The Future of Nostalgia* (New York: Basic Books, 2001), xiii.

3. Boym, *Future of Nostalgia*, 4.

4. See Raymond MacDonald, David J. Hargreaves, and Dorothy Miell, *Musical Identities* (Oxford: Oxford University Press, 2002) for a productive discussion of the role of music in the construction of identities.

5. Regula Qureshi, "How Does Music Mean? Embodied Memories and the Politics of Affect in the Indian Sarangi," *American Ethnologist* 27, no. 4 (2000): 810.

6. Ivo Oliveira, "Music: A Lens to Cultural Identity," *Fair Observer Arts & Culture*, January 26, 2012, http://www.fairobserver.com/360theme/music-lens-cultural-identity.

7. Andy Bennett, "Music, Space and Place," in *Music, Space and Place*, ed. Sheila Whiteley, Andy Bennett, and Stan Hawkins (Aldershot: Ashgate Publishing, 2005), 4.

8. For a more detailed discussion on Turkish filmmakers in Germany, see also Ayça Tunç, "Three Generations of Turkish Filmmakers in Germany: Three Different Narratives," *Turkish Studies* 12, no. 1 (2011): 117–129.

9. Ayhan Kaya and Ferhat Kentel, "Euro-Turks: A Bridge or a Breach between Turkey and the European Union? A Comparative Study of French-Turks and German Turks," Centre for European Policy Studies, Brussels, January 2005, 6, http://www.ceps.eu/book/euro-turks-bridge-or-breach-between-turkey-and-european-union-comparative-study-french-turks-an.

10. Alison Landsberg identifies the characteristics of prosthetic memory as follows: "It is not authentic or natural but rather derived from engagement with mediated

representations (seeing a film, visiting a museum, watching a television show). . . . These are sensuous memories produced by an experience of mass mediated representations. . . . Calling it 'prosthetic' signals its interchangeability and exchangeability and underscores its commodified form. . . . A sensuous engagement with the past, which prosthetic memory enables, is the foundation for more than simply individual subjectivity; it becomes the basis for mediated collective identification and for the production of potentially counterhegemonic spheres." See Alison Landsberg, "Prosthetic Memory: The Ethics and Politics of Memory in an Age of Mass Culture," in *Memory and Popular Film*, ed. Paul Grainge (Manchester: Manchester University Press, 2003), 149–150. In this sense, prosthetic memory is available for anybody who would like to reach it instead of being in the possession of one particular social group. Yet it should be noted that it will possibly be consumed differently by those who feel they have a claim to that history, as against those who do not. That is, a black British teenager would possibly engage differently with a school trip to a museum of slavery than his contemporary white classmate.

11. Qureshi, "How Does Music Mean," 811.

12. See Sujata Moorti, "Desperately Seeking an Identity: Diasporic Cinema and the Articulation of Transnational Kinship." *International Journal of Cultural Studies* 6, no. 3 (2003): 355–376.

13. Hamid Naficy, *Accented Cinema: Exilic and Diasporic Filmmaking* (Princeton: Princeton University Press, 2001), 152.

14. Deniz Göktürk,"Sound Bridges: Transnational Mobility as Ironic Melodrama," in *European Cinema in Motion: Migrant and Diasporic Film in Contemporary Europe*, ed. Daniela Berghahn and Claudia Sternberg (London: Wallflower Press, 2010), 219.

15. Boym, *Future of Nostalgia*, 50.

16. See Martin Greve, "Music in the European Turkish Diaspora," in *Music in Motion: Diversity and Dialogue in Europe*, ed. Bernd Clausen, Ursula Hemetek, and Eva Sæther (London: Transaction Publishers, 2009), 115–132 for an instructive analysis of the versatile Turkish music scene in Germany.

17. Dorit Klebe, "Kanak Attak in Germany: A Multiethnic Network of Youths Employing Musical Forms of Expression," in *Manifold Identities: Studies on Music and Minorities*, ed. Anna Czekanowska, Ursula Hemetek, Gerda Lechleitner, and Inna Naroditskaya (London: Cambridge Scholars Press, 2004), 165.

18. Martin Stokes, *The Arabesk Debate: Music and Musicians in Modern Turkey* (Oxford: Clarendon Press, 1992), 1.

19. This particular choice of a German actress to play a Turkish girl challenges ethnically defined and often stereotypical casting practices.

20. The film's similarity in terms of theme, genre and narrative strategies to another diasporic film *Bend It Like Beckham* (2002) by Gurinder Chadha should be noted here.

21. "Upcoming Director Buket Alakus Talks about Her Turkish Background, Her Family and Her Films," *Young Germany*, October 24, 2006, http://www.young-germany.de/nc/news-verwaltung/news-singleview/article/upcoming-director-buket-alakus-talks-about-her-turkish-background-her-family-and-her-films.html.

22. Thomas Solomon, "Whose Diaspora? Hybrid Identities in Turkish Rap in Germany" (paper presented at the 14th Nordic Migration Researchers' Conference in Bergen, November 2007), 3. It should be noted here that hip-hop and rap are mostly used interchangeably and the difference between the two constitutes a great debate in the pertinent music milieu. Simply put, they are related but different music genres. For instance, they both involve rhyming lyrics sung to a beat, but they differ in their messages and outlook about society's future, rap being relatively more depressive, etc. Also see Thomas Solomon, "Hardcore Muslims: Islamic Themes in Turkish Rap in Diaspora and in the Homeland," *Yearbook for Traditional Music* 38 (2006): 59–78 for a specific discussion of Islamic themes in Turkish rap in diaspora.

23. See Homi K. Bhabha, *The Location of Culture* (London and New York: Routledge, 1994) and "The Other Question: Difference, Discrimination, and the Discourse of Colonialism," in *Black British Cultural Studies: A Reader*, ed. Houston A. Baker, Jr., Manthia Diawara, and Ruth H. Lindeborg (Chicago: University of Chicago Press, 1996), 87–107 for a discussion of the concept of "third space."

24. Bhabha, *Location of Culture* and Bhabha, "Other Question."

25. Levent Soysal, "Rap, Hiphop, Kreuzberg: Scripts of/for Migrant Youth Culture in the World City Berlin," *New German Critique* 92 (2004): 63.

26. See Klebe, "Kanak Attak in Germany and Soysal, "Rap, Hiphop, Kreuzberg" for a detailed discussion of the concept of "Kanak" and how it was mobilized as an intellectual ghetto movement.

27. Qureshi, "How Does Music Mean," 811.

28. Deniz Göktürk, "Beyond Paternalism: Turkish German Traffic in Cinema," in *The German Cinema Book*, ed. Tim Bergfelder, Erica Carter, and Deniz Göktürk (London: BFI Publishing, 2002), 254.

29. Daniela Berghahn, "No Place Like Home? Or Impossible Homecomings in the Films of Fatih Akin," *New Cinemas* 4, no. 3 (2006): 147.

30. Translated and quoted in Göktürk, "Sound Bridges," 215.

31. See Charlotte Christina Fink, "Heating Up: Border Crossings and Identity Formation undergone *In July* (2000)," in this volume for another analysis of the film.

32. My translation of the lyrics of the song performed by Melek.

33. See Jeff Smith, *The Sounds of Commerce: Marketing Popular Film Music* (New York: Columbia University Press, 1998).

34. Philip Drake, "'Mortgaged to Music': New Retro Movies in 1990s Hollywood Cinema," in *Memory and Popular Film*, ed. Paul Grainge (Manchester: Manchester University Press, 2003), 193–194.

35. My translation of the lyrics of the soundtrack heard in the scene.

36. Also, despite being raised in Turkey, Tarkan was born in Alzey, Germany, in 1972 as the son of a Turkish guest worker family.

37. My translation of the lyrics of the soundtrack heard in the scene.

38. Alexander Hacke worked with Akın for *Head-On*, too.

39. Göktürk, "Sound Bridges," 231.

40. Arjun Appadurai, *Modernity at Large: Cultural Dimensions of Globalization* (Minneapolis: University of Minnesota Press, 2003), 10.

Works Cited

Appadurai, Arjun. *Modernity at Large: Cultural Dimensions of Globalization.* Minneapolis: University of Minnesota Press, 2003.

Bennett, Andy. "Music, Space and Place." In *Music, Space and Place*, edited by Sheila Whiteley, Andy Bennett, and Stan Hawkins, 2–7. Aldershot: Ashgate Publishing, 2005.

Berghahn, Daniela. "No Place Like Home? Or Impossible Homecomings in the Films of Fatih Akin." *New Cinemas* 4, no. 3 (2006): 141–157.

Bhabha, Homi K. *The Location of Culture.* London and New York: Routledge, 1994.

——. "The Other Question: Difference, Discrimination, and the Discourse of Colonialism." In *Black British Cultural Studies: A Reader*, edited by Houston A. Baker, Jr., Manthia Diawara, and Ruth H. Lindeborg, 87–107. Chicago: University of Chicago Press, 1996.

Boym, Svetlana. *The Future of Nostalgia.* New York: Basic Books, 2001.

Drake, Philip. "'Mortgaged to Music:' New Retro Movies in 1990s Hollywood Cinema." In *Memory and Popular Film*, edited by Paul Grainge, 183–200. Manchester: Manchester University Press, 2003.

Ghosh, Bishnupriya, and Sarkar Bhaskar. "The Cinema of Displacement: Towards a Politically Motivated Poetics." *Film Criticism* 20, nos. 1–2 (1996): 102–113.

Göktürk, Deniz. "Beyond Paternalism: Turkish German Traffic in Cinema." In *The German Cinema Book*, edited by Tim Bergfelder, Erica Carter, and Deniz Göktürk, 248–256. London: BFI Publishing, 2002.

——. "Sound Bridges: Transnational Mobility as Ironic Melodrama." In *European Cinema in Motion: Migrant and Diasporic Film in Contemporary Europe*, edited by Daniela Berghahn and Claudia Sternberg, 215–234. London: Wallflower Press, 2010.

Greve, Martin. "Music in the European Turkish Diaspora." In *Music in Motion: Diversity and Dialogue in Europe*, edited by Bernd Clausen, Ursula Hemetek, and Eva Sæther, 115–132. London: Transaction Publishers, 2009.

Higbee, Will. "Beyond the (Trans)national: Towards a Cinema of Transvergence in Postcolonial and Diasporic Francophone Cinema(s)." *Studies in French Cinema* 7, no. 2 (2007): 79–91.

Kaya, Ayhan and Ferhat Kentel. "Euro-Turks: A Bridge or a Breach between Turkey and the European Union? A Comparative Study of French-Turks and German Turks." Centre for European Policy Studies, Brussels, January 2005. http://www.ceps.eu/book/euro-turks-bridge-or-breach-between-turkey-and-european-union-comparative-study-french-turks-an.

Klebe, Dorit. "Kanak Attak in Germany: A Multiethnic Network of Youths Employing Musical Forms of Expression." In *Manifold Identities: Studies on Music and Minorities*, edited by Anna Czekanowska, Ursula Hemetek, Gerda Lechleitner, and Inna Naroditskaya, 162–180. London: Cambridge Scholars Press, 2004.

Landsberg, Alison. "Prosthetic Memory: The Ethics and Politics of Memory in an Age of Mass Culture." In *Memory and Popular Film*, edited by Paul Grainge. Manchester: Manchester University Press, 2003.

MacDonald, Raymond, David J. Hargreaves, and Dorothy Miell. *Musical Identities.* Oxford: Oxford University Press, 2002.

Marks, Laura U. *The Skin of the Film: Intercultural Cinema, Embodiment, and the Senses.* Durham, NC: Duke University Press, 2000.

Moorti, Sujata. "Desperately Seeking an Identity: Diasporic Cinema and the Articulation of Transnational Kinship." *International Journal of Cultural Studies* 6, no. 3 (2003): 355–376.

Mutman, Mahmut. "Up against the Wall of the Signifier: *Gegen die Wand.*" In *Shifting Landscapes*, edited by Miyase Christensen and Nezih Erdoğan, 317–333. Newcastle upon Tyne: Cambridge Scholars Publishing, 2009.

Naficy, Hamid. *Accented Cinema: Exilic and Diasporic Filmmaking.* Princeton: Princeton University Press, 2001.

——. "Situating Accented Cinema." In *Transnational Cinema: The Film Reader*, edited by Elizabeth Ezra and Terry Rowden, 111–130. London: Routledge, 2006.

Oliveira, Ivo. "Music: A Lens to Cultural Identity." *Fair Observer Arts & Culture,* January 26, 2012. http://www.fairobserver.com/360theme/music-lens-cultural-identity.

Qureshi, Regula, "How Does Music Mean? Embodied Memories and the Politics of Affect in the Indian Sarangi." *American Ethnologist* 27, no. 4 (2000): 810.

Smith, Jeff. *The Sounds of Commerce: Marketing Popular Film Music.* New York: Columbia University Press, 1998.

Solomon, Thomas. "Hardcore Muslims: Islamic Themes in Turkish Rap in Diaspora and in the Homeland." *Yearbook for Traditional Music* 38 (2006): 59–78.

——. "Whose Diaspora? Hybrid Identities in Turkish Rap in Germany." Paper presented at the 14th Nordic Migration Researchers' Conference in Bergen. November 2007.

Soysal, Levent. "Rap, Hiphop, Kreuzberg: Scripts of/for Migrant Youth Culture in the World City Berlin." *New German Critique* 92 (2004): 62–81.

Stokes, Martin. 1992, *The Arabesk Debate: Music and Musicians in Modern Turkey.* Oxford: Clarendon Press.

Tunç, Ayça. "Three Generations of Turkish Filmmakers in Germany: Three Different Narratives." *Turkish Studies* 12, no. 1 (2011): 117–129.

——. "Upcoming Director Buket Alakus Talks about Her Turkish Background, Her Family and Her Films." *Young Germany.* October 24, 2006. http://www.young-germany.de/nc/news-verwaltung/news-singleview/article/upcoming-director-buket-alakus-talks-about-her-turkish-background-her-family-and-her-films.html.

Films

A Little Bit of Freedom. Directed by Yüksel Yavuz. Cotta Media Entertainment, Peter Stockhaus Filmproduktion, and Zweites Deutsches Fernsehen (ZDF) and Zero Fiction Film GmbH. Germany, 2003.

April Children. Directed by Yüksel Yavuz. Zweites Deutsches Fernsehen (ZDF) and Zero Fiction Film GmbH. Germany, 1998.

Crossing the Bridge: The Sound of İstanbul. Directed by Fatih Akin. Corazón International, Norddeutscher Rundfunk (NDR), Panfilm, Pictorion Pictures GmbH and Intervista digital media GmbH. Germany, 2005.

En Garde. Directed by Ayşe Polat. X-Filme Creative Pool and Zweites Deutsches Fernsehen (ZDF). Germany, 2004.

Head-On. Directed by Fatih Akin. Wüste Filmproduktion, Bavaria Film and Soda Pictures. Germany, 2004.

In July. Directed by Fatih Akin. Wüste Filmproduktion, Argos Filmcilik Turizm and Quality Pictures. Germany, 2000.

My Sorrowful Village. Directed by Kemal Görgülü. dostFilm and ESAV. Germany, 2005.

Offside. Directed by Buket Alakuş. Wüste Filmproduktion and Das kleine Fernsehspiel. Germany, 2004.

Rage. Directed by Züli Aladağ. Colonia Media Filmproduktions GmbH and Westdeutscher Rundfunk (WDR). Germany, 2006.

Short Sharp Shock. Directed by Fatih Akin. Wüste Filmproduktion and Zweites Deutsches Fernsehen (ZDF). Germany, 1998.

Tour Abroad. Directed Ayşe Polat. Mira Filmproduktion Bremen GmbH and Zweites Deutsches Fernsehen (ZDF). Germany, 1999.

Yasemin. Directed by Hark Bohm. Hamburger Kino-Kompanie, Hark Bohm Filmproduktions KG and Zweites Deutsches Fernsehen (ZDF). Germany, 1988.

IV

GROWING UP ON THE ROAD

CROSSING BORDERS AND IDENTITY FORMATION

10

Heating Up

Border Crossing and Identity Formation in Fatih Akin's In July *(2000)*

Charlotte Christina Fink

THE GERMAN FILM *IN JULY* (*Im Juli*), written and directed by Fatih Akin in 2000, is a romantic comedy that revolves around the developing romance between a young street vendor, Juli (Christiane Paul), and prospective teacher Daniel (Moritz Bleibtreu). *In July* is more than a mere love story, however; it vividly depicts the complex system and interplay of borders and border crossings on the European continent, and illustrates how they relate to identity formation in the "New Europe" in the twenty-first century.

The story opens in Hamburg, Germany, when Juli sells Daniel an enchanted ring picturing a sun, telling him that the woman destined to be his true love will be wearing a sun. Shortly thereafter, Daniel meets Melek (Idil Üner), who is wearing a T-shirt with a sun but is leaving for Istanbul the next day. Thinking Melek is his one and only, Daniel spontaneously decides to go after her and drives to Turkey. Along the way, he picks up Juli, who is hitchhiking to get away for the summer. Juli and Daniel must overcome numerous obstacles and disorientations throughout the course of their cross-European journey in order to ultimately end up as a couple—a thinly veiled reference to the challenges and prospects associated with European enlargement and cultural diversity. The two main characters' destination—Turkey, adjacent to, but not yet part of the European Union (EU)—enables the film to also address the EU's borderlines and conceptualizations of the lands beyond as "outside."

Applying theories of identity formation to the context of European borders, this chapter will discuss the ways in which the borders and border crossings encountered by Juli and Daniel are linked to "real-world" European borderlines and borderlands, and the formation of a European identity in the twenty-first century.

Borders, Border Crossing, and Identity Formation

Borders exist as real and imaginary boundaries, limitations, or obstacles in various contexts. They represent and provide a frame of reference for individuals and collectives alike, and are, therefore, intrinsically tied to identity and the behavior that stems from that identity. Processes of identity formation, then—on both micro and macro levels[1]—are associated not only with the creation and maintenance of borders but on the subsequent crossing of those borders, as well.[2]

Assuming that identity formation requires a "sense of personal continuity and of uniqueness from other people . . . in addition to . . . membership in various groups—familial, ethnic, occupational, and others,"[3] the activity around borders contributes to this process vis-à-vis encounters with those stereotypically defined as "Other." Such encounters are rooted, as Goffman notes, in closely held expectations about values, norms, and ideals, highlighting previously unarticulated notions of "self."[4] Similarly, Frederick Barth has claimed that the

> boundary canalizes social life—it entails a frequently quite complex organization of behaviour and social relations. The identification of another person as a fellow member . . . entails the assumption that the two are fundamentally "playing the same game." . . . On the other hand, a dichotomization of others as strangers . . . implies a recognition of limitations on shared understanding, differences in criteria for judgment of value and performance, and a restriction of interaction to sectors of assumed common understanding and mutual interest.[5]

Identity, then, is not fixed, but rather, continuously undergoes challenges, changes, and adjustments.[6] In every respect, border crossing highlights the scope of what is and what is not part of that identity, formulating and reformulating respective role ascriptions and expectations as part of ongoing social discourse.

In the context of the EU, the de- and reconstruction of a New Europe is undoubtedly predicated on the establishment and concurrent abolishment of borders in all respects. By its definition, the formation of a European identity requires change and adjustment. However, the transformations and modifications the twenty-first century has brought to European states have certainly revitalized discussions about the quality of cultural and national borders, as well as the significance of inner and outer European borderlines.

European Borderlines, Borderlands, and Formulating a New Europe

With regard to the European Union, Ivaylo Ditchev argues that "increasing the speed of human flows produces more difference rather than less, in the same way the result of global warming is more extreme weather."[7] It is argued that European enlargement and increased mobility generally induce a de- and reconstruction of the meaning and significance of European borderlines and border crossings.[8] Based on the concept of cultural borderlands—the assumption that borderlands are created when two or more cultures "inhabit" the same territory while maintaining the "original" cultures—this suggests an expansion of the notion of borderlands to the framework and context of formulating a European identity.[9]

Countries and cultures that were formerly recognized as Other or outsiders are now insiders and part of the EU.[10] Accepting a new member country from the borders of Europe into the EU—changing its status from outside to inside the union—fundamentally changes the act of crossing its borders. They suddenly become not merely border crossings into that country but, more importantly, crossings into the EU, which forcefully insists on the distinction between those who are part of it and those who are not.[11]

Politics, the economy, and social rights are adjusted so that they correspond to EU norms, while EU laws and regulations are implemented in ways that complement the original system. The two systems coexist but also interact, simultaneously emphasizing the differences, as well as the interaction and interdependency, between the two. Borderlands are also created across the EU, as disparities in wages, taxes, or judicial systems spur discussions on a supranational level. Student and tourist flows, encouraged by cross-cultural exchange programs and borderless travel, facilitate and reinforce the creation and maintenance of borderlines because, as Ditchev asserts, "mobility in this case . . . is based on international, regional, or cultural difference. Experience abroad is considered to be a resource: the fact of trans-border mobility thus reinforces rather than weakens borders."[12]

Internal and external cultural borderlands thus seem to represent the very core of Europe's identity problem, that is, "the uncertainty about who actually counts as European [or, who is more European than others and why], lack of strong participatory democracy in the EU system," as well as "ideological and material concerns about whether Europe will be a welfare state or a market-only economy."[13] As the formation of the EU has evolved around economic and political interests, recent financial turmoil has had an effect on not only the countries in question but also the entire EU and its member countries. Crises like these put a strain on EU identity politics fueled by and based on various nationalities encapsulated by the attribution "European." Indeed, it has been observed that "Europe is multiple; it is always home to tensions between numerous religious, cultural, linguistic, and political affiliations, numerous readings of history, numerous modes of relations with the rest of the world."[14] Thus, the meaning and significance of European borderlines and subsequent border crossings are surely at the very core of discussing the New Europe and European identity. Consequently, debates regarding EU-Turkey relations, for example, have been revolving around the question of whether Turkey is European enough to be part of the EU, particularly with regard to religion, freedom of speech, and the rule of law.[15] This question, however, remains absent from *In July*, which instead uses its narrative to highlight the wide array of cultural differences within the New Europe.

Heating Up: *In July*

European borders and border crossings in *In July* are represented as being interrelated and interdependent throughout the film. The crossing of geographical and physical borders accompanies the crossing of (inter)personal borders, as well as borders of perception, reality, and the law: as real or outer borders are crossed, so are imaginary and inner borders, and vice versa.

The first borderline encountered encompasses the seemingly irreconcilable differences in personality, lifestyle, behavior, outlook, and appearance between Juli and Daniel. Juli is highly optimistic, enthusiastic, laid back, relaxed, impulsive, and wears casual clothes and dreadlocks. After all, her name is Juli (July in English), which invokes the height of the summer and freedom from responsibility. She lives from day to day, enjoys life to the fullest, and has a lot of trust in people. Daniel, on the other hand, is a well-put-together prospective German high school mathematics teacher, an embodiment of the rational and thoughtful approach that he generally uses to tackle life's questions. When one of his students complains about him wanting to teach and discuss mathematical problem statements at the very last day of the school year, he responds, "Why—what else would we do?" When Juli asks him for his interpretation of the sun, for example, he delivers a coherent scientific explanation, while she emphasizes its symbolic value of light and luck. Despite his love for jazz and preference for reading books on his balcony—which hint at a more Romantic, contemplative side of his personality—Daniel is a rationalist who feels most comfortable in a well-organized and straightforward environment.

The pair's long trek across Europe—and its borders—leads to their bonding and eventual love for each other. As they travel from Hamburg through

Bavaria, Austria, Hungary, Romania, and Bulgaria to Turkey, their relationship continuously develops and progresses, and Daniel evolves, as well.

Physical borders are established, as well as crossed, several times in the film. When the pair is forced to share a single bed in rural Bavaria, for example, Daniel finds it "uncomfortable and hot," but when they get even closer to spoon, Daniel's discomfort is overcome and he falls asleep right away. When the pair crosses the border into Austria, Leo (Jochen Nickel), a truck driver, asks Juli to dance with him during a stop at a roadside restaurant. When Leo pulls her uncomfortably close, to the point that he seems to assault her, Daniel hits him and then recoils in shock: "My god, I just got into a fight. . . . I despise violence!" Throughout the narrative, Daniel gradually becomes more comfortable crossing the borders that separate lawful from transgressive behavior. He smokes marijuana for the first time with Juli on the Danube; steals two cars, a van in Budapest and "a bad guy's car" in Romania; illegally crosses the borders of Bulgaria and Turkey; and breaks out of prison at the Bulgarian-Turkish border.

All border crossings in the film rely on a catalyst or additional facilitating narrative element, which serves as a metaphorical immigration officer. Illegal substances serve as a particularly significant tool for expanding, or crossing, the borders of personality, perception, and imagination: getting high with Juli on the ship, Daniel actually opens up to her, makes jokes, and seems to feel very comfortable with himself, very real and down-to-earth. Similarly, in Budapest when a woman named Luna (Branka Katic) picks him up after he

Figure 10.1. Crossing physical borders without a doubt is a prerequisite of Daniel and Juli's bonding as a couple. *In July* (Koch Lorber Films).

is thrown from the ship and drugs him, the constraints of reality crack again as Luna, Melek, and Juli appear and bewilder him. Under the influence, one woman seamlessly becomes another, to the point where they all seem to become one.[16]

Juli appears to be the ultimate catalyst as she herself functions as the epitome of border crossings, while at the same time representing an individual without any borders.[17] Her enthusiasm about going abroad and experiences hitchhiking far beyond Europe make her the ultimate crosser of literal, geographic borders. Wearing dreadlocks and colorful clothes and working at a flea market, she also crosses cultural borders, defying conventional expectations about appearance and lifestyle, particularly with regard to gender. On the other hand, the film leaves her background a mystery, framing her as a borderless being who seems to simply float from here to there and feels at home wherever she goes.

Thus, Juli propels and addresses border crossing as much as she exposes, establishes, and reinforces borders. When she meets Daniel and he is hesitant about buying a ring that he seems to like, she blatantly challenges him, "If you like it, then why don't you fight for it?" She is the one who states at the very beginning that "he [Daniel] has something deep inside that wants to get out," foretelling his imminent identity reformation. Encouraging him to trust her, she teaches him to trust others, as well as himself, in order to ultimately become more confident.

Figure 10.2. While Daniel is determined to jump over the river he mistakes for the Danube, Juli knows that the real obstacle is still ahead of them. *In July* (Koch Lorber Films).

Identity Forming Roles of Inner and Outer Borders

The de- and reconstruction of the EU's inner borders becomes apparent when Juli tells her friend in Hamburg that she just wants to get away. Her friend asks in disbelief, "What if the first car is going to *Bavaria*? You'll go then to *Bavaria*?" While Germany's inner borders seem significant to, and are reinforced by, her two companions, Juli is trying to deconstruct the borderline; to her, it does not make a difference whether she is in Hamburg or Munich, since "the sky is blue wherever you go."[18]

Inner borders are also addressed when the question arises of how to get to Istanbul after the car breaks down. Standing in front of a map of Europe, Juli and Daniel illustrate the saying "All roads lead to Rome,' as they trace numerous ways to get to Turkey.[19] While the map conveys national and geographical borders and how they may be crossed (by land or by sea), it also provides a site where associated obstacles and limitations can be projected onto them. Daniel's statement that "there is war [in Yugoslavia]," citing it as the reason why another route is chosen, illustrates that there is a border overlaid on the national border that distinguishes between non-Yugoslavian (that is, nonwarring, European, EU) territory on the one hand and Yugoslavia on the other.[20]

For speakers of German, inner borders are further illustrated through different languages and variations of German, in particular, those from Hamburg, Bavaria, and Austria because the language that Juli and Daniel hear facilitates their interpretation of what they see. Thus, German-speaking audiences know not only what region Juli and Daniel are currently visiting but also the local and national identities to which those regions are home.[21] These linguistic differences, however, do not pose a challenge to the pair whatsoever. They are able to overcome other language-related boundaries and borderlines as well through the use of English. In this sense, English functions as an inter- and supra-national element in various contexts, enabling communication and interaction inside Europe and also outside the EU's borders, on the one hand affirming language differences and barriers, but on the other, overcoming them.

Inner borders of Europe are also depicted through the lens of economics. Luna's run-down van with an "Ex-Yugo" bumper sticker and a horse-drawn carriage on an unpaved road in Hungary, for example, both hint at the economic borders of Europe and the EU. Images of Hungary's agricultural landscape, signaling "backwardness" and lack of industrialization, suggest obstacles to the country's then future accession to the EU.[22] This continues later, when Daniel wakes up after Luna has drugged and left him in the Hungarian countryside. He finds himself facing an old farmer with a gun who defends his property, at first thinking Daniel intends to rob him. Once he realizes that Daniel means him no harm and has crossed the border of his property unintentionally, however, he offers the disoriented young man aid and even takes him to Budapest, suggesting that good-natured collaboration and trust resolve many situations.[23]

Despite this experience, it is Daniel himself who demonstrates mistrust and scant regard for the Other as the main characters' eastward journey continues. Looking for a car to steal from a "bad guy" in Romania, he suspects all those he sees of being murderers and states, "They all look like criminals." Later, when he is faced with the prospect of entering Turkey undocumented, the threat of the unknown, non-EU Other he will find there looms—large and frightening—in his mind. "No passport, no Romania," he declares. "No passport, no Bulgaria. I'm fed up. The Turks are probably five times worse than the Bulgarians. If the Bulgarians fuss around like this, what will the Turks do?"

"No passport, no Romania" is one of the key scenes in the film, as it not only points to borders and border crossings as the main theme of the narrative, but also addresses the question of who configures and has control over a border, as well as who is allowed to cross that border and how. An ironic twist in the scene is the fact that the director Fatih Akin himself poses as the officer at the Hungarian–Romanian border to whom Daniel is trying to explain his situation: his passport was stolen, but he needs to cross the border to Turkey.

Figure 10.3. No passport, no Romania: Only by repeating Juli's vows is Daniel able to "get married" to her and cross the Hungarian-Romanian border. *In July* (Koch Lorber Films).

Akin's character sets up the framework for Daniel's border crossing: Daniel needs to get "married" to Juli, who unexpectedly appears on the other side of the gate, and to give a wedding "present" to Akin, his car. At the same time, however, the filmmaker actively calls the entire border crossing procedure into question.

United in Diversity?

The film's tag line, "Can Daniel follow the sun from Hamburg to the Bosporus by Friday to meet his love?" not only summarizes the plot but also suggests a multifaceted sociocultural analysis with regard to borders and border crossings. First, as Juli and Daniel travel from northern Europe to Turkey, their journey establishes a significant connection between the border cities of Hamburg, located at the northern border of Germany and continental Europe, and Istanbul, which not only borders the EU but is, in itself, a borderland, situated on two different continents. As the plot resolves, this connection grows stronger, more interwoven, and more interdependent.

Received notions of history use the Ottoman Empire's wars with Eastern Europe—that began in the thirteenth century and continued up to the early nineteenth—to frame European relations with Turkey in terms of perpetual conflict. Within Asia Minor, they depict the Muslim Turks as seeming to prevail and gradually pushing Christian minorities back toward the northeast.[24] True Europeanness, in this view, is constituted by ethnic and racial ties to a particular nation-state.[25] Within this context, discussions of the integration of Turkish immigrant minorities into European states and possible membership of Turkey itself in the EU presuppose nation-states and Christendom as the two pillars of European civilization, leaving both possibilities unlikely. The film subverts this view of national identity, framing it instead in a way that renders the binary opposition "Europeanness" and "Turkishness" irrelevant. Germany and Turkey are depicted, in the film, as encompassing and embracing a rich diversity of cultures, as well as the wide array of cultural differences. *In July* notes the existence of economic borders and differences but suggests that their existence does not hinder identity formation. The two worlds do not oppose but, ultimately, complement one other.

Significantly, because of the experiences Daniel gains, his goals and expectations are altered along the way, and he loses interest in Melek, realizing that Juli is his one and only. When he arrives in Turkey, he has become stronger, more aggressive, and more proactive pursuing his love interest. In that sense, Turkey stands not only for an ending to a tumultuous journey of self-discovery that goes against both reason and experience, but also for the beginning of the promising relationship between two souls who have found each other. While one is challenged not to lose hope and faith or give in to disappointment, the other needs encouragement and affirmation to become more self-aware and confident. Daniel needs to let go and simply follow his "guiding light" so that everything can fall into place in the end, although he does not know anything about the woman he pursues.

Likewise, time constraints propel the story forward as there is a deadline that Daniel is determined to meet in order to "get it right." From the moment that Melek tells Daniel that she is going to Istanbul to meet her true love under the bridge spanning the Bosporus, his goal is to get there in time to present himself as her one and only true love. Only his determination to follow Melek, and reach the bridge "in time," brings him together with Juli. Had Daniel decided, at the outset, that Melek was unattainable, he would likely never have given Juli a second thought. Even though they nominally come from the same country, they appear as different as night and day; everything about them seems inherently different and insuperable. Throughout, and by means of, their journey, however, they get to know, and love, one another despite—and perhaps also because of—their differences.

Placed within the context of discussions about nation states and regional identities in the European Union, it seems clear that aversion or lack of understanding within countries and within regions of Europe need to be overcome in order to be open to other perspectives, approaches, and goals.[26] Yet more importantly, finding oneself depends on encountering outsiders and stepping outside one's homeland and comfort zone. For Daniel and Juli, the road to such self-discovery and love does not end at the German-Austrian border, but goes all the way down to the Sea of Marmara. The fact that Daniel ends up with Juli as opposed to Melek plays a significant role in the narrative: the German narrative only becomes complete because of its steady Turkish counterpart. Melek serves as a catalyst for her fellow Germans to connect with their identities. Clearly, the ultimate European question Who are we? cannot be answered single-handedly, but requires an Other to shape the process of self-discovery.

Notes

1. For micro-level approaches, see particularly Erik Erikson's (1959) eight stages of psychosocial development and contemporary approaches to this theory by, for instance, Klimstra (2010). For current discussions about collective identities in Europe see, for example, Eder and Spohn (2005), Karolewski (2011), or Risse (2010).

2. See, for instance, Vila (2000), Nitsiakos, et al. (2008), Cheng (2008), or Brickhouse and Potter (2001).

3. Bonnie Strickland, *The Gale Encyclopedia of Psychology* (Detroit: Gale, 2000), 322.

4. Erving Goffman, *Encounters: Two Studies in the Sociology of Interaction* (Indianapolis: Bobbs-Merril, 1961), 19.

5. Frederick Barth, *Ethnic Groups and Boundaries: The Social Organization of Cultural Difference* (Boston: Little, Brown and Company, 1969), 15.

6. See for example George (1993), Demo (1992), and Erikson (1959).

7. Ivaylo Ditchev, "Crossing Borders,"*Eurozine*, August 31, 2006, 1, http://www.eurozine.com/articles/2006-08-31-ditchev-en.html.

8. Compare Frederick Barth's conclusion over forty years ago that "it is clear that boundaries persist despite a flow of personnel across them", and that "stable, persisting, and often vitally important social relations are maintained across such boundaries, and are frequently based on the dichotomized ethnic statuses. In other words . . . cultural differences can persist despite inter-ethnic contact and interdependence" (Barth, *Ethnic Groups*, 9–10).

9. See Kellner (1995) as well as Rosaldo (1993): "More often than we usually care to think, our everyday lives are crisscrossed by border zones, pockets and eruptions of all kinds. . . . Along with 'our' supposedly transparent cultural selves, such borderlands should be regarded not as analytically empty transitional zones but as sites of creative cultural production that require investigation." Renato Rosaldo, *Culture and Truth: Remaking Social Analysis* (London: Routledge, 1993), 207–208; quoted in Scott Michaelsen and David E. Johnson, eds., *Border Theory: The Limits of Cultural Politics* (Minneapolis: University of Minnesota Press, 1997), 50–51.

10. Compare the continuous expansion of a European Union since its formation in the 1950s, particularly in the 2000s.

11. Based on the fact that in 2010, Istanbul was one of the EU's cultural capitals without Turkey being an actual member but a candidate country, it may well be that Turkey is no member *just yet*. Indeed, in his report to the European Parliament in March 2012, the European Commissioner for Enlargement and European Neighbourhood, Stefan Füle, acknowledges, "[A] fair assessment of the important challenges that Turkey is taking on in the area of judiciary and fundamental rights." See Stefan Füle, "Opening Remarks in European Parliament Debate on Turkey, 28 March 2012," Brussels: European Parliament, 2012, http://www.europarl.europa.eu/meetdocs/2009_2014/documents/d-tr/dv/0420_06/0420_06en.pdf.

12. Ditchev, "Crossing Borders," 3.

13. Janelle G. Reinelt, "Performing Europe: Identity Formation for a 'New' Europe," *Theatre Journal* 53, no. 3 (2001): 369.

14. Étienne Balibar, *We, the People of Europe? Reflections on Transnational Citizenship* (Princeton: Princeton University Press, 2004), 5.

15. For the EU enlargement criteria in regard to practiced democracy, human rights, and minorities, see European Commission's Directorate General for Enlargement, "European Commission-Enlargement-Accession Criteria," accessed November 22, 2012, http://ec.europa.eu/enlargement/policy/glossary/terms/accession-criteria_en.htm.

16. Questioning the Ancient Greeks' three-part-system of continents, Herodotus remarked that "[a]nother thing that puzzles me is why three distinct women's names should have been given to what is really a single landmass." See Herodotus, *The Histories* (Harmondsworth: Penguin Books, 1954), 285; quoted in Martin W. Lewis and

Kären E. Wigen, *The Myth of the Continents: A Critique of Metageography* (Berkeley and Los Angeles: University of California Press, 1997), 22. Likewise, in this scene well-defined constructed identities are put into question as the women's portrayals progressively coalesce. Indeed, we acknowledge the existence of three individuals: On the one hand, Juli and Luna, who represent the unity of the sun and the moon, whilst also standing for Western versus Eastern Europe. On the other hand there is Melek, whose name means angel in Arabic and who may be of Turkish origin, but is from Berlin. Yet we do not know anything further about them and their backgrounds, and this does not seem to matter. To us, all three women become beings without borders inhabiting a single landmass: Europe.

17. This again relates to the essence of her name with regard to July, a month that was named after and introduced by the Roman Empire's straightforward and adamant emperor Julius Caesar.

18. Comic irony hereby lets this interaction be read differently as the comical aspect of this issue can only be understood within the wider regional and national context. Thus, audience-related cultural borders are created and reinforced.

19. Note the implication of Istanbul as the "center" of (Daniel and Juli's) Europe: just as Rome was the center of the Roman Empire and literally, all roads led to Rome, it is suggested that Istanbul, situated at the margins of Europe, may become the center and capital of a New Europe. This not only accounts for a significant reversal of the notions of "center" and "margins," but also implies a shift in the notion and standard of "true" Europeanness.

20. Interestingly, as we see Juli and Daniel in front of the map, the scene's setup appears like the Ludo board game. While the map represents the board, Juli and Daniel seem to represent the tokens that need to race from start to finish, or else, A to B, figuring out a strategy how to get there, but also being subject to noncontrollable situations and incidents (like dice rolls).

Also, regarding my previous remarks about cultural borderlands of Europe, it seems worth pointing out that this particular scene can only be understood and make sense in relation to the EU's political setup of the time of the narrative. As of 2013, Slovenia is already a member state of the EU while Croatia, Macedonia, Montenegro, and Serbia are official candidate countries; Bosnia and Herzegovina entered negotiations concerning a possible accession to the EU in 2003; Kosovo's independence was declared in 2008 and affirmed by the International Court of Justice in 2010. Thus, despite the fact that the countries of former Yugoslavia may still be unfamiliar and predominantly war-related territory to many people, the statement that "there is war [in Yugoslavia]" is applicable to the time when the narrative is set only.

21. At this point it seems essential to again point out the role of irony here as non-German speakers or else, nonnative speakers are most likely not able to distinguish the various regional dialects of German, let alone their implications for the respective speakers and their cultural or else regional and national identity. This, interestingly enough, in turn represents the affirmation and exposure of the border of language and groups all German native speakers together while simultaneously also categorizing and labeling them into several subgroups of German, which in turn fuels and affirms local identities.

22. Membership negotiations with Hungary but also with Bulgaria, the Czech Republic, Estonia, Latvia, Lithuania, Poland, Romania, Slovakia, and Slovenia; Romania

and Bulgaria entered the EU in 2004 and the others, in 2007. All negotiations started in December 1997.

23. As part of a lecture regarding the Hungarian EU-experience in 2009, the head of the Department of Agriculture and Rural Development, László Vajda, stated that after becoming an EU member state in 2004, there are still negative and positive tendencies toward the EU as the critical aspect is and has been to balance national priorities with the character of the EU food sector. There is "market access for Hungarian agri-food products . . . but our market became also exposed and unprotected at the same time." See László Vajda, "Hungarian Experience on the Way to the EU, Before and After Accession," June 13, 2009, http://ec.europa.eu/agriculture/events/zagreb2009/vajda_en.pdf.

24. Lewis and Wigen, *The Myth of the Continents*, 24–25.

25. Chase Cavanaugh, "Turkey's Difficult Entry into the European Union," *Washington Review of Turkish & Eurasian Affairs*, February 2011, http://www.thewashingtonreview.org/articles/turkeys-difficult-entry-into-the-european-union.html.

26. "To overcome" in this context means to be acknowledged yet diminished in importance with regard to decision making processes.

Works Cited

Balibar, Étienne. *We, the People of Europe? Reflections on Transnational Citizenship.* Princeton: Princeton University Press, 2004.

Barth, Frederick. *Ethnic Groups and Boundaries: The Social Organization of Cultural Difference.* Boston: Little, Brown and Company, 1969.

Brickhouse, Nancy W., and Jennifer T. Potter. "Young Women's Scientific Identity Formation in an Urban Context." *Journal of Research in Science Teaching* 38, no. 8 (2001): 965980.

Cavanaugh, Chase. "Turkey's Difficult Entry into the European Union." *Washington Review of Turkish & Eurasian Affairs,* February 2011. http://www.thewashingtonreview.org/articles/turkeys-difficult-entry-into-the-european-union.html.

Cheng, Hsin-I. *Culturing Interface: Identity, Communication, and Chinese Transnationalism.* New York: Peter Lang, 2008.

Demo, David H. "The Self-Concept over Time: Research Issues and Directions." *Annual Review of Sociology* 18 (1992): 303–326.

Ditchev, Ivaylo. "Crossing Borders."*Eurozine*, August 31, 2006. http://www.eurozine.com/articles/2006-08-31-ditchev-en.html.

Eder, Klaus, and Wilifried Spohn, eds. *Collective Memory and European Identity: The Effects of Integration and Enlargement.* Aldershot: Ashgate Publishing, 2005.

Erikson, Erik H. *Identity and the Life Cycle: Selected Papers.* New York: International University Press, 1959.

European Commission's Directorate General for Enlargement. "European Commission-Enlargement-Accession Criteria." Accessed November 22, 2012. http://ec.europa.eu/enlargement/policy/glossary/terms/accession-criteria_en.htm.

Füle, Stefan. "Opening Remarks in EP [European Parliament] Debate on Turkey, 28 March 2012." Brussels: European Parliament, 2012. http://www.europarl.europa.eu/meetdocs/2009_2014/documents/d-tr/dv/0420_06/0420_06en.pdf.

George, Linda K. "Sociological Perspectives on Life Transitions." *Annual Review of Sociology* 19 (1993): 353–373.

Goffman, Erving. *Encounters: Two Studies in the Sociology of Interaction*. Indianapolis: Bobbs-Merril, 1961.

Herodotus. *The Histories*. Harmondsworth: Penguin Books, 1954.

"*In July*." IMDb. Accessed November 22, 2012. http://www.imdb.com/title/tt0177858/.

Karolewski, Ireneusz P. *Citizenship and Collective Identity in Europe*. London: Routledge, 2011.

Kellner, Douglas. *Media Culture: Cultural Studies, Identity and Politics between the Modern and the Postmodern*. London: Routledge, 1995.

Klimstra, Theo A., Koen Luyckx, William W. Hale III, Tom Frijns, Pol A. C. van Lier, and Wim H. J. Meeus. "Short-Term Fluctuations in Identity: Introducing a Micro-Level Approach to Identity Formation." *Journal of Personality and Social Psychology* 99, no. 1 (2010): 191–202.

Lewis, Martin W., and Kären E. Wigen. *The Myth of the Continents: A Critique of Metageography*. Berkeley and Los Angeles: University of California Press, 1997.

Michaelsen, Scott, and David E. Johnson, eds. *Border Theory: The Limits of Cultural Politics*. Minneapolis: University of Minnesota Press, 1997.

Nitsiakos, Vassilis, Ioannis Manos, Georgios Agelopoulos, Aliki Angelidou, and Vassilis Dalkavoukis, eds. *Balkan Border Crossings: Second Annual of the Konitsa Summer School*. Berlin: LIT Verlag, 2008.

Reinelt, Janelle G. "Performing Europe: Identity Formation for a 'New' Europe." *Theatre Journal* 53, no. 3 (2001): 365–387. http://muse.jhu.edu/journals/theatre_journal/v053/53.3reinelt.html.

Risse, Thomas. *A Community of Europeans? Transnational Identities and Public Spheres*. Ithaca, NY: Cornell University Press, 2010.

Rosaldo, Renato. *Culture and Truth: Remaking Social Analysis*. London: Routledge, 1993.

Scott, A. O. "Movie Review: *In July*." *New York Times Online*, December 7, 2001. http://movies.nytimes.com/movie/review?res=9C01EED7133CF934A35751C1A9679C8B63.

Strickland, Bonnie B., ed. *The Gale Encyclopedia of Psychology*. 2nd ed. Detroit: Gale, 2000.

Vajda, László. "Hungarian Experience on the Way to the EU, Before and After Accession." June 13, 2009. http://ec.europa.eu/agriculture/events/zagreb2009/vajda_en.pdf.

Vila, Pablo. *Crossing Borders, Reinforcing Borders: Social Categories, Metaphors and Narrative identities on the U.S.-Mexico Frontier*. Austin: University of Texas Press, 2000.

Film

In July. Directed by Fatih Akin. Germany, 2000.

11

Lost Children

Images of Childhood on the German-Polish Border in Christoph Hochhäusler's This Very Moment *(2003) and Robert Gliński's* Piggies *(2009)*

Jakub Kazecki

WHEN SELECTING A LOCATION for the narrative of *This Very Moment* (*Milchwald*, 2003), Christoph Hochhäusler, the director and co-writer of the film,[1] was searching for an area that would include elements both familiar and foreign to German audiences: a geographical space in close proximity to German urban regions but, at the same time, characterized by unsettling strangeness and exoticism. His choice of the German-Polish borderland, located less than sixty miles from Germany's largest city, Berlin, offered unique possibilities for storytelling because, as Hochhäusler noted, "many Germans do not know Poland, amazingly. It is a direct neighbor . . . [but] the language is very different, it is really a different cultural space. It is certainly the strongest of all German borders. . . . [The other side] is a place of a complete openness: everything can happen there."[2]

In Hochhäusler's interpretation, the German-Polish border functions as a divide between the rational and predicable world and the realm of unexpected scenarios. The other side, like a fairy-tale forest, remains unknown and dangerous, but that is also one of its main magnetic attractions. A similar depiction of the border in another contemporary film, the German-Polish co-production *Piggies* (*Ich, Tomek*, 2009) by Robert Gliński, provokes questions about the impulses that have led the directors to propose such images of the border as the dividing line between two worlds. In both films, the border invites transgression and promises a learning experience—an experience of growing up and growing wiser—but also has the potential to destroy the life of the trespasser.

That, however, is not the only parallel between the two films. Hochhäusler's reading of the border, located within the narrative structure of a fairy tale, also defines the choice of the main character for his story: only a child can attempt such a transgression into a strange land. In both films, *This Very Moment* by Hochhäusler and *Piggies* by Gliński, through the child protagonist, the geographical space of the borderlands turns into a domain of childhood, dependent on specific cinematic and narrative codes of representation and characterized—from the point of view of the adult audiences—by an amalgamation of the familiar and the Other. Through its analysis of the two productions, this chapter explores different representations of childhood on Germany's eastern peripheries and proposes reading them as metaphors that enforce the politically loaded notion of the border line as a "frontier": the outer edge of the civilized area subjected to conquest and colonization, and sometimes, as in *Piggies*, also a domain of physical violence resulting from the clash of two cultures.

The focus on two films released in the 2000s that place their narratives on the Eastern German border is not coincidental. The decade witnessed an increased interest by German filmmakers in an area that was subjected to rapid political and social changes. The transformations in Central Europe after 1989, including the reunification of Germany in 1990 and the expansion of the European Union (EU) by ten countries in 2004—among them Germany's two direct neighbors, Poland and the Czech Republic—brought about an intensified border exchange in the east. This exchange motivated many German filmmakers to position their works against the backdrop of the border opening and use the controversies around the vanishing border as a source of narrative tension and conflict. At the same time as individual, business, and cultural relationships with Germany's neighbor to the east intensified in the late 1990s and 2000s, audiences were also ready to be more receptive about depictions of the borderland. In addition to *This Very Moment* and *Piggies*, the films *Grill Point* (*Halbe Treppe*, 2002) by Andreas Dresen, *Distant Lights* (*Lichter*, 2003) by Hans-Christian Schmid, *Schröder's Wonderful World* (*Schröders wunderbare Welt*, 2006) by Michael Schorr, and *Polska Love Serenade* (2008) by Monika Anna Wojtyllo are examples of this surge in interest in the German-Polish borderland.[3]

The "New Europe": The Other(ed) Child

On December 21, 2007, passport checks were abolished on Germany's border to Poland and the Czech Republic, allowing the latter two countries' citizens to freely move within the EU's Schengen zone.[4] The Schengen Agreement marked a symbolic end to the postwar order of Europe: the border control at the limits of "Old Europe" had disappeared.[5] Polish mass media and state and local government officials responded to the border opening with enthusiasm, interpreting the event as a natural and long-desired step in the expansion of the EU, often formulated as "returning home to Europe."[6] Focusing on the positive, these voices omitted issues of illegal trading and migration around the main border crossings Görlitz/Zgorzelec and Frankfurt an der Oder/Słubice, while German media more often expressed concern about long-standing controversies associated with the Oder and Neisse border rivers. The German commentators articulated potential problems, such as a further increase in criminal activities after the border opening, an influx of undocumented migrants and cheap labor, and a worsening of the economic situation of the local population, stressing all too often an assumed civilizational discrepancy between Germany and Poland, that is, between the good "old" and the newest addition to the continental family: the New Europe.[7] The underlying metaphors in these and similar reactions—the Old Europe as grown-ups, the New Europe as children returning home[8]—constitute one of the basic components of EU expansionist discourse. The metaphor of the "ages" of Europe offers a point of entry for conceptualizing the systemic changes in the Eastern European countries: there is a possibility for error and transgression in the process, and the New Europe, similar to childhood, is also the domain of the Other.

This conjunction of the political and social transformation within childhood also opens a wide range of political cinematic responses that take advantage of the traditional tropes, motifs, and narrative solutions of representing childhood on screen. In cinema (starting with the "first important film about a child, *The Kid* [1921]" by Charlie Chaplin[9]), child protagonists are often used as ciphers for adult anxieties, fantasies, and fears. In such projections, the child is presented as different from adults (innocent and vulnerable), while at the same time acting as a projection screen for adult emotions. This projection remakes the child in the image of the adult and, at the same time, alters him or her in a way: "the child and childhood, and indeed children themselves, occupy a situation in which they are 'other': other to the supposedly rational, civilized, 'grown up' human animal that is the adult."[10]

A consequence of this Otherness of the child in film is the problem of agency. Films about and with children are reflections on a period of human life that is interpreted as a transitional stage in a linear development, with its expected completion in adulthood: "the cinema's depiction of childhood has been an essentially *adult* construction. In depicting childhood, the cinema . . . has generally excluded . . . the voice that could speak with first-hand authority on the subject: namely, the child him/herself."[11] Therefore, images of childhood in cinema amount to nothing but a "set of ideological assumptions about childhood," and childhood is seen as "a transcendental period of human life."[12]

This Very Moment of Border Transgression

Reading *This Very Moment* against the two overlapping backgrounds of EU expansionist discourse and of childhood representations in culture as the domain of the Other allows for a political interpretation of the borderland images in Hochhäusler's work.[13] The film uses the narrative structure of the Brothers Grimm's *Hänsel and Gretel* to tell the story of Sylvia (played by Judith Engel), who, during a shopping trip to neighboring Poland, dumps her two stepchildren, Lea (Sophie Charlotte Conrad) and Konstantin (Leonard Bruckmann), on the side of the road. Although the gesture is meant only as a temporary punishment, she soon loses the children. After coming back home to Germany, she is afraid to tell her husband, Josef (Horst-Günter Marx), about her behavior, and the children roam on the Polish side of the border until Kuba Lubiński (Mirosław Baka), a traveling sales manager, finds them. Kuba first wants to take Lea and Konstantin to the police, but, after seeing on TV that Josef is offering a reward for any information about his lost children, the salesman decides to earn some money on the side and deliver the children to Josef himself.

By using both narrative and aesthetic devices, Hochhäusler draws a very strong divide between the two countries and cultures. Following the paradigm of frontier,[14] the director takes advantage of both the intertextual echoes of his story and the linguistic and cultural Otherness of Poland. The viewers' interpretation of the children's first encounter with a Pole is preconditioned by the reception of the well-known *Hänsel and Gretel* story. The hungry children find an unlocked truck in the middle of the forest and food set up on a table in front of it (the equivalent of the gingerbread house from the Grimm's tale). The truck belongs to Kuba, who is just taking a dinner break on the road before heading to the area motels with a supply of sanitary products. Even when Kuba, after the first brief moment of speaking Polish and scaring the children, switches to familiar German and invites the children to join him at the table in a friendly manner, an element of uncertainty about his intentions remains. The audience's misgivings are confirmed when good-hearted Kuba, motivated by a stroke of greed, refuses to let the children go. The German spoken by the Pole is revealed as an instrument of deception. The representation of languages in *This Very Moment* becomes an indicator of the director's position on the divisions between the characters as unbridgeable: they do be-

Figure 11.1. ***This Very Moment*: Lea and Konstantin get lost in the lush vegetation in Poland. Courtesy of Filmgalerie 451.**

long to different worlds. The Polish spoken in the film remains untranslated and contributes to the isolation of the characters.

Before a word of Polish is even articulated in the story, however, the Otherness of Poland is already manifested in the landscape. On the other side of the border, the power lines that characterize the German landscape disappear and are replaced by a thick green forest. Wheat fields are ready for harvest, pollen dust is slowly carried by the wind, and birds are singing. The sleepy high-summer landscape is a dreamy vision of an unreal and wild land, vital and full of possibilities, yet threatening.

The foreign area is linked to Germany by the road system, a device created to control nature and put it on track—a civilizing effort to provide a connection between people, but, as used by Hochhäusler, also a metaphor for linear (and normalized) personal development. When the children get lost, they are going away from the road, pushed off by the oncoming reaping machine, and disappear in the road ditch. The night spent in the forest is the only time when the children are deprived of any social contacts, truly lost in the middle of nowhere in a state of suspension and despair. Kuba, who finds the children, takes Lea and Konstantin with him on the trip to Poland. The children experience the roads and streets of the new country from his truck. The strangeness of the foreign land is mediated through their point of view: the traditional annual August pilgrimage to the Catholic monastery in Częstochowa on the side of the road appears inexplicable and fascinating in its exoticism. The masses of pilgrims praying, singing, and marching with Polish and EU flags and blocking the city streets seem like a chaotic disturbance to the rules of traffic: an intervention of nature, invading the roads and lifting the civilizatory order.

The contrast between Polish and German spaces as domains of vitality and infertility, respectively, is amplified through the depiction of Sylvia and Josef's house: a brand-new black-and-white building, characterized by clean lines and symmetrical design, with a concrete driveway and a carefully trimmed front yard. The interior of the house is cold and sterile, with the blinds half-closed, lights off, unfinished walls, and furniture still factory wrapped. The rooms are submerged in a blue-tinted light and ghostly quiet. The house is also a space of intimacy bordering on entrapment, which mirrors Sylvia's state and explains her wish for a chance at a new life without the burden of her stepchildren. The spaces where Sylvia has abandoned the children are characterized by the cycle of nature and a maternal principle. Rich in vegetation and eroticized, they are clearly a counterpoint to the emptiness of the father's house. Several visual elements on the Polish side of the border remind the audience of Sylvia's denial of her parental duties and her symbolic infertility: the stork appearing in Sylvia's path when she reflects on her moment of hostility toward Lea and Konstantin; the church celebrations of harvest and pilgrimage to Mary, the Mother of God; the caring maternal figures who feed the hungry children; and Kuba's pregnant girlfriend (Hanna Kochańska), completely absorbed in her nesting activity of picking the color for the baby's room.

Hochhäusler depicts the rejection of vitality, which is associated with Germany, as a dominant feature in the relationship between Josef and Sylvia. The incident exposes the faults of their marriage, but the crisis of their relationship caused by Sylvia's secret is also a crisis of the lifestyle of their social class, guided by materialistic values and striving to keep up the conservative image of woman as homemaker and caregiver and man as provider and protector. The disappearance of the children is, as in another Grimm's fairy tale, *The Ratcatcher*, a punishment for the behavior of the middle-class parents. Unlike the original *Hänsel and Gretel* tale, it is not dire financial circumstances that force Sylvia to abandon the children in the woods but rather her focus on her own comfort. The crossing of the state border (in accordance with the paradigm of frontier that promises to award a risky gamble with large personal gain) offers Josef and Sylvia a rare chance of redemption. They would be able to find the children if they gave up the egotist attitude, if they relinquished their own positions and opened up communication—not only with each other, but also with people on the other side of the border—without employing the colonial attitude of cultural and economic dominance. The figure of the father, in particular, is coded colonially here. His brutal strategy of conquest and symbolic takeover—offering ransom money for the children as the solution to the problem—seems out of place in Poland and, in the end, yields no results. The language of the film reinforces the reading of his efforts as a colonializing move. His own search for Lea and Konstantin is associated with a landscape deprived of any vegetation, as he seems to turn the places he visits in Poland into an asphalt and concrete desert. Josef, always in his business suit, symbolizes the greed and technological progress of the West. He looks for the children in an empty open-air theater or an enormous abandoned parking lot with streetlamps like bizarre concrete flowers.

Although the moment of transgression and facing the Other appears to be a chance for communication between the two adults, Sylvia cannot overcome her fear of being honest, because it would destroy the appearances of a wholesome family and create discomfort in her life. Torn between acknowledging to her husband that she failed as a stepmother and lied to him and keeping up the illusion, she falls silent and numb. Frustrated by his wife's muteness and sensing her betrayal, Josef leaves Sylvia, deserting her in a dark hotel room that replicates the setting of their empty household.

The film ends with an image of the children wandering on an empty road, still in Poland, walking into the unknown. But they are not lost and helpless

Figure 11.2. Children in wonderland: Polish landscapes as a mirror to German reality in *This Very Moment*. Courtesy of Filmgalerie 451.

anymore: they have gained a certain kind of independence, after Kuba releases them from his truck, frightened by their ingenuous attempt to kill him. It is Lea and Konstantin's choice to stay on the other side of the border. The children's refusal to return to Germany is the ultimate failure of both parents, who could not transform into a different social model.

This Very Moment, as a tale with no happy ending, has a distorting effect on the class-coded images of German family normalcy and material wealth.[15] The story offers no closure and no redemption. Instead, it brings about a destabilizing absence and forces the viewers of this "fairytale in fear and color"[16] "to remain suspended in the narrative, or to veer off back into the fairytale world, the fantastic world or real forest,"[17] in a state of discomfort that allows for a critical position.

Three Little *Piggies* and the German Wolf

Similar to *This Very Moment*, *Piggies* by Robert Gliński ends with a violent act that robs the audience of a feeling of redemption. The story of fifteen-year-old Tomek (Filip Garbacz), a Polish youth who lives near the Sieniawka border crossing to Germany, follows a fatal trajectory of cause and effect that leads him to commit murder. Tomek discovers that his best friend, Ciemny (Daniel Furmaniak), earns pocket money by selling his body to German pedophiles and decides to join the business. In the border area, where the standard of living is low and unemployment high, prostitution appears to Tomek as the best way to help out his mother (Dorota Wierzbicka), who has serious financial difficulties and is threatened with losing her job. He also feels that giving expensive presents to materialistic Marta (Anna Kulej), his first big love, is the only option to ensure her interest. One of Tomek's clients brutally rapes him, and the boy plots a revenge on the pimp, on his friend Ciemny who has drawn him into the criminal world, and, in the end, on the client himself. He turns from a good student and member of the church youth club into a murderer by killing the man who raped him.

By bringing the example of child prostitution to his German and Polish viewers (the film is a German and Polish co-production), Gliński wants to point out a problem that emerged in the economic transformation of Poland after 1989 but has been suppressed in public debate: "It is a taboo topic. Polish society and the Polish politicians don't say anything about it. There is no public discussion, although this prostitution is visible everywhere. I placed the story at the German-Polish border. The problem is, however, also in larger Polish cities, in shopping malls. Young boys and girls are hanging around there and offering themselves to rich customers, for a cell phone or a leather jacket."[18]

The English title *Piggies* is a direct translation of the Polish slang expression *świnki*, describing these teenagers who sell their bodies for presents and money. *Świnki*, and not the equivalent of the German *Ich, Tomek* (I, Tomek), is also the title of the film in the Polish distribution. According to the intentions of the director, this title draws the viewers' attention to the main problem of the story. But *Piggies* cannot be compartmentalized as a contemporary social drama shot in almost documentary style and set in the very specific realities of the German-Polish borderland of the late 2000s, although many critics have focused only on this aspect.[19] The setting of the film in time and place is only seemingly authentic. Both the director and the writer of the screenplay, Joanna Didik, point out that the story is set in Gubin/Guben, a small border city in the proximity of Frankfurt an der Oder.[20] The scenes in the film indicate, however, a geographical site more blurred in its contours: some images testify to the fact that Tomek lives in the city, but the actual border crossing the audience sees (with its large name sign in view) is Sieniawka/Zittau, over ninety miles to the south of Gubin. Equally unclear is the location of the story in time. The fact that some of the key events in the film take place on the historical day on which passport controls at the border are abolished would suggest that story occurs in December 2007. However, the audience sees spring landscapes and witnesses the outdoor festivities that follow the opening of the border (typical for the day of the accession of Poland to the EU in May 2004), as well as the annual Catholic youth meeting in which Tomek participates (always taking place in May or June). In addition, Tomek and Marta's trip to the Love Parade in Berlin (typically in July) also distorts this chronology.

The displacement of the story on the map and in time indicates that Gliński wants to depart from factual authenticity and aims at a more universal message for his story. This departure from specificity allows *Piggies* to be interpreted as a morality play placed in borderlands understood not as much as a geographical or historical space, but as a metaphorical playground of the struggle between good and evil. As Gliński formulates it,

> in the moment when the borders . . . between countries disappeared . . . the consequence was the pushing of limits within us, the moral limits. [The film shows] that people change, that the traditional morality changes, that a blowjob is a normal kind of job for these young people, who don't see anything immoral about it. I think it's a big change of social norms, and a story about it needed to be told: many young people take a shortcut . . . and they don't have any moral distance or a moral reflection. . . . [The film] shows a problem that emerges in Poland in many places: the moral code changes.[21]

Gliński identifies the border opening with the abolishing of moral restrictions. This has the biggest impact on the children. Within the narrative

Figure 11.3. The celebration of the border opening and the first transgression: Tomek abused by a pedophile in *Piggies*. Courtesy of Fabryka Obrazu. Photo by Piotr Bujnowicz.

structure of a morality play, *Piggies* sets up an ensemble of symbolic characters and personified forces that assault the weaknesses of the protagonist or at least fail to provide him with guidance and support. Tomek is a gifted language student and astronomy fan; his dream is to get a telescope for his astronomy club. But neither his German teacher and club advisor, Weber (Rolf Hoppe), nor the leader of his Catholic youth group, the charismatic priest (Marek Kalita), can offer much help in purchasing the expensive instrument, as both are focused on their goals for the group, not on the individual needs of its members. The institutions of school and church fail the boy. In addition, Tomek cannot count on his parents, who are preoccupied with the struggle for the financial survival of the family (his mother) or searching for an escape from reality in soccer and alcohol (his father, played by Bogdan Koca). As a result, Tomek and the other two main characters in the film—his girlfriend, Marta, and his friend Ciemny—are put in the roles of three little "piggies," lacking the tools that would help them to resist temptation. The association with another popular fairy tale about three little pigs who build three houses of different materials is not out of place here; it provides conditions for delivering a moral message. By placing the dangers to the children across the border, on the German side (where the wealthy clients and the attractive gadgets are coming from),

Gliński casts the Germans in the role of the big bad wolf, the personified evil that contributes to the failure of traditional social institutions on the Polish side and skews the moral compass of the children.

Tomek's trip to the East, during which he takes part in the annual Catholic youth meeting in Lednica (in the heart of historical Poland, associated with the establishment of the Polish state and the country's Christianization), is contrasted with the trip to the Love Parade in Berlin, to the west. While the scenes at the youth meeting radiate lyricism and are dominated by warm tones and wide shots stressing the connection within the community, the images of the electronic music festival in Germany's capital are loaded with flashy colors and close-ups separating the transgendered and queer individuals from the crowd, emphasizing, in Tomek's eyes, their bizarre individuality. The Love Parade is Tomek's emanation of Germany, he "is disgusted with its forced physicality, his sexuality gets distorted before he has discovered it for himself."[22] The boy moves between the two poles, the East and the West, and the latter draws him more and more into its orbit.

This attraction to the West (Germany and the EU) is nowhere more apparent than in the way in which Gliński uses Tomek's passion for astronomy as a symbol for the loss of moral values. *Piggies* plays here upon the famous sentence by Immanuel Kant that only two things can inspire a

Figure 11.4. Between the two states: Tomek and Ciemny at the German-Polish border. Courtesy of Fabryka Obrazu. Photo by Piotr Bujnowicz.

Figure 11.5. Tomek and Marta's date at the border river. Courtesy of Fabryka Obrazu. Photo by Piotr Bujnowicz.

genuine awe in a person: "The starry heavens above me and the moral law within me."[23] The boy observes the zodiac in the firmament, longing for a larger telescope, but turns away from the sky when he meets Marta in the local club, the Zodiac. From that moment on, Marta directs Tomek's attention toward the shiny objects she desires, objects symbolically reflecting light and not possessing it. She asks him to give her one thousand euros for bleaching her teeth and convinces him to buy her a glittery pair of shoes. The euro, with its design encompassing the twelve stars of the EU (the same number as the constellations in the zodiac), becomes the new object of Marta and Tomek's awe. The moral code vanishes with the dream of watching stars in the sky, and the children discover that, within this ethical void, nothing is forbidden anymore—and nothing *does* seem to have any negative consequences.

Cautionary (Fairy) Tales for Adults?

Samantha Lay, in her study of British social realist films—which also frequently made working-class children the central protagonists—expresses the view that this narrative solution inevitably

> poses new questions for audiences, critics and theorists. How do we identify with a twelve-year-old girl or a six-year-old-boy? Are we more distanced because we cannot directly align or identify with their world view, or are we being addressed as parents or potential parents? Are working class parents being addressed, or are these films merely reminding middle class audiences of how lucky their own children are? What position are we being invited to take—observer or social worker?[24]

The same questions, arising from the assumption of cinematic childhood as ideological construction, can be directed to the creators of *This Very Moment* and *Piggies*. Robert Gliński offers his audience a social drama in documentary style. At the outset, however, his film passes a moral judgment by taking advantage of the binary structures of the morality play, inviting the audience into the protagonist's struggles. *Piggies* depicts the border as a line between good and evil forces, as well as a frontier that incorporates conquest and exploitation, which appear as intrinsic to the spreading of the free market economy and liberalization. The story of abuse and rape fits into the paradigm of colonization and eroticization of the Other side, but it also nods at the commoditization of everything, including the human body. The violation of Tomek's innocence (significantly, his first client places euro banknotes on his crotch for Tomek to pick up) marks his initiation in both sexual and economic senses, paralleling the sexual abuse and multilevel exploitation accompanying the expansion of the EU. This traumatizing transgression is the reason why Tomek smashes his rapist's head in the final scene of the film, lacking faith in the law enforcement and justice institutions. Gliński uses the figure of Tomek as an "example of one dimensional critique of capitalism. . . . the victim becomes the victimizer the moment he plays 'the game'."[25] In contrast to Gliński's intentions, however, the clash between the visual style of a social drama and the highly symbolic coding of the German-Polish borderlands creates an estrangement, which prevents the audience from taking the position of engaged social activist. The role of the audience is limited to that of a mere observer of the fatal causality of Tomek's journey.[26]

In the similarly symbolic narrative structure of the fairy tale of homecoming with no happy ending, Hochhäusler has found a vehicle for his engagement of the audience, not only as protectors of childhood but also as social critics, for whom cinema can serve as a subversive and transformative impulse. The subversion is enveloped in the nostalgic topos of a missing child and in the way in which this topos is placed in the borderlands, which are interpreted here as an area destabilizing in its Otherness.[27] In *This Very Moment*, the topos does not encompass a fantasy of family values and family structure that is typical for the nostalgic reconstruction of the lost home, truth, and tradition. In Svetlana Boym's terms, the nostalgia in Hochhäusler's film is reflective, not restorative.[28] The accent is on *algia* and as such has the power of social criticism: "Reflective nostalgia thrives in algia, the longing itself, and delays the homecoming—wistfully, ironically, desperately. . . . Restorative nostalgia protects the absolute truth, while reflective nostalgia calls it into doubt."[29]

In Hochhäusler's film, passing the German-Polish frontier and going beyond it is not just a trip across the geographical divide but, more importantly, a rupture in the conventional narratives of family, progress, and expansion, having a politically subversive—and intentionally distressing—effect on the German audience. In both film narratives, children are (ab)used in order to convey political commentary. It is left to the viewer to question where one can draw the borderline.

Notes

1. With Benjamin Heisenberg, the director of *Schläfer* (*Sleeper*, 2005) and *Der Räuber* (*The Robber*, 2010). Hochhäusler's co-operation with Heisenberg dates back to 1998, when they co-founded (with Sebastian Kutzli) the film magazine *Revolver*, one of the most influential film periodicals in Germany. For an overview of their work on *Revolver*, see "*Revolver*," *Colophon*, September 22, 2006, http://www.welovecolophon.com/archive/?mag_id=206.

2. Christoph Hochhäusler, "Interview mit dem Regisseur," in *Milchwald*, DVD. (Stuttgart and Berlin: Filmgalerie 451, 2004).

3. The list of German productions can be completed by another representation of borderlands, *Hochzeitspolka* (*Wedding Polka*, 2010), by Lars Jessen. In this film, however, the German-Polish tensions associated with Germany's border to the east are played out on Poland's border with the Ukraine, possibly reflecting on the shift of the EU border and the displacement of the same economic and social issues to the east. For a discussion about earlier depictions of German-Polish border and the images of Poland in German cinema, see Konrad Klejsa, Schamma Schahadat, and Christian Nastal, eds., *Deutschland und Polen: Filmische Grenzen und Nachbarschaften* (Marburg: Schüren Verlag, 2011).

4. "Schengen Area," European Commission Home Affairs, October 16, 2012, http://ec.europa.eu/dgs/home-affairs/what-we-do/policies/borders-and-visas/schengen/index_en.htm.

5. The term *Old Europe* was first used by U.S. Secretary of Defense Donald Rumsfeld in January 2003 to differentiate between the European countries that supported the 2003 invasion of Iraq (the New Europe) and the opponents of the intervention and the largest member states of the EU from before its expansion, in particular, Germany, France, and the United Kingdom. See Office of the Assistant Secretary of Defense (Public Affairs), "Secretary Rumsfeld Briefs at the Foreign Press Center," U.S. Department of Defense, January 22, 2003, http://www.defense.gov/transcripts/transcript.aspx?transcriptid=1330.

6. See, among many others, the articles in the Polish newspapers and weekly magazines emphasizing the image of Poland's return to Europe without borders: Andrzej Seweryn, "Polska wróciła do domu," *Dziennik*, December 21, 2007, http://wiadomosci.dziennik.pl/opinie/artykuly/123268,polska-wrocila-do-domu.html; ab, "Powrót Polski do serca Europy," *Wprost*, December 5, 2007, http:/www.wprost.pl/ar/119100/Powrot-Polski-do-serca-Europy/; Jacek Pawlicki, "My w bezgranicznej Europie," *Gazeta Wyborcza*, December 9, 2007, http://wyborcza.pl/dziennikarze/1,84228,4746510.html.

7. Even if the German media show the advantages of the border openings, the image of concerned citizens is recurring: "Statt grenzenloser Sicherheit befürchten viele Bürger grenzenlose Kriminalität" ("Instead of security without borders many citizens fear unlimited criminality") in Hannelore Crolly, "Keine Angst vor dem Europa ohne Grenzen," *Die Welt*, December 6, 2007, sec. Politik, http://www.welt.de/politik/article1436505/Keine-Angst-vor-dem-Europa-ohne-Grenzen.html.

8. One of the most prominent examples of using these metaphors in the official discourse is the emotional statement of French President Jacques Chirac at the emergency EU summit in Brussels in February 2003, where the EU's involvement in the U.S. intervention in Iraq was discussed. Chirac called the position of the countries supporting the U.S. stance on Iraq "childish" and noted that "it is not well-brought-up behavior" and that these countries "missed a great opportunity to shut up." See Oana Lungescu, "Chirac Blasts EU Candidates," *BBC News*, February 18, 2003, http://news.bbc.co.uk/2/hi/europe/2774139.stm; "'New Europe' Backs EU on Iraq," *BBC News*, February 19, 2003, http://news.bbc.co.uk/2/hi/europe/2775579.stm. The reactions in the criticized countries also used the vocabulary of childhood, e.g., in Latvia: "perhaps we were not raised properly," "perhaps there are some in Paris who want to be the patriarch of Europe's 'family.'" See "Chirac Sparks 'New Europe' Ire," *BBC News*, February 19, 2003, http://news.bbc.co.uk/2/hi/europe/2780881.stm.

9. Named the "first important film about a child" by Ruth M. Goldstein and Edith Zornow, *The Screen Image of Youth: Movies About Children and Adolescents* (Metuchen, NJ: Scarecrow Press, 1980), vii.

10. Karen Lury, *The Child in Film: Tears, Fears and Fairytales* (New Brunswick, NJ: Rutgers University Press, 2010), 1. Owain Jones interprets childhood (also using Levinas and Derrida's terminology of the Other) in a similar way: "Otherness . . . does not just mean simple separation and unknowability. It is a more subtle idea of the knowable and unknowable, the familiar and the strange, the close and the distance." See Owain Jones, "'True Geography [ ] Quickly Forgotten, Giving Away to an Adult-Imagined Universe:' Approaching the Otherness of Childhood," *Children's Geographies* 6, no. 2 (2008): 197. André Bazin notes that it is precisely this mixture of familiar and strange that makes childhood a desirable object of adult contemplation. In his essay about *Germany, Year Zero* by Roberto Rossellini (which features a child protagonist), Bazin expresses the opinion that "children's films fully play on the ambiguity of our interest in these miniature human beings. . . .[They] treat childhood precisely as if it were open to our understanding and empathy; they are made in the name of anthropomorphism." See André Bazin, "*Germany, Year Zero*," in *Bazin at Work: Major Essays & Reviews From the Forties & Fifties* (New York: Routledge, 1997), 121.

11. Neil Sinyard, *Children in the Movies* (New York: St. Martin's Press, 1992), 11–12.

12. David Lusted, "Introduction," in *Kidstuff: Childhood and Cinema: Notes to Accompany the Season of Films Programmed Under the Title "Seen but Not Heard"* (London: Institute of Contemporary Arts Cinema, 1979), n.p.; quoted in Joe Kelleher, "Face to Face with Terror: Children in Film," in *Children in Culture: Approaches to Childhood*, ed. Karín Lesnik-Oberstein (New York: St. Martin's Press, 1998), 29.

13. Hochhäusler has, in fact, indicated that he wants his film to be interpreted politically. However, most of the critical responses focused on the aesthetic qualities of his work without connecting them with the politics of *This Very Moment*. Marco Abel describes its aesthetics as "viral politics" which "tends to appeal directly to the nervous system by affecting viewers through submitting them to a modulation of intensities to which we have no choice but to respond." Marco Abel, "Tender Speaking: An Interview with Christoph Hochhäusler," *Senses of Cinema* 42 (February 13, 2007), http://sensesofcinema.com/2007/42/christoph-hochhausler/. See also the analysis by Kristin Kopp that highlights the politics of the film in the context of other Berlin School productions, the post-1990 films that advance the aesthetics of cinema within German narrative filmmaking: Kristin Kopp, "Christoph Hochhäusler's *This Very Moment*: The Berlin School and the Politics of Spacial Aesthetics in the German-Polish Borderlands," in *The Collapse of the Conventional: German Film and Its Politics at the Turn of the Twenty-First Century*, ed. Jaimey Fisher and Brad Prager (Detroit: Wayne State University Press, 2010), 285–292. A survey of critical reception of *This Very Moment* is also included in Sandra Calkins, "*Milchwald*": *Hänsel und Gretel in der Spätmoderne: Eine Analyse von Christoph Hochhäuslers Filmdebüt* (München: GRIN Verlag, 2007), 23–24.

14. The frontier, a term used in border studies for historical and present-day colonial encroachments, signifies the meeting point between the known and the alien land. It is a product of colonial discourse that implies the opportunity to push forward, explore the new land, and benefit, economically or socially. The risk connected with this type of border crossing is quite significant: the escapades on "the other side" are intrusions into the unknown beyond the German comfort zone.

15. In their discussion of films about lost children, Debbie Olson and Andrew Scahill point out the destabilizing effect of a story about lost children who do not return home. Such narrative, deprived of a happy ending, "continues to frame stories about children and childhood as a multitextured cultural space that is, quite often, discombobulating. As in the old myths and tales, such lost child narratives today do not always end happily ever after and instead, often reveal a sinister and secret underside, a lingering shadow that distorts and alters the 'normal' cultural spaces of childhood." See Debbie Olson and Andrew Scahill, "Introduction," in *Lost and Othered Children in Contemporary Cinema*, ed. Debbie Olson and Andrew Scahill (Lanham, MD: Lexington Books, 2012), x.

16. The tagline of the film: "Ein Märchen in Angst und Farbe."

17. Lury, *The Child in Film*, 136.

18. Wolfgang Martin Hamdorf, "Ein Sozialdrama: *Ich, Tomek* als polnisch-deutsche Koproduktion," *Fazit* (Deutschlandradio Kultur, June 8, 2010), http://www.dradio.de/dkultur/sendungen/fazit/1200260/ (my translation).

19. See, for example, the readings that place the story in specific historical circumstances and interpret it as pure social drama focusing mainly on the quasi-documentary style of the film and authenticity of location: "[Gliński] approaches this moving and at the same time shocking social drama with a cool and almost documentary distance which amplifies its effect even more." Axel Schock, "*Ich, Tomek*: Für die Liebe auf den Kinderstrich," *News.de*, June 9, 2010, http://www.news.de/medien/855060120/fuer-die-liebe-auf-den-kinderstrich/1/. See also Nina Scholz, "Wünsche erfüllen," *Jungle World: Die linke Wochenzeitung*, June 10, 2010, http://jungle-world.com/artikel/2010/23/41107.html; Christina Bylow, "Wenn alle versagen," *Berliner Zeitung*, June 11, 2010, http://www.berliner-zeitung.de/archiv/der-film--ich--tomek--handelt-von-kinderprostitution-wenn-alle-versagen,10810590,10722520.html; Angelika Nguyen, "*Ich, Tomek* von Robert Glinski (Polen/Deutschland)," *OST:BLOG*, June 11, 2010, http://www.ostblog.de/2010/06/ich_tomek_von_robert_glinski_p.php.

20. Robert Gliński emphasizes that Joanna Didik, the author of the screenplay and his student at the National Higher School of Film, Television, and Theatre in Łódź, was born and lived in Gubin for twenty years and "practically wrote the story about her school friends." It reinforces the impression that the film is set exclusively in Gubin/Guben. See Ewa Szponar, "Robert Gliński: W moim filmie nie ma kłamstwa," *Onet Film*, May 19, 2011, http://film.onet.pl/wiadomosci/publikacje/wywiady/robert-glinski-w-moim-filmie-nie-ma-klamstwa,1,4336067,wiadomosc.html [my translation]; "Robert Gliński o swoim najnowszym filmie," *PolskieRadio.pl*, May 19, 2011, http://www.polskieradio.pl/24/1022/Artykul/370056,Robert-Glinski-o-swoim-najnowszym-filmie-Swinki-(galeria).

21. *Filmweb rozmawia z Robertem Glińskim* (video) (FilmWebTV, 2011), http://www.youtube.com/watch?v=N-ScNL2VLi0&feature=youtube_gdata_player [my translation].

22. Bylow, "Der Film 'Ich, Tomek'" (my translation).

23. Immanuel Kant, *Critique of Practical Reason*, ed. Mary J. Gregor (Cambridge: Cambridge University Press, 1997), 133.

24. Samantha Lay, *British Social Realism: From Documentary to Brit-Grit* (London: Wallflower Press, 2002), 109; quoted in Stella M. Hockenhull, "Wednesday's Child: Adolescent Outsiders in Contemporary British Cinema," in *Lost and Othered Children in Contemporary Cinema*, ed. Debbie Olson and Andrew Scahill (Lanham, MD: Lexington Books, 2012), 49.

25. Scholz, "Wünsche erfüllen" (my translation).

26. Scholz interprets the one-dimensionality of *Piggies* as its main flaw. Gliński "has made a flawless social drama, his overzealous didacticism has choked an interesting material. . . . The pedagogical dramaturgy presents the life of the young man as one-way street and therefore does not leave the viewer any room for interpretations. Gliński makes an unbelievable film out of a pretty believable story. . . . [He] proceeds with his depiction of the situation at the border in a similar way. The viewer sees Germany with its grotesque brutal face of sparkling capitalism, while the Polish side is shaped by any lack of perspectives. The Germans in the film appear as greedy capitalists, the Poles as eternal losers who want to do something but don't know how. Instead of trying to make these contrasts accessible to viewers by showing how Tomek makes

sense of them, Gliński loses himself in the dichotomies of national stereotypes that are impossible to resolve: here, the grabby Germans—over there, the Poles who look at Germany with envy" (Scholz, "Wünsche erfüllen" [my translation]).

27. Hochhäusler admitted in the interview with Abel that the contrasts between the German and Polish landscapes, manifested, for example, in the images of Sylvia's sterile house against the wild vegetation of the other side of the border, "are signs that the viewer is supposed to read and that one can and should read politically. Germany changed a lot as a result of the reunification and the liberalization of Eastern Europe. By and large, I think this was stimulating, but at times frightening as well, and it led to a lot of pain, since every change is painful to some degree. I also perceived it as an awakening, and in any case you can see this transformation affecting German cinema." See Abel, "Tender Speaking."

28. Emma Wilson notes that "the difference between the two lies in the belief (or lack thereof) in the possibility of restoration, the return of the missing child, the reinstatement of a system of family values." See Emma Wilson, *Cinema's Missing Children* (London: Wallflower Press, 2003), 14.

29. Svetlana Boym, *The Future of Nostalgia* (New York: Basic Books, 2002), xviii.

Works Cited

ab. "Powrót Polski do serca Europy." *Wprost*, December 5, 2007. http:/www.wprost.pl/ar/119100/Powrot-Polski-do-serca-Europy/.

Abel, Marco. "Tender Speaking: An Interview with Christoph Hochhäusler." *Senses of Cinema* 42 (February 13, 2007). http://sensesofcinema.com/2007/42/christoph-hochhausler/.

Bazin, André. "*Germany, Year Zero*." In *Bazin at Work: Major Essays & Reviews From the Forties & Fifties*, 121–124. New York: Routledge, 1997.

Boym, Svetlana. *The Future of Nostalgia*. New York: Basic Books, 2002.

Bylow, Christina. "Wenn alle versagen." *Berliner Zeitung*, June 11, 2010. http://www.berliner-zeitung.de/archiv/der-film--ich--tomek--handelt-von-kinderprostitution-wenn-alle-versagen,10810590,10722520.html.

Calkins, Sandra. *"Milchwald": Hänsel und Gretel in der Spätmoderne: Eine Analyse von Christoph Hochhäuslers Filmdebüt*. München: GRIN Verlag, 2007.

"Chirac Sparks 'New Europe' Ire." *BBC News*, February 19, 2003. http://news.bbc.co.uk/2/hi/europe/2780881.stm.

Crolly, Hannelore. "Keine Angst vor dem Europa ohne Grenzen." *Die Welt*, December 6, 2007, sec. Politik. http://www.welt.de/politik/article1436505/Keine-Angst-vor-dem-Europa-ohne-Grenzen.html.

Filmweb rozmawia z Robertem Glińskim (video). FilmWebTV, 2011. http://www.youtube.com/watch?v=N-ScNL2VLi0&feature=youtube_gdata_player.

Goldstein, Ruth M., and Edith Zornow. *The Screen Image of Youth: Movies about Children and Adolescents*. Metuchen, NJ: Scarecrow Press, 1980.

Hamdorf, Wolfgang Martin. "Ein Sozialdrama: *Ich, Tomek* als polnisch-deutsche Koproduktion." *Fazit*. Deutschlandradio Kultur, June 8, 2010. http://www.dradio.de/dkultur/sendungen/fazit/1200260/.

Hochhäusler, Christoph. "Interview mit dem Regisseur." In *Milchwald*. DVD. Stuttgart: Filmgalerie 451, 2004.

Hockenhull, Stella M. "Wednesday's Child: Adolescent Outsiders in Contemporary British Cinema." In *Lost and Othered Children in Contemporary Cinema*, edited by Debbie Olson and Andrew Scahill, 47–65. Lanham, MD: Lexington Books, 2012.

Jones, Owain. "'True Geography [ ] Quickly Forgotten, Giving Away to an Adult-Imagined Universe:' Approaching the Otherness of Childhood." *Children's Geographies* 6, no. 2 (2008): 195–212.

Kant, Immanuel. *Critique of Practical Reason*. Edited by Mary J. Gregor. Cambridge: Cambridge University Press, 1997.

Kelleher, Joe. "Face to Face with Terror: Children in Film." In *Children in Culture: Approaches to Childhood*, edited by Karín Lesnik-Oberstein, 29–54. New York: St. Martin's Press, 1998.

Klejsa, Konrad, Schamma Schahadat, and Christian Nastal, eds. *Deutschland und Polen: Filmische Grenzen und Nachbarschaften*. Marburg: Schüren Verlag, 2011.

Kopp, Kristin. "Christoph Hochhäusler's *This Very Moment*: The Berlin School and the Politics of Spacial Aesthetics in the German-Polish Borderlands." In *The Collapse of the Conventional: German Film and Its Politics at the Turn of the Twenty-First Century*, edited by Jaimey Fisher and Brad Prager, 285–308. Detroit: Wayne State University Press, 2010.

Lay, Samantha. *British Social Realism: From Documentary to Brit-Grit*. London: Wallflower Press, 2002.

Lungescu, Oana. "Chirac Blasts EU Candidates." *BBC News*, February 18, 2003. http://news.bbc.co.uk/2/hi/europe/2774139.stm.

Lury, Karen. *The Child in Film: Tears, Fears and Fairytales*. New Brunswick, NJ: Rutgers University Press, 2010.

Lusted, David. "Introduction." In *Kidstuff: Childhood and Cinema: Notes to Accompany the Season of Films Programmed Under the Title "Seen but Not Heard,"* n.p. London: Institute of Contemporary Arts Cinema, 1979.

"'New Europe' Backs EU on Iraq." *BBC News*, February 19, 2003. http://news.bbc.co.uk/2/hi/europe/2775579.stm.

Nguyen, Angelika. "*Ich, Tomek* von Robert Glinski (Polen/Deutschland)." *OST:BLOG*, June 11, 2010. http://www.ostblog.de/2010/06/ich_tomek_von_robert_glinski_p.php.

Office of the Assistant Secretary of Defense (Public Affairs). "Secretary Rumsfeld Briefs at the Foreign Press Center." U.S. Department of Defense, January 22, 2003. http://www.defense.gov/transcripts/transcript.aspx?transcriptid=1330.

Olson, Debbie, and Andrew Scahill. "Introduction." In *Lost and Othered Children in Contemporary Cinema*, edited by Debbie Olson and Andrew Scahill, ix–xiv. Lanham: Lexington Books, 2012.

Pawlicki, Jacek. "My w bezgranicznej Europie." *Gazeta Wyborcza*, December 9, 2007. http://wyborcza.pl/dziennikarze/1,84228,4746510.html.

"*Revolver*." Colophon, September 22, 2006. http://www.welovecolophon.com/archive/?mag_id=206.

"Robert Gliński o swoim najnowszym filmie." *PolskieRadio.pl*, May 19, 2011. http://www.polskieradio.pl/24/1022/Artykul/370056,Robert-Glinski-o-swoim-najnowszym-filmie-Swinki-(galeria).

"Schengen Area." European Commission Home Affairs, October 16, 2012. http://ec.europa.eu/dgs/home-affairs/what-we-do/policies/borders-and-visas/schengen/index_en.htm.

Schock, Axel. "*Ich, Tomek*: Für die Liebe auf den Kinderstrich." *News.de*, June 9, 2010. http://www.news.de/medien/855060120/fuer-die-liebe-auf-den-kinderstrich/1/.

Scholz, Nina. "Wünsche erfüllen." *Jungle World: Die linke Wochenzeitung*, June 10, 2010. http://jungle-world.com/artikel/2010/23/41107.html.

Seweryn, Andrzej. "Polska wróciła do domu." *Dziennik*, December 21, 2007. http://wiadomosci.dziennik.pl/opinie/artykuly/123268,polska-wrocila-do-domu.html.

Sinyard, Neil. *Children in the Movies*. New York: St. Martin's Press, 1992.

Szponar, Ewa. "Robert Gliński: W moim filmie nie ma kłamstwa." *Onet Film*, May 19, 2011. http://film.onet.pl/wiadomosci/publikacje/wywiady/robert-glinski-w-moim-filmie-nie-ma-klamstwa,1,4336067,wiadomosc.html.

Wilson, Emma. *Cinema's Missing Children*. London: Wallflower Press, 2003.

Films

Distant Lights (*Lichter*). 2003. Directed by Hans-Christian Schmid. Germany, 2003.

Grill Point (*Halbe Treppe*). Directed by Andreas Dresen. Germany, 2002.

The Kid. Directed by Charlie Chaplin. United States, 1921.

Piggies (*Ich, Tomek/Świnki*). Directed by Robert Gliński. Germany, Poland, 2009.

Polska Love Serenade. 2008. Directed by Monika Anna Wojtyllo. Germany, 2008.

Schröder's Wonderful World (*Schröders wunderbare Welt*). Directed by Michael Schorr. Germany, 2006.

This Very Moment (*Milchwald*). Directed by Christoph Hochhäusler. Germany, 2003.

Wedding Polka (*Hochzeitspolka*). 2010. Directed by Lars Jessen. Germany, 2010.

12

Orphans, Violence, and Identity

Transnational Travel in Cary Fukunaga's Sin Nombre *(2009), Denis Villeneuve's* Incendies *(2010), and François Dupeyron's* Monsieur Ibrahim *(2003)*[1]

Karen A. Ritzenhoff

Perhaps we will discover that this love story
Has roots in violence and rape
And that in turn,
The brute and the rapist
Had his origin in love.[2]

—Wajdi Mouawad, *Scorched*

A DESPONDENT FATHER COMMITS SUICIDE; a mother dies and leaves letters that send her children on a search for hidden identity; another parent plunges to his death from the roof of a train while trying to cross the border to safety. The loss of parents and exposure to violence are traumas shared by the protagonists of the three transnational films discussed in this chapter. As survivors, the children must cross borders, explore, and forge new identities, independent from their roots.

Moises Schmitt (Pierre Boulanger), the main character in *Monsieur Ibrahim* (directed by François Dupeyron, 2009), is the son of orthodox Jewish parents who abandon him in Paris; at the outset of the film, his mother runs away with another man, and his father commits suicide. In *Sin Nombre* (directed by Cary Fukunaga, 2009), sixteen-year-old Honduran Sayra (Paulina Gaitán) travels through Mexico en route to the United States and is orphaned along the way. In *Incendies* (directed by Dennis Villeneuve, 2010), twins Jeanne and Simon Mawan (Mélissa Désormeaux-Poulin and Maxim Gaudette) grow up in Canada as members of the Lebanese diaspora but, prompted by the death of their mother, begin a journey of discovery that uncovers a terrible secret about her history and their parentage.

All three films debunk myths of nationhood and the accompanying essentializing notions of national belonging. Although they each contrast diasporic communities in western culture (Europe, Canada, United States) with distinctly religious and hybrid cultures (Middle East, Central America, Turkey), their main focus is not on portraying fundamental cultural differences. There are no exotic "Others"[3]—only the messy, hybrid, and confusing reality of identity in the twenty-first century.

The young heroes and heroines, whose ages range from fourteen to twenty-two, share similar senses of grief and anger, as well as liberation, as they reshape their own identities, creating new ones independent of their childhoods. It appears as though they are free of preconceived constructs dictated by parents, but in many ways, their life courses are still charted by their parents' values, beliefs, and actions.

The characters in these exilic films negotiate crossings from South to North (across the Mexican-American frontier) and East to West (from the Middle East to Canada), as well as of intra-European and Asian borders. Although distinctly different in narrative and tone, each story showcases the ways in which young people explore and connect with their cultural roots, while at the same time recognizing that, in a global society, they can choose identities independent of their heritage. It is no longer bloodlines that bind individuals to each other, but rather newly imagined, chosen communities.

These key thematic features interlock at different points, crystallizing around such topics as sexuality, violence, religion, silence, and secrets. The journeys in *Incendies* and *Sin Nombre* are not sugarcoated. *Monsieur Ibrahim* looks, at times, like a fairy tale of cultural symbiosis for adults, but shares many themes with the others. The three films represent alternative tales about coming to terms with the realities of a global community[4] during a time when immigration laws, ideological wars, and policies regarding refugees sharply divide political opinion in Europe/France, Canada, and the United States. In this way, each of these films adds to the ongoing dialogue about diasporic cultures in dominant western societies.

Plot Arcs

In *Monsieur Ibrahim*, Moises redefines his identity in the parental void, becoming the local "Arab" after his adoption by Monsieur Ibrahim.[5] At the outset of the film, Moises lives with his depressed father in a small, dingy apartment filled with books, in a poor, multicultural neighborhood of Paris, the "Rue Bleue."

Moises has a strong affinity for the quartier's prostitutes: they not only soothe his budding sexual appetite for pay, but also provide him with a sense of shelter, since his own mother abandoned him in childhood. The women work on Moises's side of the street, curiously watched by the boy from his bedroom window, whereas Monsieur Ibrahim (Omar Sharif) has his deli/shop across the street, also visible from the same window. The frame of the picturesque blue street is a wide, establishing shot, where the prostitutes are soliciting clients in the foreground, while Ibrahim solicits clients for his grocery business in the background. For both, transactions for "goods and services" are based on the exchange of money. The teenage protagonist eventually crosses the geographical and symbolic border from one side of the street to the other, leaving his father, childhood, prostitutes, and Jewishness behind. The film explores these developments as Moises becomes "Momo," and eventually "Mohammed" and is adopted by Monsieur Ibrahim, emotionally as well as legally, after his father dies. The film concludes with a long journey by car from Paris to Turkey, where Ibrahim, too, eventually dies after an accident. In the aftermath, Momo inherits the store and the Qur'an, assuming his adoptive father's lifestyle and religious identity.

In *Sin Nombre*, Sayra crosses the border from Mexico to the United States with the help of a so-called coyote. Her father, a native of Honduras and undocumented migrant in the United States, had recently been deported but returned to his hometown to pick up his estranged teenage daughter, seeking to bring her illegally across the border to the United States, where she would have access to an economically better life. The father dies when he falls from the roof of one of the trains, but even before this accident, Sayra has chosen her own path, abandoning her father and an uncle traveling with them and following instead her new companion, Willy, nicknamed "El Casper" (Edgar Flores). She meets El Casper during her journey through Mexico atop the train (see the cover image of this volume). He is a member of a violent drug gang, the *Mara Salvatrucha*, but when the leader of the gang, "Lil' Mago" (Tenoch Huerta) kills his girlfriend (Diana García) during an attempted rape, El Casper seeks revenge.

Lil' Mago is a predator who attacks migrants on trains and steals their belongings. When he menaces Sayra and her family, El Casper slashes the gang lord's throat and throws him off the moving train. A grateful Sayra trusts her rescuer, and the pair bond, but she is left on her own when, as they attempt to cross the border, he is caught and brutally gunned down by his fellow gang members—led by his own protégé, eleven-year-old "El Smiley" (Kristyan Ferrer)—in retaliation for Lil' Mago's murder. Although Sayra seems to be attracted to El Casper, no romance develops. He is still emotionally tied to his deceased girlfriend and regards himself as doomed to die, as well. He has

Figure 12.1. El Casper joins Sayra and her father (see background) on their journey on top of a train in Mexico in *Sin Nombre*. He is covered in blood. *Sin Nombre* (Scion Films).

become "nameless" (*sin nombre*) because he gave up his birth name when joining the gang that eventually dispatches him in an execution-like murder ritual.

At the end of the film, Sayra traverses a long stretch of bland, green-brown grass on foot and approaches the asphalt-covered outskirts of a large, generic American shopping mall, somewhere in California. Her father had urged her to memorize a phone number that would connect her to her stepmother in New Jersey, also an undocumented migrant. Sayra approaches a pay phone,

Figure 12.2. Sayra reaches the United States and enters a generic shopping mall in *Sin Nombre*. She calls from a pay phone. *Sin Nombre* (Scion Films).

her tormented face reflected in the shiny surface of the phone apparatus, and dials the number. Someone picks up on the other end and the film fades to black.

America may be the land of opportunity, but director Fukunaga frames it as an alienating consumer paradise without heart. Sayra has left "paradise"[6] behind to end up in the asphalt jungle of a mega-mall parking lot alone. Her passage to a new world is not idealized or romanticized. Instead, Fukunaga provides a somber scenario of the dangerous border crossing in contemporary culture.

In *Incendies*, the twins' father, Nihad (Hussein Sami), is also their biological older brother, who, without knowing her identity, had assaulted their imprisoned mother for years as her sadistic guard. He had been given up at birth—the illegitimate son of a Palestinian refugee and the then-sixteen-year-old Nawal Mawan (Lubna Azabal)—and was raised in a Christian orphanage. When the orphanage was overrun and burned down by a Muslim militia group, Nihad was spared and trained as a sniper. He renamed himself to embrace his new Muslim identity and is now called Abu Tharek (Abdelghafour Elaaziz). As a sniper during the Lebanese Civil War, he kills children and civilians without mercy. When his ruthless violence becomes controversial, Abu Tharek once again changes identity and is recruited by a Christian-run prison, where he becomes an infamous torturer.

Ostracized by her ancestral village for taking a Palestinian lover (who was later murdered by her Christian brothers), Nawal joined the Muslim underground and murdered a prominent, but corrupt, Christian leader. Imprisoned for fourteen years, she was known as "the woman who sings"—celebrated as one who was caged but whose spirit was never broken. Nawal's decision to work for the Muslim-run underground was made after she witnessed the brutal murder of a busload of Muslim civilians by the Christian militia. The bus went up in flames as she tried in vain to save a young girl. Only when she held up a crucifix was she spared by the corrupt Christian soldiers, who accept her as one of their own, redeemed from the status of Other. The once-cherished symbol of the cross is tainted by this violent incident, though, and the disillusioned Nawal quickly discards it.

Abu Tharek and Nawal meet at the outset of the film. While swimming at a public pool, Nawal recognizes the tattoo on Abu's heel—three black ink spots, placed there by her grandmother before handing over the baby to the orphanage—and realizes that her son was also her torturer. She suffers a stroke and dies.

Nawal's twins travel to Lebanon to uncover their mother's dark history.[7] Despite their mother's tragic and violent heritage, Jeanne and Simon end up embracing her past.[8] This crossing of religious and national boundaries dissolves the strictly held beliefs that hatred cannot harbor love and that religious heritage prevails over kinship.[9]

Throughout the diverse journeys they depict, these three films ask overarching existential questions: What happens when all the firmly established constructs of identity dissolve? Who is left, and what is there to become? The following sections explore three sets of themes that are central to the films' framing of those questions and to the answers that they offer: orphanhood and diaspora; rites of passage and transformations; and silence and letters.

Orphanhood and Diaspora

Benevolent prostitutes; a warm-hearted, cheating grocery store owner of Sufi heritage; a dangerous but kind Mexican drug dealer; and a lethal Middle Eastern sniper living quietly in Canada are all characters that drive the action in these three films about intercultural and national borders. Although these characters exist only on the margins of western societies, their stories about diasporic experiences are at the center of the films' narratives thanks to their relevance to the process of identity formation for each of the respective teenage protagonists. The existence of these outcasts intersects in encounters with the orphaned heroes and heroines that are sometimes soothing, other times disturbing. The orphans cross and re-cross boundaries, national and psychological, unaware of the interconnected histories and violent conflicts that will confront them. All are on journeys of discovery that will lead them to cross the boundaries of their identities while physically crossing borders. And in a transnational world, it seems that there is almost no line that cannot be crossed. Once one is immersed in the generic metropoles of the new world, outside the realm of passports, birth certificates, and data entry,[10] the possibilities for a new identity seem limitless.

Orphans are adrift in the world without the means to sustain themselves, and displaced orphans are doubly at loss—they must negotiate identities vis-à-vis their families and both their natal and adopted states. Members of a diaspora often accentuate their national origins, holding their heritage close and celebrating cultural markers such as dialects, food, festivals, song, rules, and rituals of marriage. The orphans in these three films, however, with their youthful detachment from their homelands, have not succumbed to the standard motifs of exile. They change names, they mark themselves, or they obliterate the markings done to them. In the case of *Incendies*, Abu Tharek is marked at birth by the ink spots on his heel. Only eleven years old, *Sin Nombre*'s El Smiley chooses to have his lower lip tattooed with the insignia of his violent gang after the execution of El Casper marks his full embrace of his new

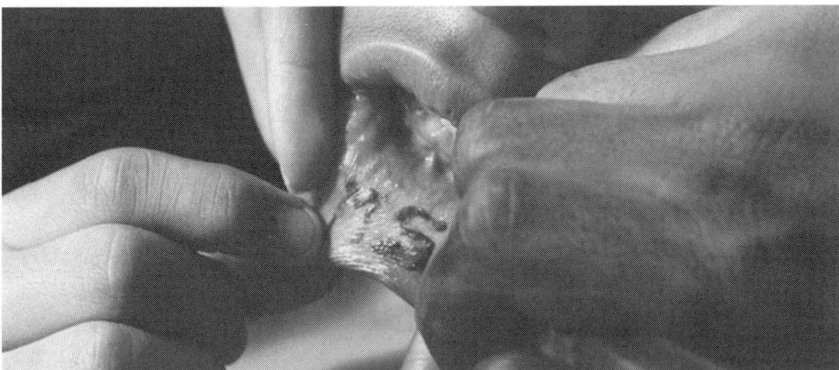

Figure 12.3. El Smiley is marked at the end of *Sin Nombre* with the insignia of his violent gang on the lower lip. *Sin Nombre* (Scion Films).

family, the *Mara Salvatrucha*. El Casper has also numerous tattoos: one of the markings below his eye is a teardrop that indicates that he has murdered someone. He tries to scratch it off while he is fleeing with Sayra but cannot erase the marking.

Border crossings play a significant role in the development of all three narratives. Journeys that involve border crossings are often seen as metaphors for the search of identity, adventure, and personal growth. Ultimately, though, the abyss created by the loss of parents is filled with new meaning, transgressing religion, cultural belonging, and kinship. Transnational travel assumes the encounter with cultural heterogeneity, and film, as a visual medium,

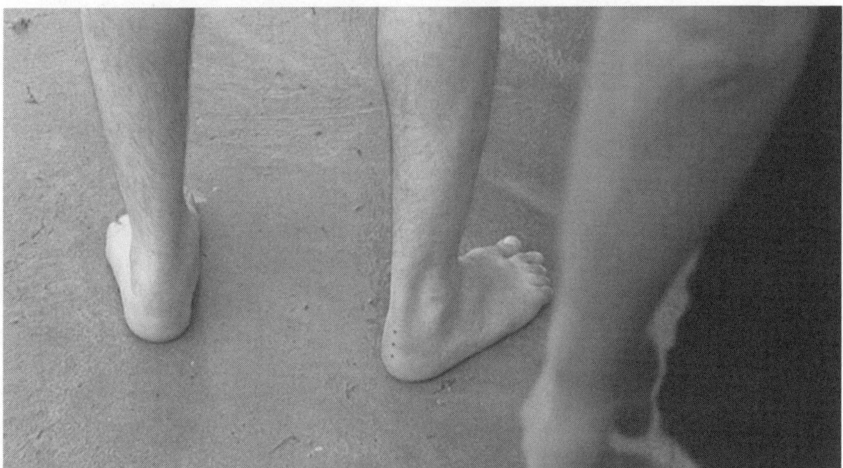

Figure 12.4. The heel of the son/brother/father has been tattooed with three ink spots at birth in *Incendies*. *Incendies* (micro scope).

seems uniquely equipped to represent difference. These three commercial feature-length films showcase elements of intercultural cinema by focusing on the crossing of borders, both literally and metaphorically.[11] In each of these cinematic narratives, however, border crossings are linked to carnage, blood, risk, death, and suffering.

Rites of Passage and Transformations

The protagonists physically cross borders on their journeys to self-discovery as well as venturing beyond personal boundaries. Rather than following in their parents' footsteps, the orphans negotiate their individual senses of being and belonging. The fourteen-year-old Moises in *Monsieur Ibrahim* seeks refuge and satisfaction with the prostitutes of the Rue Bleue.[12] The film opens with the loss of virginity: Moises breaks the piggy bank his father had given him and crosses the street to Monsieur Ibrahim's grocery story to change the coins into bills. He then buys one of the many prostitutes who work directly in front of his apartment window in his multicultural Parisian, working-class, predominantly Jewish neighborhood.[13] Moises desires a beautiful African prostitute, a clear symbol of French colonial history, but he cannot afford to pay her at the

Figure 12.5. Momo pays a black prostitute thirty francs. He can only "afford" her services after pawning his father's books. The meager contents of his piggy bank was not enough. *Monsieur Ibrahim* (ARP Sélection).

outset: her services cost thirty francs, a sum well beyond his piggy-bank budget. Eventually, he pawns his dead father's books and is able to pay.

For Momo, the warmth, gentleness, and embrace of the whores—some of whom try to mimic the style of actress Brigitte Bardot in 1960s post-Algerian France—are substitutes for his absent mother.[14] This façade is complicated in one scene, when the actress (Isabelle Adjani) visits the quartier to play one of her film roles, that of a prostitute. Since the Rue Bleue is a safe haven for real-life prostitutes of different cultural and ethnic backgrounds, the appearance of the famous French actress is doubly intriguing: as she mirrors the whores for her film role, they, in turn, are trying to mimic her.

Monsieur Ibrahim asks Bardot for an exaggerated sum of money in payment for a bottle of water when she enters his store, thirsty after her shoot on the Rue Bleue. Later, a similar exchange of money is depicted several times between Momo and the prostitutes. At the outset of the film, he relates, "Two hundred francs—that's what a girl costs in the Rue de Paradis. It was the price of becoming a man." A later exchange between Momo and the black prostitute to whom he is attracted is depicted in almost an identical way as the exchange between Ibrahim and Bardot, illustrating the interrelationship of commerce, nationality, and desire: Bardot is a global icon of sexuality and a French national fantasy, as well as part of a dominant white culture; the prostitute serves a parallel function, as an icon of France's colonial history of exploitation in Africa. When Momo requests the services of the prostitute, they are paid for by income that the teenager generates through pawning the books that tie him to his father and his Jewish intellectual heritage.[15] Having severed that tie, Momo aligns himself with members of a colonized French people, through his choices of sexual partner and mentor.[16]

The fact that Momo desires the "services" of a member of a diasporic culture is disconnected from the veneer of exploitation: not only does he pay the requested fee but he also sheds his own religious and cultural heritage to align with the subaltern class in his Jewish neighborhood. While the film is devoid of violence—the element that most distinguishes it from the other two films discussed in this chapter—it portrays cultural violence and a minority culture that is suppressed by the dominant French population.

The three movies utilize hybrid storytelling devices and distinct visual metaphors to illustrate how orphaned teenagers and young adults navigate a changing global community. In each case, border crossings are accomplished by rites of passage, wherein identities, statuses, and affiliations shift and transform. *Incendies* opens with Nawal Mawan's unexpected death as a sixty-year-old in Canadian exile, but later scenes show a younger Nawal living through several such rites of passage. These flashbacks depict her victimization during her country's civil war—subject to torture, rape, and prison due to her shifting allegiances between religious factions—and reveal her torturer and rapist to be her own biological son. The memories are unlocked, for her, by an unexpected sign of one such long-ago border crossing: three ink spots, burned into the heel of the newborn child of a teenage Christian Lebanese woman and her Muslim Palestinian lover.

Coming to terms with Nawal's death and the layers of past identities it hints at lead her twins into transformative moments of their own. Jeanne and Simon Marwan undergo their own rites of passage as they travel to their mother's country of origin in the Middle East and are exposed to the hardships and perils of village life during a religiously based civil war fueled by prejudice and antagonism. Their journey leads them to members of the Muslim underground, who disclose their Christian mother's fate at the hands of her malignant torturer and the secret of their own identities.

Sayra in *Sin Nombre* suffers from homesickness, hunger, sleep deprivation, and loss. Her journey takes her steadily further from her Honduran home and into steadily less-familiar spaces, culminating in the desolate American parking lot wasteland. She is witness (indirectly) to her father's exile from the United States and eventually witnesses the execution of her young new friend El Casper by members of his own gang. Her transformation into an independent young woman in a foreign land has been inextricably linked to danger and suffering, and the potential for a different, happier experience is, at the end of the film, tenuous at best, as she reaches out to re-create a sense of "family."

In *Monsieur Ibrahim*, Moises experiences his own rite of passage when he is taken into the mountains to Ibrahim's birthplace, a Sufi village in "the Golden Crescent," exposing him to an entirely different world and religion.[17] Ibrahim takes his young friend to a cloister and introduces him to the tradition of male dancers, so-called dervishes. Rather than being a bystander, the teenager immerses himself in the culture. He not only witnesses what he experiences but also participates: one of the iconic scenes of the exposure to cultural alterity is this riveting dance that unleashes emotions of forgiveness in Momo.[18]

The ritual of the dervishes is a key moment in experiencing cultural difference for Momo. This scene also exposes the viewer to male dancers who display an unusual rite of masculinity that is rarely represented in mainstream movies. In this moment, Momo transcends the boundaries of his own heritage and is able to reconcile with his parents in the act of moving and whirling. He purges himself of an "earthly reference point" in order to embrace a different state of belonging: finding peace in a spiritual rite of passage. At the end of the movie, Momo has not bonded with a different form of family (such as a gang) but has carved out his own sense of identity and asserted his independence.

Unlike Momo's experiences, the rites of passage experienced by the male characters in *Incendies* and *Sin Nombre* are terrifyingly violent. Nihad's transition from boyhood to manhood (and from Christian to Muslim) in *Incendies* is marked by his training as a sniper and his transformation from an innocent into a slayer of innocents. His boyhood world, the orphanage, collapses into rubble and flames at the moment of this border crossing. His re-crossing of the Christian-Muslim border draws him into another level of brutality as he trades the detachment and isolation of the sniper for the intimacy of the torturer. In *Sin Nombre*, El Casper is part of a border gang in Mexico whose members are all isolated from their families and join the larger "family" of fellow criminals who rob, torture, rape, and kill those families who, like Sayra's, try to cross the border to the United States illegally. Once accepted to the gang, the members are covered with tattoos, given weapons, trained in ground warfare, and given a new name.

The outset of the film shows a new recruit, the eleven-year-old who will be renamed El Smiley, being introduced into the "family" under the eye of the ruthless gang leader. His initial welcome is a cruel mass beating where he is kicked and humiliated by his new peers until he lies bloodied and wounded on the ground. The next rite of initiation is a killing, an execution: he is required to shoot a member of a rival gang who has been captured and held in a cage like an animal. The gang offers El Smiley shelter and protection but requires absolute loyalty to its brutal leaders. The boy's place in the gang is confirmed—its bonds rendered permanent and unbreakable—by his role in the assassination of El Casper, the apostate.

Silence and Letters

In *The Skin of the Film* (2000), Laura U. Marks discusses the use of silence as a common strategy employed by directors of intercultural films, to indicate the constraints of representation. *Incendies* seems to visualize this strategy of distancing and argues that the silence in the film (that is here written into the script), opens fissures of cultural understanding. In both *Monsieur Ibrahim* and *Incendies*, letters play a key role bridging that silence. *Incendies*' narrative opens with a lawyer reading Nawal's will to the twins and closes with the pair again reading their mother's letter.[19] Her words provide the motivation for the film's narrative, as Jeanne and Simon set off in search of their father and older brother, only to ultimately realize that they are one and the same.[20] The final shot of the movie shows the father/brother/son, Nihad/Abu Tharek, standing at his mother's/victim's grave, framed as the subjective, detached point of view of an observer—seeming more like a snippet from a surveillance camera than part of the film's visual language. Since there is no encounter between the twins and their father/brother after the delivery of the envelopes, viewers can assume that it is Jeanne and Simon who are looking on while Nihad visits Nawal's grave.

Nawal's letters indicate that she does not want to have her name engraved on her tombstone until her secret is revealed to the twins. Here, we find a thematic parallel to *Sin Nombre*. This "absence of name" in both films points to lost parental identity. The twins bear their mother's name; the fact that their father is also their mother's son and bears that same last name is a horrifying coincidence. Nawal embodies a legacy of anger among different generations of women who, in the predominantly patriarchal culture of the Middle East, have to subject themselves to the authority of fathers (and brothers), and so bearing the name of the mother has a symbolic function. The twins follow in her footsteps, not in the violent legacy of their biological father.

The discovery of letters is also a key feature in *Monsieur Ibrahim*. Momo's father leaves him with only a note tucked underneath a plate in the kitchen and a pile of cash when he departs their apartment. Shortly afterward, the father commits suicide. His note to Moises declares that he felt he was "not cut out" to be a father. After Ibrahim passes away, Momo also receives a letter from him, handed over by the executor of the estate. It is similar to the final letter from Nawal to her twins, reflecting the hope of a parent for the healing and psychological sheltering of the child left behind. In this way, the letters assist the orphans in both *Incendies* and *Monsieur Ibrahim* to cross the borders between their most private and public selves. The memorized telephone number in *Sin Nombre*, though not a tangible document, plays a similar role. When

Figure 12.6. The twins read a letter inherited from their mother. *Incendies* (micro scope).

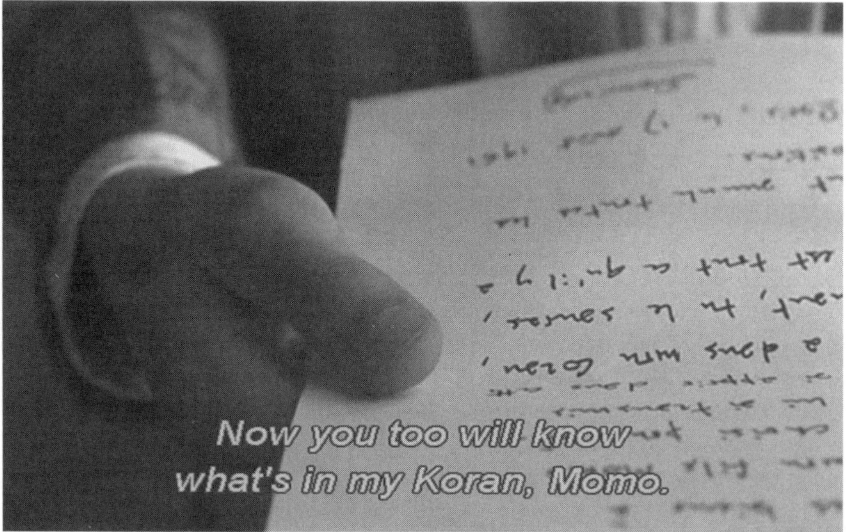

Figure 12.7. Momo reads Monsieur Ibrahim's letter after the death of his adoptive father. *Monsieur Ibrahim* (ARP Sélection).

Sayra calls the number in the final sequence of the movie, it allows her to connect with her stepmother and thereby with the legacy of her deceased father.

When Momo returns to Paris for the execution of Monsieur Ibrahim's will, he is handed not only the letter, but also the Qur'an with two dried blue flowers. On the surface, these could be the flowers mentioned in the longer title of Schmitt's short story. Metaphorically, they also refer to the prostitutes who work in the Rue Bleue, where Ibrahim built his livelihood among other migrants in the French postcolonial diaspora.

Momo actually encounters his biological mother, who comes to find her son, but refuses to reveal himself to her and she goes along with the charade, knowing that he is hiding his true identity.[21] The insecurity and awkwardness the mother feels toward her "lost" son is different from the kind exchange between the token mother figures, the "flowers" of the Rue Bleue, and the teenager. The literary version of the tale concludes with the adult Momo looking back as a narrator: "[M]y mother comes to see me. She calls me Mohammed so that I won't get angry and she asks me for news from Moises, which I give her."[22] "Arabs" are perceived to be at the bottom of this pecking order, linked to the tumultuous colonial French past.[23] And so, the film poetically negotiates identity between the subaltern and dominant French cultures.

Even though Monsieur Ibrahim wants to be seen by Momo as a Muslim, he accepts his status as the local Arab in the diasporic culture of the Rue Bleue.

The role of Momo in the film carries the fairy-tale quality of cultural immersion and adaptability: he is able to assume a different religious identity, choose his own family (Monsieur Ibrahim and the Flowers of the Rue Bleue), and conform to the prescribed attitude of members of a diasporic culture who subordinate themselves to dominance. By denying his birth mother the opportunity to reconnect with her son, Moises, he is manifesting his own choice of difference in a country where "Frenchness" is regarded as a national virtue.

Momo does not choose Monsieur Ibrahim's Qur'an as a means of converting to Muslim culture; instead, he aligns himself deliberately with another minority group, also marginalized by the dominant French national, Catholic culture. Momo thus imposes on himself, by choice, an isolation that is imposed on other characters, in other films, by circumstance. And despite this isolation, Momo eventually crafts a new identity for himself. Even though critics may contend that the overall storyline is trite and full of cultural clichés, the elements of identity formation are indicative of a modern global society where borders are being erased. The film depicts an idealized version of the hybrid world we live in, but it is, nevertheless, offering points of entry to describe the life of subordinate, diasporic cultures, embedded (harmoniously) in western societies. In this way, *Monsieur Ibrahim* adds to this global cinematic dialogue, although not as poignantly as the more political *Incendies* and *Sin Nombre* would five years later.

Conclusion

Parental lineage and bloodlines are replaced by voluntary identity formations in a global community. The three films discussed in this chapter arise from different points of origin, but share similar tropes to describe transnational identity formation: the journey; the lost, parentless, and orphaned child; and, in the case of *Incendies* and *Monsieur Ibrahim*, the interchangeability of identities generally considered to be "basic" and "natural," such as religion. The journeys of the young protagonists in *Incendies*, *Sin Nombre*, and *Monsieur Ibrahim* entail physical travel across borders and countries, but they are also symbolic of traversing difference in the mind in order to recognize one's heritage.

The price for safety is high: it is paid for with indifference and distance in interpersonal relationships. The films illustrate the undercurrents that diverse populations struggle with in order to make sense of the dominant culture in which they seek refuge, debunking the notion of romantic, restorative migration. In each, silence and namelessness play a significant role. Moises changes his name to indicate his new identity. El Casper is renamed by his gang and then marked to die. The twins reclaim their Middle Eastern cultural identity and listen at the end to their mother's silence. Intercultural knowledge is described by all three filmmakers as a tactile, sensory, and auditory experience, revealing—through tattoos, dance, and even silence—codes that are usually inaccessible to mainstream cinema audiences. Viewers learn to relate to the protagonists in new ways that enhance their understanding of global diasporic cultures, allowing them to identify with orphans who would have otherwise stayed invisible.

Notes

1. Many thanks to Chez Liley, Jakub Kazecki, Cynthia J. Miller, Kathy Hermes, and Alexandra Maravel for their suggestions and insights in the editing of this chapter and their compassion with the topic of border crossings. Thanks also to my students in the honors course on "World Cultures/Post-War Europe in Film" as well as "Women and Film" in the fall semester 2012.

2. Wajdi Mouawad, *Scorched*, trans. Linda Garboriau (Toronto: Playwrites Canada Press, 2009), 134–135.

3. Edward Said describes the romantic fascination of the postcolonial "West" with a mythical and exotic cultural destiny of the Middle East in *Orientalism*. Written over thirty years ago, long before the threat of terrorism had turned many countries in the Middle East into potential enemies and created a broad anti-Arab sentiment in the United States and Europe, Said's book dismantled the notion of nation-building as an ideological construct that is fraught and solely employed to secure a power differential between the "First" and developing world. See Edward Said, *Orientalism* (New York: Vintage, 1979).

4. See Jack Zipes, *The Irresistible Fairy Tale: The Cultural and Social History of a Genre* (Princeton: Princeton University Press, 2012).

5. See more about Sufism in Stephanie Ann Boyle, "*Sheikat and Haggat*: Female Sufi Mystics in Modern Egypt," in *Sex and Sexuality in a Feminist World*, edited by Karen A. Ritzenhoff and Katherine A. Hermes (Newcastle: Cambridge Scholars Publishing, 2009), 384–396.

6. This term is used by Sayra in a dialogue with girlfriends in Honduras, a scene that was cut from the final print of the film. It is available in the "Extras" section on the DVD release of *Sin Nombre*.

7. The author of the original theater play, Wajdi Mouawad, who was born in Lebanon, insists that the exact locale should stay anonymous to indicate that the trauma of civil war transgresses specific national borders in the Middle East. In the preface to the publication of his play *Scorched*, Mouawad writes about the close collaboration with his stage actors: "*Incendies* continues to explore the question of origins . . . only within the space of fiction, of make-believe, of the imagination, did the actors and characters not merge completely. . . . We talked about territory, reconstruction, the war in Lebanon,

about Noah and Abitibi. We talked about divorce and marriage, about theatre and God. We talked about the world today, about the war in Iraq, but also about the world of yesterday: the discovery of the Americas." See the preface "A Ruthless Consolation," in Mouawad, *Scorched*, iii–v.

8. Wajdi Mouawad, the author of *Scorched*, has Nawal write in a letter to her children: "Perhaps we will discover that this love story has roots in violence and rape and that in turn, the brute and the rapist had his origin in love" (Mouawad, *Scorched*, 134–135).

9. This is similar to a more recent film, *The Other Son* (*Le fils de l'autre*, 2012) by Lorraine Levy that tells the story of two eighteen-year-old teenagers who had been swapped by mistake in a hospital in Haifa at birth. Joseph (Jules Sitruk) is raised in Tel Aviv as the son of affluent Jewish parents—a French mother who works as a medical doctor and an Israeli father who has political influence as a general in the Department of Defense in the army and oversees permits for Palestinians to cross the border. Yacine (Medhi Dehbi) grows up with an older brother, Bilal (Mahmood Shalabi), and younger sister in Palestine, as the son of an affectionate father and a loving mother. He returns from his studies in Paris and wants to pursue an education as a doctor in the diaspora that offers him professional opportunities to eventually found a hospital in his home town in the West Bank. The film begins with Joseph trying to enroll in the mandatory Israeli military service where his identity is proven with a blood test. It reveals that genetically he is not related to his parents. This is when the switching of the babies is uncovered. The film shows not only the many border crossings of the protagonists but also the fact that religious identity or the stereotypes of the enemy do not override the family ties. *The Other Son* realistically depicts the pitfalls of neighboring nations who are fighting against each other, where the inhabitants live in constant fear of each other. Joseph is being told by an old rabbi where he seeks advice that he would have to convert to remain a Jew. Yacine, however, due to his Jewish mother, has another birth right. The film shows that blood ties do not connect the family members as firmly as the understanding of kinship. In some ways, Joseph and Yacine are also unsettled and uprooted but gain two sets of parents instead of being orphaned. The hatred felt by Bilal as the older brother dissolves into solidarity and the cultural gap is bridged. See Roger Ebert, "*The Other Son*," *Chicago Sun-Times*, October 24, 2012, http://rogerebert.suntimes.com/apps/pbcs.dll/article?AID=/20121024/REVIEWS/121029989/1023.

10. As documented in Lorraine Levy's film *The Other Son*.

11. Laura U. Marks writes in *The Skin of Film* that directors of intercultural and diasporic cinema need to find "new forms of expression and new kinds of knowledge." See Laura U. Marks, *The Skin of the Film: Intercultural Cinema, Embodiment, and the Senses* (Durham, NC: Duke University Press, 2000), 7. She states that *intercultural* "indicates a context that cannot be confined to a single culture. It also suggests movement between one culture and another, thus implying diachrony and the possibility of transformation" (p. 6). Ultimately, Marks contests that intercultural cinema is marked by "silence, absence, and hesitation" and that there is a "search for the language with which to express cultural memory" (p. 21). See also Loshitzky (2010); Nacify (2001); Durovicová and Newman (2010); and Naficy (1999).

12. The fact that the street is the Blue Street is significant because it is a part of the protagonist's sense of identity. The street is not really blue. One of the last sentences in the short story by Eric-Emmanuel Schmitt, "Monsieur Ibrahim and the Flowers of the Koran," on which the film is based, describes the identity of Momo: "So, now I am Momo, the one who has the grocery store in the Rue Bleue, the Rue Bleue that isn't blue." See Eric-Emmanuel Schmitt, *Monsieur Ibrahim and the Flowers of the Koran* (New York: Other Press, 2003), 52. At the end of the movie adaptation, Momo opens the cover of the Qur'an that he has inherited from Monsieur Ibrahim and sees two blue flowers. The prostitutes on the Rue Bleue are also depicted as flowers.

13. The blue street is also a metaphor for two different lives as well as borders: when Momo crosses the street to Monsieur Ibrahim's store, he also crosses into a different world with values other than his father's (commerce versus education), religion as well as culture. This can be compared to *My Beautiful Launderette*, a classic in transnational or "accented cinema" from the United Kingdom in 1985. In this movie Omar, the son of intellectuals from Pakistan, is attracted to his uncle Nassar's successful business dealings and gets hired to first work in the family owned car wash, then in the launderette business. Omar's father is a formerly prominent journalist turned unemployed alcoholic and rejects the fact that his son is washing other people's underwear, a trade that could be seen as being similar to running a grocery store after hours and on Sundays. Similar to Moises and his father in *Monsieur Ibrahim*, education is contrasted with small business ambition. Moises sells off his father's books and prefers to assume the role of the Arab.

14. In the short story Momo explains, "With Monsieur Ibrahim and the prostitutes I felt warmer, lighter" (Schmitt, *Monsieur Ibrahim*, 13). See also Russell Campbell, *Marked Women: Prostitutes and Prostitution in the Cinema* (Madison: University of Wisconsin Press, 2006).

15. Schmitt, *Monsieur Ibrahim*, 6–7.

16. It is important to note that shortly after the film's release in 2003, France was rocked by protests and riots that erupted in the Parisian suburbs over the institutionalized disadvantage of recent migrant groups (i.e., access to education and jobs), punitive immigration laws, and a rise of right-wing extremist parties such as Le-Pen's, whose members were elected into mainstream administrative positions and as representatives in local and national parliaments. In October 2005, Parisian suburbs—so-called *banlieues*—populated by a high percentage of migrants went up in flames as protestors of North African descent set cars aflame and defaced public buildings. A state of emergency was declared by then-president Jacques Chirac and his conservative government, as the riots spread to public housing projects across the country.

17. See more about Sufism in Boyle, "*Sheikat and Haggat.*"

18. Eric-Emmanuel Schmitt describes the sensation of dancing and twirling with the male performers in his short story *Monsieur Ibrahim and the Flowers of the Koran* that is the basis for the movie: "'You see, Momo! They're whirling around, they're turning around their own heart, the place where God is present. It's like a prayer.' 'You call that a prayer?' 'Of course, Momo. They lose their earthly reference point, the heaviness we call equilibrium, and they become torches that are consumed in a huge fire. Try it, Momo, just try it. Follow me.' . . . 'So, Momo, did you feel good things?'

'Yeah, it was incredible. My hate was draining away. If the drums hadn't stopped I might have tried to justify my mother's case'" (Schmitt, *Monsieur Ibrahim*, 45).

19. In her last (written) words, Nawal explains, "[T]he women in our family are trapped in anger. I was angry with my mother, just as you are angry with me. And just as my mother was angry with her mother. We have to break the thread" (Mouawad, *Scorched*, 134). And she concludes, "'Janine, Simon, where does your story begin? At your birth? Then it begins in horror. At your father's birth? Then it is a beautiful love story. But if we go back farther, perhaps we will discover that this love story has roots in violence and rape, and that in turn, the brute and the rapist had his origin in love. . . . Why didn't I tell you? There are truths that can only be revealed when they have been discovered. You opened the envelope, you broke the silence. Engrave my name on the stone and place the stone on my grave.' Your mother. Simon: 'Janine, let me hear her silence.' *Janine and Simon listen to their mother's silence. Torrential rain. The end*" (Mouawad, *Scorched*, 134–135).

20. Wajdi Mouawad writes in his theater play, on which the film is based, what Nawal Marwan leaves as a legacy: "All my assets are to be divided equally between the twins Janine and Simon Marwan, my offspring, flesh of my flesh" (Mouawad, *Scorched*, 6). However, she requests an unusual burial that leaves her children puzzled: "Let no stone be placed on my grave, nor my name engraved anywhere. No epigraph for those who don't keep their promises. And one promise was not kept. No epigraph for those who keep the silence. And silence was kept. No stone. No name on the stone. No epitaph for an absent name of an absent stone. No name" (Mouawad, *Scorched*, 8). Furthermore, these directions to the children are being followed with the handing over of two envelopes. Janine receives a letter that she is supposed to deliver to her father: "Find him and give him this envelope" (Mouawad, *Scorched*, 8). Simon gets a similar envelope that is written to his brother and Janine's with the same request. "Once the envelopes have been delivered to their recipients, you will be given a letter. The silence will be broken. And then a stone can be placed on my grave. And my name engraved on the stone in the sun" (Mouawad, *Scorched*, 8–9). The theater play then states the stage direction of "long silence." Simon reacts aggressively to his mother's demands: "'She had to piss us off right to the very end! That bitch! That stupid bitch! Goddamn fucking cunt! Fucking bitch! She really had to piss us off right to the very end! For ages now, we've been thinking, the bitch is going to croak any day now, she'll finally stop fucking up our lives, the old pain in the ass! And then, bingo! She finally croaks! But, *surprise*! It's not over yet! Shit! We never expected this. Christ! She really set us up, calculated everything, the fucking whore! I'd like to kick her corpse! You bet we are going to bury her face down! You bet! We'll spit on her grave.' *Silence*" (Mouawad, *Scorched*, 9).

21. Schmitt describes the encounter in his short story: "She looks at me intently, trying to scan my features. She is scared, very scared. 'And who are you?' 'Me?' I feel like having fun. It's incredible how people can get themselves in such a state, especially after thirteen years. 'Me, they call me Momo.' Her face shatters. Laughing, I add: 'It's a diminutive for Mohammed.' She becomes even paler than the paint on my baseboards. 'Oh really? You're not Moses?' 'Oh no, you shouldn't confuse the two, Madame. Me, I'm Mohammed'" (Schmitt, *Monsieur Ibrahim*, 35).

22. A secondary plot barely emerges in the film adaptation: Moises's father had invented the existence of a supposedly more perfect elder brother, "Popol," to shame his son into submission. Momo reveals to his mother: "Recently, I told her that Moises had found his brother Popol again and they had left on a trip together and that, as far as I could tell, we wouldn't see them any time soon. Perhaps it wasn't worth discussing any more. She thought for a long time—she is always on her guard with me—then she murmured gently: 'After all, maybe it's better that way. There are some forms of childhood you should leave behind, that need healing'" (Schmitt, *Monsieur Ibrahim*, 50–51). Once Momo has children, his biological mother invites the "Arabs" to her house where she lives with her second French husband. "What is certain is that it is a little strange to have two teachers from the state education system receive Mohammed, the grocer, but then again, why not? I'm not racist" (Schmitt, *Monsieur Ibrahim*, 51). Momo's statement that he is "not racist" points to the ambivalence of being welcomed into the home of members of the French state employees, representatives of an accepted hierarchy.

23. Mohammed concludes, "So, now I am Momo, the one who has the grocery store in the Rue Bleue, the Rue Bleue that isn't blue. In everybody's eyes I am the local Arab. In the grocery business, being Arab means being open at night and on Sundays" (Schmitt, *Monsieur Ibrahim*, 52). Although Monsieur Ibrahim is described in Schmitt's short story as being "the only Arab in a Jewish street" (Schmitt, *Monsieur Ibrahim*, 7), he corrects the boy at the outset of their friendship: "I'm not an Arab, Momo. I'm from the Golden Crescent. I'm a Muslim" (Schmitt, *Monsieur Ibrahim*, 8–9).

Works Cited

Boyle, Stephanie Anne. "*Sheikat and Haggat*: Female Sufi Mystics in Modern Egypt." In *Sex and Sexuality in a Feminist World,* edited by Karen A. Ritzenhoff and Katherine A. Hermes, 384-396. Newcastle: Cambridge Scholars Publishing, 2009.

Campbell, Russell. *Marked Women: Prostitutes and Prostitution in the Cinema*. Madison: University of Wisconsin Press, 2006.

Durovicová, Natasa, and Kathleen Newman, eds. *World Cinemas, Transnational Perspectives*. New York: Routledge, 2010.

Ebert, Roger. "The Other Son." *Chicago Sun-Times*. October 24, 2012. http://rogerebert.suntimes.com/apps/pbcs.dll/article?AID=/20121024/REVIEWS/121029989/1023.

Marks, Laura U. *The Skin of the Film: Intercultural Cinema, Embodiment, and the Senses*. Durham, NC: Duke University Press, 2000.

Naficy, Hamid. *An Accented Cinema: Exilic and Diasporic Filmmaking*. Princeton: Princeton University Press, 2001.

———, ed. *Home, Exile, Homeland: Film, Media, and the Politics of Place*. New York: Routledge, 1999.

Loshitzky, Yosefa. *Screening Strangers: Migration and Diaspora in Contemporary European Cinema*. Bloomington: Indiana University Press, 2010.

Mouawad, Wajdi. *Scorched*. Translated by Linda Garboriau. Toronto: Playwrites Canada Press, 2009.

Said, Edward. *Orientalism*. New York: Vintage, 1979.
Schmitt, Eric-Emmanuel. *Monsieur Ibrahim and the Flowers of the Koran*. New York: Other Press, 2003.
Zipes, Jack. *The Irresistible Fairy Tale: The Cultural and Social History of a Genre*. Princeton: Princeton University Press, 2012.

Films

Incendies. Directed by Denis Villeneuve. Canada, France, 2010.
Monsieur Ibrahim. Directed by François Dupeyron. France, 2003.
My Beautiful Laundrette. Directed by Stephen Frears. United Kingdom, 1985.
The Other Son (Le Fils de l'Otre). Directed by Lorraine Levy. France, Israel, 2012.
Sin Nombre. Directed by Cary Fukunaga. United States, Mexico, 2009.

V

NARRATIVE TRANSGRESSIONS

CROSSING GENRES AND BORDER CROSSINGS

13

What the Images Cannot Show

The Letters in Montxo Armendáriz's Letters from Alou *(1990)*

María Lourdes Casas

IN THE 1980S, SPANIARDS STARTED to notice the increased numbers of immigrant workers who came from Africa to the streets of Madrid and Barcelona. While some of these workers were first perceived with mild exoticism and curiosity, or even conservative paternalism (referred to as *los negritos*, "the little blacks"), soon these perceptions shifted to contempt, stereotyping, blatant discrimination, and racism. Spanish movies began addressing the social implications of the immigrant experience and its impact on the social fabric of Spain. Since that time, a growing number of films have dramatized the migration of Africans (and later Latin Americans) to Spain and have problematized the act of crossing borders, not only as a geographical and physical process, but also a cultural, social, and identity-shaping process. Foremost among these is *Las cartas de Alou* (*Letters from Alou*), written and directed by Montxo Armendáriz in 1990, the first immigration-themed film made in Spain by a Spanish director.[1]

Las cartas de Alou focuses on the four eponymous letters written by the main character. While crossing borders across different territories and societies, these letters also cross generic borders between cinematographic and written texts. This chapter focuses on the director's use of the letters as narrative vehicles: first as a means of delivering messages or meanings that images cannot convey, and second, as an illustration of the complex, and often fraught, relationship between native and immigrant cultures. The connection—or disconnection—of the letters' content and the accompanying images is essential to the politics of the film.

Spain has only recently become an immigrant-receiving nation, yet staggering numbers of immigrants have crossed the country's borders in recent years. In only the last fifteen years, more than six million were added to a native population of around forty million, due to an economic upswing that began in 1997 and lasted for over a decade.[2] Most of these immigrants were North Africans and Latin Americans who came to work in Spain's astonishing construction boom, which collapsed in 2009. However, the origins of this surge of workers across the country's borders can be traced to the mid-1980s, when the first wave of immigrants from Africa arrived in Spain. While some traveled around urban centers with no steady jobs selling petty merchandise, most moved to rural areas to take agricultural jobs created by modernization and the migration of native Spaniards to urban centers. Armendáriz's film maps the struggles in integration and cultural alienation suffered by this first wave of new immigrants. Additionally, the film opened the door to a series of movies made by Spaniards whose main subject was the immigration experience in their country. As Schroeder-Rodríguez notes, "[T]hirty such independent films have been produced [in Spain] since 1990."[3]

Las cartas de Alou tells the story of Alou (Mulie Jarju), a young Senegalese man who goes to Spain looking for a better life. The film follows Alou's indoctrination into immigrant life and education on how to work the system. The film takes the "journey film" format, as Alou traverses the country and survives multiple misadventures. First, he arrives in Almería on the Spanish south coast on a *patera*.[4] After his arrival, he lives and works as an undocumented migrant, first as a greenhouse worker in Almería. Looking for a better salary, he moves to Barcelona (Catalonia) where his friend Mulai (Akonio Dolo) has been living for several years and promises to help him, but his trip is cut short when he is robbed while sleeping in a train station in Madrid. He must once again find work in order to continue his travels to Barcelona. Alou's misadventures draw him into the world of Madrid's immigrants and their gray market economy, until he sets out again for Barcelona. Once there, Mulai's Spanish wife, Rosa (Rosa Morata), tells Alou that Mulai has gone to Lleida (in the west of Catalonia) to work during the fruit-picking season, so Alou continues on in search of his friend.

Once in Lleida, Alou finds not only Mulai and work but also love, with the beautiful barmaid Carmen (Eulalia Ramón). His life here, however, is still fraught with difficulty. Carmen's father (Albert Vidal) disapproves of their relationship, and Alou's boss is bigoted and abusive toward the immigrant workers in his employment. Alou rails against this discrimination and loses his job. Forced to return to Barcelona, Alou travels between the two cities to continue his relationship with Carmen. One day, as the pair is saying their goodbyes at the train station, Alou is arrested by the Spanish police and deported for not having a work permit. In spite of these trials, the film ends with the image of Alou ready to embark again on a small boat to return to Spain.

Las cartas de Alou's narrative is structured by the four letters that Alou writes to share his immigrant experience in Spain. The letters tell the audience about his work as an undocumented migrant and some personal experiences with Spaniards, while standing as proof of the racism he suffers. Two of these letters are addressed to his parents, who remained in his native Senegal; the other two are addressed to his friend Mulai who, at that time, had been living in Barcelona, Spain, for several years. The audience knows the content of each letter through Alou's voice-over. It is also through the letters that the audience comes to know Alou and how he understands his experience as an immigrant.

Before discussing the content of each letter and the role they collectively play in the development of the film, I want to point out some features that illustrate the director's intentionality. First, the language used in the film is Spanish, with the exception of four short periods in which the audience hears the content of the letters in Alou's voice-over using his native African language, Wolof.[5] This technique "produces a linguistic alienation that can be overcome only with the reading of the subtitles"[6] and, consequently, has a distancing effect between the main character and the audience. Alou himself writes the letters, a strategy that Armendáriz uses to break the stereotype of the illiterate immigrant. Furthermore, the four letters "denote Alou's command of various narrative registers; they carefully filter information, depending on to whom they are addressed";[7] the letters sent to his parents are formal and intimate in contrast with the ones sent to his friend Mulai, in which he reflects on his social and cultural experiences as an immigrant. A delicate symmetry is revealed in the use of the letters, as well: the first and last letters open and close, respectively, the film, while the other letters appear roughly thirty minutes apart, creating a framing device for the narrative. A closer look at the letters' content and their correlation with images will give us a better understanding of the director's political stance, denouncing the outrageous conditions of African immigration in Spain in the 1980s.

The First Letter: Alou from Africa to His Friend Mulai in Spain

Before the content of the first letter is presented in the narrative voice-over, viewers see an image of the open sea at night and a ship in the distance. As the camera moves closer to the ship, several men become apparent, trying to send a small boat, a *patera*, into the sea's waters. The next image shows Alou leaving the ship's hold, while the audience hears the content of the first letter, written prior to his departure from Senegal:

> My dear friend, Mulai. I decided to follow your advice. The other day I told my father: "I will quit this job. I cannot live with what I earn." "What will you do?," he asked me. "I will leave the country. Some did it before and did well." My father said nothing. He looked very serious and left. At night, he asked me, "When are you going?" "Next month," I said. He nodded and fell asleep. My mother was crying all week. "Do not cry," I told her. "I'm not your only son. The other six will stay with you." She looked very sad and said, "None of your brothers has your voice or your name. If one day I want to see you, whom should I call?" I did not know what to answer back. I was sad; I had taken a decision and had to keep it. I hope to see you soon and hug you soon. Your friend, Alou.[8]

The contents of all the letters are juxtaposed with background images that relate to the texts in varying ways and degrees. In the case of Alou's first letter, there is a clear discrepancy between the text and the images: they share simultaneity in the film, but they do not narrate the same time in Alou's biography. While the letter, sent to Mulai, provides the narrative's backstory, the images evoke the dangerous conditions of his present-day journey, creating an explicit contrast between the sentimentality and emotions of "home" and the danger and uncertainty of migratory displacement. The crossing is not only a geographical border but also one of identity. This border separates Alou as an individual, with a distinct identity, personal history, and social context in his homeland, from Alou as an immigrant in Spain, subject to brutal conditions, racial prejudices, and a collective identity as undocumented "Other." The clashing and blending of dissonant images and narratives at the film's opening highlights the stark contrast between the two worlds, but at the same time signals the ultimate effacement of the border between them, through its symbolic depiction of Alou inhabiting both sides of his identity at the same time. Just as he traverses the border between Africa and Europe, he will also cross the border between "insider" and "outsider," through the process of integration, building his own personal and affective history in Spain.

The Second Letter: Alou from Spain to His Parents in Africa

The film's second letter is addressed to Alou's parents and is written once he has settled in Madrid. Images preceding the letter show Alou with other African immigrants in a boardinghouse. Alou explains to his new African friends how, while selling petty merchandise on the streets, he had to run away from the police. One of his comrades also teaches him to say the words *rain* and *umbrella*, suggesting that the road to success is through linguistic integration. Through the bedroom window, we see the rain, as if conjured by the word, and for the first and only time, we also see the actual writing of the letter:

> Dear Parents, I am writing this letter to tell you how I feel here. I'm fine. How is the rain this year? Has it rained a lot or little? I would also like to know how harvest was this year. I work every day without problems and I am learning to speak and to understand these people. Here, if you see a friend, you do not go home for tea. You get together with him in a bar and talk. Every night I sell in bars. Bars with girls are the best places to sell. The clients will buy from me many things to please the girls. The more drunk they are, the more things they buy for them. One day I was lucky. A man told me: "I'll buy the whole box." He was very drunk and I did not believe him. He began to give the girls all the merchandise I had. He gave me 20,000 pesetas and said, "Is this enough for you, *moreno* [dark-skinned person]?" I took the money and I left before he passed out. I always think of you. I miss you. I'd like to go back and find you in good health. I hope I will see you soon. I love you. God bless you. Your son who is always thinking of you.

This second letter begins in a nostalgic tone, as he asks his parents about their situation back home, and ends using the same sentimental attitude to say goodbye to his parents. Both the beginning and ending of the letter express what Deveny describes as "feelings that are common to the recent immigrant: missing his family, and hoping to return home soon."[9] However, the content of this second letter introduces interesting aspects in Alou's assimilation process. First, to avoid causing them pain, Alou lies to his parents and says he is working without problems. However, the images associated with the letter tell a different story: of Alou selling cheap watches, bracelets, and other trinkets at the bars and nightclubs in Madrid and running from the police. Second, Alou mentions two elements that seem to indicate successful integration: his acquisition of the Spanish language and knowledge of Spanish customs. Alou is aware that he needs to know the language to work, and he makes great efforts to learn it. However, when he tells his parents about the deep-rooted Spanish custom of socializing in bars, the film reveals that this is cultural knowledge he possesses, but does not put into practice. Alou may recognize the custom, but neither he nor any other Senegalese in the film adopt this habit—all continue to drink tea at home, following their culture's tradition. His commentary on Spaniards' social lives revolving around bars instead of homes, producing, implicitly, more superficial social relations, contrasts with the more intimate relationships he has with his friends, drinking tea inside a house. The director uses the distance between image and narrative in order to emphasize a cultural difference that might otherwise go unnoticed by

Spanish viewers. Finally, within this overall narrative, Alou has interspersed a story about a drunken man purchasing all the merchandise he had for twenty thousand pesetas.[10] This is not a banal comment—it makes Alou an acute observer of Spain's material excess and waste—and can be further interpreted as Armendáriz's criticism of the waste that occurred during Spain's years of economic prosperity.

The Third Letter: Alou from Spain to His Parents

Alou's third letter is the last one addressed to his parents and is written once he is established in Barcelona. The images that precede the letter show Alou in a bar with his friend Mulai, who seems to have assimilated well enough to create social networks and secure a steady job in the manufacturing industry. Mulai takes Alou to a clothing sweatshop and gets him a night job. The audience hears Alou's voice-over narrating the letter, while images show his training on how to use the sewing machine:

> Dear Parents, I hope my letter reaches you in perfect health. Here it's cold, especially in the place where I work. Now, I sew clothes in a shop with others. We work at night. My friend Mulai knows the owner of the workshop. One day he told the owner: "Let us, the *morenos* [dark-skinned person], work overnight. This way you will have more clothes to sell," and he agreed. Mulai knows these people very well. His wife is a girl from here. I live with them. I got a room with a friend and pay them. Mulai's wife prepares food for us. I do not like how she cooks and I told Mulai: "I want to cook my own food." He replied angrily: "If you live in my home, do what I say." It is true that he is making money of us, but he is not a bad friend. I am sending you money with a friend who returns to our country. He will tell you how we live here. He will also give you my regards.

The next scene shows Alou training a new worker how to use the machine, documenting, in turn, Alou's job promotion and assimilation. This third letter is the one that matches most closely with images: Alou and other Africans sewing at night in the cold, Alou living in Mulai and Rosa's house, giving a bottle of milk to Rosa and Mulai's child, and paying money for the room he occupies with another African. Finally, we see an image of Alou sending money to his parents with a fellow countryman. Both words and images here acknowledge immigrants' hard work and living conditions.

There are, however, other issues in this third letter not rendered visible by the film's images. These center on Alou's stories involving Mulai: his exploitation of Alou and his fellow Africans and the dangers of immigrants' overidentification with the dominant group in their host land. Mulai has jumped over racial borders, as he behaves, in Alou's words, like a white man, using the same racial insults used by Spaniards in reference to Africans (*moreno*, black-skinned).

Alou, the letter demonstrates, has also changed through the immigrant experience. His earlier focus on stability and family, so much in evidence in his first letter, has receded into the background, crowded out by his struggles to survive. Previous letters have chronicled Alou's affective self but have simultaneously been dissociated from images that portray his material conditions. In this third letter, however, this affective identity is absent. The letters, which have, until now, been the register of intimate experience and memories of his homeland, are no longer at a disconnect from the visual register, reinforcing commentary on Alou's working conditions and exploitation and erasing the border between the two.

The Fourth Letter: Alou from Africa to His Friend Mulai in Spain

Alou's last letter is addressed to Mulai and is written from Senegal after Alou's deportation. Images preceding the letter show Alou and Carmen leaving the boardinghouse where they have just made love. Carmen discloses that she is determined to tell her father that she is leaving home to live with Alou. While they are saying goodbye at the train station, the police arrive and ask for Alou's documents. Unable to produce any, he is arrested and thrown in a van. The content of the last letter is revealed while Alou and other Africans leave their cells and walk down the prison hallway on their way to the airport to be deported:

> Mulai, when I came to Spain for the first time, my father told me: "You know nothing about that country. To you it's like barren land. Take care of it with tender and you will have good harvest." Now, after knowing it, I wonder, why don't these people accept us? Why do they believe we all are criminals? They say that we, black people, sell drugs. If some do, that is no reason to blame them all. The truth is that our presence bothers them, and so they send us away. They do not like us, but do not want to tell us why. They put us on a plane and sent us back to Africa. I was delighted to see my family again and return to my country. But this is not my place. I do not like this life. The other day I told my father: "Now I know how to deal with the whites. I'm going back. I want to find a place to live for the rest of my days. You've been lucky." If you see Carmen, tell her that, God willing, I hope to see her and hug her soon. A kiss to you and Rosa. I love you. A friend, Alou.

Alou remembers the hopeful words uttered by his father before he embarked on his journey. Then, he reflects on his stay in Spain, characterized by alienation and persecution because of racial prejudices. The letter explains his abusive deportation but, at the same time, chronicles that although his love for his parents has not changed, his affinity for his homeland has vanished, prompting him to attempt a return to Spain by any means. In fact, the last scene portrays Alou on a North African beach, paying a man to help him crossing over to Europe for a second time, starting the cycle of immigration again.

This last letter is not accompanied by images that illustrate its contents, except for a brief moment. In the precise instant in which Alou writes, "They put us on a plane and sent us back to Africa," an Iberian Airlines plane takes off on-screen. Interestingly, this airplane image-text marks a dividing line in his letter's content. The first half deals with Alou's reflection on his experiences in Spain and the lessons he has learned, such as his new understanding of Spaniards' blatant racism, typified by unfair stereotyping and criminalization toward Africans. He asks himself, "Why don't these people accept us?" and has an answer at the ready: "The truth is that our presence bothers them and so they send us away. They do not like us, but do not want to tell us why."

During this reflection on intolerance, background images show a group of illegal immigrants exiting a police station and being forced into a law enforcement van that will take them to the airport. These images are well-known to Spanish viewers and do not require explanation, so rather than verbalizing this scene through Alou's letter, Armendáriz uses the text of the letter to emphasize his social criticism by adding the layer of Alou's intimate reflections about his innocence, on top of the stereotyping criminalization. This produces, in turn, a severe critique of the fantasy performed by law enforcement operatives of restoring social order by cleansing the Spanish national body of immigrants. Rather, these images reinforce the unfair criminalization of undocumented migrants.

The second part of the letter contains Alou's reasons for attempting to return to Spain. Once again, the background images show a familiar event that does not need words: the moment in which Alou is about to go back aboard a small boat that will make a crossing to Europe again. Alou has, effectively, already made the crossing—finding it impossible to remain in Senegal after building a new identity in Spain.

The letters' narratives are straightforward. They register, in chronological fashion, the stages of Alou's experience from his initial crossing to Spain to his final deportation and decision to return to Europe. At the same time, they provide an account of a nostalgic longing for his homeland that slowly dissolves, as he settles down and starts climbing up the social ladder by means of a steady job, cultural assimilation, and the creation of a love relationship.

As we think about these four letters—their sequential position in the film, form, content, and connection to the background images—it is possible to group them into pairs. In the first and last, we see a clash between images and text, a disconnect between the time of writing and the time of narration, and a sharing of the same image: Alou ready to get into a boat toward the Spanish coast. Both are reflections of Alou outside Spain but with one important difference: the first depicts Alou as innocent and naïve; the second, however, portrays a mature Alou, reflective and able to analyze the racism he has seen and experienced in Spain. The Alou who is returning to Spain for the second time is not the same man as the one who wrote the first letter in eager anticipation of a new life.

The first letter portrays Alou as a distinct subject with a specific family history, the film's images show, however, an individual dispossessed of his personal identity as he shares with other immigrants the same appalling conditions during their crossing into Spain. The fourth letter operates similarly: the cinematography focuses on the harsh deportation process, while the text centers at the same time on a critique of the unfair stereotyping of Africans as criminals. But now, Alou is presented as a caustic expert who knows how to decode Spanish racial mechanisms that may possibly grant him more stability when he returns to Spain for the second time.[11] Together, they use Alou's subjectivity to confront the audience with the blatant racism of Spaniards themselves, forcing them to analyze and critique their own racial prejudices. In this sense the film is also a reflection about Spanish society, which is not portrayed in a positive light.[12]

The second and third letters demonstrate a greater connection with the images on screen, and both refer to the present time of the action (Alou's experiences in Madrid and Barcelona). This correlation makes sense, since their function is to inform Alou's parents of his current situation. In these two letters the connection between text and image is more intimate, particularly when letters address familiar aspects known to the audience: Africans as sellers on the streets or immigrants working in appalling conditions in sweatshops. However, the text diverges from the film's images when it seeks to emphasize aspects that may be beyond the audience reflections: for example, the cultural estrangement created by Spaniards meeting at bars (as remarked in the second letter) or the different food they prepare (as emphasized in the third letter). Here, the text provides information not conveyed by images themselves, ensuring that the audience is aware of cultural differences.

If we understand the border as a dividing line that separates not only lands but identities, in *Las cartas de Alou* we see a process of erasure of the line that separates Alou's distinct identities at the time he crosses the geographical divide between Africa and Europe. However, the four letters highlight and clarify what is perhaps not so obvious in the images or, conversely, is so obvious for the viewers that they may not see the problems they contain. The combinations of text and images duplicate the message in order to reinforce Armendáriz's political criticism of the appalling immigrant conditions. And even more interestingly, the movie starts and ends with a clash of letters and images that reinforces the radical displacement from one side of Alou's identity to another. Through this manipulation of the connection between narrative text and image, Armendáriz is telling us that there are times when a picture by itself is definitely not worth a thousand words.

Notes

1. See Isabel Ramón Santaolalla, *Los "Otros": etnicidad y "raza" en el cine español contemporáneo* (Saragossa and Madrid: Prensas Universitarias de Zaragoza and Ocho y Medio, 2005), 120. Montxo Armendáriz was born in Olleta (Navarre) in 1949. When he was six, he moved to Pamplona (Navarre). He is well-known for feature films like *Tasio* (1984), *27 horas* (1986), *Las cartas de Alou* (1990), *Historias del Kronen* (1995), *Secretos del corazón* (1997) *Silencio roto* (1999), *Obaba* (2005), and *No tengas miedo* (2011). However, he started his filmmaker career with shorts such as *Paisaje* (1980) and *Carboneros de Navarra* (1981). Armendáriz's cinema addresses issues related to marginalized groups in Spanish contemporary society such as youngsters involved with drugs, delinquency and sex, immigrants, and abused children.

2. For official figures see "Press Release, 3 June 2009: Estimate of the Municipal Register at 1 January 2009, Provisional data," Instituto Nacional de Estadística, June 3, 2009, http://www.ine.es/en/prensa/np551_en.pdf.

3. Among these we find *Las cartas de Alou* (*Letters From Alou*, dir. Montxo Armendáriz, 1990), *El techo del mundo* (dir. Felipe Vega, 1995; *Bwana* (dir. Imanol Uribe, 1996), *Tomando té* (*Two for Tea*, dir. Isabel Gardela, 2000); *Salvajes* (*Savages*, dir. Carlos Molinero, 2001), and *Poniente* (dir. Chus Gutiérrez, 2002). Schroeder adds three recent documentaries that also deal with the immigration experience in Spain: *Extranjeras* (dir. Helena Taberna, 2003), *Si nos dejan* (*If They Let Us*, dir. Ana Torres, 2005), and *Pobladores* (dir. Manuel García Serrano, 2006). Also from 2003 is *Europlex*, a twenty-minute video-documentary by Ursula Biemann in collaboration with the anthropologist Angela Sander, about the different activities that women who cross the border between Spain and Ceuta and Melilla do, such as smuggling clothes and domestic service. See Paul A Schroeder-Rodríguez, "Migrants and Lovers: Interculturation in *Flowers from Another World*," *Jump Cut: A Review of Contemporary Media* 50 (2008), http://www.ejumpcut.org/archive/jc50.2008/FloresOMundo/text.html.

4. Literally, a small boat used to hunt ducks.

5. Wolof is a language of the West-Atlantic branch of the Niger-Congo language family. It is spoken in Senegal, Gambia, and Mauritania.

6. Santaolalla, *Los "Otros,"* 123.

7. Isolina Ballesteros, *Cine (ins)urgente:Textos fílmicos y contextos culturales de la España posfranquista* (Madrid: Fundamentos, 2001), 219.

8. Translation of the four letters into English is mine. The original letters are introduced in the film in Alou's voice-over in his original African language. The audience gets the letters content by means of Spanish subtitles.

9. Thomas G. Deveny, *Migration in Contemporary Hispanic Cinema* (Plymouth, UK: Scarecrow Press, 2012), 28.

10. Twenty thousand pesetas (former currency in Spain before the euro) equal around 120 euros. However, the purchasing power of twenty thousand pesetas at the end of the 1990s was higher than 120 euros today. Twenty thousand pesetas in 1990 could roughly be a third of an average Spanish salary.

11. Regarding stereotypes there is another significant difference between *Las cartas de Alou* and the other movies that treat immigration. In Armendáriz's movie there is little mythologizing of the black character, as it does not conform to stereotypes of the black males in the sense of being primitive and physically and sexually superior. See Doreen O'Connor-Gómez, "Spectacle and Violence: Immigration in Spain Today," *Hispania* 91, no. 1 (2008): 268. It is interesting in this regard a note by Isabel Santaolalla about an exclusive screening of the film that took place in San Sebastián for the Senegalese community. After the film, the general comment from the audience was positive because the movie showed their reality as it was. This confirms that absence of mythologizing noted by O'Connor-Gómez. See Santaolalla, *Los "Otros,"* 121.

12. Chema Castiello, "Inmigrantes en el cine español: el caso marroquí," in *Atlas de inmigración en España, Atlas 2004: Taller de Estudios Internacionales Mediterráneos*, edited by Bernabé López García and Mohamed Berriane (Universidad Autónoma de Madrid: Madrid, 2004), 426.

Works Cited

Ballesteros, Isolina. *Cine (ins)urgente:Textos fílmicos y contextos culturales de la España posfranquista.* Madrid: Fundamentos, 2001.

Castiello, Chema. "Inmigrantes en el cine español: el caso marroquí." In *Atlas de inmigración en España, Atlas 2004: Taller de Estudios Internacionales Mediterráneos,* edited by Bernabé López García and Mohamed Berriane, 425–427. Universidad Autónoma de Madrid: Madrid, 2004. http://www.iemed.org/documents/atlaspresentacio.pdf

Deveny, Thomas G. *Migration in Contemporary Hispanic Cinema.* Plymouth, UK: Scarecrow Press, 2012.

O'Connor-Gómez, Doreen. "Spectacle and Violence: Immigration in Spain Today." *Hispania* 91, no. 1 (2008): 267–268.

"Press Release, 3 June 2009: Estimate of the Municipal Register at 1 January 2009, Provisional data." Instituto Nacional de Estadística. June 3, 2009. http://www.ine.es/en/prensa/np551_en.pdf.

Santaolalla Ramón, Isabel. *Los "Otros": etnicidad y "raza" en el cine español contemporáneo.* Saragossa and Madrid: Prensas Universitarias de Zaragoza and Ocho y Medio, 2005.

Schroeder-Rodríguez, Paul A. "Migrants and Lovers: Interculturation in *Flowers from Another World*." *Jump Cut: A Review of Contemporary Media* 50 (2008). http://www.ejumpcut.org/archive/jc50.2008/FloresOMundo/text.html.

Films

Bwana. Directed by Imanol Uribe. Spain, 1996.
El techo del mundo. Directed by Felipe Vega. Spain, 1995.
Europlex. Directed by Ursula Biemann and Angela Sander, 2003.
Extranjeras. Directed by Helena Taberna. Spain, 2003.
Flores de otro mundo. Directed by Iciar Bollaín. Spain, 1999.
Las cartas de Alou. Directed by Montxo Armendáriz. Spain, 1990.
Pobladores. Directed by Manuel García Serrano. Spain, 2006.
Poniente. Directed by Chus Gutiérrez. Spain, 2002.
Salvajes. Directed by Carlos Molinero. Spain, 2001.
Si nos dejan. Directed by Ana Torres. Spain, 2005.
Tomando té. Directed by Isabel Gardela. Spain, 2000.

14

Reflections on China and Border Crossings in Jia Zhang-ke's *Unknown Pleasures* (2002) and *Still Life* (2006)

Sean Allan

Chinese leader Mao Zedong attempted, during the Cultural Revolution of the early 1970s, to reestablish power through the disruption of everyday urban life—including, importantly, the closure of universities—and the denunciation of all things labeled capitalist or bourgeois. After Mao's death in 1976, however, a faction of the Chinese Communist Party led by Deng Xiaoping established a market economy, reopened the universities, and reopened China to other cultures' influences. The fifth generation of Chinese filmmakers, who entered the film academy of Beijing University during the early years of this post-Mao era, came of age during the Cultural Revolution and were profoundly shaped by it. Director Chen Kaige, whose film *The Yellow Earth* (*Huang tu di*, 1985) was the fifth generation's first major work, had denounced his own father as an enemy of progress. Much of Chen's work combines an effort to understand China's past with an effort to understand the Cultural Revolution.

Jia Zhang-ke was inspired to become a filmmaker when, in his early twenties, he saw Chen's *The Yellow Earth*. His reputation as a leading member of the sixth generation of Chinese filmmakers was established by his short student film "Xiao Shan Going Home" and expanded by a series of narrative fiction films referred to collectively as the Fenyang trilogy: *Xiao Wu* (1997), *Platform* (*Zhan Tai*, 2000), and *Unknown Pleasures* (*Ren Xiao Yao*, 2002).[1] Jia's insistence on shooting these early films outside the Chinese government's cinema system—without permits or official approval—is part of what earned him attention from world audiences, which often celebrated his work as courageous. Beginning with his 2004 film *The World* (*Shijie*), all of his productions have been made with government approval, but they continue to address issues that make the Chinese government uncomfortable.[2]

Born in 1970, Jia directly experienced the Cultural Revolution only as a young child but is well aware of its effects because of his family's experiences. He was raised in Fenyang, a city in Shanxi province in the north of China whose citizens are typical of the rural Chinese who move to bigger cities to find opportunity and provide for their families. Immigrant laborers have limited rights in the city; they are for the most part forced to take work in factories or at construction sites. Jia combines these life and family experiences with the concerns of the previous generation, producing a keen understanding of how people live through and with change—including, importantly, the effects of these changes on individual (subjective) consciousness. We can also claim, given the influence of *Yellow Earth*, that Jia is interested in how these concerns with change and the rural-urban divide relate to how those same concerns played out in the past.

This chapter will explore the varieties of borders and border crossings in two of Jia Zhang-ke's films, in order to delineate Jia's insights into contemporary China and rural Chinese lives. *Unknown Pleasures* takes place among the aimless young people of Jia's own hometown, while *Still Life* (*San xia hao ren*, 2006) concerns rural subjects more focused on or resigned to dedicating their lives to urban labor. Jia uses borders primarily to show how the changes in China since 1976 have affected the lives of rural Chinese negatively; he also considers the way in which these changes provide some tools to rural Chinese people to help them develop a sense of their own personal identity.

Jia's work examines the new subjectivities of post-Maoist China within the liminal space of the various borders between rural and urban China—geographic, cultural, and legal—and the new desire for individual identity that becomes possible within that space. These border crossings function at two levels. First is the level of narrative, in which the story presented plays with the borders between realism and editorializing: telling a story about how things are that functions as an implied argument about why they are that way. Second is the level of agency, in which characters navigate a cultural landscape and process cultural material in ways that function on the border between wisdom and ephemera, enlightenment and mere interest in trivia, a border resulting from the confusion caused by the magnitude of changes in China's recent past. The characters who struggle to make their way in these cultural borderlands are left confused and vulnerable by the ceaseless, pervasive changes they experience there.

Known Borders: The Films

Jia's *Unknown Pleasures*, filmed and set in 2002 in his hometown of Fenyang, is his most focused study of the effects of globalization on post-Mao China.

The film is a lament on the state of affairs in China and is openly sympathetic to its subjects and their failed efforts to create their own identities freely and effectively. The film is principally about the dreams of three characters who are barely out of high school. Bin Bin (Wei Wei Zhao) is a recent graduate who lives with his mother, a divorced and struggling factory worker. He attempts to hide the recent loss of his job, but when his mother discovers his deception, Bin Bin makes amends by promising to join the military to ensure a decent future for himself. Bin Bin spends his time either with his school-age girlfriend, Yuan Yuan (Qing Feng Zhou), or his male friend Xiao Ji (Qiong Wu). Xiao Ji is a recent high school graduate, as well. He lives with his father and brother, both of whom work at a factory. Xiao Ji himself doesn't have a job, and he spends most of his time on his motorcycle or with Bin Bin.

One day Xiao Ji and Bin Bin go to a performance advertising Mongolian King Liquor. The lead dancer is a woman named Qiao Qiao (Zhao Tao). Xiao Ji is smitten. The twenty-year-old Qiao Qiao is pursuing a career as a dancer and entertainer, but she seems to be exploited by managers who give her work: they delay payment whenever possible. Qiao Qiao's manager and boyfriend, Qiao San (Zhubin Li), is Qiao Qiao's former physical education teacher, the current leader of a criminal gang, and a pimp. As much as Qiao Qiao claims to be free to pursue pleasure and fulfillment, film viewers see that Qiao San has control over her.

Xiao Ji tries to impress Qiao Qiao. He helps her get money to pay for her father's hospital visit and creates a cosmopolitan image for himself through his knowledge of American cinema, in the form of Quentin Tarantino's 1994 film *Pulp Fiction*. However, when Xiao Ji tries to confront Qiao San over his treatment of Qiao Qiao, he fails and is beaten up by Qiao San's gang. Ultimately, Xiao Ji needs his own savior: Bin Bin, who prevents a second confrontation when he sees that Qiao San is armed with a gun.

Menacing as Qiao San is, he is eventually no longer a threat, meeting his end offscreen in a car accident. The lovers share temporary bliss in a small hotel, where Qiao Qiao introduces Xiao Ji to philosophies of pleasure and the self through the teachings of Zhuangzi. She draws a butterfly, which Xiao Ji takes with him and places over his heart after they part.[3] Xiao Ji's romantic yearning is for naught—Qiao Qiao vanishes from his life as unexpectedly as she appeared.

Bin Bin's romantic life also becomes fraught. His plan to join the military is dashed when a blood test reveals that he has hepatitis. When his girlfriend Yuan Yuan attempts to connect with him romantically before traveling to Beijing to study, he is unresponsive. What she interprets as his rejection is, in fact, an effort to save her from both his hepatitis and his dim future as a rural Chinese with no college or military prospects.

After Yuan Yuan leaves, Bin Bin and Xiao Ji make a feeble attempt to rob a bank. The bank guard quickly arrests Bin Bin. Xiao Ji escapes on his motorcycle, and when it runs out of gas, Xiao Ji simply leaves it on the side of the road and boards a bus to places unknown. Bin Bin is taken to the police station. The film ends when the policeman at the station forces Bin Bin to sing a song. Bin Bin sings the Richie Jen love song "Unknown Pleasures," a symbol of the happiness in which he no longer believes.

The film's title signals Jia's view of the way traditional culture and popular culture are vitiated by the impulses unleashed by globalization and unfettered consumer culture. The term *unknown pleasures* is multivalent. It can refer, both alternately and simultaneously, to the noise of popular culture, the way in which popular culture is processed individually, or the way in which ideas are trivialized. The use of Hong Kong singer Richie Jen's song "Unknown Pleasures," present in the film's diegetic sound, is a prime example. Its first use is as part of Qiao Qiao's dance performance promoting Mongolian King Liquor. The song is little more than foreground noise, not unlike the loud lottery announcement the audience hears earlier outside Xiao Ji and Bin Bin's hangout, a promotion of false dreams. This highlights the ways popular culture is trivialized—a mere come-on to convince consumers to buy Mongolian King Liquor.

Yet, the very same song can provide a sense of identity and hope, however fleeting it may be. When Bin Bin and Yuan Yuan use the video rental room to watch videos, rather than as a place for furtive sexual relations, their most intimate moment occurs when they hold hands and sing the lyrics of "Unknown Pleasures" together, making the song's commitment to romantic love their own. The scene offers hope that popular culture can serve as something other than merely the product of a crass libidinal economy, as the pair avoids cheap sex in a culture that places too much value on cheapness of all types.

When Bin Bin sings "Unknown Pleasures" again, in the police station after his arrest for attempted bank robbery, it is a response to the assault on his dignity and to a tragedy that seems predestined, an exemplification of the sense that there is, in Bin Bin's words, "No fucking future."

Although *Unknown Pleasures* does not blame the sad fates of its protagonists on the music of Hong Kong's Richie Jen, it is less sympathetic to the introduction of bootlegs of American film into the culture. The primary action of the film derives from a misreading of Quentin Tarantino's film *Pulp Fiction*, an imported film that impresses Xiao Ji. In a sense, it is his misreading of the "coolness" championed by *Pulp Fiction* that leads to the bank robbery. The conceit of misread popular culture establishes Jia's insights into the dangers and limits of self-fashioning; it suggests that the flood of popular and global culture products need not necessarily be "junk," but that they are difficult to process and contextualize within the framework provided by traditional culture. The conceit manifests the literal and conceptual borders between rural and urban. Xiao Ji is not exactly a rube, but he does not have the ability to use popular culture to effectively fashion a sense of self, the result of new cultural directives that flood the market with liquor, illegal DVDs of foreign films, and limited visions of traditional culture.

Xiao Ji notes that Qiao Qiao resembles *Pulp Fiction*'s Mia Wallace, and this resemblance is concretized when the audience sees Qiao Qiao perform in an underground club a dance similar to Mia's famous dance, the techno song playing a motif from *Pulp Fiction*'s opening credits music. The resemblance is important, because if Xiao Ji does not understand Mia Wallace, he cannot understand Qiao Qiao, whose resemblance to Mia is part of what attracts him to her.

The link also helps to establish Qiao Qiao's flawed self-fashioning, an example of an incompletely understood aspect of traditional Chinese culture. She embraces a more traditional sensuality following the philosopher Zhuangzi's concept of unknown pleasures, an interpretation of Taoism's embrace of "the Way" (understanding the forces of life as part of life's ineffable flow) as a pursuit of personal happiness. But it is too difficult for her to distinguish between the sustaining sensibility of Zhuangzi and the cheap thrills of the cultural landscape. Rather than understand "unknown pleasures" as a method to avoid unnecessary stress by engaging with the Way, she instead embraces hedonism, mistaking the new false pleasures (and the stresses they impose) as sources for her liberation. She has chosen a look that links to the West and personal freedom, but the look will not necessarily free her. She is struggling to self-fashion within the context of the rural-urban border, for she lacks the power either to contextualize the messages of American culture or to process the wisdom of Zhuangzi's call to intelligent hedonism. Her predicament shows that the cacophony of influences on the rural subject makes self-fashioning an insurmountable challenge. The purpose is to keep the rural subject's sense of self and labor power contingent.[4] Even in a story that does not seem to be about work, it is useful to interpret the ways in which the characters represent the deep economic divisions in China.

Qiao Qiao's boyfriend and pimp Qiao San embodies a pervasive, yet unrecognized, form of evil. The new market economy and its concomitant contribution to individual self-deception makes pimping particularly attractive and makes those who seek to be free—particularly rural people—especially vulnerable to the pimp and confidence man, two figures functioning within the gray market economies that dominate the landscape of Fenyang. Qiao San transforms from a teacher into a pimp and gangster, corrupting his former student Qiao Qiao as he makes his own transition. Qiao San's transgressive personality ties to a long tradition of criticism of Chinese authority, the implied argument being that the tyrannical teacher trope found in criticisms of the feudal- and Confucian-era influences on China has moved from the classroom into the new economy: the manipulative teacher is now a manipulator of both the market and the mind.[5]

It is within the logic of this shift in tropes that we may understand the scenes involving curiously repetitive acts of abuse, such as Xiao Ji being repeatedly slapped by Qiao San's men, or Qiao Qiao being repeatedly pushed back by Qiao San into her seat on their bus during an argument. The tools for identity formation provided by popular culture are prone to such significant manipulation that efforts to self-invent and live freely could very well result in running in circles and subjecting oneself to repeated punishment. This sort of encouraged self-deception ultimately leads to acts of faux agency—in the case of this film, Xiao Ji and Bin Bin's belief that they are acting like Americans by robbing a bank.

Jia's later film, *Still Life*, features a more diverse set of rural characters, moving beyond tragic fools like Xiao Ji, Bin Bin, and Qiao Qiao and metaphors for evil like Qiao San. In *Unknown Pleasures*, Jia's subjects' efforts to self-fashion in meaningful ways were always failures. They eventually realize that their dreams will forever be deferred, so they give up. The film returns to the more hopeful themes of self-fashioning that animated Jia's second film, *Platform*. Ian Johnston, in his essay on *Still Life*, notes that "*Still Life*'s two protagonists . . . are better survivors, more tenacious, and their fates have none of the sense of failure, of coming to a dead end, that marks Jia's other films."[6] Through the protagonists Shen Hong (Zhao Tao) and Han Sanming (played by himself), the audience experiences a variety of border spaces and experiential realities for rural subjects of the area. The former is a nurse looking for her husband (Zhubin Li), a man who has been doing gray market work in the Three Gorges area and has been avoiding his wife for two years, while the latter is a man from Fenyang searching for a long-disappeared wife and daughter, his only clue to their whereabouts an address that is now underwater because of the Three Gorges dam project.

The film's rural space is literally flooded, forced to give way to urban construction, with the flooding also serving as a metaphor for changes forced by the influx of new people and money.[7] Relocation offices become literal border spaces, and the small kindnesses and cruelties—offers of help and refusals of the same, senses of hopelessness and perseverance—in the interactions among characters highlight a number of experiential realities within border space and among rural subjectivities, as they manage the changes wrought by the market economy, the attendant presence of gang violence, and the absence of family members.

Johnston identifies Han Sanming's dignity: "Sanming's relentless tenacity is expressed above all through his body. . . . He is in a way a very passive figure. . . . But there's an inner strength to Sanming that drives him to persevere."[8] Complementing Sanming's perseverance is the minor character Brother Mark, a local who helps Sanming find both a job and Sanming's estranged wife. Brother Mark's good nature helps situate Jia's section titles: "Tea," "Toffee," "Tobacco," and "Liquor." These items are typically used as small gifts and consumed as simple pleasures. In the film, however, these gifts are not always accepted when offered, and they do not always give pleasure when consumed, belying a sense of uncertainty about how things work in contemporary China and how people might relate to one another. Brother Mark loves another simple pleasure: cinema. He fashions an identity and attitude through the character of Brother Mark (Chow Yun-Fat) in John Woo's 1986 Hong Kong gangster film *A Better Tomorrow*, seeing himself, like the character, as a nostalgic figure who champions other dreamers. Brother Mark's consumption of cinema tacitly connects to objects of exchange and consumption by demonstrating that the tools for conviviality, like toffee and tobacco, may be part of the corrupting and corruptible market, but they can also be sources of identity and providers of personal pleasures. Brother Mark ultimately becomes a victim of the world as it has become, killed from either a construction accident or a murder carried out by gangsters running the gray market designed to look like an accident, yet he has crafted an identity for himself beyond merely that of an oppressed rural laborer. Similarly, Shen Hong also perseveres by escaping her failed marriage to her husband. She finalizes their separation by insisting to him that she has taken a lover. She has not, but the use of the gambit implies that the idea of romance can give one agency, as it allows her to move on with her life.

Overall, however, it seems that perseverance is the best that can be achieved through effective self-fashioning. The characters of *Unknown Pleasures* wanted liberation. They failed, and their souls were crushed. They lacked the tools and discipline of Han Sanming and Brother Mark, and they lacked, as well, the proper sense of scope. It is the perseverance of Sanming, the dissimulation and perseverance of Shen Hong, and the self-fashioning of Brother Mark that embody the possibility for rural subjects to maintain their dignity and humanity despite their economic exploitation, and Jia celebrates this. Yet Jia's perspective on rural Chinese is bittersweet, for in its celebration of rural perseverance there is also a recognition that seemingly nothing further can be accomplished.

The economic exploitation of the rural subject, along with the legal standards that forever prevent a "rural" person from forming an "urban" identity even if that person resides and works in an urban space, combine to create a sense of alienation. Sanming and Brother Mark avoid this alienation by reshaping themselves, and Shen Hong ultimately escapes the alienating effects of a failed marriage, but they cannot escape forces that define them as alien to the urban space and the space as alien to them. Jia conveys the force of the border between rural and urban with two visual jokes: at one point a UFO flies past Sanming. At another point, a building near Shen Hong turns out to be an alien ship in disguise, and the ship flies away after Shen Hong walks past it. These jokes underscore the rural subject and his or her embodied navigation of spaces and borders as the true grounding for the contemporary Chinese spirit. The images identify the rural Chinese subject's alienation and imply that rapid change has rendered the landscape utterly alien, even to those who have always called the Three Gorges home.[9]

Jia's Sense of Beauty, and Ours

Despite the sardonic fabulism of Jia's UFO imagery, Ian Johnston contends that "[t]he inspiration for *Still Life* lies in documentary."[10] Establishing shots of the landscape and human movement seem to present everyday life rather than dramatized action, and the camera's unobtrusiveness, because it is so different from the active camera work that guides viewers through popular narrative film, invites viewers to interpret the visuals as if they were nonfiction.[11] The complex way in which Jia combines documentary filmmaking (rather than just a visual sense similar to the documentary filmmaking style) with fiction in his later films requires an inquiry beyond the scope of this chapter; however, Jia's later work will continue making inquiries into borders by connecting presentations of real life to fictional storytelling. The fictional turns and moments of instability in these more recent films work like the UFO motif in *Still Life*, interrupting documentary-style realism and making problematic the nature of truth telling as a means to better understand what is real. In the border between fiction and nonfiction filmmaking, perhaps there is a space in which to view a greater possibility for the rural Chinese subject beyond basic perseverance and survival. Following a similar logic, the image that ends *Still Life*, an image of a man walking a tightrope from one nearly demolished building to another, exemplifies both the border navigations that Jia's films feature and the ways in which the striking image complements and transmogrifies the film's realistic mood and style.

The use of a fantastic image as the coda to a realistic film fittingly symbolizes Jia's attitude toward borders. His films reveal a commitment to understanding and presenting the struggles that rural Chinese are undertaking in post-Mao China, while at the same time stressing the intensity of rural China's experiential reality. Life is a tightrope walk. The position between rural and urban borders does not just challenge a rural subject's sense of belonging; it is dangerous, requiring constant balance and movement.

The fraught image of the tightrope also exemplifies Jia's desire to show that many of China's transformations create new ways for rural Chinese to be exploited and manipulated. Jia's figures struggle with difficult material situations, as well as with their own thoughts and desires—thoughts and desires they do not necessarily have control over and which they do not have the tools to understand. Throughout, these may be seen as struggles with borders: not just between the rural and urban, but also between the global and the local, tradition and modernity, and people and ideas.

Yet Jia's stories are not unmitigated tragedies, for that would fail to appreciate rural Chinese lives or recognize their humanity, their triumphs, and their failed efforts. Jia's stories offer glimmers of hope in which aspects of the new circumstances and new ways of life within China can be used by rural Chinese to form personal identities—identities from which they might maintain a sense of dignity, understand how to treat others humanely, and develop a sense of how to persevere through continuing changes and struggles. Ultimately, they traverse a border between hope and despair, a space in which perseverance may, paradoxically, open the door to greater possibilities. Han Sanming and Brother Mark's methods of perseverance do not exhaust those possibilities. Bin Bin and Yuan Yuan's singing along to a romantic love song is also a moment of self-fashioning: fleeting, but holding out the hope that others could find a way to sustain it. Beneath the surface, as Doris Lim and others have noted, romantic songs have sustained everyday Chinese lives in the post-Mao period. The day belonged to Deng Xiaoping and market reforms, but the night belonged to Taiwanese torch song singer Teresa Teng.[12] Shen Hong frees herself by appealing to romance, as well, and with her freedom comes the possibility for further development of her identity and her sense of romance. Yet the risk remains that she may fail as Qiao Qiao failed, falling victim to a false and limiting sense of love and pleasure. For the rural Chinese, every path is a tightrope, a liminal space between conceptual borders. There is a certain beauty to watching a tightrope walk; Jia's hope is that the beauty arrests the viewers and moves them to think further.

Notes

1. Kevin B. Lee, "Jia Zhangke," *Senses of Cinema* 25 (2003), http://www.sensesofcinema.com/2003/great-directors/jia/.

2. Biographical and historical information can be gleaned from reference sources or survey books. The information is presented to help the reader understand the context under which Jia Zhang-ke grew up. The discussion of Jia's relationship to Chinese government censors does not factor into further discussion, but it is relevant to readers to the degree that they engage with Jia's films, personal and group understandings of Jia films, and the institutions that determine what films and directors will receive

a world audience. Regarding the Chinese government, the foundational myth of the Chinese revolution was that it was a people's victory, in particular a victory made possible by the heroism of rural Chinese. Any sort of text that highlights the contemporary poor treatment of rural Chinese could challenge this myth or convince people that the revolution has been betrayed.

3. The butterfly is another symbol associated with Zhuangzi, an ancient Chinese philosopher who famously wondered if his dream about being a butterfly is actually the butterfly's dream about being him.

4. In the context of the film, cultural and economic forces want Qiao Qiao to forever market Mongolian King Liquor, her wages and her dreams to dance more meaningfully always deferred.

5. One of the best delineations of the corrupt feudal lord and corrupt teacher motif as it is understood in popular Chinese consciousness is Lu Xun's story "Nostalgia." See Lu Xun, "Nostalgia," in *The Real Story of Ah-Q and Other Tales of China: The Complete Fiction of Lu Xun*, trans. Julia Lovell (London: Penguin Books, 2009), 1–14.

6. Ian Johnston, "Still, Life: Looking at Jia Zhang-ke's Recent Masterpiece." *Bright Lights Film Journal* 58 (2007), http://www.brightlightsfilm.com/58/58stilllife.php.

7. To understand this idea, think of a place like Tibet. It's considered to be under attack because the area is being changed by the immigration of Han Chinese and the introduction of investment money. The immigration and investment work together to replace traditional Tibetan culture with consumer culture. In the case of this essay, we are applying the specific narratives we've heard about the commercialization of special places and applying it to rural China in general.

8. Johnston, "Still, Life."

9. Those who lived in nearby rural villages have their home identity taken from them through submersion or eminent domain: the ground beneath their feet is now urban, but they remain rural subjects and hence are out of place.

10. Johnston, "Still, Life."

11. This sense of documentary-style grounding also helps to situate Jia's movement toward more directly documentary-style forms in his later films, *24 City* (2008) and *I Wish I Knew* (2010).

12. Doris Lim, "Teresa Teng, The Singer Not the Song?" Musicouch, January 17, 2011, http://musicouch.com/genres/folk/teresa-teng-the-singer-not-the-song/.

Works Cited

Johnston, Ian. "Still, Life: Looking at Jia Zhang-ke's Recent Masterpiece." *Bright Lights Film Journal* 58 (2007). http://www.brightlightsfilm.com/58/58stilllife.php.

Lee, Kevin B. "Jia Zhangke." *Senses of Cinema* 25 (2003). http://www.sensesofcinema.com/2003/great-directors/jia/.

Lim, Doris. "Teresa Teng, The Singer Not the Song?" Musicouch. January 17, 2011. http://musicouch.com/genres/folk/teresa-teng-the-singer-not-the-song/.

Xun, Lu. "Nostalgia." In *The Real Story of Ah-Q and Other Tales of China: The Complete Fiction of Lu Xun*, translated by Julia Lovell, 1–14. London: Penguin Books, 2009.

Films

24 City (*Er shi si cheng ji*). Directed by Jia Zhang-ke. China, Hong Kong, Japan, 2008.
A Better Tomorrow (*Yung hung bon sik*). Directed by John Woo. Hong Kong, 1986.
In the Mood for Love. Directed by Wong Kar-wai. Hong Kong, France, 2000.
I Wish I Knew (*Hai shang chuan qi*). Directed by Jia Zhang-ke. China, 2010.
Pickpocket (*Xiao wu*). Directed by Jia Zhang-ke. Hong Kong, China, 1997.
Platform (*Zhan tai*). Directed by Jia Zhang-ke. Hong Kong, China, Japan, France, 2000.
Pulp Fiction. Directed by Quentin Tarantino. United States, 1994.
Still Life (*San xia hao ren*). Directed by Jia Zhang-ke. China, Hong Kong, 2006.
Unknown Pleasures (*Ren xiao yao*). Directed by Jia Zhang-ke. South Korea, France, Japan, China, 2002.
The World (*Shijie*). Directed by Jia Zhang-ke. China, Japan, France, 2004.
"Xiao Shan Going Home (Xiao shan hui jia)." Directed by Jia Zhang-ke. China, 1995.
Yellow Earth. Directed by Chen Kaige. China, 1985.

15

Border Imaging

Revealing the Gaps between the Reality, the Representation, and the Experience of the Border

Katie Davies

INSPECTING THE BRITISH BORDER through a western prism of political sovereignty, this chapter focuses upon one particular sociopolitical flashpoint shared by hundreds of civilians and members of the British Armed Forces. Between 2007 and 2011 the small English market town of Wootton Bassett became a site for British repatriation ceremonies. The repatriation ceremonies were initiated and continued by the community in order to pay respect to the British soldiers killed in Afghanistan, by marking the passage and return of their dead bodies to the United Kingdom. Through a critique of the short video work *The Separation Line,* which I filmed while participating in the ceremonies, a portrait of the small English town, its people, and their way of demarcating a political border through performance is explored. By focusing on these ceremonies, I will unpack an initial definition of border as a power structure and how video practice can render visible this usually invisible border type. Through the performance of the ceremonies, the town became a symbol of political edict, national identity, and sovereignty. I will explain how the video work transcends these symbolic machinations because those involved (both within and observing the video work) maintain a position of performer and participant. This position as an inclusive act allows the sharing of an experience and is in opposition to the dividing and restructuring mechanisms of the border.

As a beginning, I should offer a brief sketch as to how my contribution to this volume has developed. As a practice-driven researcher and artist, my position is one of production, of construction, and of a critical understanding of the border polemic through the development of an artist's video practice. I sometimes belong to, but stand apart from, the groups featured in my video work, in order to engage with people who are either bound by geopolitical circumstance or liberated from certain structural obligations. For several years I have been researching and lecturing on issues related to border zones. My previous video projects have included working with the UN Armistice Commission and United States Forces in Korea to research and film the Korean border from within the Korean Demilitarised Zone in 2008. In 2009 I documented the journey and experience of the British citizenship ceremonies, facilitated by the British Home Office, Sheffield City Council, and Yorkshire ArtSpace. Attracted by political transformations that dictate how society, territory, and political debate are controlled, my work aims to realize the sensation of a border as an experience of artifice and human division, in order to propose alternative relations between social, historical, and economic episodes. My aim is to address whether a contemporary experience of border can be understood as an involvement within a polis of power, and how research through an artistic practice can render visible this invisible and legislative structure. This forms part of an ongoing investigation into the restructuring activities created by border spaces.

The Separation Line attempts to project its audience into the midst of the repatriation ceremonies that took place at Wootton Bassett, positioning the viewer as witness to this collective experience, an experience that brings the war overseas home by rendering it undeniably present. As an installation, *The Separation Line* constitutes a single screen that lasts the actual duration of the repatriation ceremony. A montage of fourteen different ceremonies, the installation presents the repetition of this ceremony as a toll that increased as each dead soldier returned. It also highlights the necessity of a ceremonial commemoration as this political border interrupts and divides the flows of everyday life.

Throughout my research, it has certainly not been my primary concern to refute the validity of political and personal arguments as to whether the British Armed Forces should be active within Afghanistan. This was discussed through news media speculation and, furiously, within the town, right up until the moment at which the ceremonies started. Initiated by the townsfolk with the intention of paying respect to the dead soldiers killed in combat and returning from war, the repatriation ceremonies also highlighted the implications of conflict. This gave rise to an almost manic media presence within the town as news correspondents clambered about broadcast vans, sending back reports from High Street,[1] which often concealed as much as they revealed (their own, overwhelming presence, included). The aligning of political agendas became apparent within the news coverage of the repatriations with the media predilection for reducing the ceremonial reality to an ideological symbol, thrusting the issue into a lengthy oratory around military operations, government legislation, and geopolitics.

My investigative practice was not an isolated initiative as I relied on the knowledge and testimonies of local and key figures from the Royal British Legion and the town council, who initiated the tributes, as well as colleagues in the artistic and academic field with whom I had theoretical and aesthetic discussions.

My motivation was to study the repatriations from a local position or "street level," with the aim of contributing to different understandings of the ceremony. Filming alternative aspects and perspectives to those of recent documentaries and media coverage, the HD video work and archive present a picture of the repatriations that has not, to date, been presented at a local, national, or international level. John C. Welchman, the author of *Rethinking Borders* (1996), defines *border* as a conduit of power driven across the territory of differential traces,[2] and it is the observation of border as an intervention of power, forming a bounded process of repetition within the town, that sits at the center of this research.

Figure 15.1. Soldiers of the 5th Battalion Argyll and Sutherland Highlanders, Royal Regiment of Scotland gather at the curb of Wootton Bassett High Street, waiting for the repatriation ceremony of Private Joseva Saqanagonedau Valabua, January 11, 2011. Video still from *The Separation Line*. Katie Davies.

Royal Wootton Bassett and the Military Community

My attention was drawn toward the ceremonies in August 2010 when, standing among the growing crowds on either side of High Street, I understood a community dynamic that I recognized from my own childhood; that secular and social structure of the extended military family, or more precisely in this case and my own, the Royal Air Force (RAF).

I became fascinated with the repatriations ceremonies because of what they made visible and apparent to me. I recognized within the townsfolk that I met at Wootton Bassett, who were mostly employed by the British Armed Forces in some respect, a group of individuals who were living, as I had, within the culture of a small market town that is "Other" to that of their military upbringing. There was an aura of my own experience present—not only of a market town situated one mile from an operational air force base, but also of belonging to a military culture that somehow renders its members expatriate as they leave and enter civilian life. This distinction between military and civilian life may be slight, but its impact is significant nonetheless.

I was intent on capturing through moving image the individual instances of human interrelatedness and the multiplicity of structural ties that I recognized

Figure 15.2. From left to right: The television and BBC news broadcaster Harry Gration, a photojournalist and members of the Royal Marines Cadets gather on Wootton Bassett High Street, waiting for the repatriation of Private Martin Bell of the 2nd Battalion, Parachute Regiment, February 3, 2011. Video still from *The Separation Line*. Katie Davies.

as present within the ceremonies. An apparent social bond within the gathering was visible, organized in hierarchies of caste, class, and rank, or oppositions of gender, age, and political leanings. The townsfolk were engaged and performing as ceremonial participants, communicating their inherited mannerisms as signals, both as a conscious and unconscious posturing. The mirroring of body language across the street, a shift between standing to attention and at ease, the wringing of hands behind the back, and most notably the rocking from the heels to the balls of the feet and eventual lifting up straight on the toes were all postulated, communicated by the civilians who were attending. During the two-hour gathering and subsequent ten-minute ceremony lay all of those contradictory features, affording humans the capacity to laugh and cry together: the language of commemoration. I began, in 2010, and continued over a period of fourteen months, to witness the transformation of Wootton Bassett to Royal Wootton Bassett and to understand the town as a microcosm of British tendencies.[3]

A multiplicity of sociopolitical and economic models, displaying opposing values but interrelating needs. The need for society as structured, differentiated, and separating individuals in terms of "more" or "less" appears as relevant now as when Queen Victoria bequeathed Leamington Spa Royal more than a century ago in 1838.

The Transformation of Royal Patronage

In order to understand Wootton Bassett's transformation to Royal, it seems important to highlight the ways in which it appears to be an average middle England market town. It is a small civil parish, represented by a conservative minister of parliament and situated in the middle of the Wiltshire countryside, in the southwest of England. With a population of approximately eleven thousand, the main draw of the town is High Street, seeing little or no change since the eighteenth century. The mainly two-story buildings of the Georgian architectural era line High Street and are home to the post office, butchers, news agents, chemist, charity shops, and a handful of coffee shops. Every Wednesday is market day, comprised of twelve market stalls that pedestrianize High Street, creating the opportunity for locals to meet, chat, and chew the fat about agricultural politics, the weather, the price of a loaf, and how to defrost a fridge freezer. Yet on closer inspection, one can witness the town experiencing life at its own pace—or, more precisely, in a multiplicity of rhythms—postmen, bank clerks, security vans, and the hourly toll of the church bell. However, there was the additional, and less average, sight of large military vehicles and armed forces personnel passing southward down High Street with continuity and frequency as normal as any other traffic. As the main route into RAF Lyneham, High Street acts as a channel, funneling military lorries, Jeeps, and as I once observed, heavily armored Mastiff 2 patrol vehicles—an incongruous and alarming sight to the outsider such as myself, but a normal, almost banal, rhythm and passage to the local townsfolk. As the major employer in the area, the base has directly or indirectly employed the majority of the town's population. The base once operated as the home of the United Kingdom's military air transport, but has now handed over full tactical air transport to RAF Brize Norton in Oxfordshire, due to cuts in the Ministry of Defense.[4] With the base being home to the C-17 and C-130 Hercules aircraft, these huge aircraft flew low along High Street on their way to landing at Lyneham, only a mile away, punctuating daily rhythms with their landings and departures and dominating the skyline above the town.

The first repatriation consisted of only a few passersby, a few veterans, and the town's mayor. It did not start as an organized event, but rather, as an impromptu gathering, coordinated by town members of the Royal British Legion, which steadily grew. Shortly after this modest beginning, military families also stood and paid respects along with many people from outside the town. Before long, the town was attracting international attention, with crowds, at times, reaching over a thousand. In the ensuing four years, 167 repatriation ceremonies saw the bodies of 345 service personnel pass through the Wiltshire town. In April 2007, one of the very first of the repatriation ceremonies took place as the dead bodies of the men and women of the British Armed Forces fighting in Iraq passed through the town as part of a funeral cortège on their way to the John Radcliffe Hospital and coroners in Oxford. Four years later, due to the closure of the RAF base in Lyneham, the repatriations at Wootton Bassett were concluded.

There are now three towns in the United Kingdom that hold royal patronage, granted royal status and awarded the letters patent by the express wish of the monarch. Following Leamington Spa was Tunbridge Wells in 1909, when Edward VII bestowed his patronage on the spa town in recognition of its connections to the Stuart dynasty. In October 2011, Wootton Bassett became the first town in Britain in more than a century to be given a royal title and awarded the letters patent by the princess royal on behalf of the queen, becoming Royal Wootton Bassett. On Sunday, October 16, 2011, thousands gathered on High Street as the town received the royal patronage following a petition from British Prime Minister David Cameron, who stated that the town's dignified demonstrations of respect and mourning had shown the deep bond between the public and the British Armed Forces.[5] Her royal highness the princess royal was received by the lord lieutenant, Mr. John Bush, in full military uniform, who escorted the princess down the High Street to a stage to assemble for the parade and the presentation of the letters patent. The

Figure 15.3. British Armed Forces veterans and two members of the public gather on Wootton Bassett High Street, waiting for the repatriation of Private Martin Bell of the 2nd Battalion, Parachute Regiment, February 3, 2011. Video still from *The Separation Line*. Katie Davies.

town crier, Owen Collier, also in ceremonial uniform, announced her royal highness as she arrived at the stage.

The commemoration and ceremony that followed included parade troops, the Wootton Bassett Band, and Royal Marines Band. Following speeches, a ceremonial and historic moment arrived when the town's new flag bearing the new coat of arms was raised for the first time after the presentation of the letters patent. The master of ceremonies, Councilor Steve Bucknell, invited Canon Thomas Woodhouse to bless the coat of arms. A fly-over of the Globemaster, Hercules, and later Vulcan bomber aircraft concluded the ceremony and souvenir flags, programs, Royal Wootton Bassett crown buns, tea towels, and other memorabilia were available to buy on the day. On reflection, it appears that modern Britain is in constant change, yet has never fundamentally changed. Outside observers would be forgiven for thinking that Elizabeth I was conferring the royal title on the town, so palpable was the Crown's legacy and so traditionally timeless the rhetoric that this ceremony represented: a moment out of time.

The Ceremonial Border within the Town

During my research for *The Separation Line*, I was faced with the challenge of finding an existing definition of *border* that would be beneficial in analyzing the repatriation ceremonies as an invisible border structure. A border can be viewed as two corresponding points of control in any given conflict of interest. It can also be experienced as alternately blocking or permitting, and policed or transgressive. Welchman describes the border not as a finite spatial delineation but as a differential process of boundary articulation marked by repetition, projection, and interruption: "The border is a conduit of power driven across the territory of 'differential traces'; it is always a specific intervention in place and in time; it will always interrupt even the most self-interruptive ('laminar') of flows (desire, the corporate economy, the television signal, and so on). Yet it will always be rematerialized as a specific function of system, history, language and place."[6] With regard to Wootton Bassett he added that Wootton Bassett is a good example of a border in this expanded sense. The town has been transformed into a surrogate border by virtue of its proximity to a point of entry for military air traffic (a key feature of twentieth-century transit infrastructure, the advent of airports themselves, both military and civilian, already marks the technological re-vectoring of border spaces). Wootton Bassett emerged as a zone of public and media crystallization for the temporary ritual visibility of the border, becoming a symbolic arena of postmortem repatriation oriented around a border space that would otherwise be invisible.[7]

He also made a comparison to similar ritual visibility in the United States, noting the prohibition by the Bush administration of media representations of the bodies of American soldiers returning to U.S. airfields: "You couldn't see the coffins, you couldn't see the flags, you couldn't see anything—so it was rendered invisible. The border at that point was put into suspension by political edict. In Britain, by contrast, it has erupted into a form of quasi-folkloric visibility governed by arbitrary and contingent directives that determine the route of a procession: the bodies have to pass through this place to go somewhere else."[8] Welchman's understanding of the border as an intervention, not just in a physical sense, but also in symbolic and imaginary negotiations with place, time, and power, begins to explain the invisible and interruptive nature of a border as a construct of power relations. However, it is also important to recognize ways in which this border becomes physically represented as an articulation of homeland. In the prologue to *Routes: Travel and Translation in the Twentieth Century* (2011), James Clifford questions how the notion of home is conceived and lived in relation to practices of coming and going. He states that since 1900, transregional histories have been powerfully inflected by three connected global forces: the continuing legacies of empire, the effects of unprecedented world wars, and the global consequences of industrial capitalism's disruptive, restructuring activity. He then goes on to observe how the currency of culture and identity as performative acts can be traced to their articulation of homelands, safe spaces, and that such acts of control, maintaining coherent insides and outsides, are always tactical.[9]

It is through this distinction of assuming a position of control through a performative act that a border of power becomes a visible and physical structure. The contemporary power structures that Clifford mentions—the legacies of Empire, war, and capitalist industry—are the border thresholds represented at the repatriations, as key figures from each of these contemporary structures participated in the ceremonies. There were regular appearances from international diplomats, royalty, charitable organizations, senior military officials, war veterans, and international media correspondents, as well as writers, journalists, and image-makers like myself who attempted to make sense of the conjunction of these borders.

Given the complex sociopolitical relations between these groups, to participate was to form the line at the curb of High Street. The ceremonies represented an interruption, a crossroads that became visible when a dead soldier passed through the town, yet any political or military hierarchies became neutralized as military protocol, the sovereign state, and the general public faced the implications of conflict and mortality together.

In doing so, they rendered the invisible political and military power borders, latent within the everyday, momentarily visible. This communion

Figure 15.4. Soldiers of the 1st Battalion Irish Guards and members of the public gather on Wootton Bassett High Street, waiting for the repatriation of Matthew James Collins and Lance-Sergeant Mark Terence Burgan, March 30, 2011. Video still from *The Separation Line*. Katie Davies.

highlights a liminal[10] and social bond that, for most in the United Kingdom, has ceased to be visible in everyday life. However, it also represents a bigger story about the phenomenon of social status and sacredness, homogeneity, and comradeship—or, more precisely, the what, where, and who of public demonstration.

Representing the Border through an Artistic Video Practice

It is from this moment that *The Separation Line* attempts to render visible the ceremonial borders experienced by its participants. As a montage of fourteen different ceremonies, parallels are proposed between the cortège passing repeatedly and the flow of moving images capturing the event at the edge of the filmic shot, acting as a border between two corresponding and fixed realities. Both constitute parallels represented in spatial and temporal dimensions, but more precisely, digital space and border space are formed by, and gain meaning through, the processes that occur in relation to them. High Street is not only the setting for the ceremonies but has also come to represent the repatriations in the index of the mind—symbolizing the corresponding point of control in any given border situation.

Although High Street plays a central part in the work, there is no wider angle view or shot down the street, no alternative perspective except that of the participants' immediate view. High Street appears as a setting and in this mode becomes a trope of the aesthetic, transgressing its role as a social construct for local transport and flow. It becomes a site from which to examine the linguistics of the ceremony within the construct of digital space. When considering the representation of border dialectics as forming an opposed pairing, digital and material landscapes also must be considered as a coupling, defined by their opposition and formed perceptually and actually. This observation forms the core principle driving this research and my position, going into the field and trying to make sense of these public conventions—or more precisely, mapping a space that corresponds with a mapping of public and personal knowledge about a subject that is active and ever mobilized. The topographies that are produced within the research, both practical and theoretical, operate in multiple modes as an intended and layered relational discussion, provoking an audience to engage emotionally with the subject matter while also allowing an unpacking of layered forms of representation.

As the work is concerned with public memory, the formation of public space, and its relationship to public intimacy through the social body, *The Separation Line* is presented as a large video installation, back-projected onto a four-by-two-and-a-half-meter screen (ca. 158 by 97 inches), which sits on

Figure 15.5. The 5th Battalion Argyll and Sutherland Highlanders, Royal Regiment of Scotland observe the two minutes silence during the repatriation of Private Joseva Saqanagonedau Valabua, January 11, 2011. Video still from *The Separation Line*. Katie Davies.

the floor of the exhibition space. Installed in this way and viewed at this scale, audiences naturally stand in front of the projected image, as a gathering—a line—standing opposite and receiving the projected High Street, face-to-face with its digital participants on a human scale. The stereo soundtrack captures the left-to-right sound of the traffic and street noise, and is emitted from speakers on either side of the installed screen. Intentionally, as the author, and perhaps unintentionally on the part of the installation audience, the other side of High Street is formed by the audience, mirroring the digital ceremony participants on the other side of the road. In relation to the projection and in relation to the ceremony that is depicted, real and digital witnesses to the repatriation ceremonies face each other. As the videoed ceremony plays out with the installation audience in position, a mirroring of body language emerges as, faced by the digital participants of the ceremony, the installation audience reflects upon the faces, the voices, the passing of the body, and the collection of individuals presented, as moments of expression and emotion leak from the formal funeral procession.

The installation presents a montage of street setting, ceremonial event, exhibition space, and fourteen different repatriations. It has the potential to reveal the relationships between the digital audience within the work and the installation audience, as they reflect upon past experiences projected into the present. The artwork offers its audience the position of self-awareness, proposing a shared and multilayered cultural experience. Here, polarized military stereotypes fleetingly dissolve, as the officers and other ranks stand side by side, paying respect to the dead of their regiment, only to return to the conflict zone within days of attending the ceremony. One of the invisible borders present at Wotton Bassett is the commemoration of mortality, experienced through participation in the ritual of the repatriation ceremonies. As the soldiers stand among the people of the town, many themselves having experienced the ruin of conflict, what becomes comparable and visible is how all present, regardless of rank or profession, identify with their own mortality and moral obligations of duty within conflict. What becomes key to making this experience visible within a video practice is to make the video installation experiential: to translate the experience of the real into an encounter with the representational.

The Separation Line translates this reflection upon mortality by placing the audience in the same position as the town's participants, involving them, by virtue of sheer proximity, in the human scale installation that is ultimately representational of the event. The work alters the audience's position from passive to active and from viewer to participant.

What is important and intentional within the installation is that it is not the video image itself that makes the border visible, but rather the *experience* of the border as a liminal sensation that the installation makes perceptible. As

Figure 15.6. Soldiers of the 5th Battalion Argyll and Sutherland Highlanders, Royal Regiment of Scotland wait as the body of Private Joseva Saqanagonedau Valabua approaches from the left along Wootton Bassett High Street, January 11, 2011. Video still from *The Separation Line*. Katie Davies.

the hearse carrying the body approaches and is about to come into shot, the image cuts to black and the audience is denied its photographic representation. As they hear the hearse pass, the phenomenon of experience remains, precisely because the body as the spectacle of the ceremony has not been pacified or fetishized by my own authorial translation. For Jacques Rancière, this shared experience is at the heart of what constitutes spectacle: "[A] theatre without spectators, where those in attendance learn from, as opposed to being seduced, by images: where they become active participants as opposed to passive voyeurs."[11] To witness the passing of the hearse in the mind's eye is to participate and share an understanding of the event—an event that, at the very least, is a manifestation of our own mortality, as the last border threshold that we all have in common.

Conclusion: Toward Multiple Viewpoints

In considering the construction of public discourse, it is important to reflect on the ways in which artistic video practice can intervene in these political relationships, to resonate within the contexts of social debate and through the visual establishments that encourage these debates. Artistic videos, such as *The Separation Line*, give voice to multiple perspectives and experiences and serve to negate the ongoing reductive media assault of television and newspapers, offering the public an alternative context for discourse through artistic practice.

One way to achieve this is to position video practice within the gap left by the media, as a space for well-researched reports, observational documentary, conceptual exploration, and artistic intervention. *The Separation Line* attempts to occupy this gap. It takes a counter position—reconsidering what has already been seen, what has already been reported, and what has become immemorable—by producing an alternative representation as a quieter and less singular viewpoint. This critical and tactical approach appropriates visual languages for a different end. As video unfolds over time, it reveals a more complex temporality—the gap between the real event and the artifice of the installation, as well as the real event and the artifice of the news broadcast. Setting up this distance and challenging these representations of real experiences offers the possibility of penetrating social and theoretical discourse. It allows audiences to engage with the subject matter in both an emotional and analytical way, calling upon viewers to justify their positions in relation to the image as a political symbol.

In an address to Parliament, in which he described the repatriations as defining the deep bond between the public and the armed forces, Prime Minister David Cameron appropriated and used the town's motivation to pay respect in order to create a symbolic projection of maintaining and dictating power. He achieved this by erecting a border. Here his border operates as a restriction and builds a divide between a reality and a representation. The reality is the town's opposition to the involvement of British forces in Afghanistan; the representation is the way in which their mark of respect for those soldiers killed is transformed into support for the war on terror. Cameron's intervention disrupts the reality of the community as he crystalizes political and economic motivations into historical facts that will become the future legacy of the town. Throughout the news coverage of the awarding the letters patent, the act seemed to unite the Sovereign and the townsfolk in a show of solidarity. However, the patronage also muted potential discussion within the town around sovereignty, political obsequiousness, and military ambition. More precisely, it affirmed a sanction of power as a construct of political relations, articulating the state's control over history, language, and place: the border at the edge of the sovereign state.

The Separation Line enables individual encounters within a space that represents the timing and scale of the ceremonies themselves, a space that reveals the presence of those who attended, and finally, creates the time and space for the installation attendees to form a personal interpretation and reading of the event and all it symbolizes. Setting up this reflective space in its entirety

Figure 15.7. Soldiers of the 1st Battalion Irish Guards wait as the bodies of Major Matthew James Collins and Lance -Sergeant Mark Terence Burgan approach from the right along Wootton Bassett High Street, March 30, 2011. Video still from *The Separation Line*. Katie Davies.

reveals a more complex temporality—the gap, or distance, between reality and representation.

When presenting such conflicts of interest in modes that are analytical and emotional, artistic practice *is* the opportunity to reflect upon what it might mean to occupy more than one position or cultural identity. It can illuminate the construction of legislative borders that create artificial divides between communities, creating an autonomous space from which to question their validity and necessity. Artistic practice can reveal the voice of the outsider, and in providing a site for discussion, create an agency for those not represented by political directives but rooted in a precise physical and psychological place. For this reason, artistic interventions and observations engage deep psychic and national archetypes on their own terms and in doing so can transgress the border of a political polarization and cultural and social stereotypes by offering up alternative and multiple readings, demanding a space for alternative perspectives to be included, not excluded.

The repatriation ceremonies and subsequent patronage of Royal Wootton Bassett have now become a commodity, traded on the global market of national identity as cultural currency. The need to recognize the shifting of state identities and borders becomes essential in order to understand the parameters of national identity. To challenge these borders by stepping into their thresholds to seek them out, to look across them, and to look through them is to initiate the first stages of communication across these polarized zones: to transcend them. Through discussion, what begins to emerge is the realization that the experience of being divided is the first thing that both sides have in common.

The Separation Line can be viewed at www.theseparationline.com.

Notes

1. Name of street but also British noun meaning the main street of a town and the traditional site for shops, banks, and other businesses.

2. John C. Welchman, "The Philosophical Brothel," in *Rethinking Borders*, ed. John C. Welchman (London: Macmillan Press, 1996), 167–68.

3. The decision to "award the town with the royal prefix" was to highlight that it is "an enduring symbol of the nation's admiration and gratitude," an incorporation of the British tendencies. See Josie Ensor, "Wootton Bassett Officially Re-named Royal Town," *Telegraph* [online], October 16, 2011, http://www.telegraph.co.uk/news/uknews/theroyalfamily/8829788/ Wootton-Bassett-officially-re-named-royal-town.html.

4. The base began as the home of military transport in March of 1943.

5. David Cameron, "Address to Parliament," *BBC News Politics*, BBC News 24, March 16, 2011, 12:15.

6. Welchman, "The Philosophical Brothel," 167–168.
7. John C. Welchman, interview by author, the Arnolfini, Bristol, March 5, 2011.
8. Welchman, interview by author.
9. James Clifford, *Routes: Travel and Translation in the Late Twentieth Century* (Cambridge, MA: Harvard University Press, 1997), 7.
10. "*Adjective,* 1. relating to a transitional or initial stage of a process. 2. occupying a position at, or on both sides of, a boundary or threshold." See *The Oxford English Dictionary* (Oxford: Clarendon Press, 1991), 297.
11. Jacques Rancière, *The Emancipated Spectator* (London: Verso, 2009), 4.

Works Cited

Clifford, James. *Routes: Travel and Translation in the Late Twentieth Century.* London: Harvard University Press, 2011.

The Oxford English Dictionary. Oxford: Clarendon Press, 1991.

Rancière, Jacques. *The Emancipated Spectator.* London: Verso, 2009.

Welchman, John C. Interview by author. The Arnolfini, Bristol. March 5, 2011.

——. "The Philosophical Brothel." In *Rethinking Borders,* edited by John C. Welchman, 160–186. London: Macmillan Press, 1996.

Films

The Separation Line. Directed by Katie Davies. United Kingdom, 2012.

Index

About the Editors and Contributors

Jakub Kazecki (Bates College) teaches German language, literature, and film. He is the author of *Laughter in the Trenches: Humour and Front Experience in German First World War Narratives* (2012). His articles on the twentieth-century German literature and images of Polish-German relationships in literature, film, and visual arts have appeared in journals and edited volumes in the fields of German and Slavic Studies. His recent publications include the essay on images of the German-Polish borderlands in German cinema in the volume *Cinema and Social Change in Germany and Austria* (2012), and the article on the functions of humor and laughter in the German literature of the First World War in the collection *Expressions of the Unspeakable: Narratives of Trauma* (2013). Kazecki is currently working on a book on images of the East in the contemporary German cinema.

Cynthia J. Miller (Emerson College) is a cultural anthropologist, specializing in popular culture and visual media. Her writing and photography have appeared in edited volumes and journals across the disciplines. She is the editor of *Too Bold for the Box Office: The Mockumentary From Big Screen to Small* (2012) and co-editor of *1950s "Rocketman" TV Series and Their Fans: Cadets, Rangers, and Junior Space Men* (with A. Bowdoin Van Riper, 2012); *Undead in the West: Vampires, Zombies, Mummies and Ghosts on the Cinematic Frontier* (with A. Bowdoin Van Riper, 2012); and the award-winning *Steaming into a Victorian Future: A Steampunk Anthology* (with Julie Anne Taddeo, 2012). She serves as series editor for Scarecrow Press's Film and History series, as well as on the editorial board of the *Journal of Popular Television*. Miller is currently at work on two edited volumes: *Undead in the West II: They Just Keep Coming*, and *(Re)Locating the Frontier: International Western Films.*

Karen A. Ritzenhoff (Central Connecticut State University) is a professor of communication and a member of the Program for Women, Gender, and Sexuality Studies. She teaches courses on women and film, mass media, film history, global visual communication, American cinema, and television production. Her dissertation focused on borderlands: she analyzed the work of East German documentary filmmakers, many affiliated with the DEFA (Deutsche Film Aktiengesellschaft) studios, and how they depicted the time period before and after the fall of the Berlin Wall. She is the co-editor of *Screening the Dark Side of Love: From Euro-Horror to American Cinema* (with Karen Randell, 2012). She has also co-edited *Sex and Sexuality in a Feminist World* (with Katherine A. Hermes, 2009) and authored the monograph *Screen Nightmares: Video, Television, and Violence in Film* (2010). Ritzenhoff is currently working on projects focused on the work of Stanley Kubrick and representations of the Apocalypse in cinema.

* * *

Sean Allan received a PhD in English from the University of California, Davis. His interests include post-Vietnam-era American literature and culture, transcultural masculinities, and world cinema. He has taught composition, literature, and film in Taiwan and both coasts of the United States. Currently, he teaches literature and film courses in the English Department at Bridgewater State University in Massachusetts and at Southern Connecticut State University in New Haven, Connecticut.

Dennis Browne is an associate professor of Russian at Bates College. He received his PhD in Slavic Linguistics from the University of Virginia. At Bates College, he teaches Russian language, film, and culture courses, and seminars on Europe and the Balkans. He has published articles and reviews on language teaching and Russian rock music, and is coauthor of a book on translation and stylistics. He has also written about music and film from the western Balkans and is currently examining the works of controversial filmmaker Emir Kusturica.

María Lourdes Casas received her MA and PhD in Spanish from the University of Wisconsin–Madison. Currently she is an assistant professor at Central Connecticut State University, where she teaches Spanish language, literature, and culture. She specializes in nineteenth- and twentieth-century Spanish literature and culture. Her main research focuses on short novel collections in Spain from 1900–1936. She is also interested in Spanish contemporary cinema. She has published articles dealing with mass readership and the female characterizations in these collections. She is currently working on a book-length project about one of these collections, *La Novela Mundial*. She is also coauthor of several Spanish textbooks.

Raluca Cernahoschi is assistant professor of German at Bates College. She obtained her PhD from the University of British Columbia, Vancouver, Canada, with an analysis of postwar German poetry from Romania. Her current research focuses on the representation of the Austro-Hungarian Empire in literature and film and the interactions of cultures in the eastern borderlands of the monarchy. She has participated in several international projects and authored articles on different facets of East-Central European literature and film.

Jane Costlow is a professor of environmental studies at Bates College, with a background in the study of Russian literature and culture. She received her PhD from Yale University. She is the author of *Heart-Pine Russia: Walking and Writing the Nineteenth-Century Forest* (2012). She has also co-edited a volume of essays titled *Other Animals: Beyond the Human in Russian Culture and History* (with Amy Nelson, 2010), and has written extensively on Russian women writers. She has a special affection for the art of translation—where scholarly training joins the love of language to create bridges between multiple worlds.

Ayça Tunç Cox completed her PhD at Royal Holloway, University of London, United Kingdom, with a dissertation titled "Diasporic Cinema: Turkish-German Filmmakers with Particular Emphasis on Generational Differences." She received her MA from Ege University, İzmir, Turkey, with a thesis titled "Independent Cinema: Alternative Tendencies in Turkish Cinema in the 1990s." Having taught previously in both media arts and communication, she now works as an assistant professor in the Industrial Design Department at Izmir Institute of Technology, Turkey. Among her research interests are transnational cinema, diasporic cinema, national cinemas, European cinema, independent and alternative cinema, and new Turkish cinema. She has published several articles and four book chapters on cinema and has made several short films.

Katie Davies is a visual artist and documentary filmmaker. Through video installation, her research and artworks explore the nature of borders, indistinguishable zones, and in-between states that are in some way betwixt. Previous video projects include *38th Parallel*, working with the UN Armistice Commission and United States Forces in Korea to research and film within the Korean Demilitarized Zone in 2008 and working with the British Home Office, Sheffield City Council, and Yorkshire Artspace Society to film *Commonwealth*, a film observing British citizenship ceremonies in 2009. She is currently completing her dissertation, "Border Imaging: Realizing the Rhetoric of Sovereign Order through Artistic Video Practice," at the University of the West of England, Bristol.

Charlotte Christina Fink holds undergraduate and graduate degrees in American cultural studies, English, the social sciences, and media studies from the Karl-Franzens-University Graz, Austria. Her main areas of academic interest include sociocultural concepts of identity (particularly with regard to gender, age, culture, and ethnicity) along with communication, foreign languages, social structures, globalization, and popular culture. Fink is currently an independent scholar situated in her hometown of Graz.

Claudia Plasse is a PhD student in German and Scandinavian studies at the University of Massachusetts, Amherst. Since 2007, she has taught courses in media communication and cultural studies at Anna Maria College in Paxton, Massachusetts. Plasse has worked for twenty years as a TV and radio journalist and as a media relations specialist in Germany and in the United States. She holds a master's degree in political science, TV and film studies, and history from the University of Cologne, Germany. Among others, her research interests are German and international documentary films, documentary film production for TV, and issues of representing "reality" in documentaries and in reality TV shows.

Laila Pakalniņa was born in Liepaja, Latvia. She graduated from the Moscow University, Department of TV Journalism and, later, from the Moscow Film Institute (VGIK), Department of Film Direction. She is director and scriptwriter of twenty-one documentaries, five shorts, and four fiction features. So, she has thirty films, two children, one husband, one dog, one bicycle, and many ideas for new films. Her fiction features include *Pizzas* (*Picas*, 2012); *The Hostage* (*Ķīlnieks*, 2006); *The Python* (*Pitons*, 2003); and *The Shoe* (*Kurpe*, 1998). Her most recent documentary films include *Snow Crazy* (*Sniegs*, 2012); *33 Animals of Santa Claus* (*33 zvēri Ziemassvētki vecītim*, 2011); *On Rubiks' Road* (*Pa Rubika ceļu*, 2010); and *Three Men and a Fish Pond* (*Par dzimtenīti*, 2008). She is also the director of *The Bus* (*Autobuss*, 2004), which is discussed in this volume.

Lesley C. Pleasant teaches as an assistant professor of German at the University of Evansville, Indiana. She received her PhD in German literature from the University of Virginia. Her interests include German theater/drama and film, specifically Bergfilme, Wendefilme, and marginal cinema. Her recent publications include articles on Yilmaz Arslan's *Brudermord* (2005); a review of Knigge's *Hemingway und die Deutschen* in *The Hemingway Review*; and entries in the forthcoming *Directory of World Cinema: Germany 2* (edited by Michelle Langford). She is currently working on the uses of color in Misselwitz's *Herzsprung* (1992) and a comparison of Borchert's *Draussen vor der Tür* (1947) and Wyler's *Best Years of our Lives* (1947).

Thomas Prasch, professor and chair of the Department of History at Washburn University, received his PhD from Indiana University. Assistant editor responsible for film reviews for the *American Historical Review* from 1994 to 2004, he has edited a biannual selection of film reviews for *Kansas History* since 2001. Recent publications include "Eating the World: London in 1851" in *Victorian Literature and Culture* (2008) and "Behind the Last Veil: Forms of Transgression in Ken Russell's *Salome's Last Dance*" in *Ken Russell: Re-Viewing England's Last Mannerist* (edited by Kevin Flanagan, 2009).

Tanya Shilina-Conte is a lecturer at the University at Buffalo, New York, where she teaches a wide variety of courses in film theory, theory of film narrative, global media and culture, contemporary cinema, gender and film, and literary criticism in the departments of media study and English. She holds a PhD in English from Saint-Petersburg Herzen State University, Russia (2004) and an MA in film studies from the University at Buffalo (2012). She is the author of a book, *"Midway upon the Road": A Study of Openings in Contemporary Short Fiction* (2011), and several articles on the questions of narrative theory and practice. She is also the recipient of an award from the Ministry of Culture and Cinematography of the Russian Federation (2006).

Maruta Z. Vitols is a media historian, specializing in political documentary. Her present research interests center on cyberactivism and how new media is used for political purposes. She received her PhD in the history of art from The Ohio State University and holds an MA in cinema studies from New York University. Vitols has published articles on Latvian cinema, and her latest study on the relationships between Latvian documentaries and politics appears in *A Companion to Eastern European Cinemas* (edited by Anikó Imre, 2012). She is also a Fulbright scholar; teaches at Emerson College in Boston, Massachusetts; and was a visiting lecturer at the Franklin W. Olin College of Engineering in Needham, Massachusetts, during the 2012–2013 academic year.